Vampire Game

JUDAL

ALSO AVAILABLE FROM 🌀 TOKYOPOP®

MANGA

.HACK//LEGEND OF THE TWILIGHT BRACELET (September 2003)
@LARGE (COMING SOON)
ANGELIC LAYER*
BABY BIRTH* (September 2003)
BATTLE ROYALE*
BRAIN POWERED*
BRIGADOON* (August 2003)
CARDCAPTOR SAKURA
CARDCAPTOR SAKURA: MASTER OF THE CLOW*
CHOBITS*
CHRONICLES OF THE CURSED SWORD
CLAMP SCHOOL DETECTIVES*
CLOVER
CONFIDENTIAL CONFESSIONS*
CORRECTOR YUI
COWBOY BEBOP*
COWBOY BEBOP: SHOOTING STAR*
DEMON DIARY
DIGIMON*
DRAGON HUNTER
DRAGON KNIGHTS*
DUKLYON: CLAMP SCHOOL DEFENDERS*
ERICA SAKURAZAWA*
FAKE*
FLCL* (September 2003)
FORBIDDEN DANCE* (August 2003)
GATE KEEPERS*
G GUNDAM*
GRAVITATION*
GTO*
GUNDAM WING
GUNDAM WING: BATTLEFIELD OF PACIFISTS
GUNDAM WING: ENDLESS WALTZ*
GUNDAM WING: THE LAST OUTPOST*
HAPPY MANIA*
HARLEM BEAT
I.N.V.U.
INITIAL D*
ISLAND
JING: KING OF BANDITS*
JULINE
KARE KANO*
KINDAICHI CASE FILES, THE*
KING OF HELL
KODOCHA: SANA'S STAGE*
LOVE HINA*
LUPIN III*
MAGIC KNIGHT RAYEARTH* (August 2003)
MAGIC KNIGHT RAYEARTH II* (COMING SOON)

MAN OF MANY FACES*
MARMALADE BOY*
MARS*
MIRACLE GIRLS
MIYUKI-CHAN IN WONDERLAND* (October 2003)
MONSTERS, INC.
PARADISE KISS*
PARASYTE
PEACH GIRL
PEACH GIRL: CHANGE OF HEART*
PET SHOP OF HORRORS*
PLANET LADDER*
PLANETES* (October 2003)
PRIEST
RAGNAROK
RAVE MASTER*
REALITY CHECK
REBIRTH
REBOUND*
RISING STARS OF MANGA
SABER MARIONETTE J*
SAILOR MOON
SAINT TAIL
SAMURAI DEEPER KYO*
SAMURAI GIRL: REAL BOUT HIGH SCHOOL*
SCRYED*
SHAOLIN SISTERS*
SHIRAHIME-SYO: SNOW GODDESS TALES* (Dec. 2003)
SHUTTERBOX (November 2003)
SORCERER HUNTERS
THE SKULL MAN*
THE VISION OF ESCAFLOWNE
TOKYO MEW MEW*
UNDER THE GLASS MOON
VAMPIRE GAME*
WILD ACT*
WISH*
WORLD OF HARTZ (COMING SOON)
X-DAY* (August 2003)
ZODIAC P.I. *

For more information visit www.TOKYOPOP.com

*INDICATES 100% AUTHENTIC MANGA (RIGHT-TO-LEFT FORMAT)

CINE-MANGA™

CARDCAPTORS
JACKIE CHAN ADVENTURES (COMING SOON)
JIMMY NEUTRON (September 2003)
KIM POSSIBLE
LIZZIE MCGUIRE
POWER RANGERS: NINJA STORM (August 2003)
SPONGEBOB SQUAREPANTS (September 2003)
SPY KIDS 2

NOVELS

KARMA CLUB (COMING SOON)
SAILOR MOON

TOKYOPOP KIDS

STRAY SHEEP (September 2003)

ART BOOKS

CARDCAPTOR SAKURA*
MAGIC KNIGHT RAYEARTH*

ANIME GUIDES

COWBOY BEBOP ANIME GUIDES
GUNDAM TECHNICAL MANUALS
SAILOR MOON SCOUT GUIDES

5-12-03

VAMPIRE GAME

Volume 2

by
JUDAL

TOKYOPOP®
Los Angeles • Tokyo • London

Translator - Ikoi Hiroe
English Adaptation - Jason Deitrich
Associate Editor - Tim Beedle
Retouch and Lettering - Jennifer Nunn
Cover Layout - Aaron Suhr

Editor - Luis Reyes
Managing Editor - Jill Freshney
Production Coordinator - Antonio DePietro
Production Manager - Jennifer Miller
Art Director - Matthew Alford
Editorial Director - Jeremy Ross
VP of Production - Ron Klamert
President & C.O.O. - John Parker
Publisher & C.E.O. - Stuart Levy

Email: editor@TOKYOPOP.com
Come visit us online at www.TOKYOPOP.com

A  Manga

TOKYOPOP® is an imprint of Mixx Entertainment, Inc.
5900 Wilshire Blvd. Suite 2000, Los Angeles, CA 90036

ISBN: 1-59182-370-6

First TOKYOPOP® printing: August 2003

10 9 8 7 6 5 4
Printed in the USA

VAMPIRE GAME

A hundred years ago, King Phelios killed the Vampire King Duzell. Now, the reincarnated Duzell searches for the reincarnated Phelios to get his revenge. Some vampires just can't get over things. Duzell's search has led him to Lady Ishtar, a princess who, like most young members of the royal family, is a spoiled little snot. While she isn't Phelios' reincarnation, Ishtar is a direct descendent of the good king. She's just not a very grateful one. Unhappy with her pre-chosen role in life, Ishtar joins with the vampire Duzell, and this pernicious pair make their way to the kingdom of La Naan. Under the rule of the Lady Ramia, La Naan is also the home of her three sons, any one of which could be the reborn Phelios. Tolerating them long enough to find out, however, will be a challenge.

Table of Contents

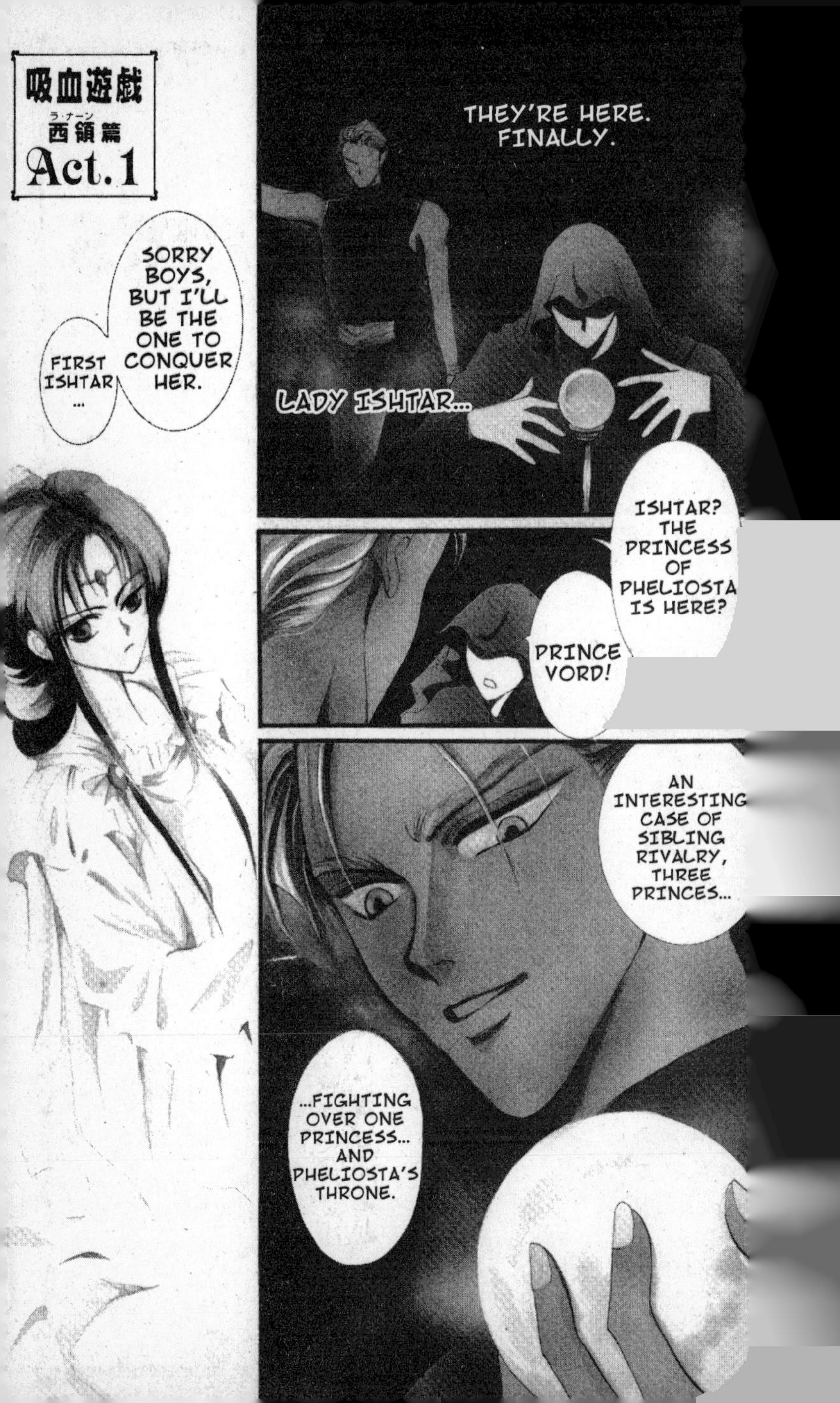
THEY'RE HERE. FINALLY.
LADY ISHTAR...
ISHTAR? THE PRINCESS OF PHELIOSTA IS HERE?
PRINCE VORD!
AN INTERESTING CASE OF SIBLING RIVALRY, THREE PRINCES...
...FIGHTING OVER ONE PRINCESS... AND PHELIOSTA'S THRONE.
吸血遊戯
ラ・ナーン
西領篇
Act.1
SORRY BOYS, BUT I'LL BE THE ONE TO CONQUER HER.
FIRST ISHTAR ...

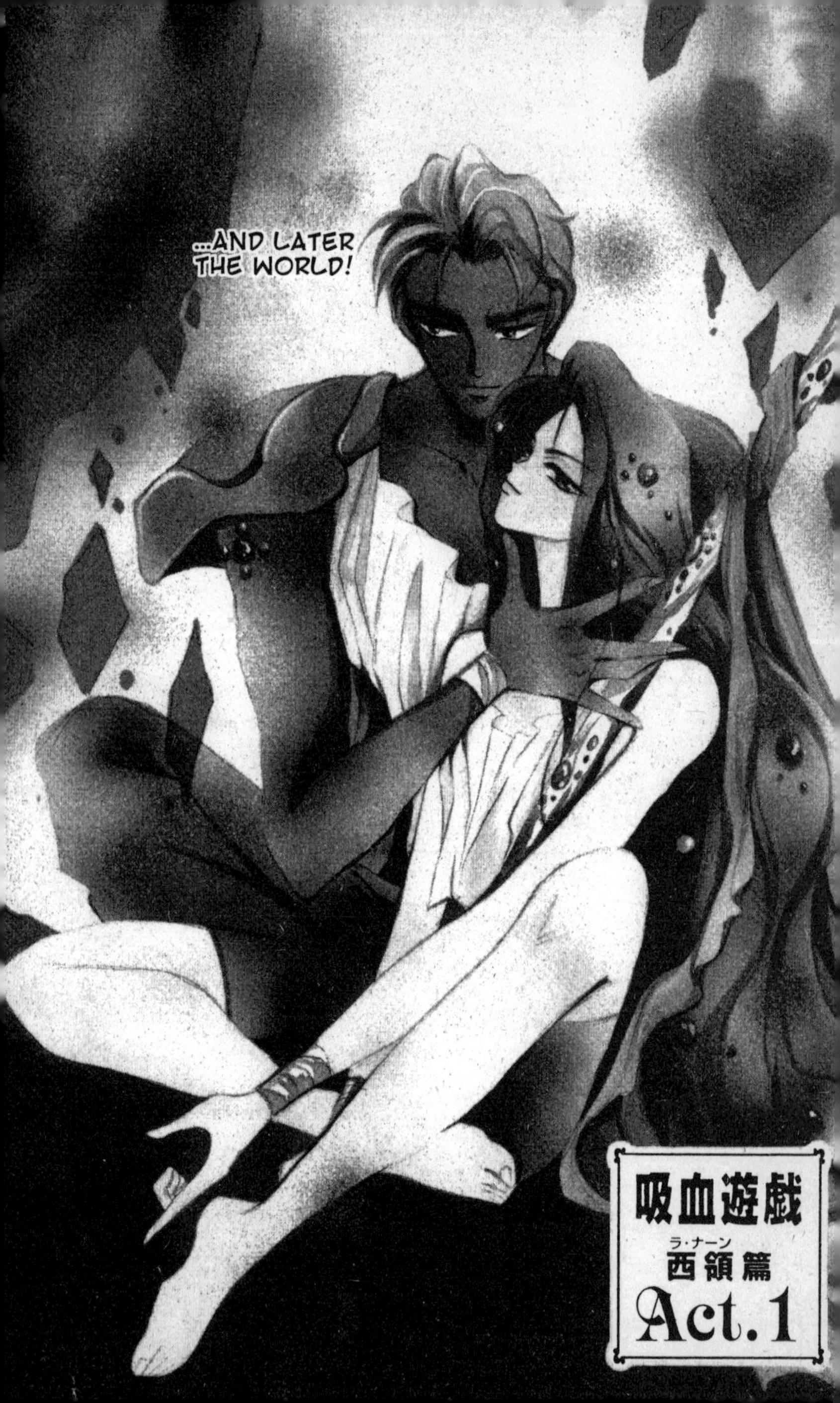
...AND LATER THE WORLD!
吸血遊戯
ラ・ナーン
西領篇
Act. 1

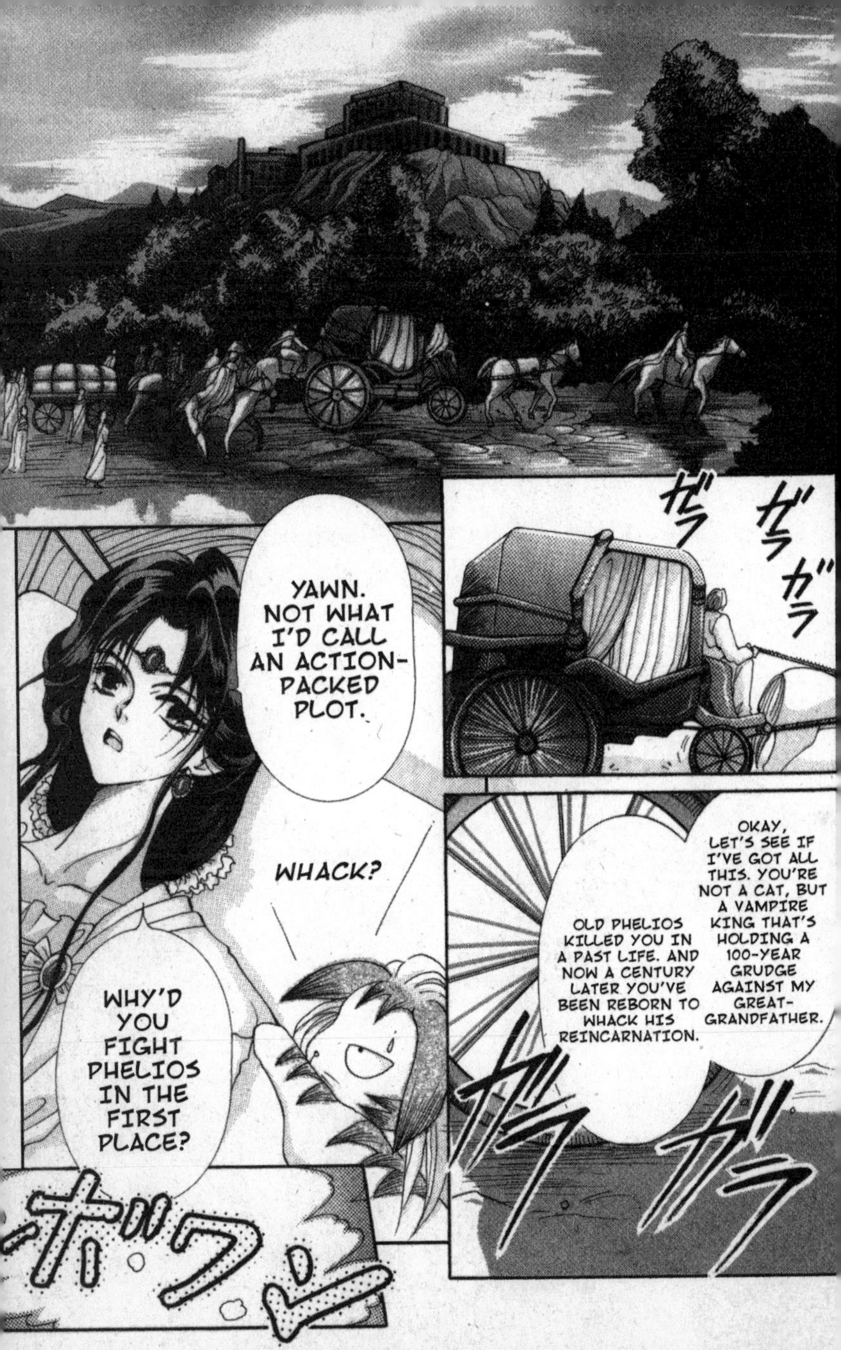
ガラ
ガラ
OKAY, LET'S SEE IF I'VE GOT ALL THIS. YOU'RE NOT A CAT, BUT A VAMPIRE KING THAT'S HOLDING A 100-YEAR GRUDGE AGAINST MY GREAT-GRANDFATHER.
OLD PHELIOS KILLED YOU IN A PAST LIFE. AND NOW A CENTURY LATER YOU'VE BEEN REBORN TO WHACK HIS REINCARNATION.
ガラ
ガラ
YAWN. NOT WHAT I'D CALL AN ACTION-PACKED PLOT.
WHACK?
WHY'D YOU FIGHT PHELIOS IN THE FIRST PLACE?
ボワン

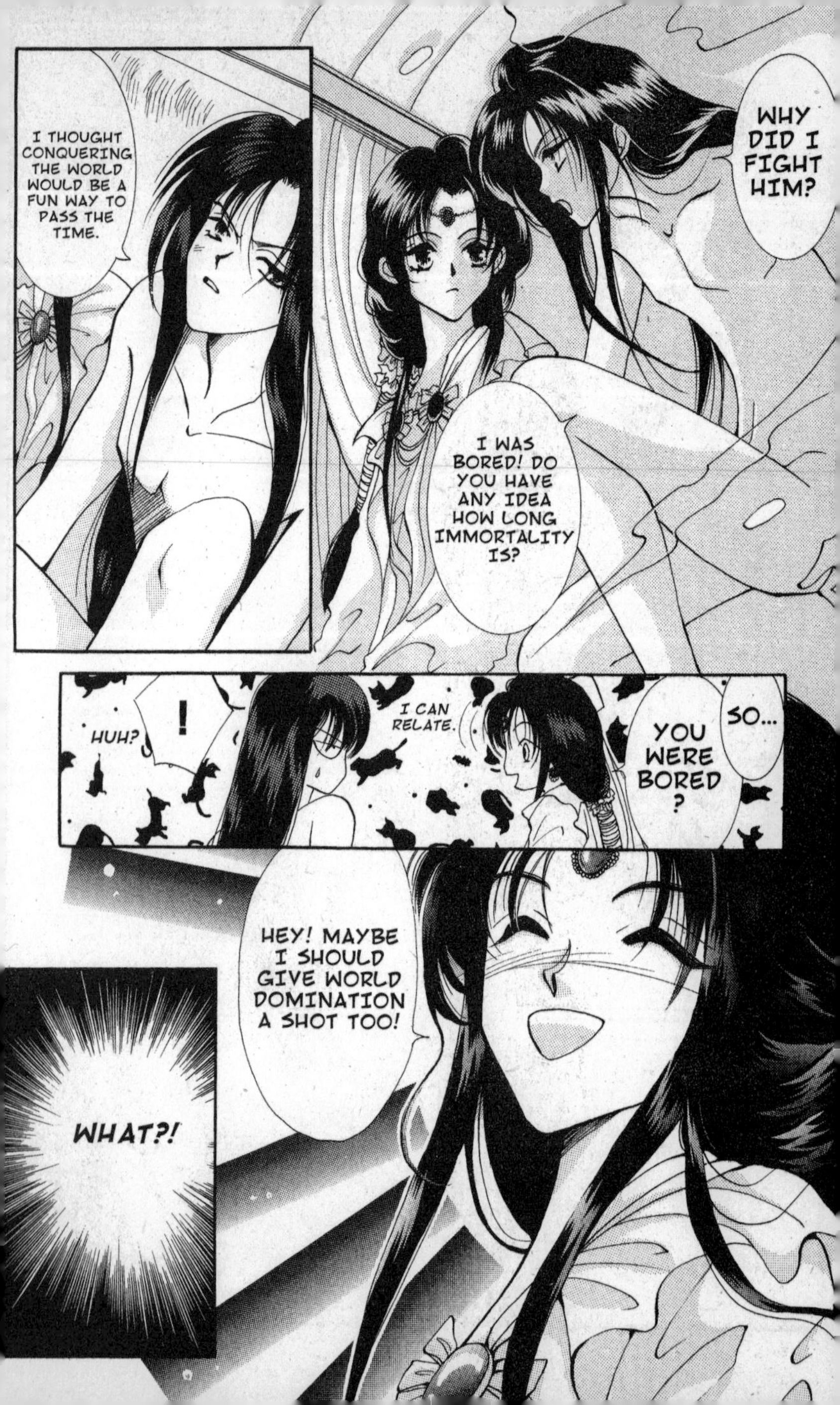
WHY DID I FIGHT HIM?
I THOUGHT CONQUERING THE WORLD WOULD BE A FUN WAY TO PASS THE TIME.
I WAS BORED! DO YOU HAVE ANY IDEA HOW LONG IMMORTALITY IS?
SO...
YOU WERE BORED?
I CAN RELATE.
!
HUH?
HEY! MAYBE I SHOULD GIVE WORLD DOMINATION A SHOT TOO!
WHAT?!

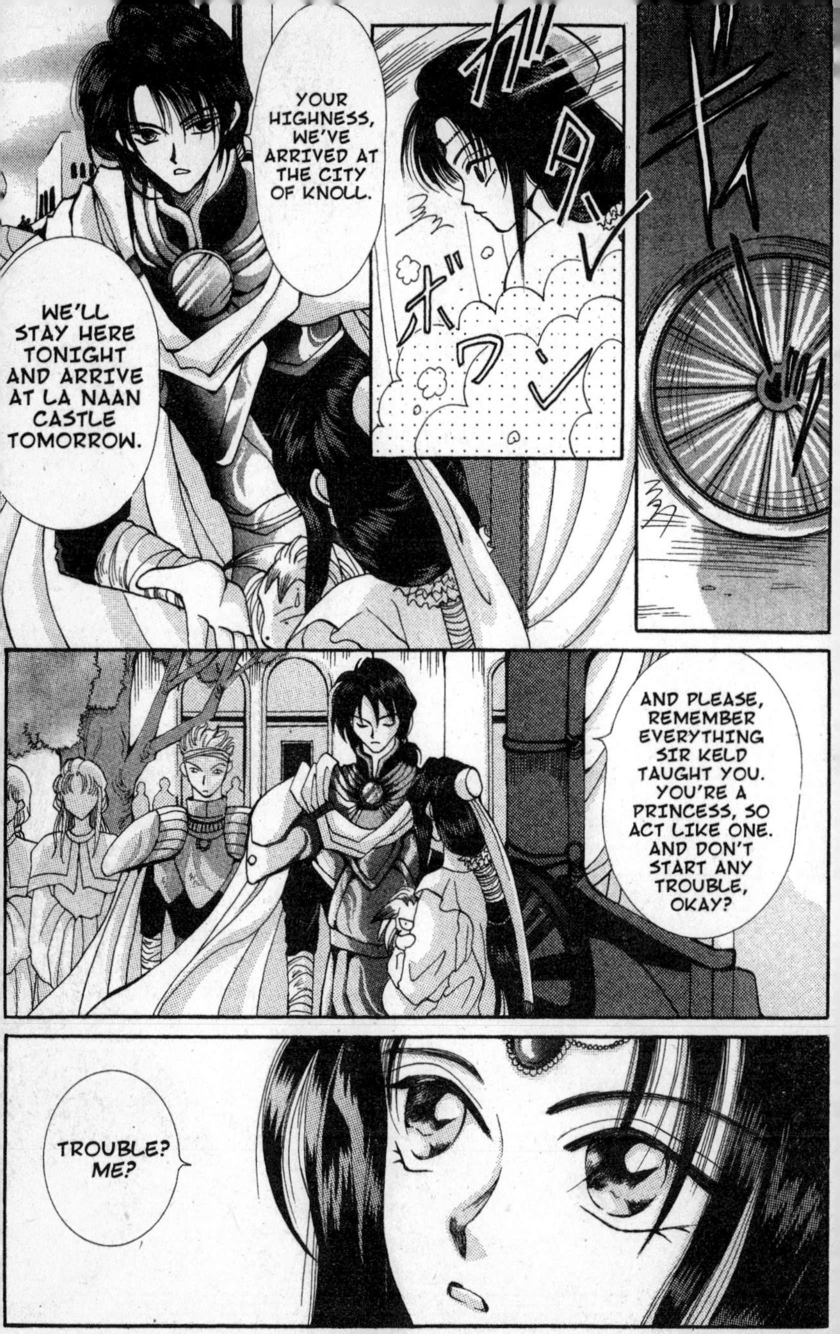
ボワン
YOUR HIGHNESS, WE'VE ARRIVED AT THE CITY OF KNOLL.
WE'LL STAY HERE TONIGHT AND ARRIVE AT LA NAAN CASTLE TOMORROW.
AND PLEASE, REMEMBER EVERYTHING SIR KELD TAUGHT YOU. YOU'RE A PRINCESS, SO ACT LIKE ONE. AND DON'T START ANY TROUBLE, OKAY?
TROUBLE? ME?

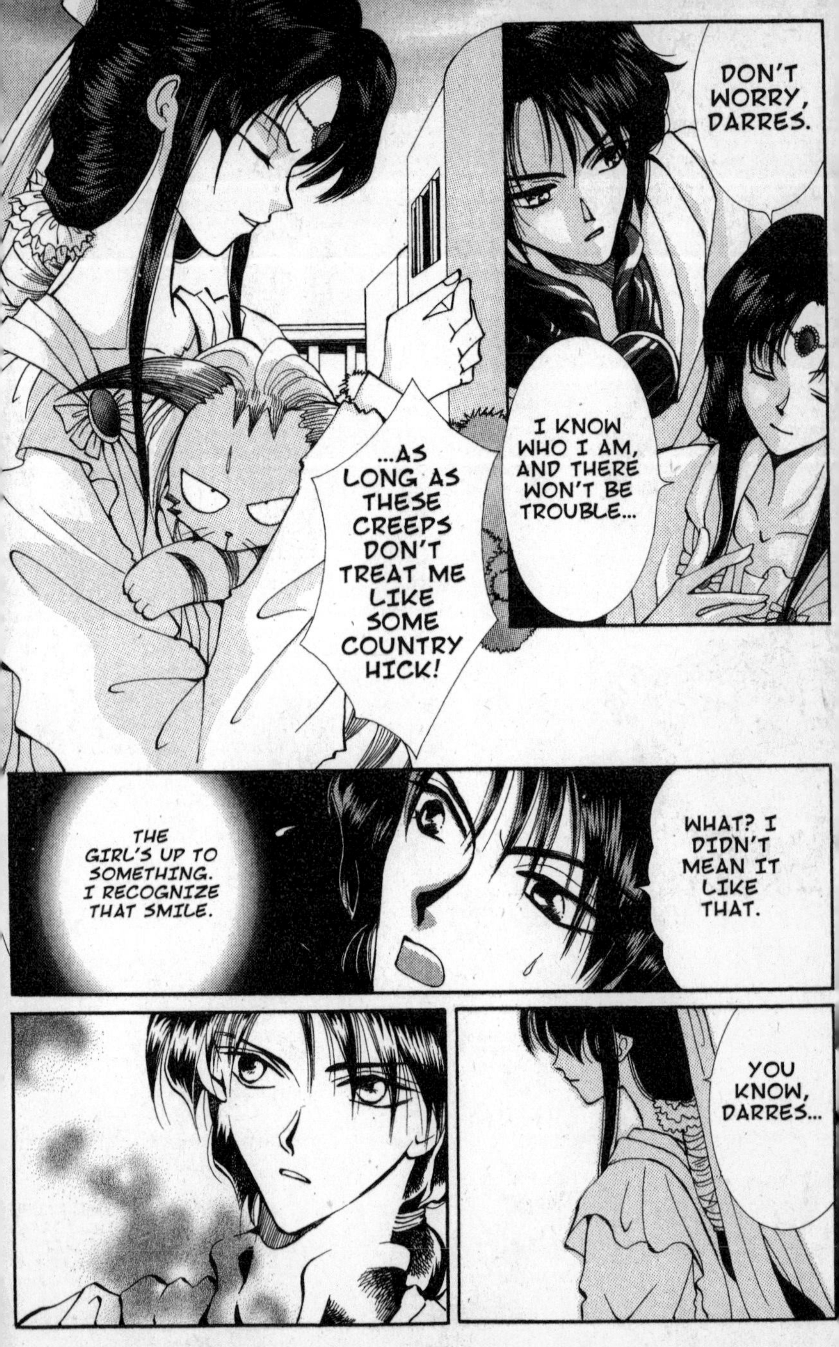
DON'T WORRY, DARRES.
I KNOW WHO I AM, AND THERE WON'T BE TROUBLE...
...AS LONG AS THESE CREEPS DON'T TREAT ME LIKE SOME COUNTRY HICK!
WHAT? I DIDN'T MEAN IT LIKE THAT.
THE GIRL'S UP TO SOMETHING. I RECOGNIZE THAT SMILE.
YOU KNOW, DARRES...

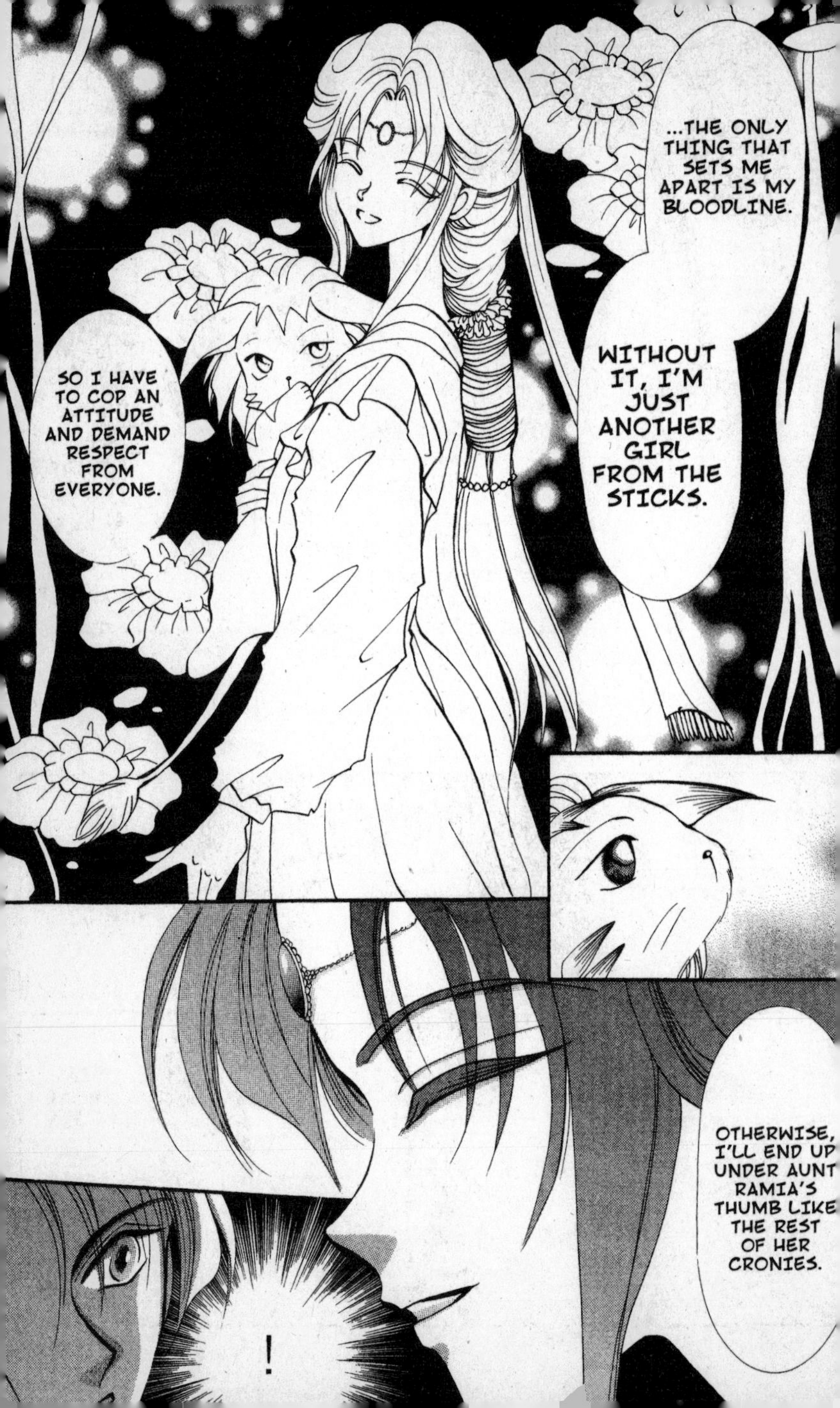
...THE ONLY THING THAT SETS ME APART IS MY BLOODLINE.
WITHOUT IT, I'M JUST ANOTHER GIRL FROM THE STICKS.
SO I HAVE TO COP AN ATTITUDE AND DEMAND RESPECT FROM EVERYONE.
OTHERWISE, I'LL END UP UNDER AUNT RAMIA'S THUMB LIKE THE REST OF HER CRONIES.
!

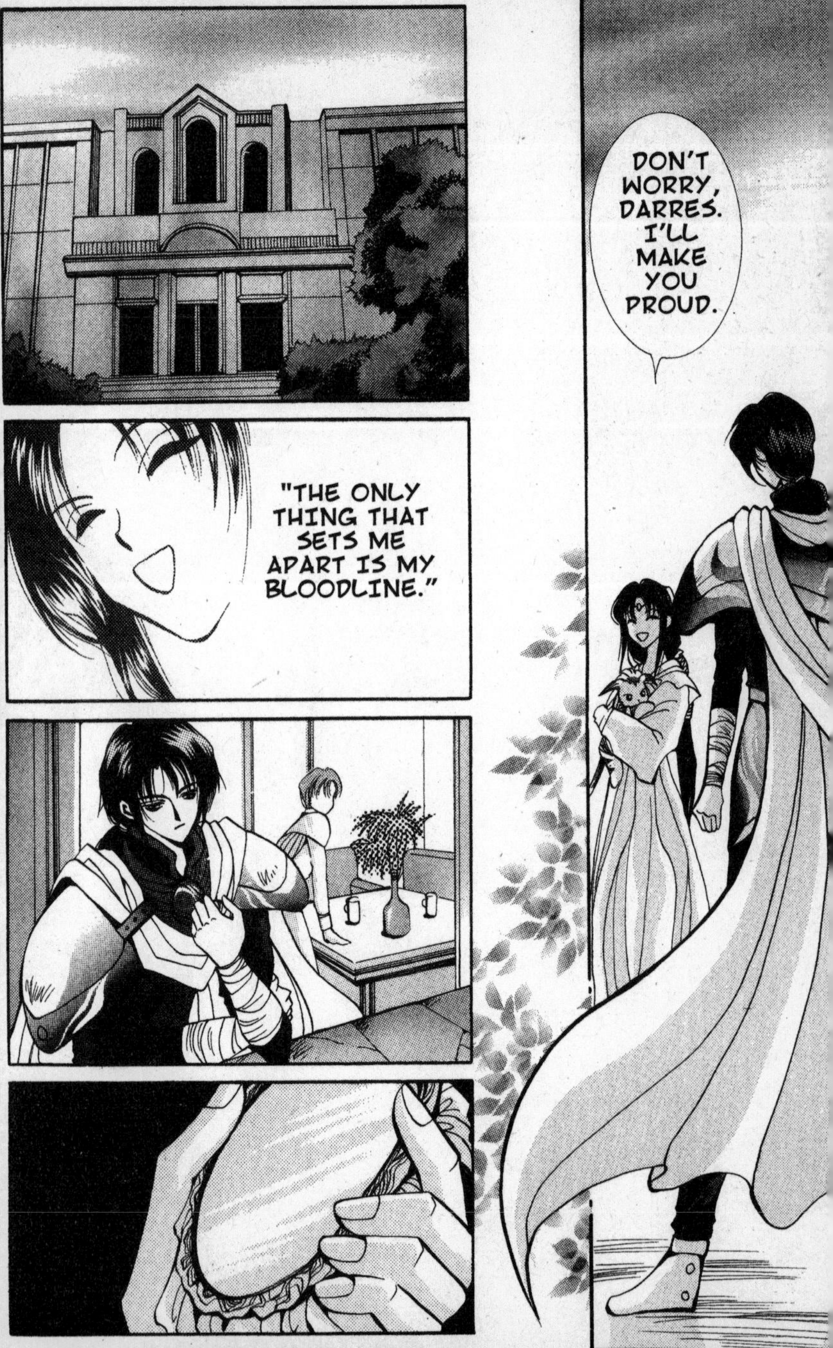
DON'T WORRY, DARRES. I'LL MAKE YOU PROUD.
"THE ONLY THING THAT SETS ME APART IS MY BLOODLINE."

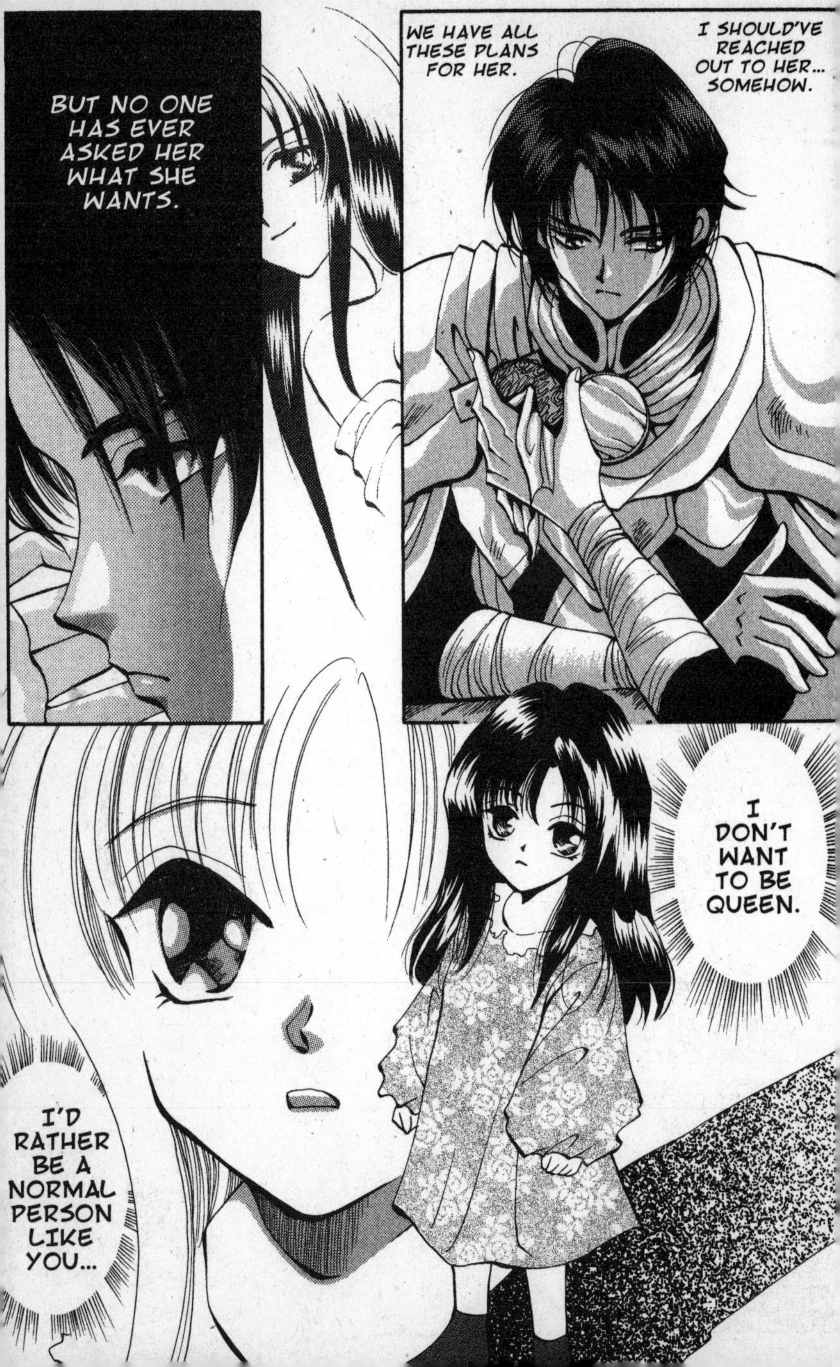
I SHOULD'VE REACHED OUT TO HER... SOMEHOW.
WE HAVE ALL THESE PLANS FOR HER.
BUT NO ONE HAS EVER ASKED HER WHAT SHE WANTS.
I DON'T WANT TO BE QUEEN.
I'D RATHER BE A NORMAL PERSON LIKE YOU...

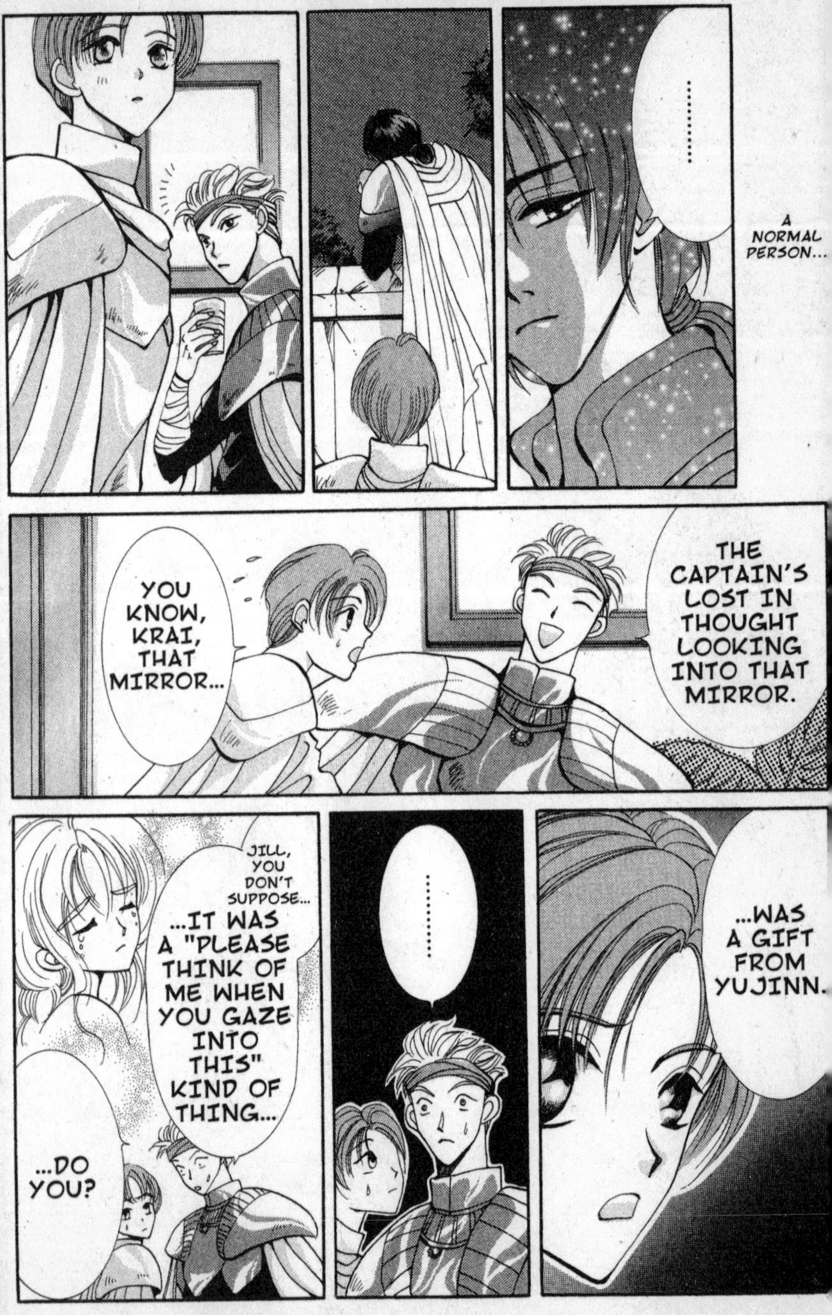
A NORMAL PERSON...
......
THE CAPTAIN'S LOST IN THOUGHT LOOKING INTO THAT MIRROR.
YOU KNOW, KRAI, THAT MIRROR...
...WAS A GIFT FROM YUJINN.
......
JILL, YOU DON'T SUPPOSE...
...IT WAS A "PLEASE THINK OF ME WHEN YOU GAZE INTO THIS" KIND OF THING...
...DO YOU?

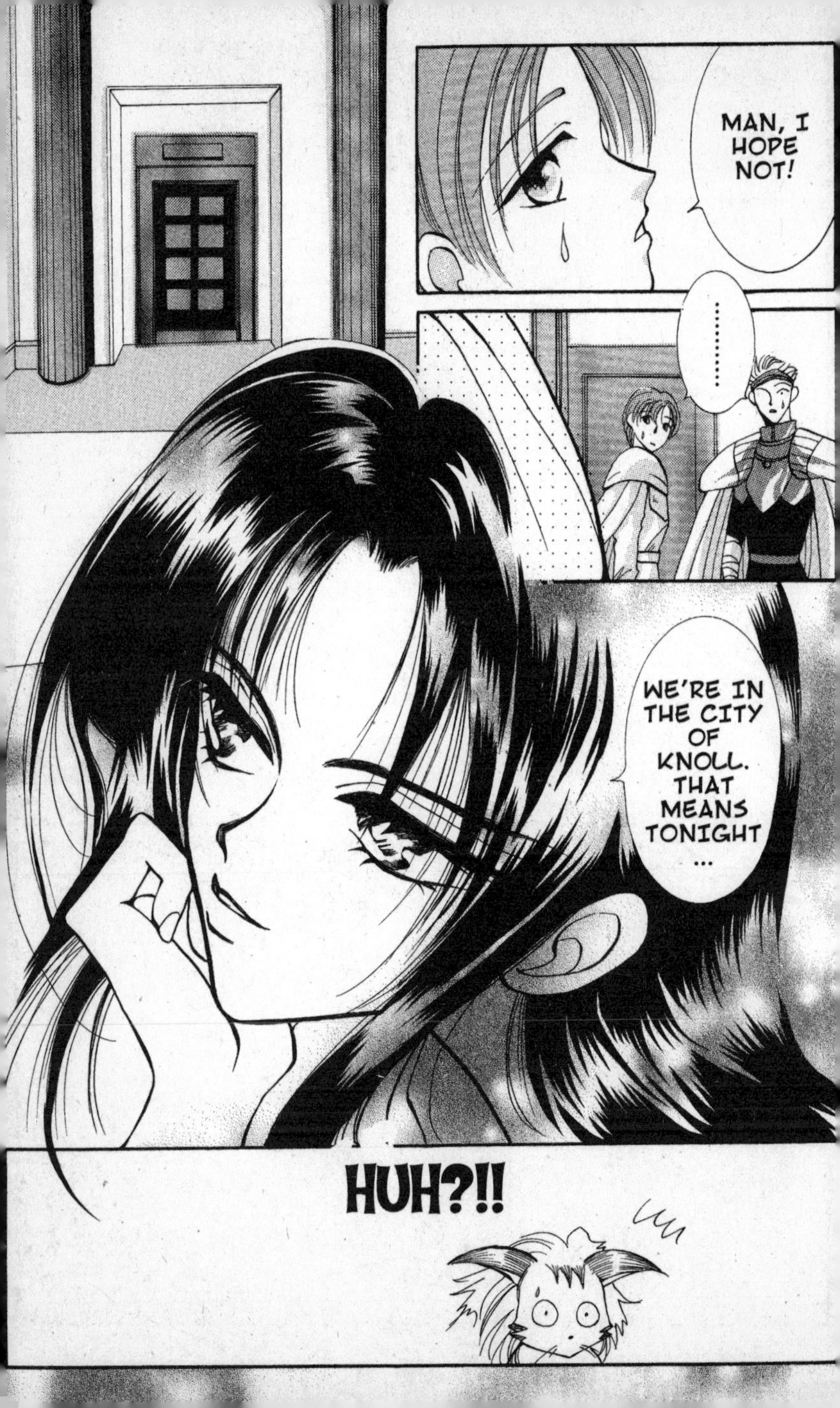
MAN, I HOPE NOT!
......
WE'RE IN THE CITY OF KNOLL. THAT MEANS TONIGHT ...
HUH?!!

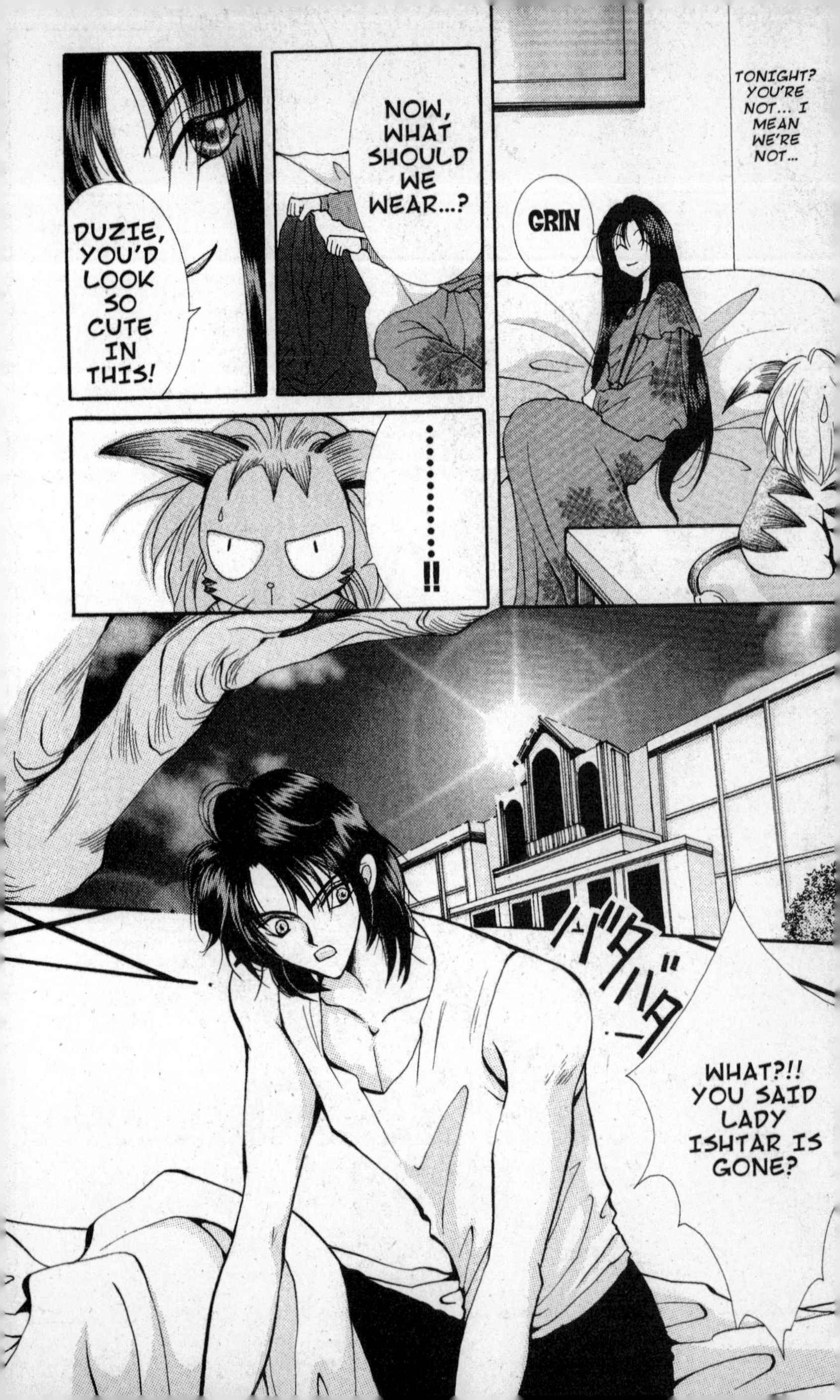
TONIGHT? YOU'RE NOT... I MEAN WE'RE NOT...
GRIN
NOW, WHAT SHOULD WE WEAR...?
DUZIE, YOU'D LOOK SO CUTE IN THIS!
..........!!
バタバタ
WHAT?!! YOU SAID LADY ISHTAR IS GONE?

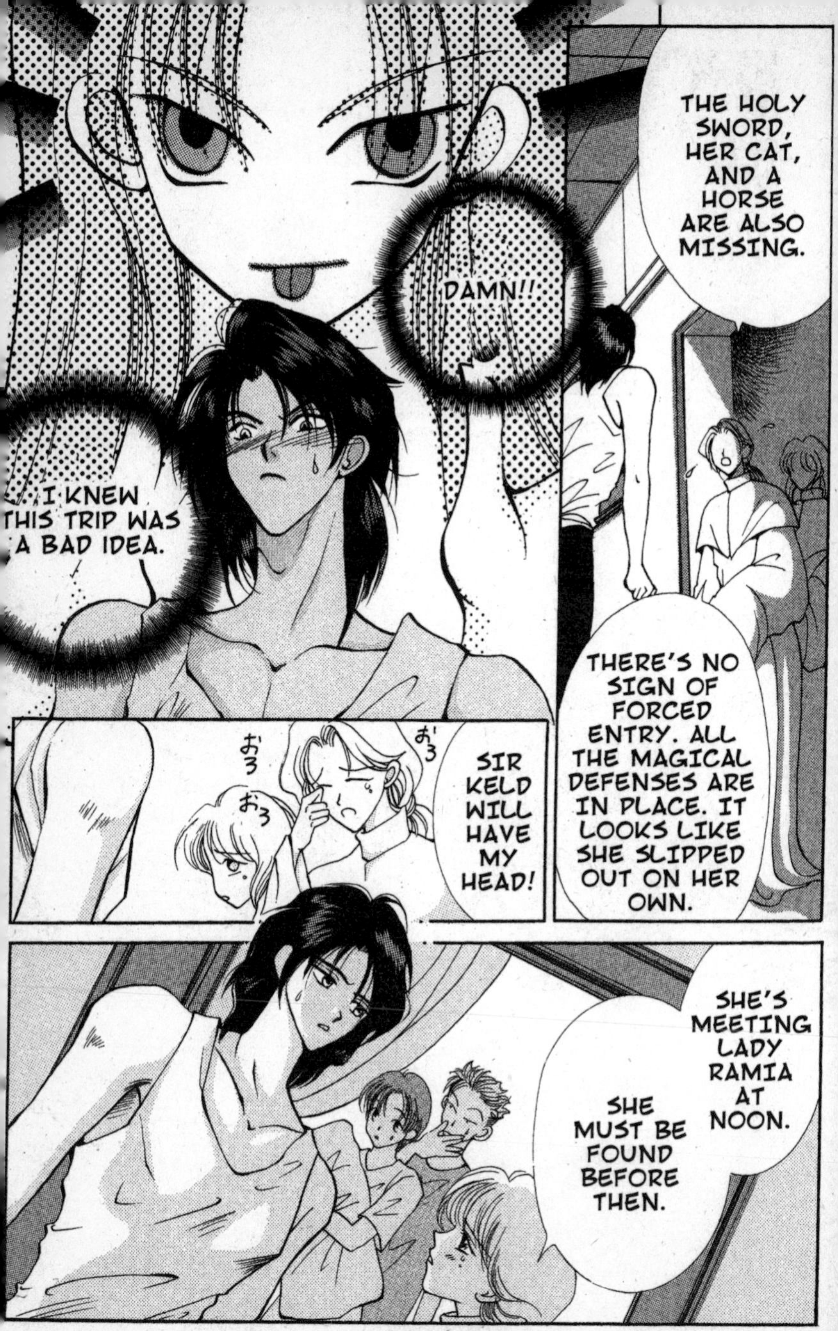
THE HOLY SWORD, HER CAT, AND A HORSE ARE ALSO MISSING.
THERE'S NO SIGN OF FORCED ENTRY. ALL THE MAGICAL DEFENSES ARE IN PLACE. IT LOOKS LIKE SHE SLIPPED OUT ON HER OWN.
DAMN!!
I KNEW THIS TRIP WAS A BAD IDEA.
SIR KELD WILL HAVE MY HEAD!
おろ
おろ
おろ
SHE'S MEETING LADY RAMIA AT NOON.
SHE MUST BE FOUND BEFORE THEN.

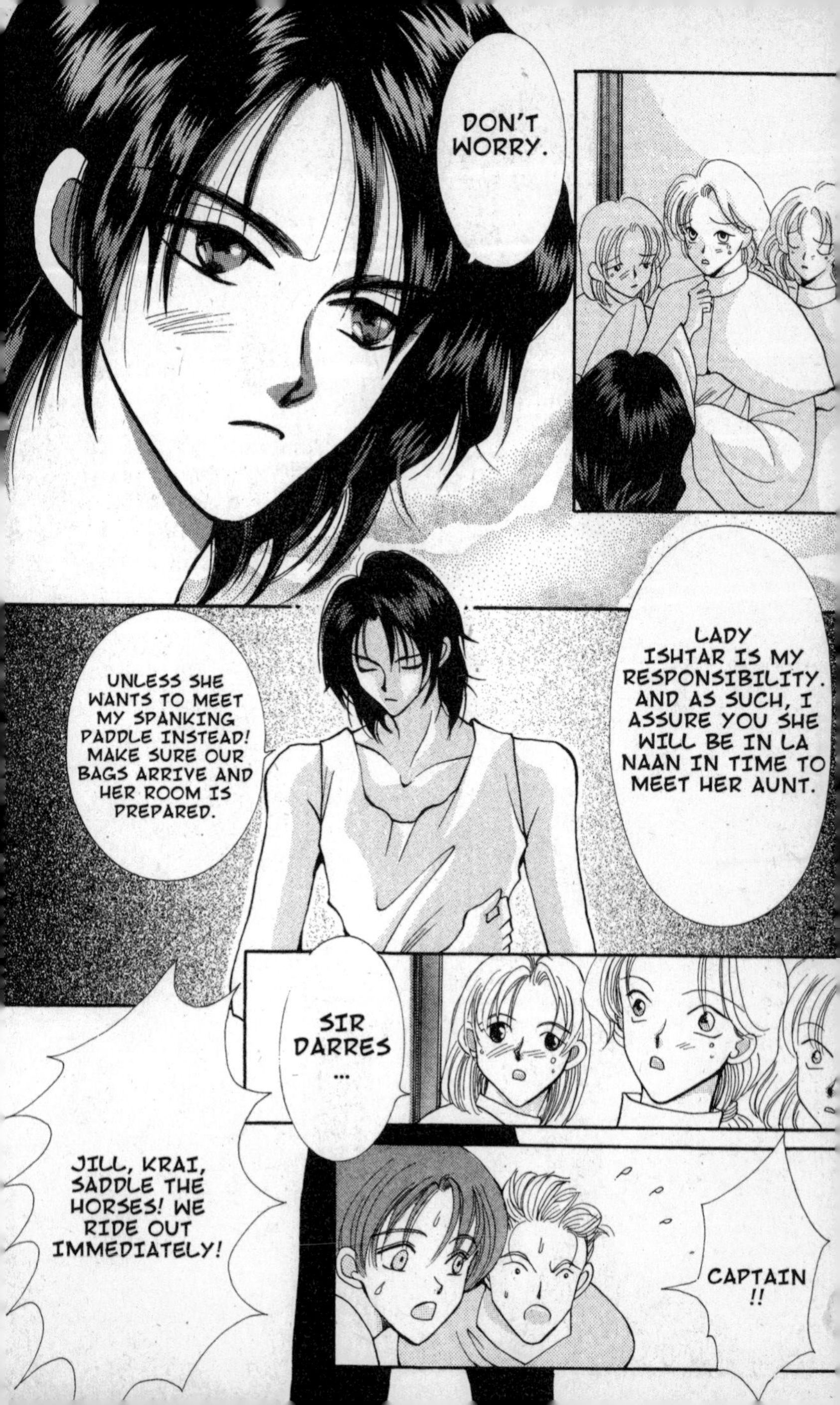
DON'T WORRY.
LADY ISHTAR IS MY RESPONSIBILITY. AND AS SUCH, I ASSURE YOU SHE WILL BE IN LA NAAN IN TIME TO MEET HER AUNT.
UNLESS SHE WANTS TO MEET MY SPANKING PADDLE INSTEAD! MAKE SURE OUR BAGS ARRIVE AND HER ROOM IS PREPARED.
SIR DARRES ...
CAPTAIN !!
JILL, KRAI, SADDLE THE HORSES! WE RIDE OUT IMMEDIATELY!

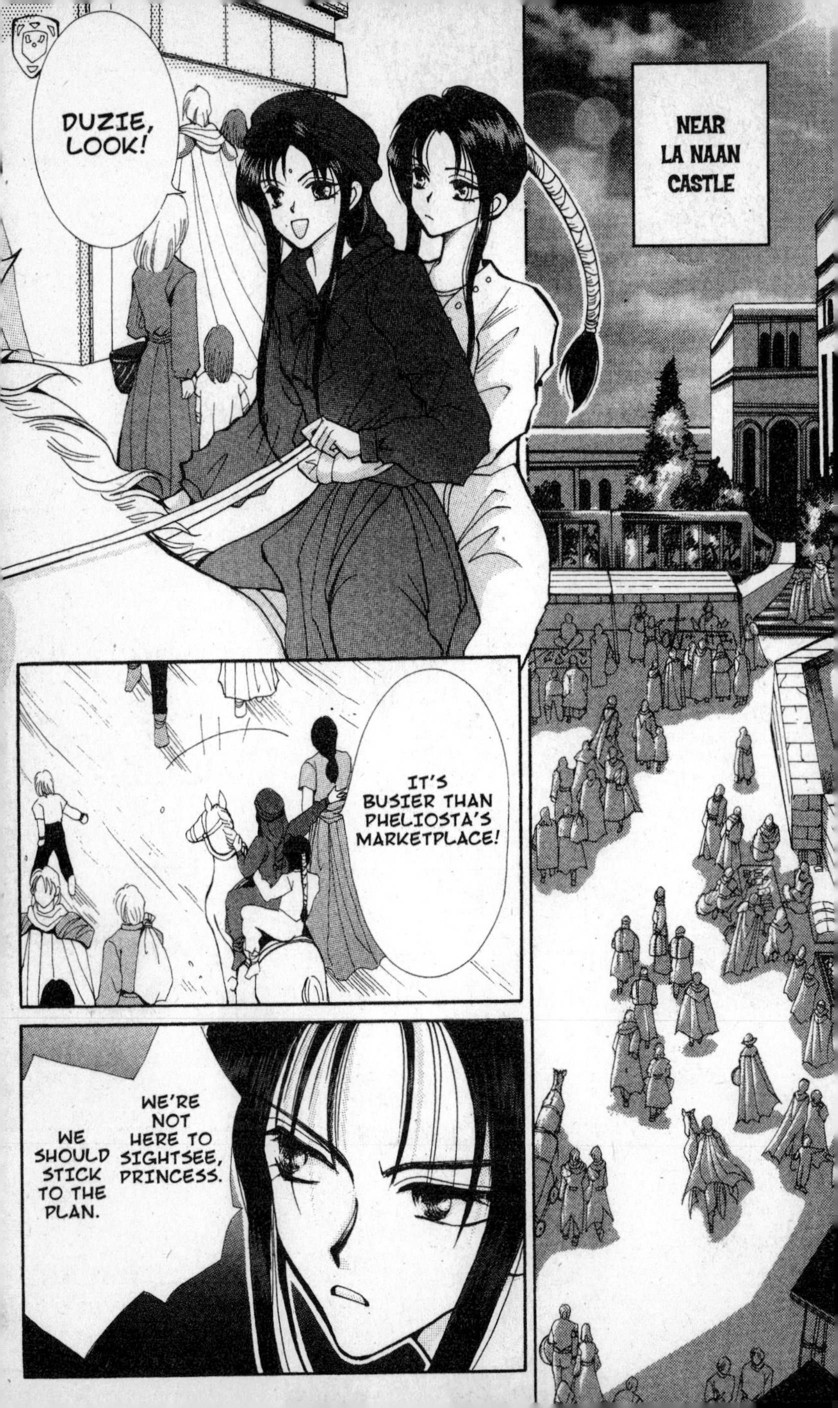
NEAR LA NAAN CASTLE
DUZIE, LOOK!
IT'S BUSIER THAN PHELIOSTA'S MARKETPLACE!
WE'RE NOT HERE TO SIGHTSEE, PRINCESS.
WE SHOULD STICK TO THE PLAN.

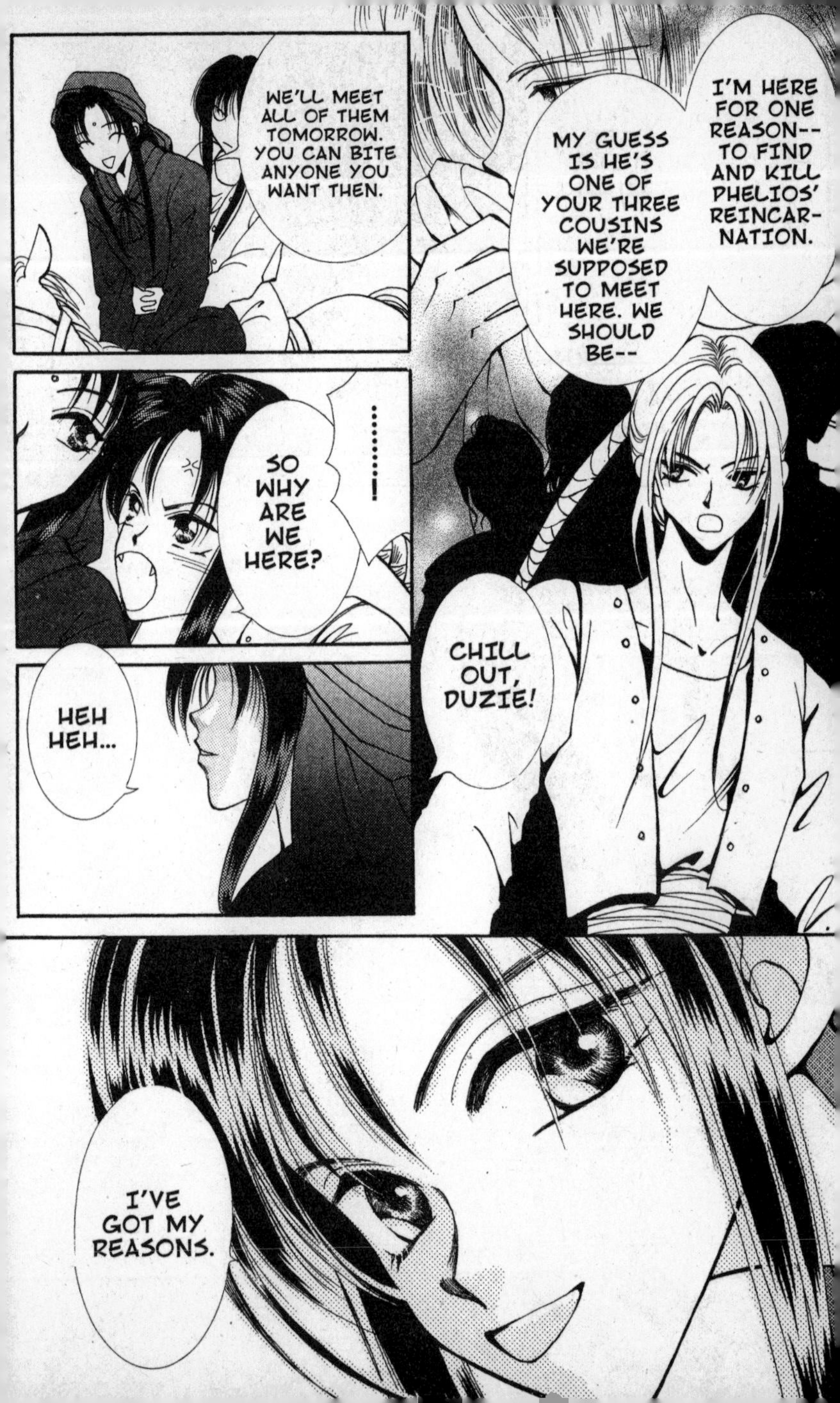
I'M HERE FOR ONE REASON-- TO FIND AND KILL PHELIOS' REINCARNATION.
MY GUESS IS HE'S ONE OF YOUR THREE COUSINS WE'RE SUPPOSED TO MEET HERE. WE SHOULD BE--
CHILL OUT, DUZIE!
WE'LL MEET ALL OF THEM TOMORROW. YOU CAN BITE ANYONE YOU WANT THEN.
......!
SO WHY ARE WE HERE?
HEH HEH...
I'VE GOT MY REASONS.

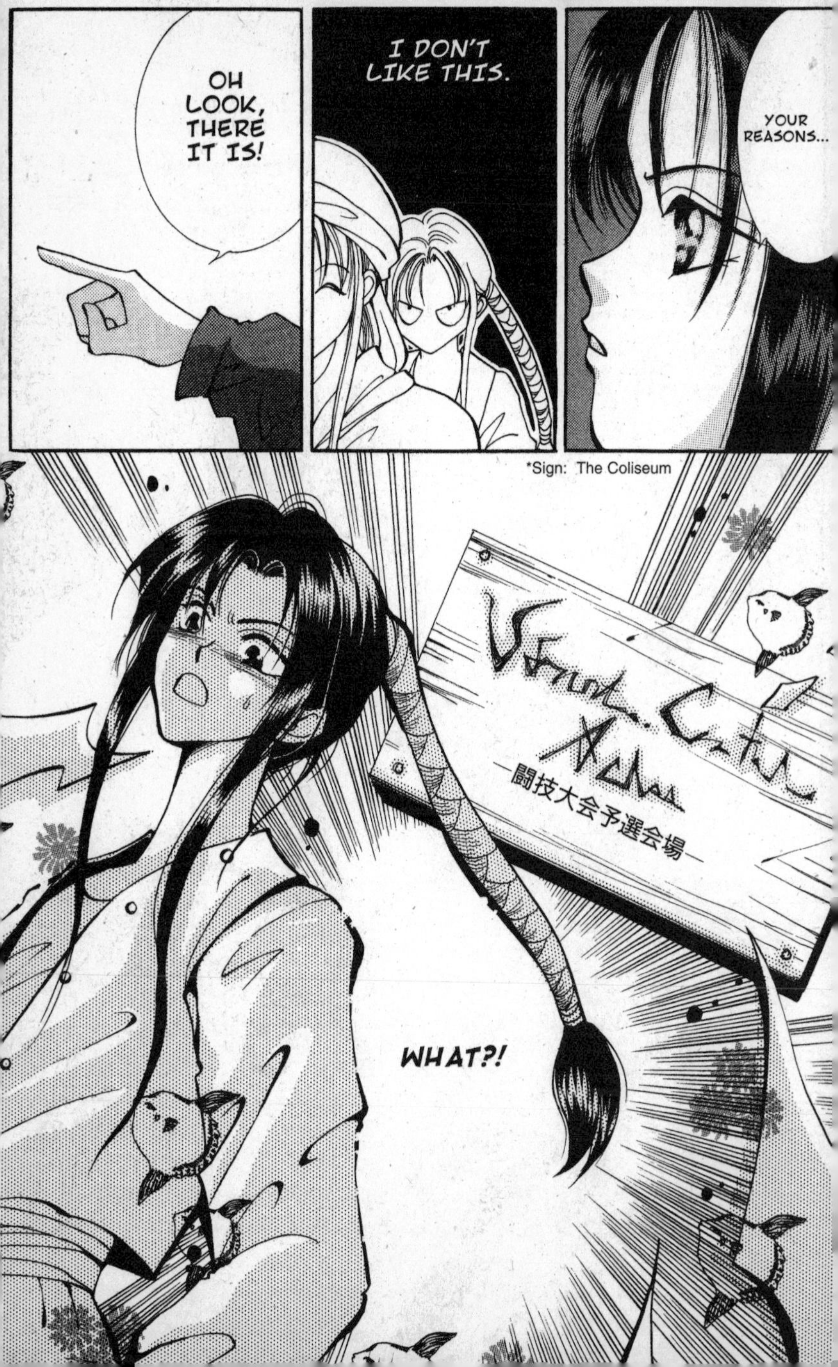
YOUR REASONS...
I DON'T LIKE THIS.
OH LOOK, THERE IT IS!
*Sign: The Coliseum
闘技大会予選会場
WHAT?!

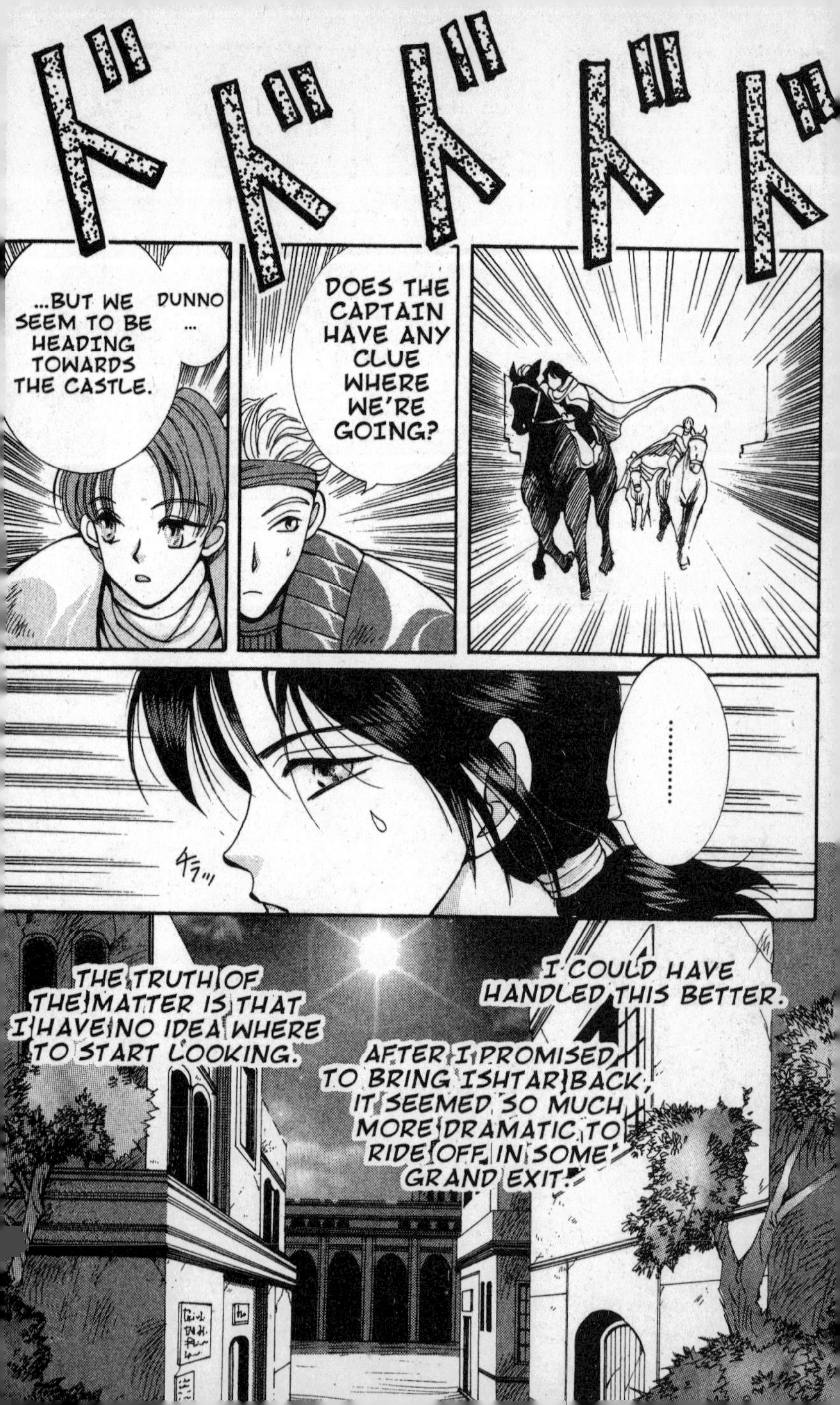
ドドドドド
DOES THE CAPTAIN HAVE ANY CLUE WHERE WE'RE GOING?
DUNNO ...
...BUT WE SEEM TO BE HEADING TOWARDS THE CASTLE.
......
I COULD HAVE HANDLED THIS BETTER.
AFTER I PROMISED TO BRING ISHTAR BACK, IT SEEMED SO MUCH MORE DRAMATIC TO RIDE OFF IN SOME GRAND EXIT.
THE TRUTH OF THE MATTER IS THAT I HAVE NO IDEA WHERE TO START LOOKING.

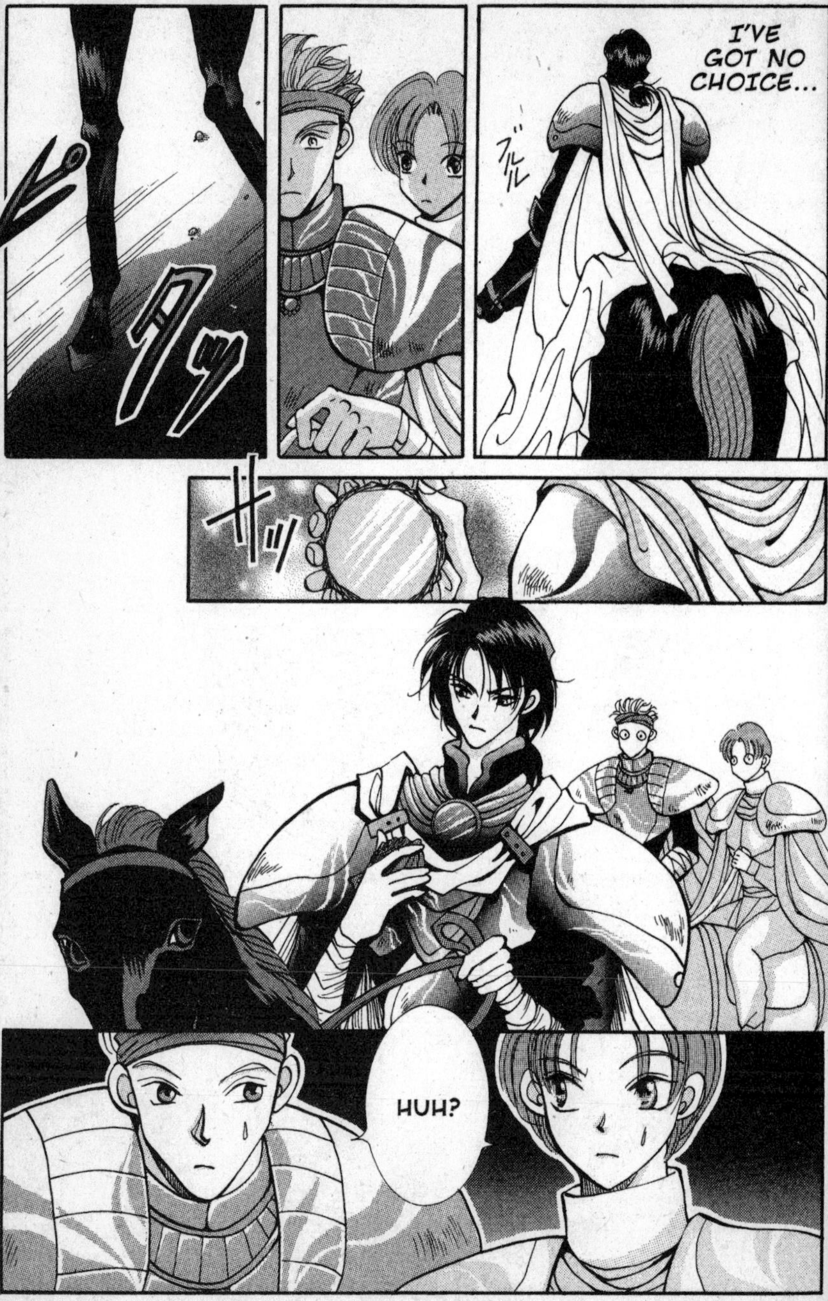
I'VE GOT NO CHOICE...
ブルル
タッ
サッ
HUH?

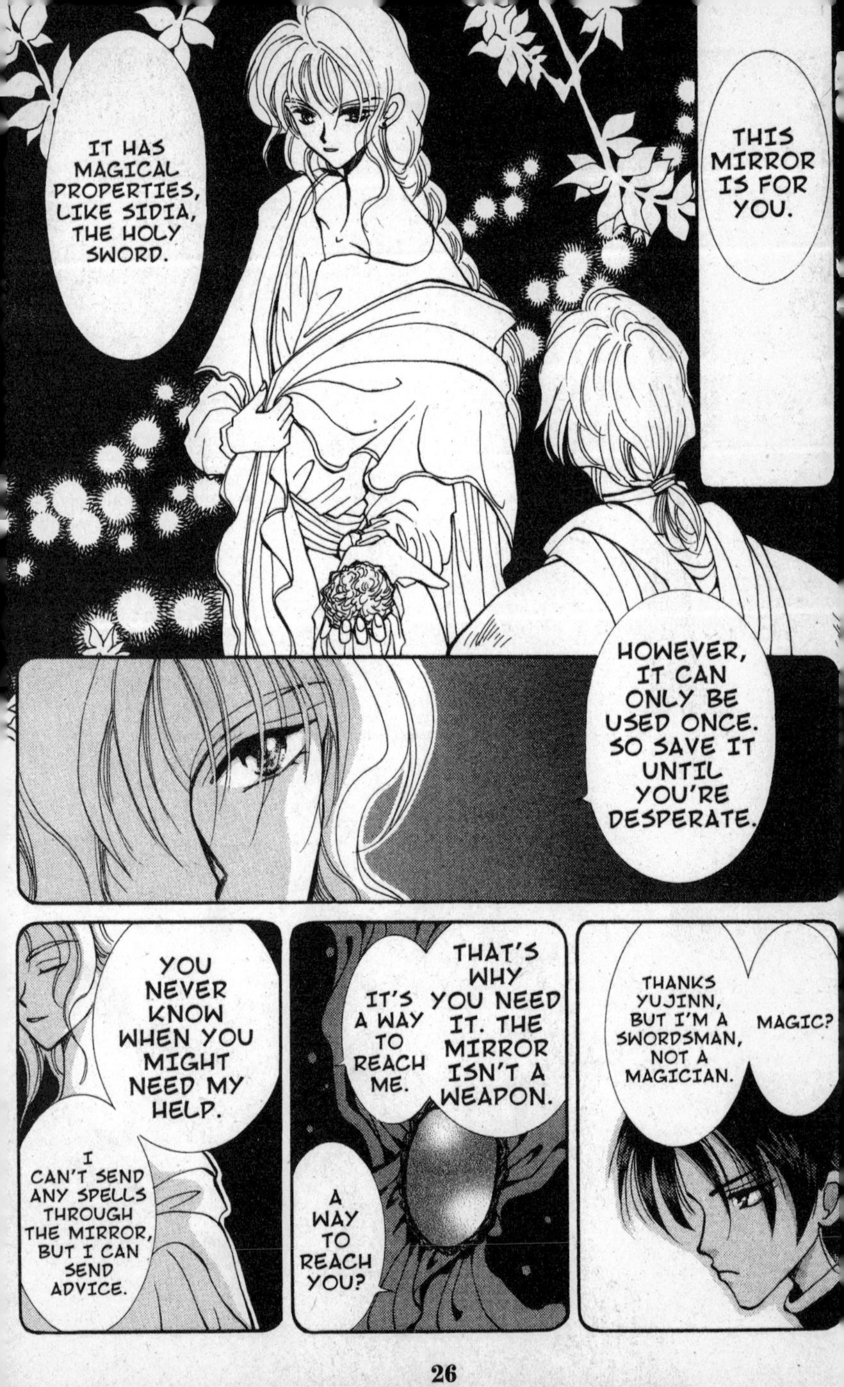
THIS MIRROR IS FOR YOU.
IT HAS MAGICAL PROPERTIES, LIKE SIDIA, THE HOLY SWORD.
HOWEVER, IT CAN ONLY BE USED ONCE. SO SAVE IT UNTIL YOU'RE DESPERATE.
MAGIC?
THANKS YUJINN, BUT I'M A SWORDSMAN, NOT A MAGICIAN.
THAT'S WHY YOU NEED IT. THE MIRROR ISN'T A WEAPON.
IT'S A WAY TO REACH ME.
A WAY TO REACH YOU?
YOU NEVER KNOW WHEN YOU MIGHT NEED MY HELP.
I CAN'T SEND ANY SPELLS THROUGH THE MIRROR, BUT I CAN SEND ADVICE.

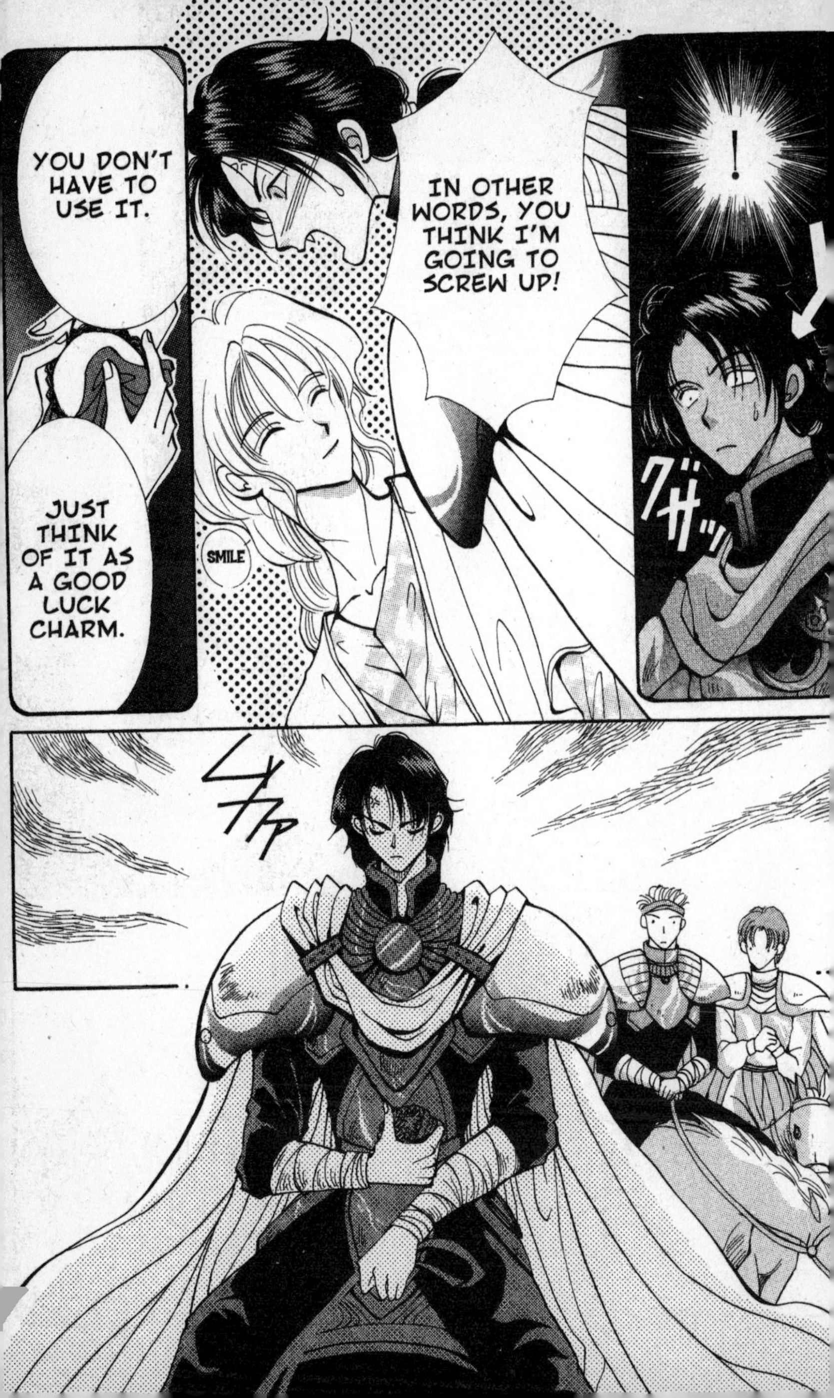
!
クザッ
IN OTHER WORDS, YOU THINK I'M GOING TO SCREW UP!
SMILE
YOU DON'T HAVE TO USE IT.
JUST THINK OF IT AS A GOOD LUCK CHARM.

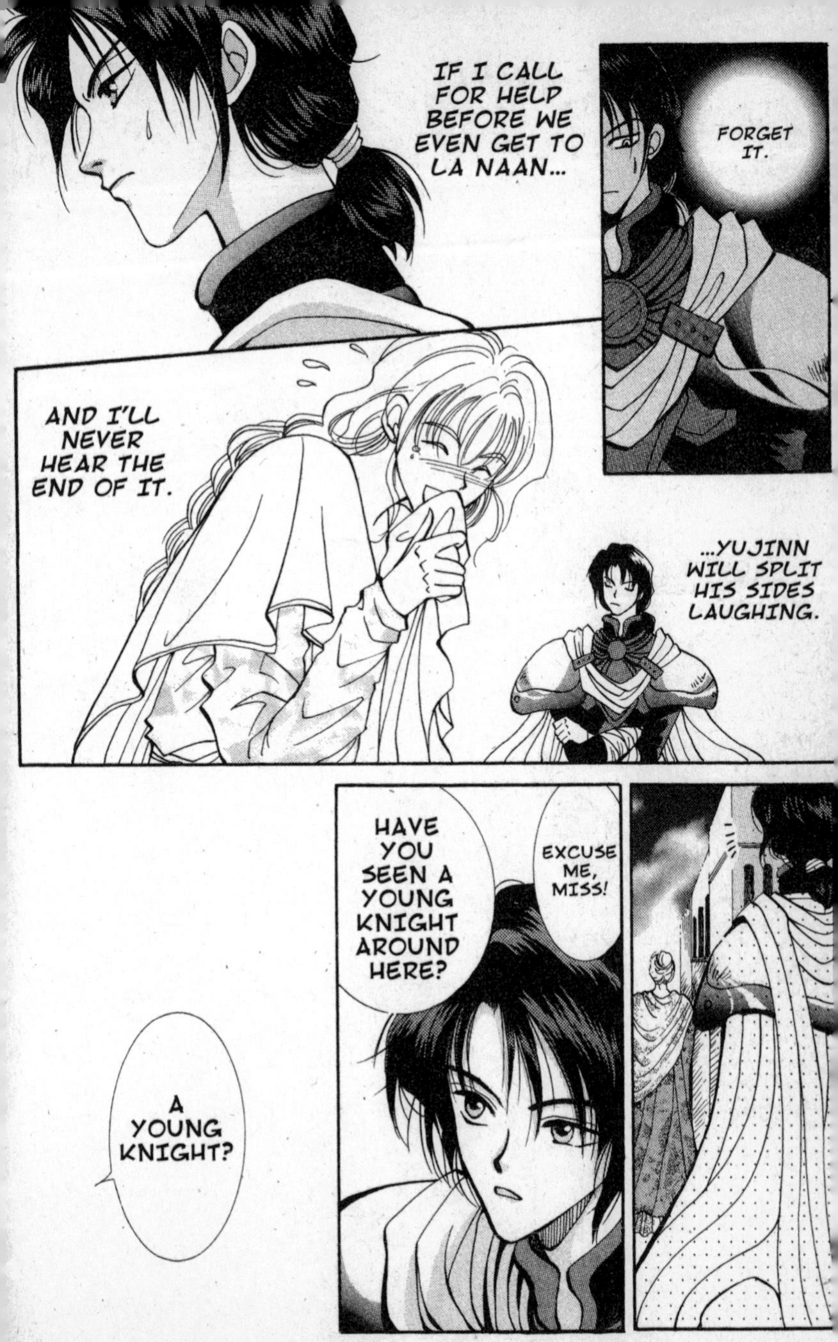
FORGET IT.
IF I CALL FOR HELP BEFORE WE EVEN GET TO LA NAAN...
...YUJINN WILL SPLIT HIS SIDES LAUGHING.
AND I'LL NEVER HEAR THE END OF IT.
EXCUSE ME, MISS!
HAVE YOU SEEN A YOUNG KNIGHT AROUND HERE?
A YOUNG KNIGHT?

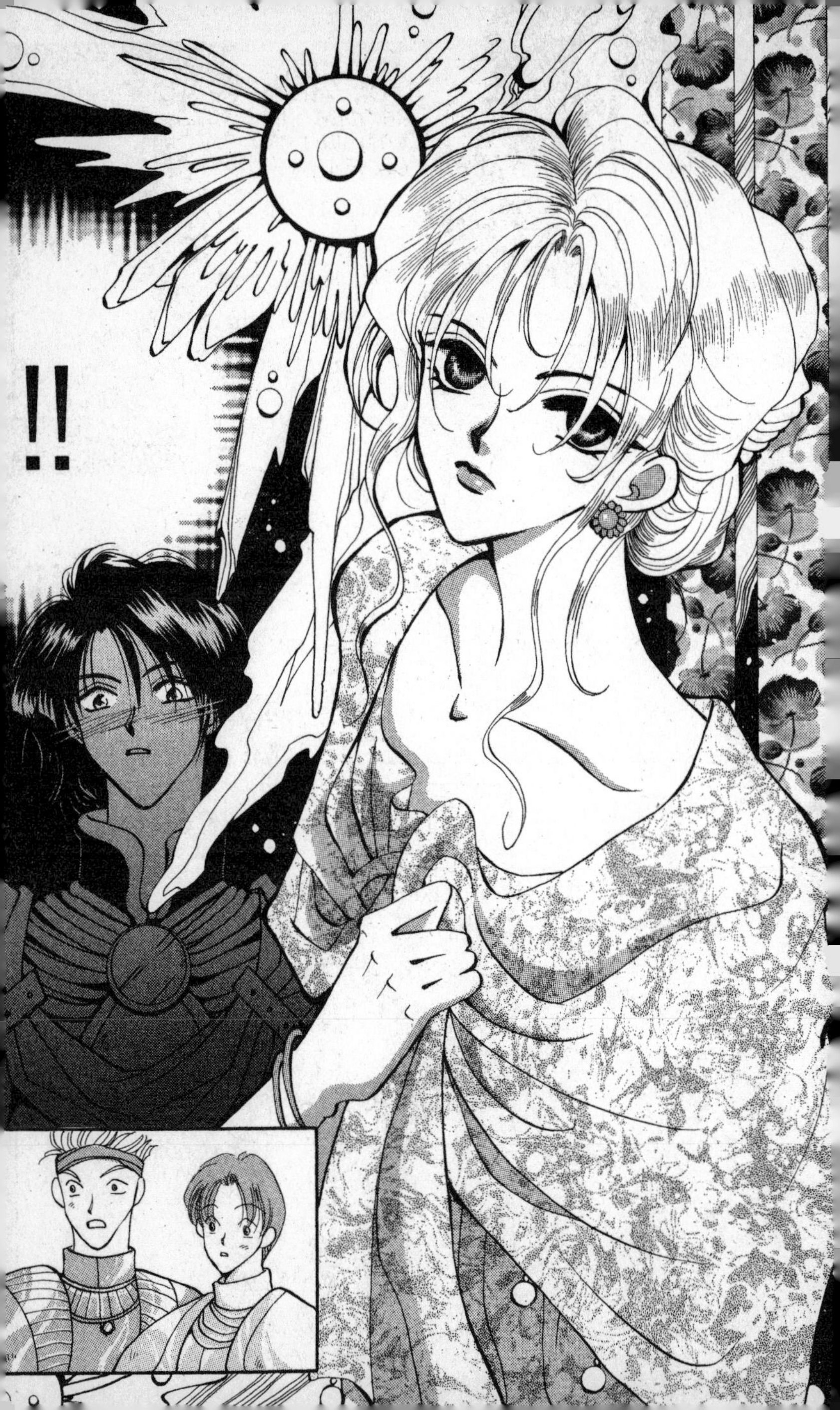
!!

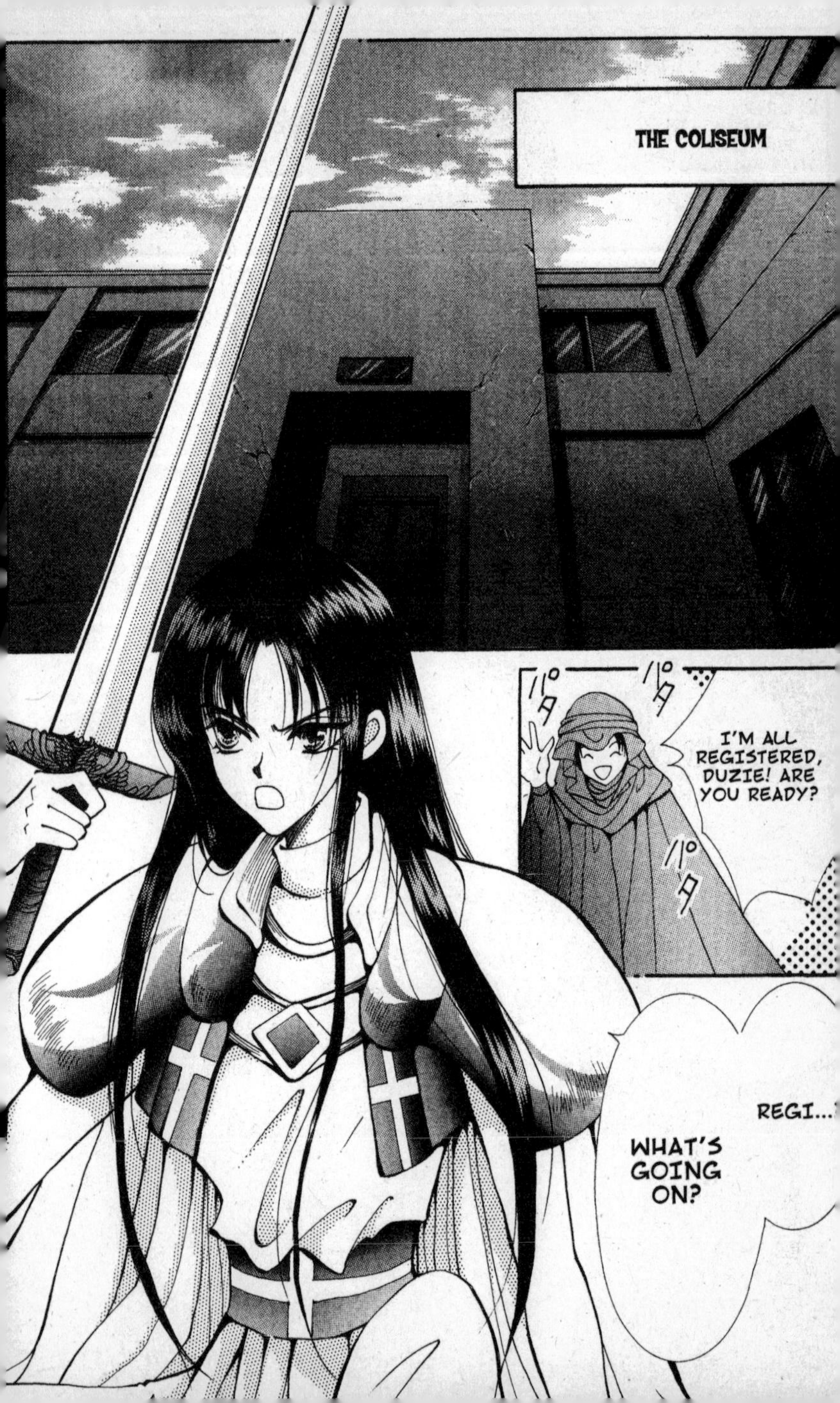
THE COLISEUM
パタ
パタ
I'M ALL REGISTERED, DUZIE! ARE YOU READY?
パタ
REGI...
WHAT'S GOING ON?

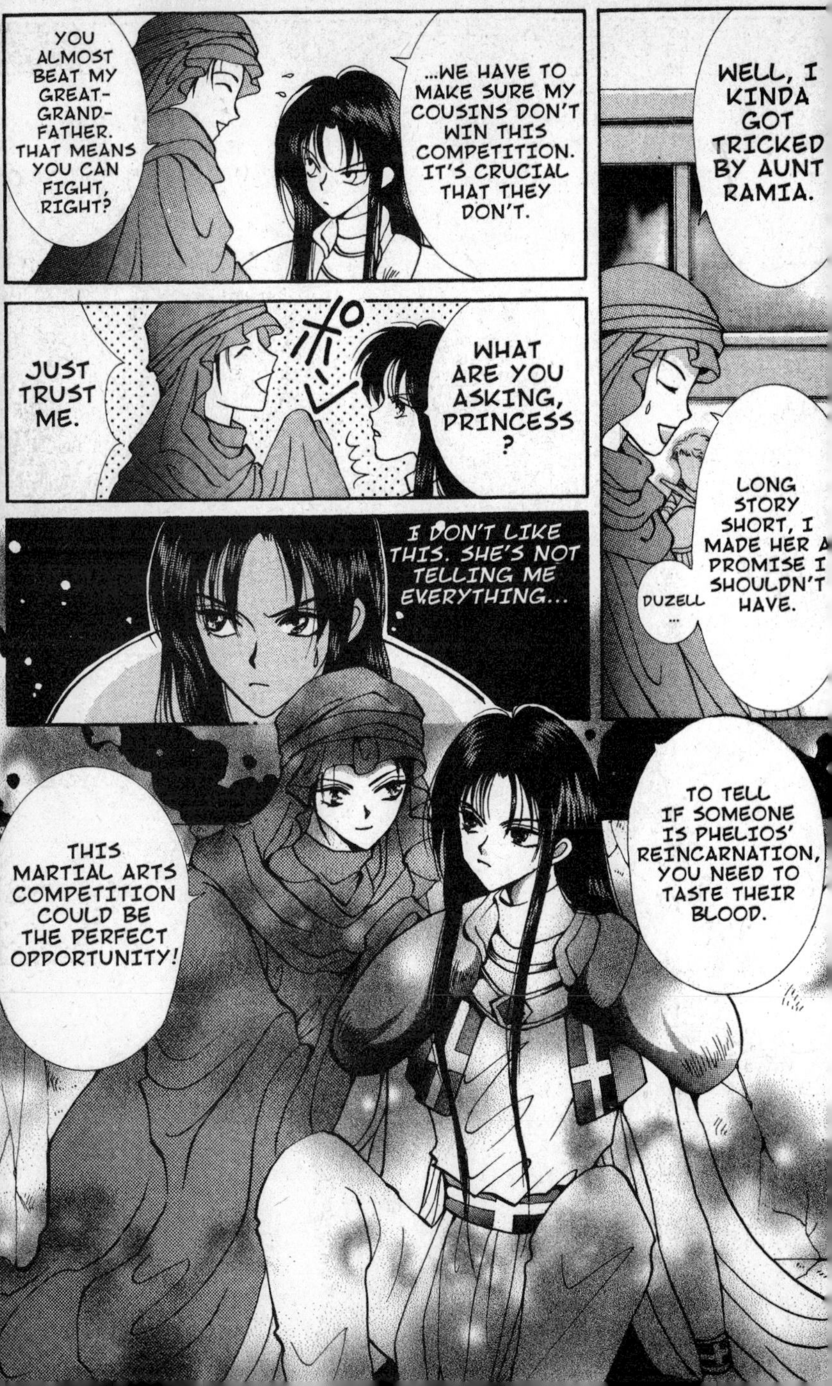
WELL, I KINDA GOT TRICKED BY AUNT RAMIA.
LONG STORY SHORT, I MADE HER A PROMISE I SHOULDN'T HAVE.
DUZELL...
...WE HAVE TO MAKE SURE MY COUSINS DON'T WIN THIS COMPETITION. IT'S CRUCIAL THAT THEY DON'T.
YOU ALMOST BEAT MY GREAT-GRANDFATHER. THAT MEANS YOU CAN FIGHT, RIGHT?
WHAT ARE YOU ASKING, PRINCESS?
ポン
JUST TRUST ME.
I DON'T LIKE THIS. SHE'S NOT TELLING ME EVERYTHING...
TO TELL IF SOMEONE IS PHELIOS' REINCARNATION, YOU NEED TO TASTE THEIR BLOOD.
THIS MARTIAL ARTS COMPETITION COULD BE THE PERFECT OPPORTUNITY!

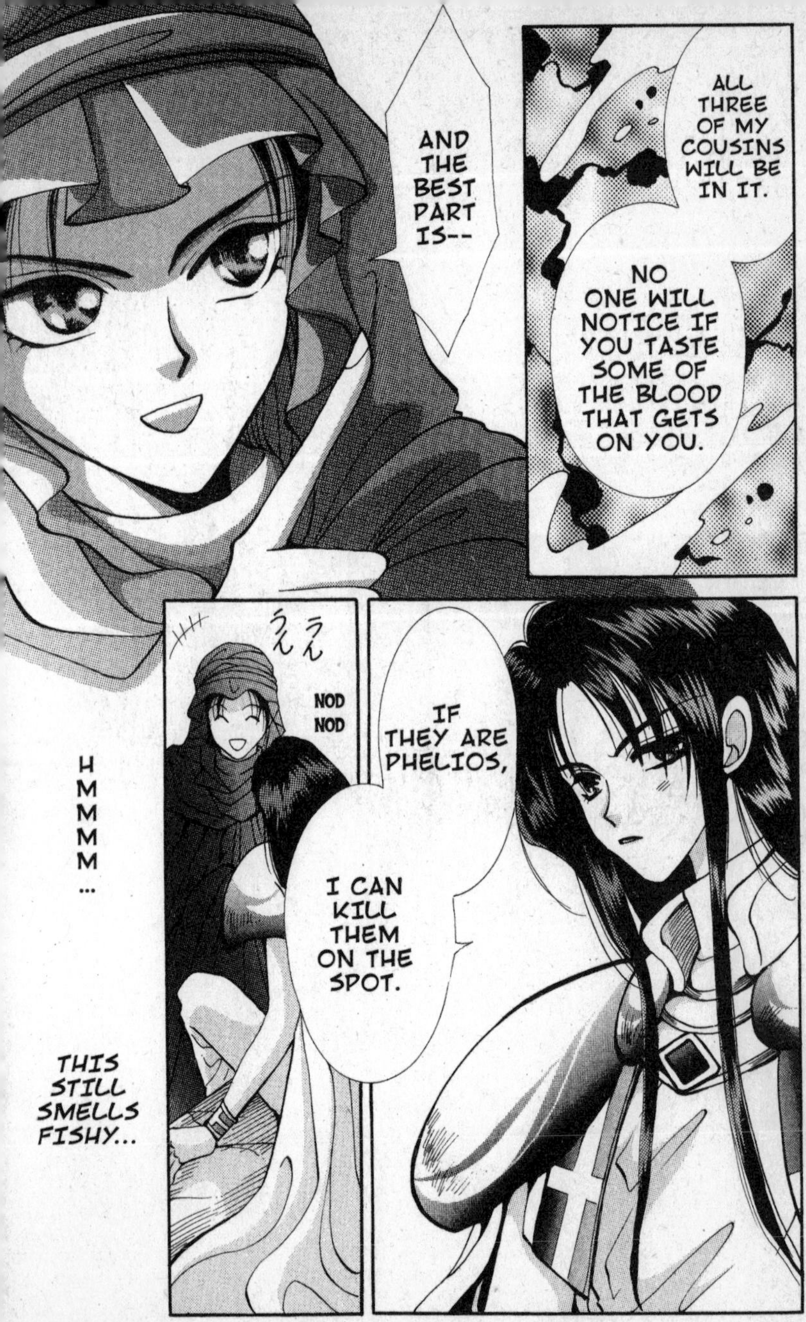
ALL THREE OF MY COUSINS WILL BE IN IT.
AND THE BEST PART IS--
NO ONE WILL NOTICE IF YOU TASTE SOME OF THE BLOOD THAT GETS ON YOU.
IF THEY ARE PHELIOS,
I CAN KILL THEM ON THE SPOT.
うんうん
NOD NOD
HMMMM...
THIS STILL SMELLS FISHY...

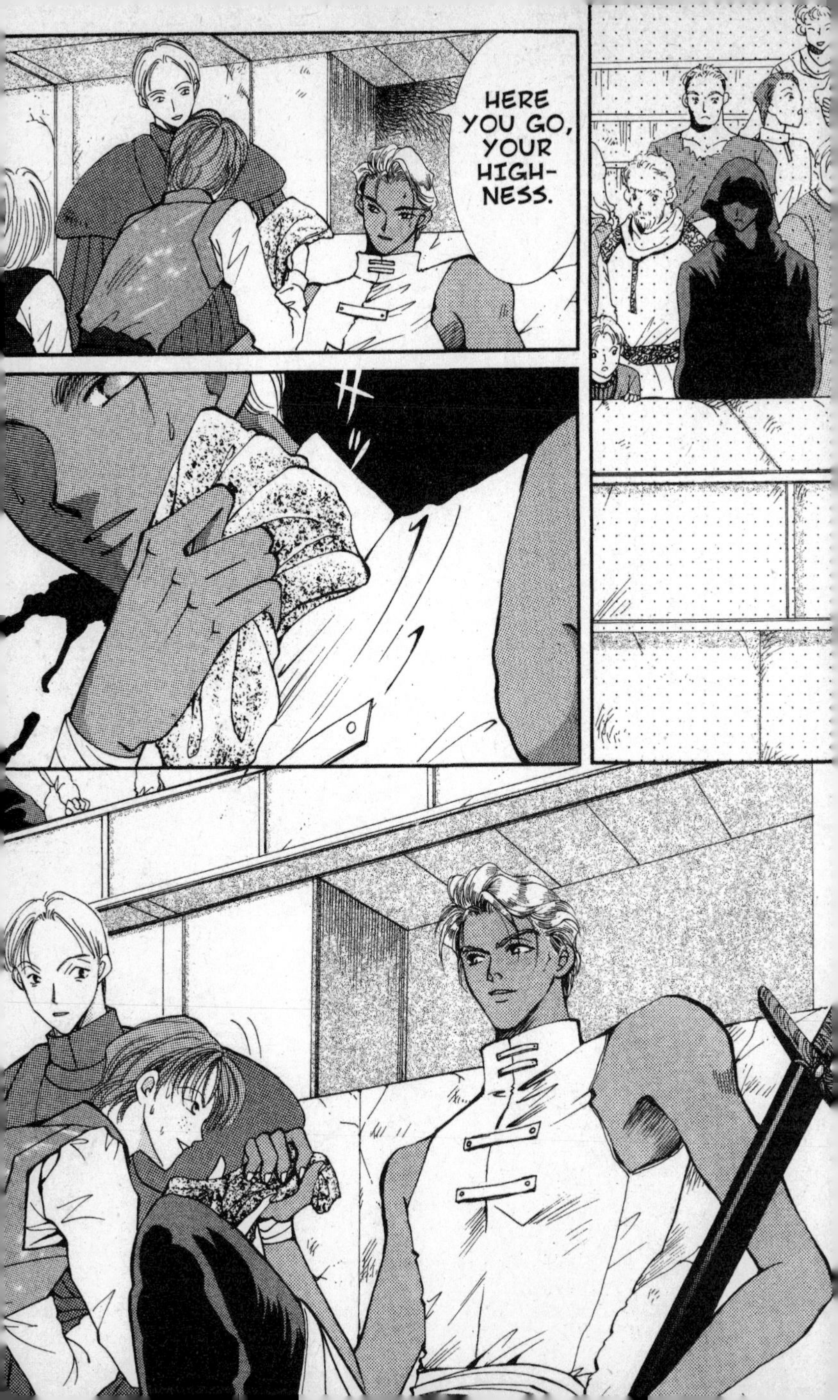
HERE YOU GO, YOUR HIGH-NESS.

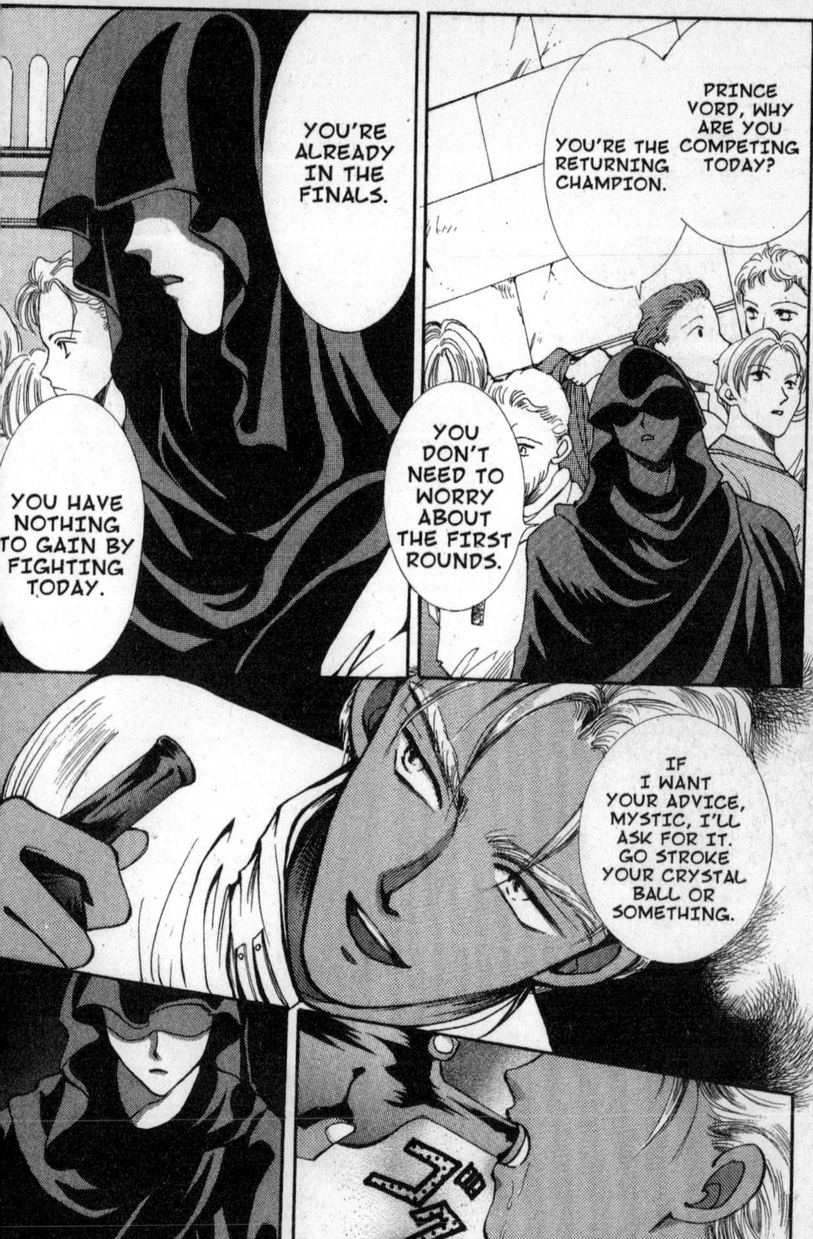
PRINCE VORD, WHY ARE YOU COMPETING TODAY?
YOU'RE THE RETURNING CHAMPION.
YOU DON'T NEED TO WORRY ABOUT THE FIRST ROUNDS.
YOU'RE ALREADY IN THE FINALS.
YOU HAVE NOTHING TO GAIN BY FIGHTING TODAY.
IF I WANT YOUR ADVICE, MYSTIC, I'LL ASK FOR IT. GO STROKE YOUR CRYSTAL BALL OR SOMETHING.

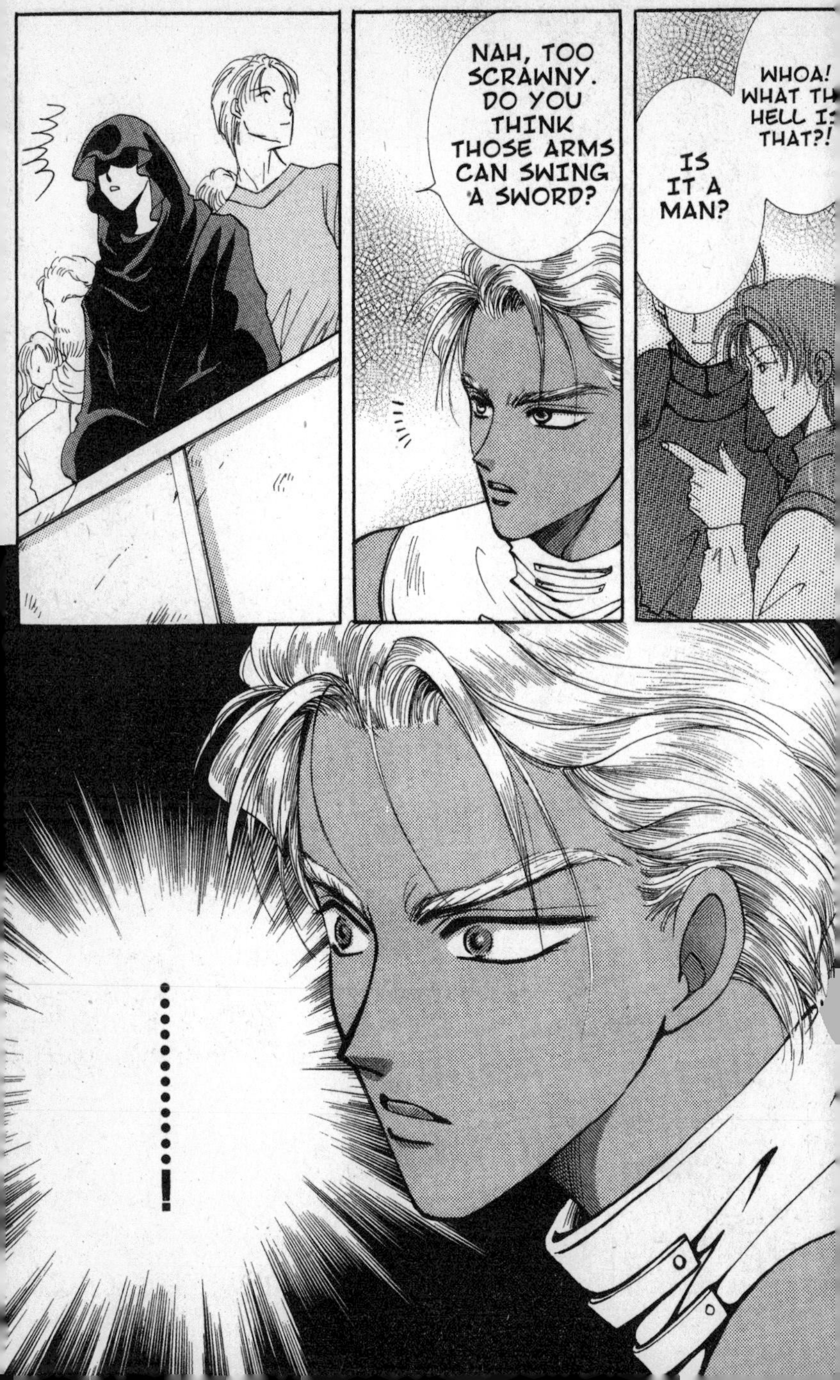
WHOA! WHAT TH HELL I THAT?!
IS IT A MAN?
NAH, TOO SCRAWNY. DO YOU THINK THOSE ARMS CAN SWING A SWORD?
......!

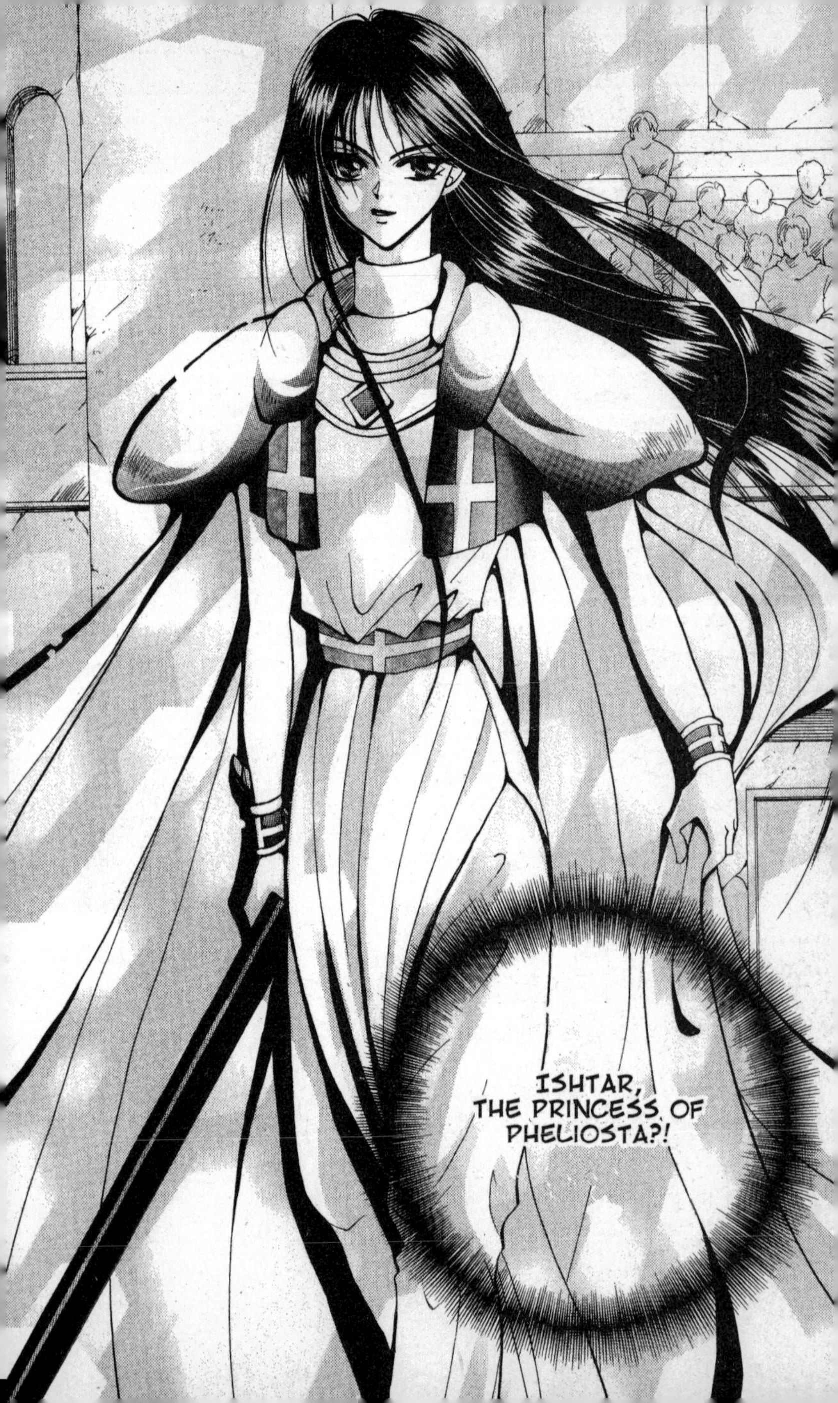
ISHTAR, THE PRINCESS OF PHELIOSTA?!

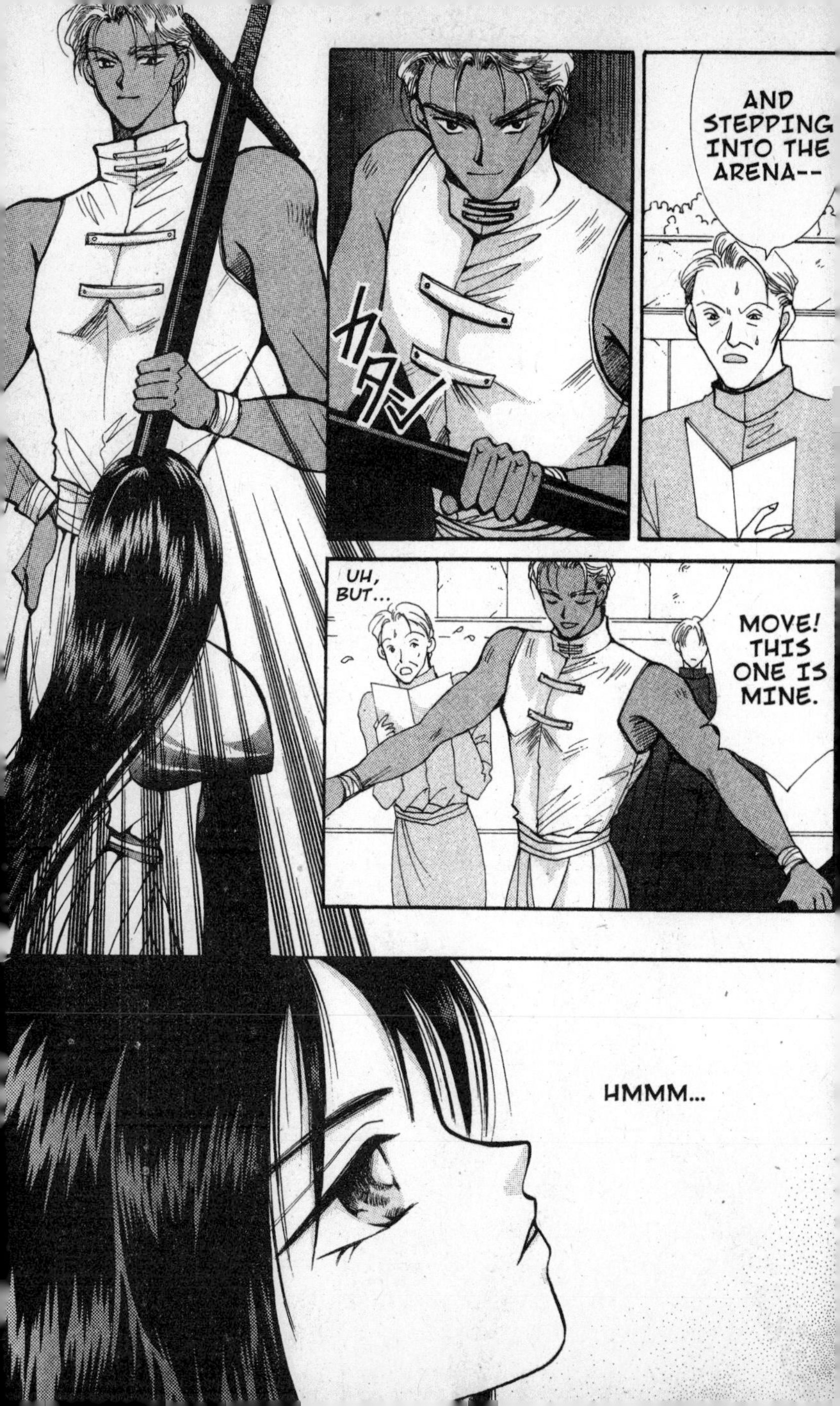
AND STEPPING INTO THE ARENA--
カタン
MOVE! THIS ONE IS MINE.
UH, BUT...
HMMM...

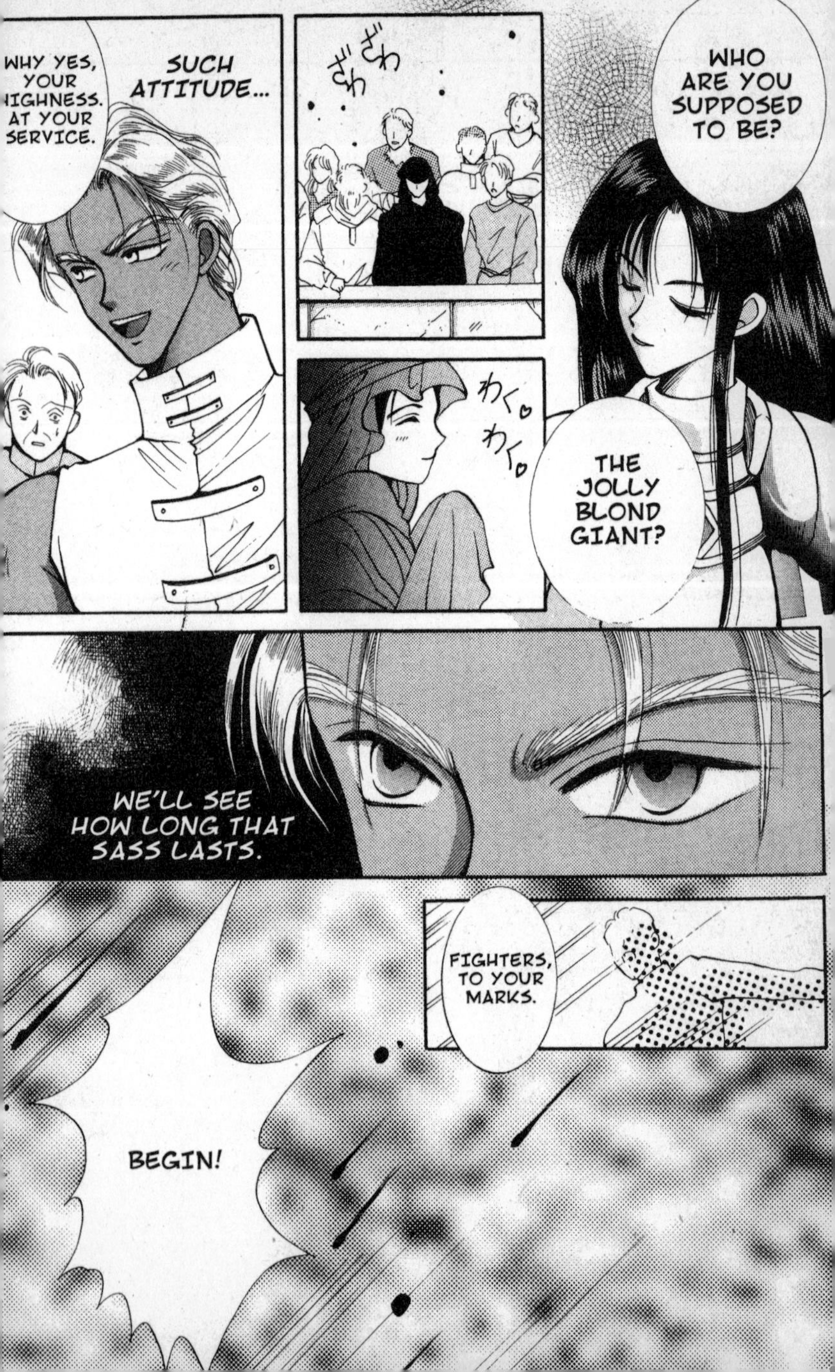
WHO ARE YOU SUPPOSED TO BE?
THE JOLLY BLOND GIANT?
ざわ ざわ
わく♡ わく♡
SUCH ATTITUDE...
WHY YES, YOUR HIGHNESS. AT YOUR SERVICE.
WE'LL SEE HOW LONG THAT SASS LASTS.
FIGHTERS, TO YOUR MARKS.
BEGIN!

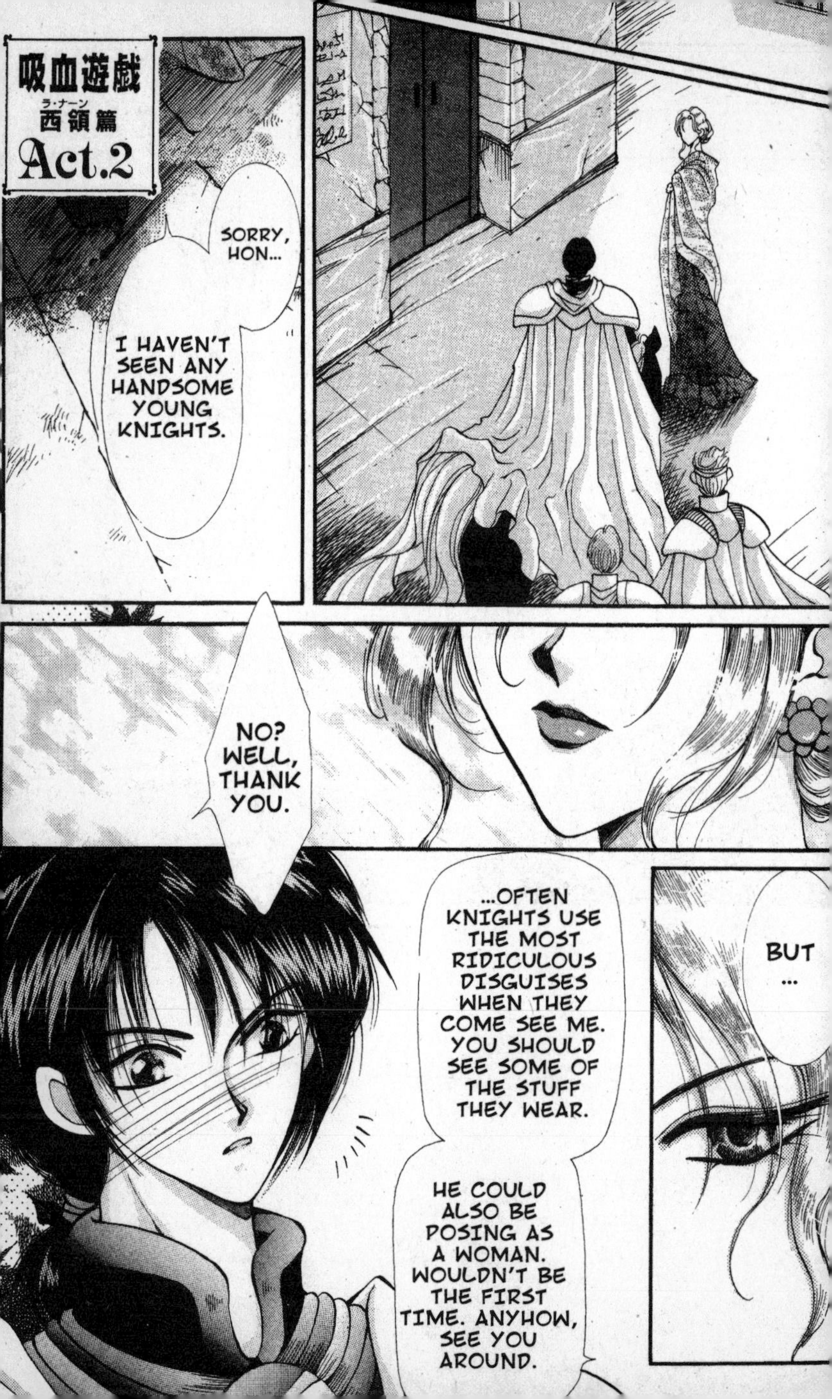
吸血遊戯
ラ・ナーン
西領篇
Act.2
SORRY, HON...
I HAVEN'T SEEN ANY HANDSOME YOUNG KNIGHTS.
NO? WELL, THANK YOU.
BUT ...
...OFTEN KNIGHTS USE THE MOST RIDICULOUS DISGUISES WHEN THEY COME SEE ME. YOU SHOULD SEE SOME OF THE STUFF THEY WEAR.
HE COULD ALSO BE POSING AS A WOMAN. WOULDN'T BE THE FIRST TIME. ANYHOW, SEE YOU AROUND.

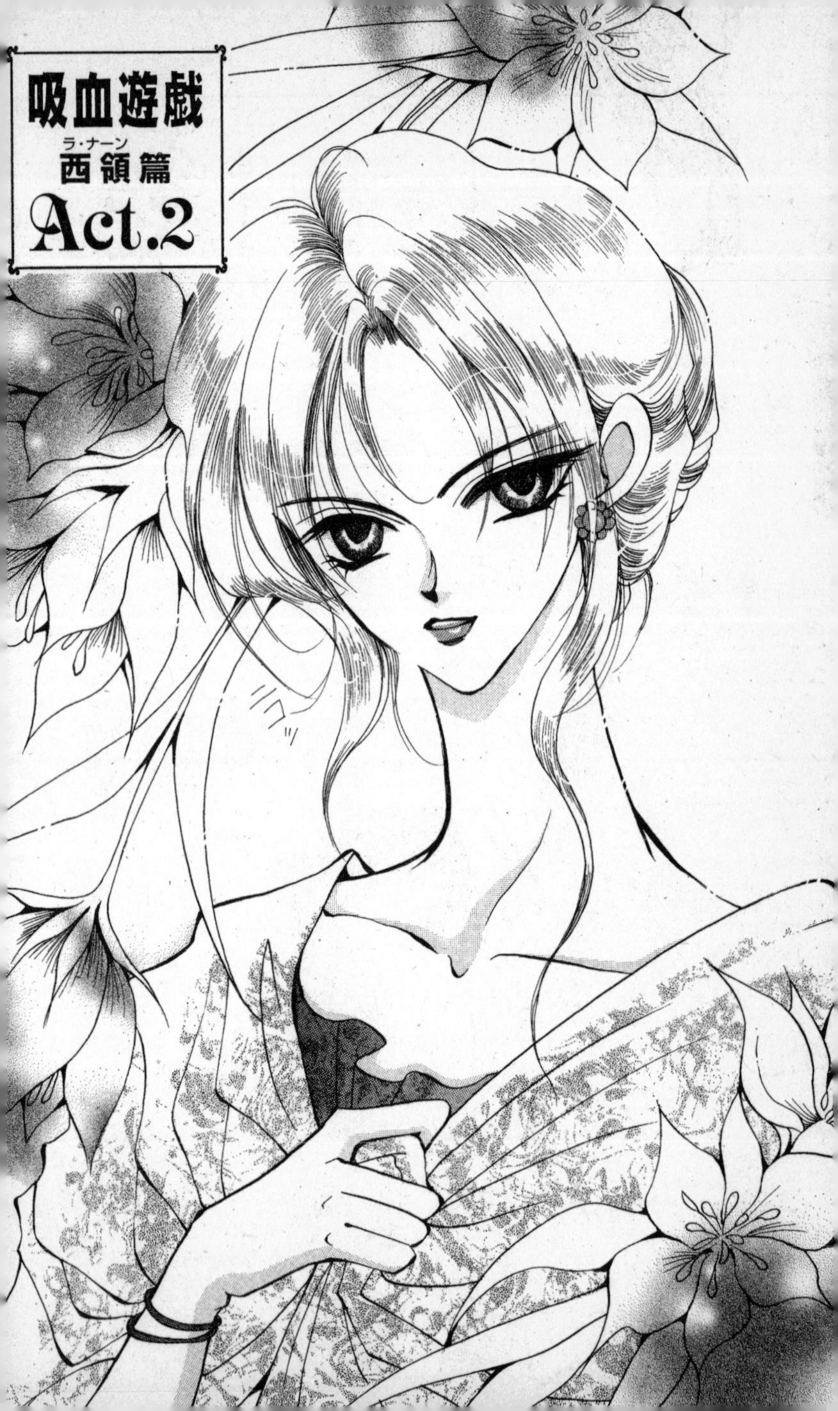
吸血遊戯
西領篇（ラ・ナーン）
Act.2

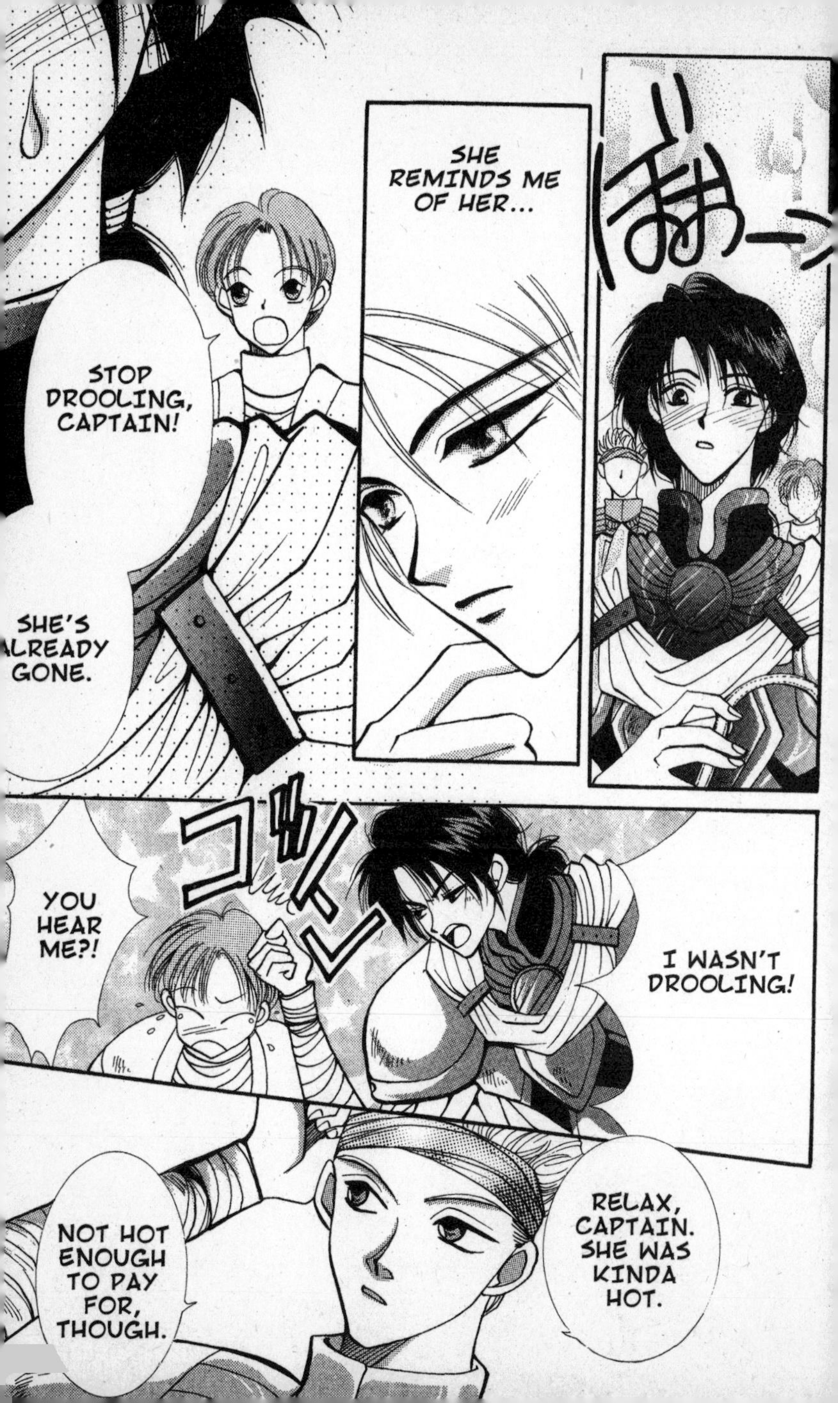
SHE REMINDS ME OF HER...
STOP DROOLING, CAPTAIN!
SHE'S ALREADY GONE.
I WASN'T DROOLING!
YOU HEAR ME?!
RELAX, CAPTAIN. SHE WAS KINDA HOT.
NOT HOT ENOUGH TO PAY FOR, THOUGH.

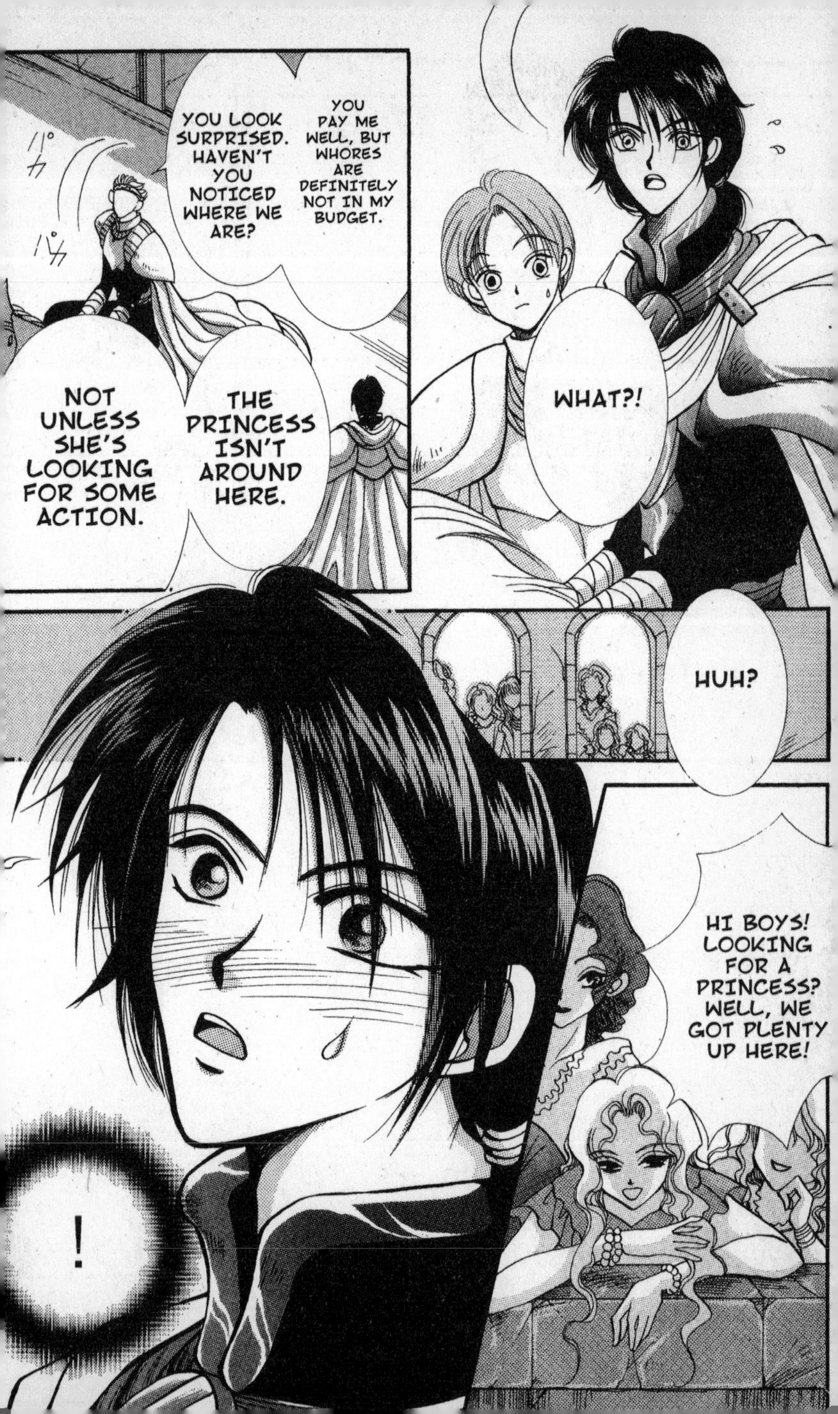
WHAT?!
YOU PAY ME WELL, BUT WHORES ARE DEFINITELY NOT IN MY BUDGET.
YOU LOOK SURPRISED. HAVEN'T YOU NOTICED WHERE WE ARE?
パカ
パカ
THE PRINCESS ISN'T AROUND HERE.
NOT UNLESS SHE'S LOOKING FOR SOME ACTION.
HUH?
HI BOYS! LOOKING FOR A PRINCESS? WELL, WE GOT PLENTY UP HERE!
!

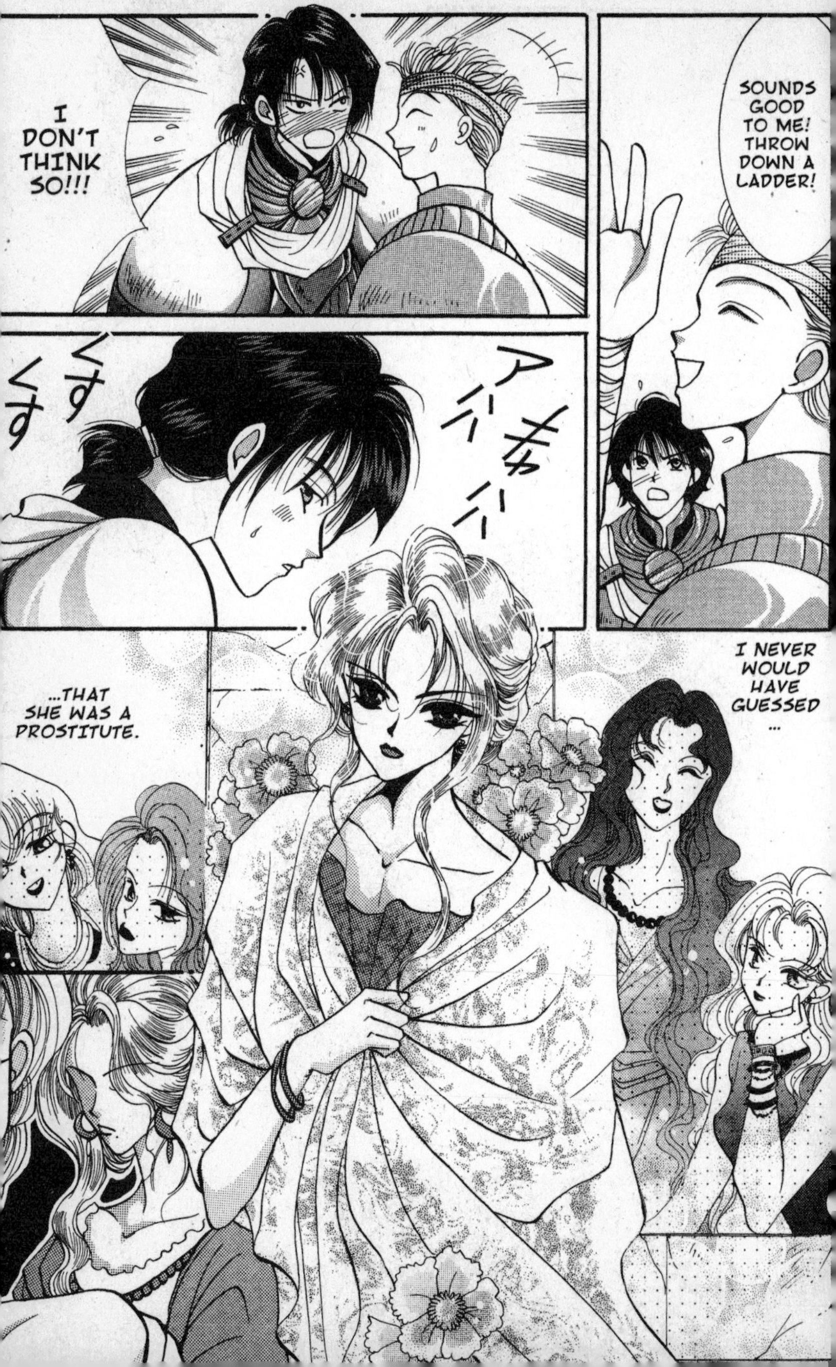
SOUNDS GOOD TO ME! THROW DOWN A LADDER!
I DON'T THINK SO!!!
アハハハ
くすくす
I NEVER WOULD HAVE GUESSED ...
...THAT SHE WAS A PROSTITUTE.

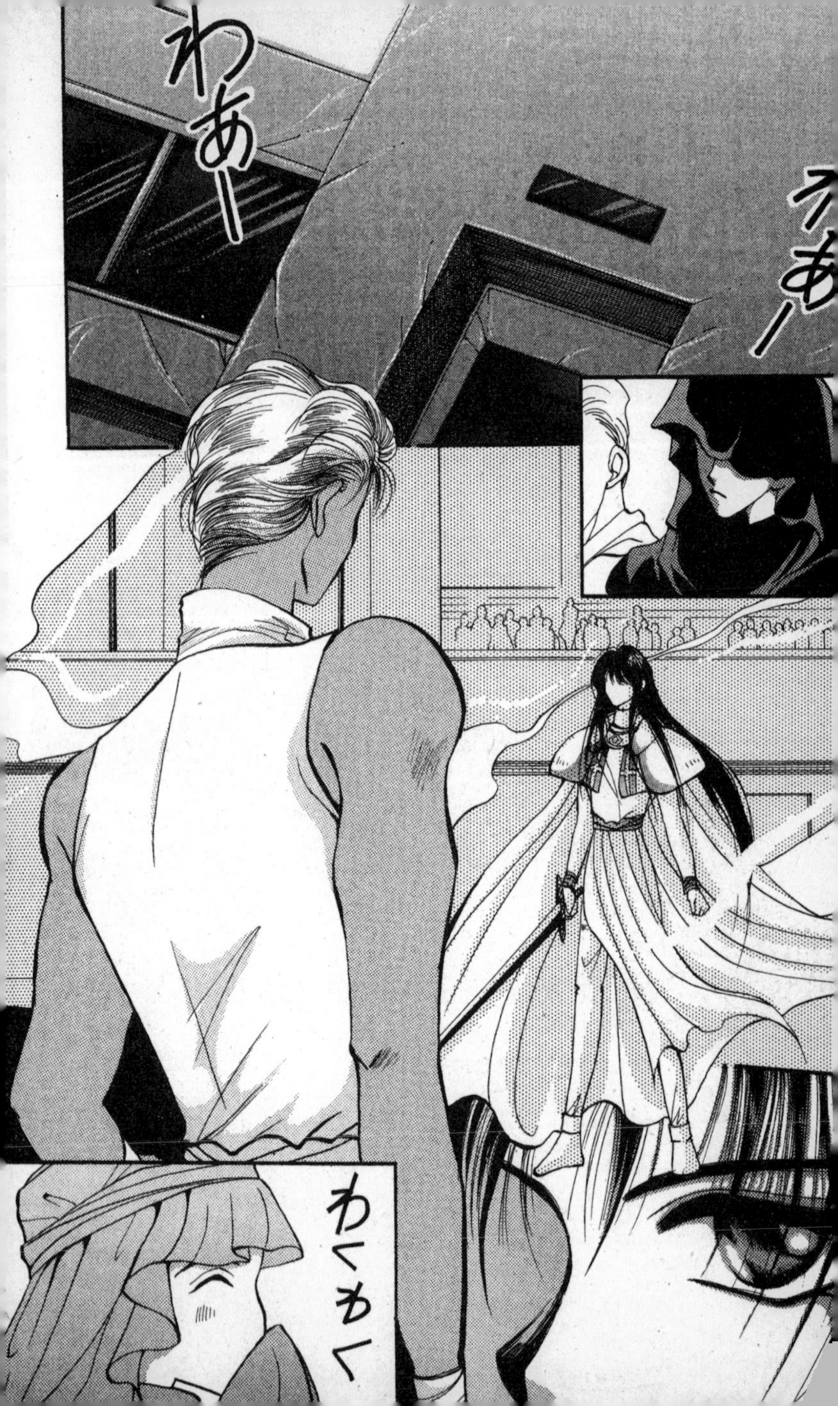
うあー
わあー
わくわく

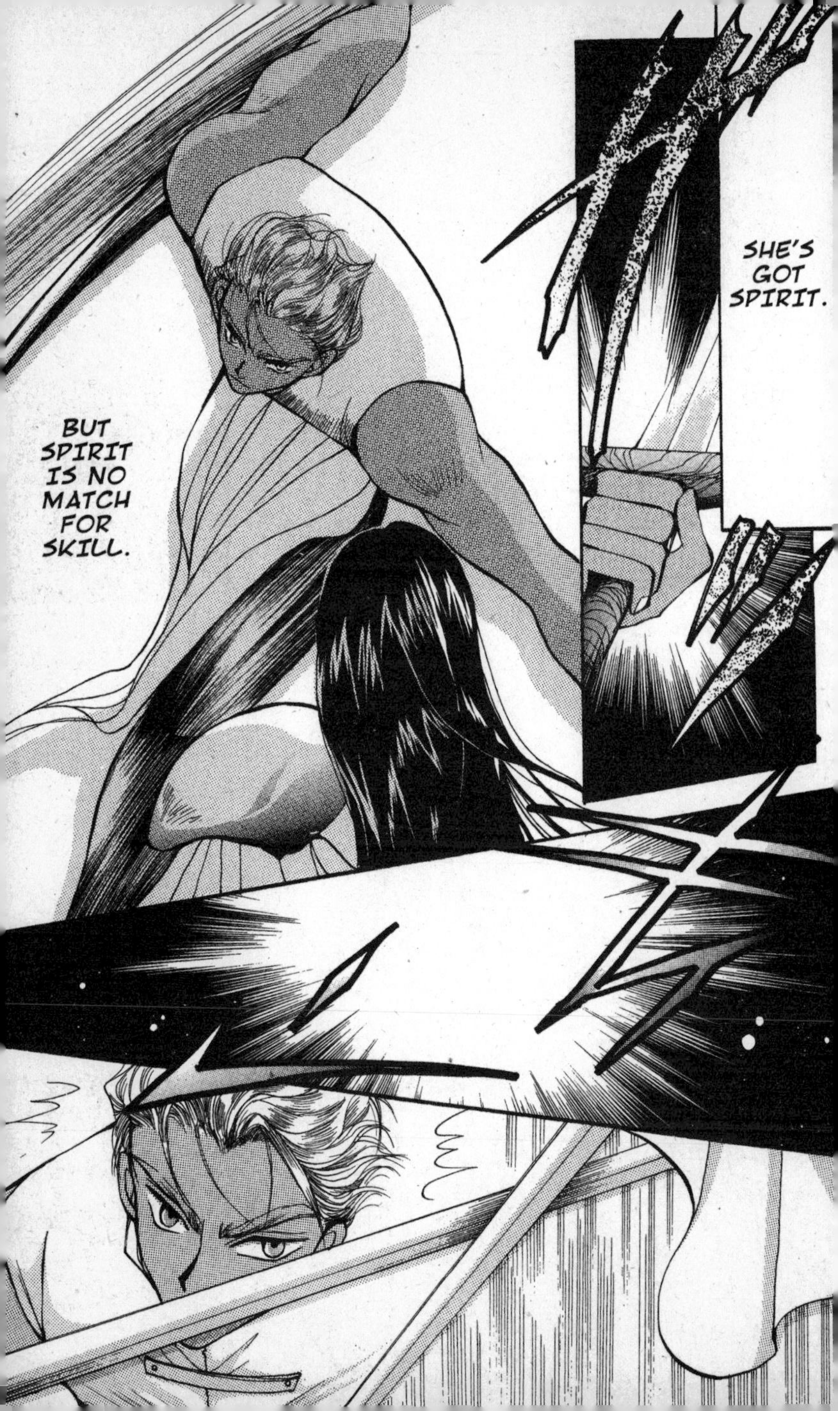
SHE'S GOT SPIRIT.
BUT SPIRIT IS NO MATCH FOR SKILL.

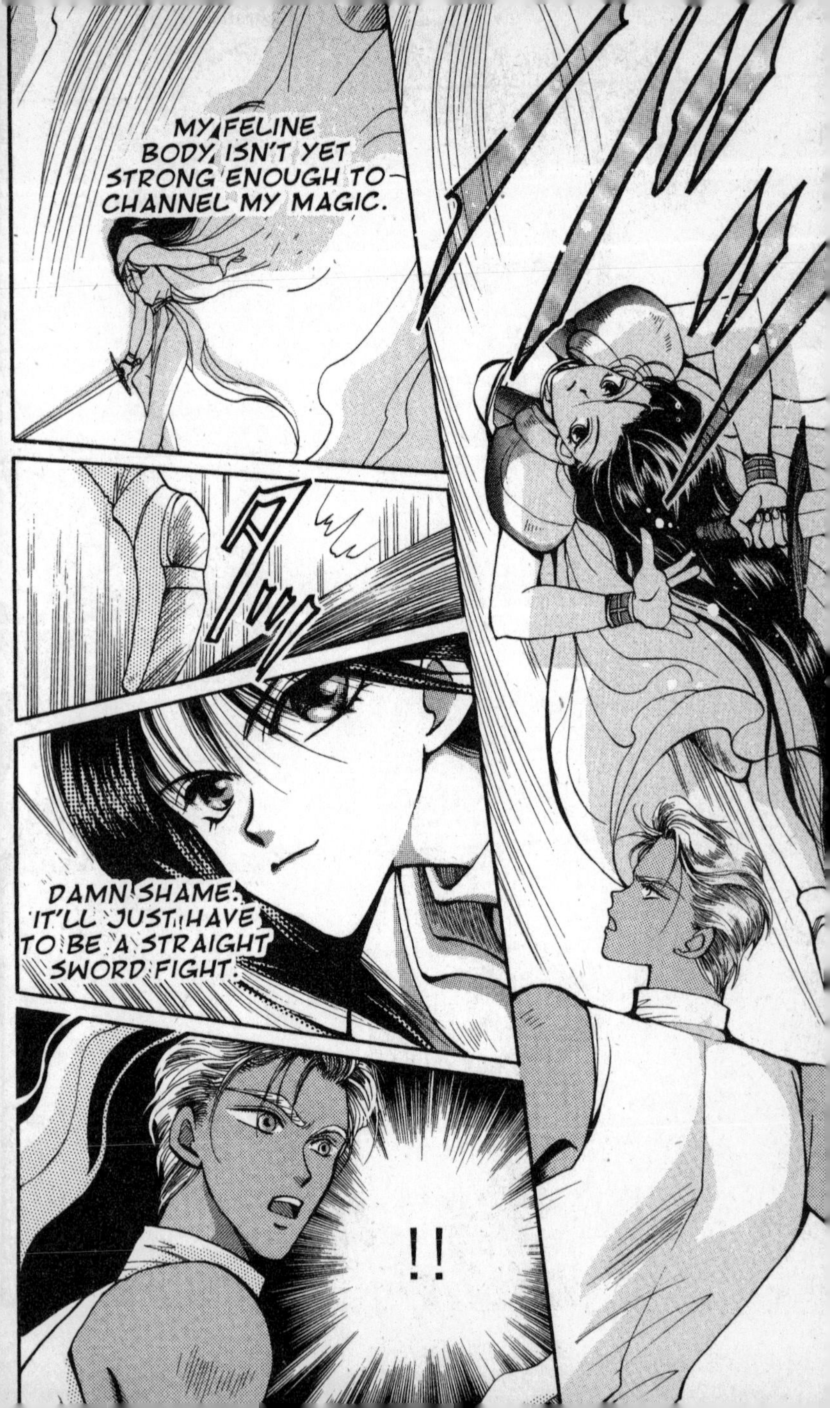
MY FELINE BODY ISN'T YET STRONG ENOUGH TO CHANNEL MY MAGIC.
DAMN SHAME. IT'LL JUST HAVE TO BE A STRAIGHT SWORD FIGHT.
!!

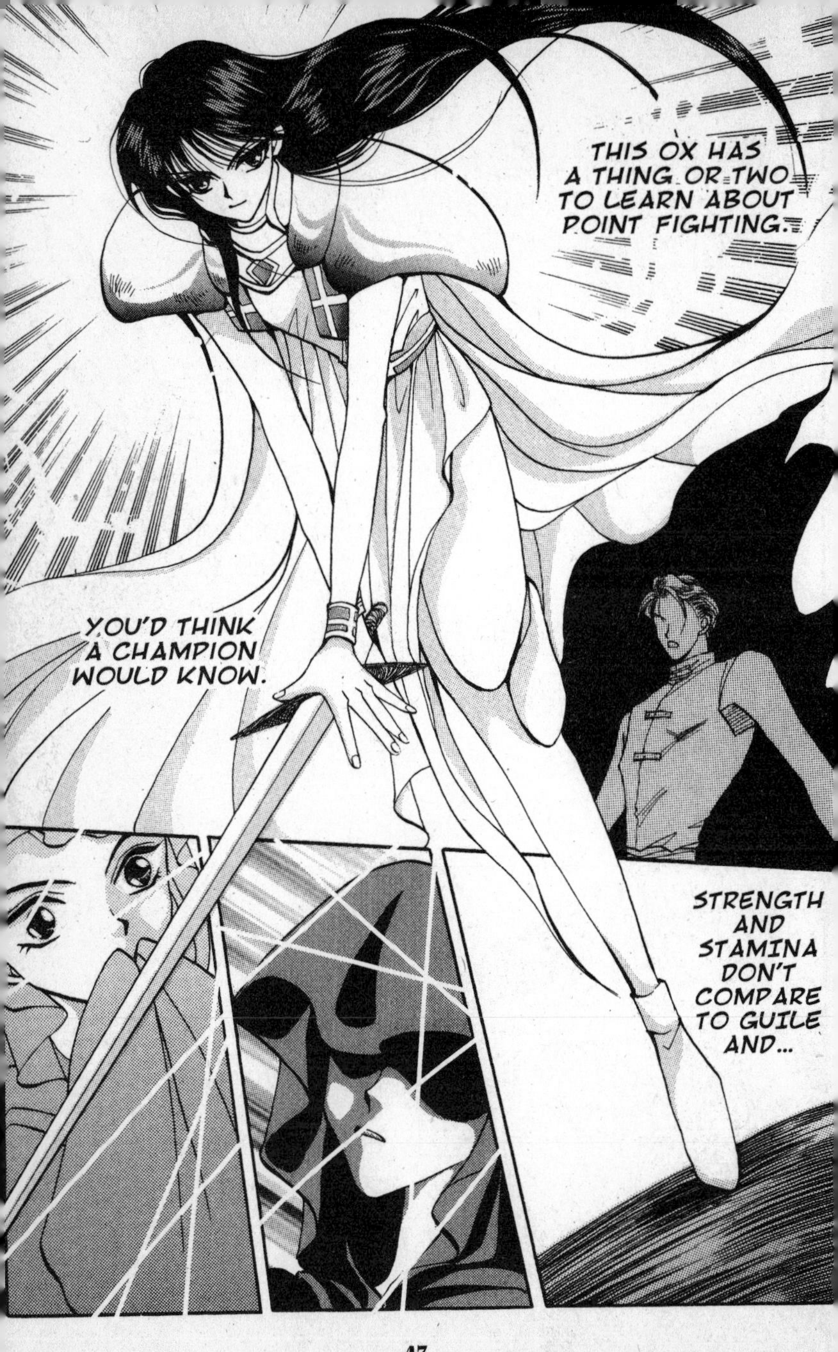
THIS OX HAS A THING OR TWO TO LEARN ABOUT POINT FIGHTING.
YOU'D THINK A CHAMPION WOULD KNOW.
STRENGTH AND STAMINA DON'T COMPARE TO GUILE AND...

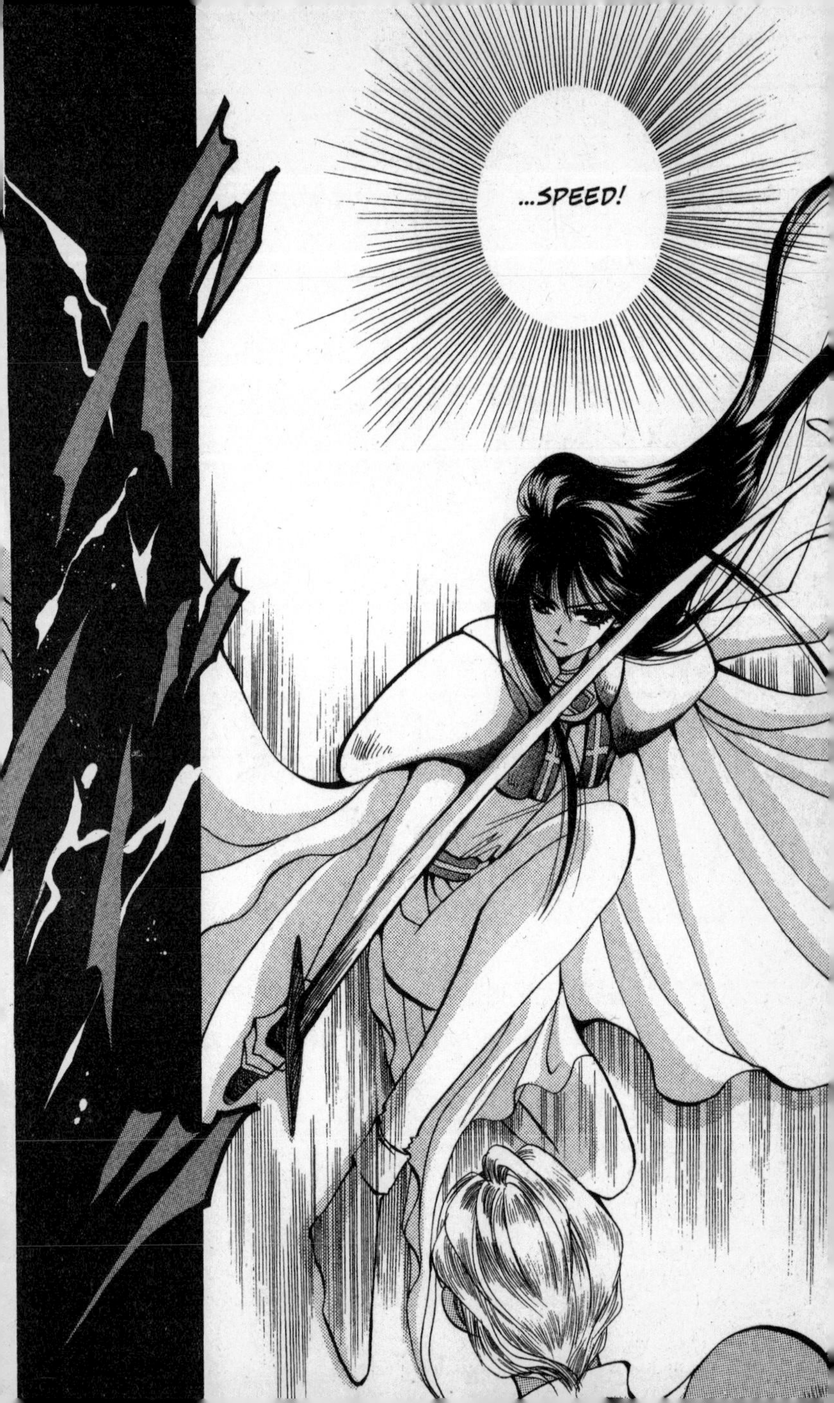
...SPEED!

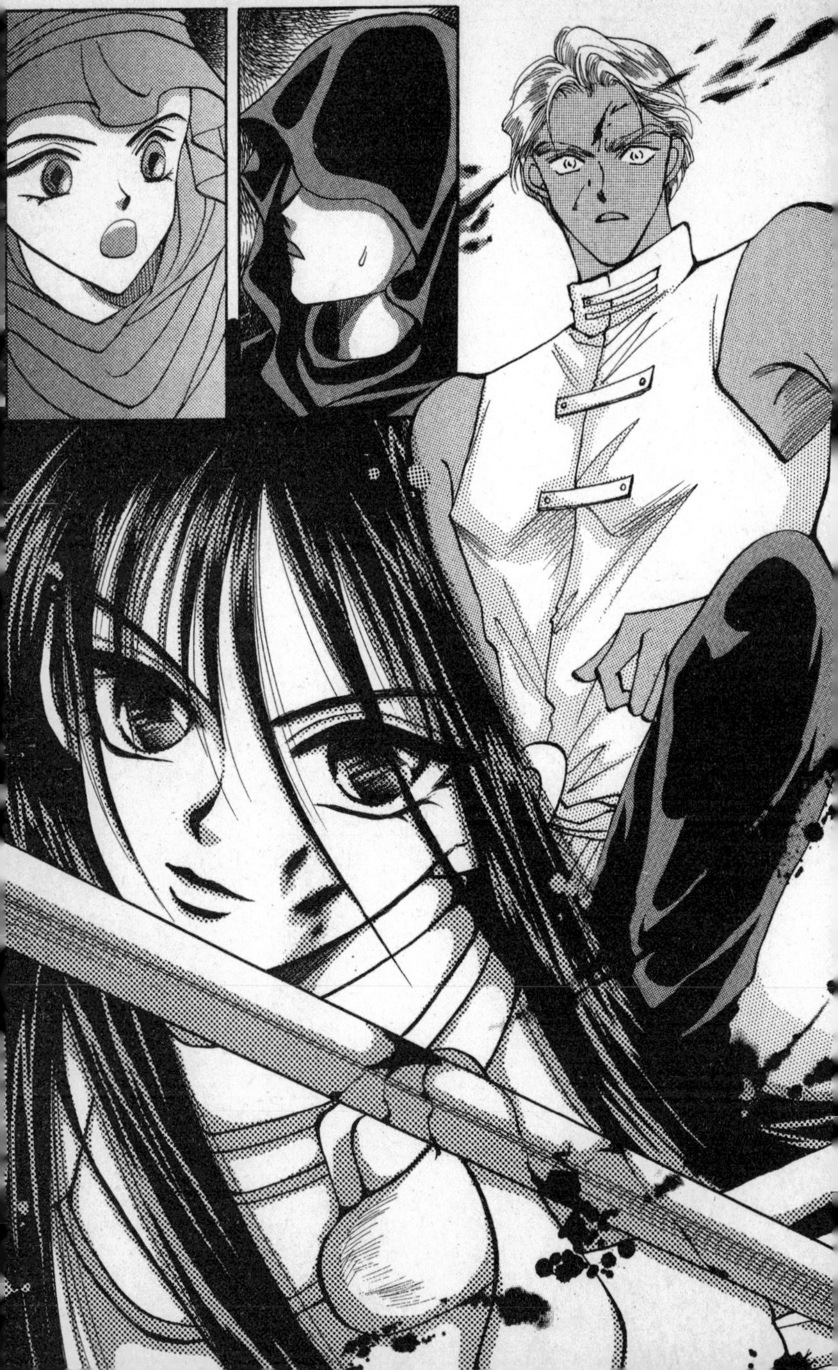

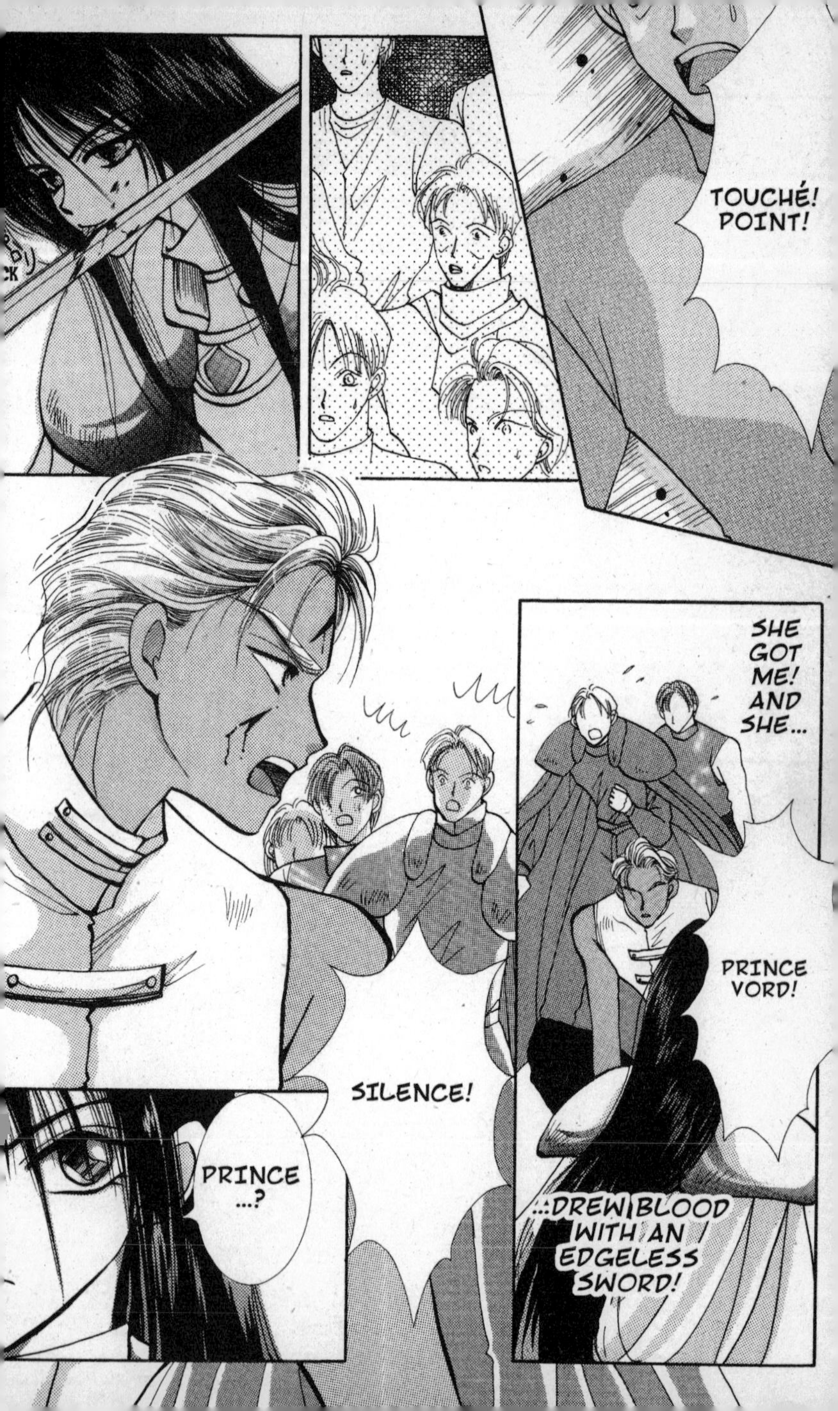
TOUCHÉ! POINT!
SHE GOT ME! AND SHE...
PRINCE VORD!
...DREW BLOOD WITH AN EDGELESS SWORD!
SILENCE!
PRINCE ...?

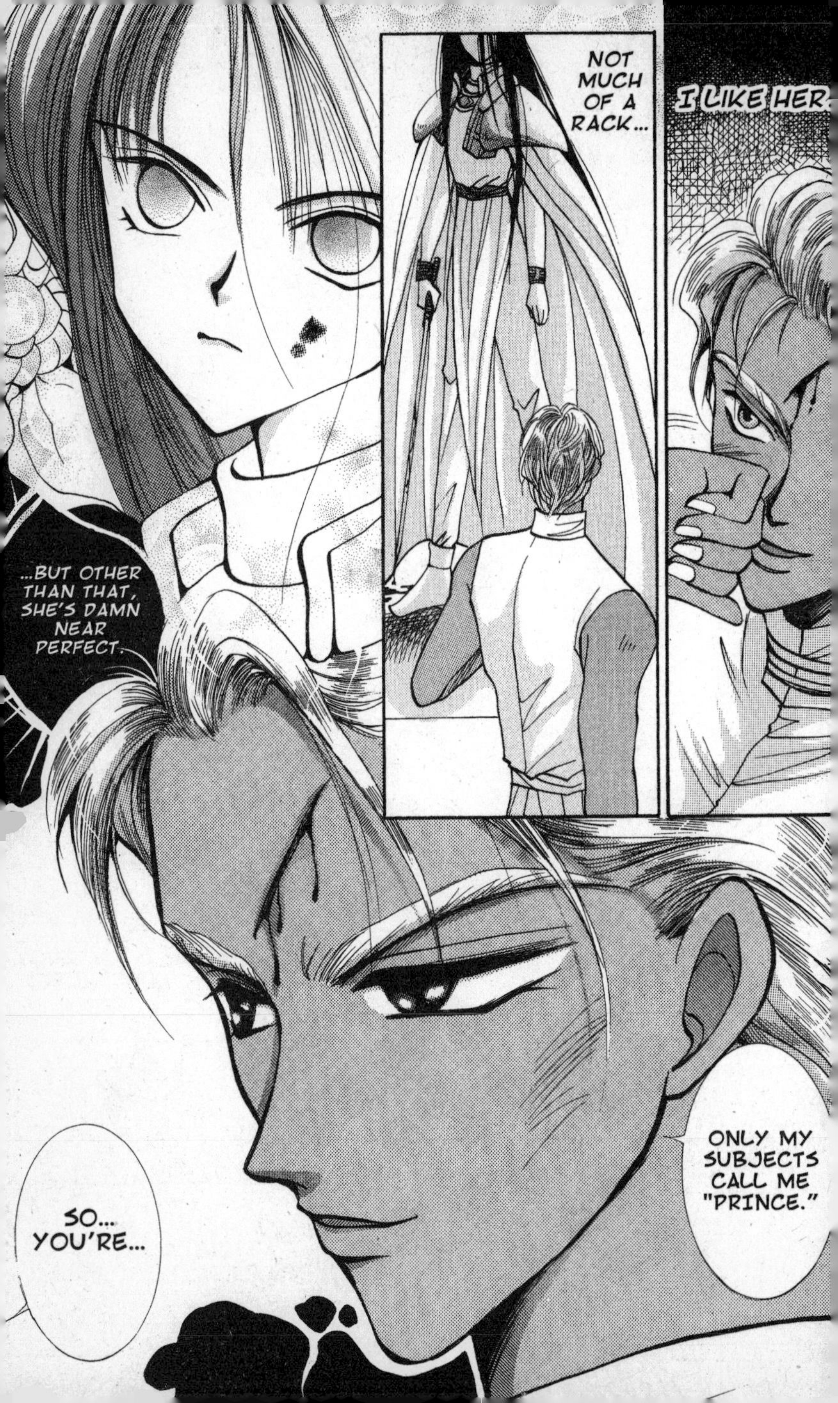
I LIKE HER.
NOT MUCH OF A RACK...
...BUT OTHER THAN THAT, SHE'S DAMN NEAR PERFECT.
ONLY MY SUBJECTS CALL ME "PRINCE."
SO... YOU'RE...

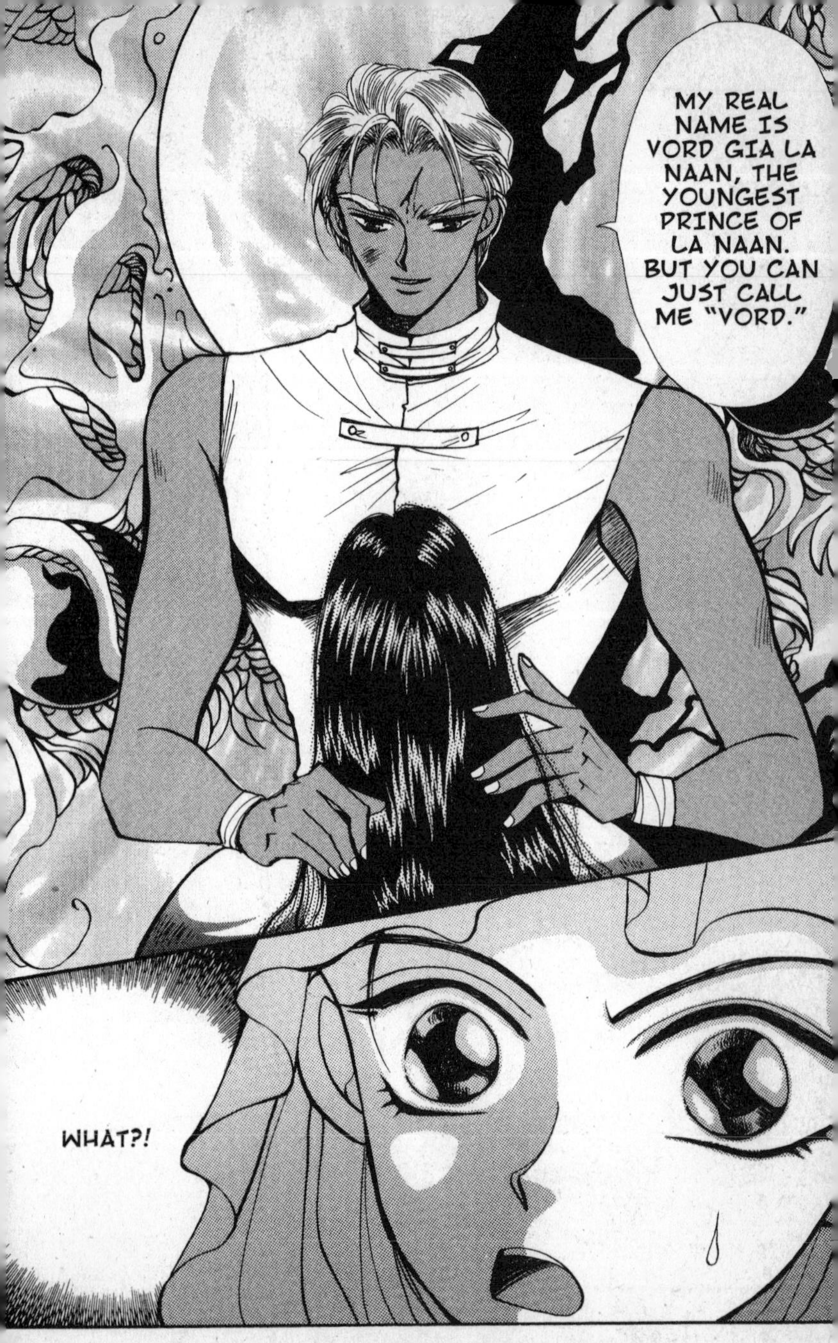
MY REAL NAME IS VORD GIA LA NAAN, THE YOUNGEST PRINCE OF LA NAAN. BUT YOU CAN JUST CALL ME "VORD."
WHAT?!

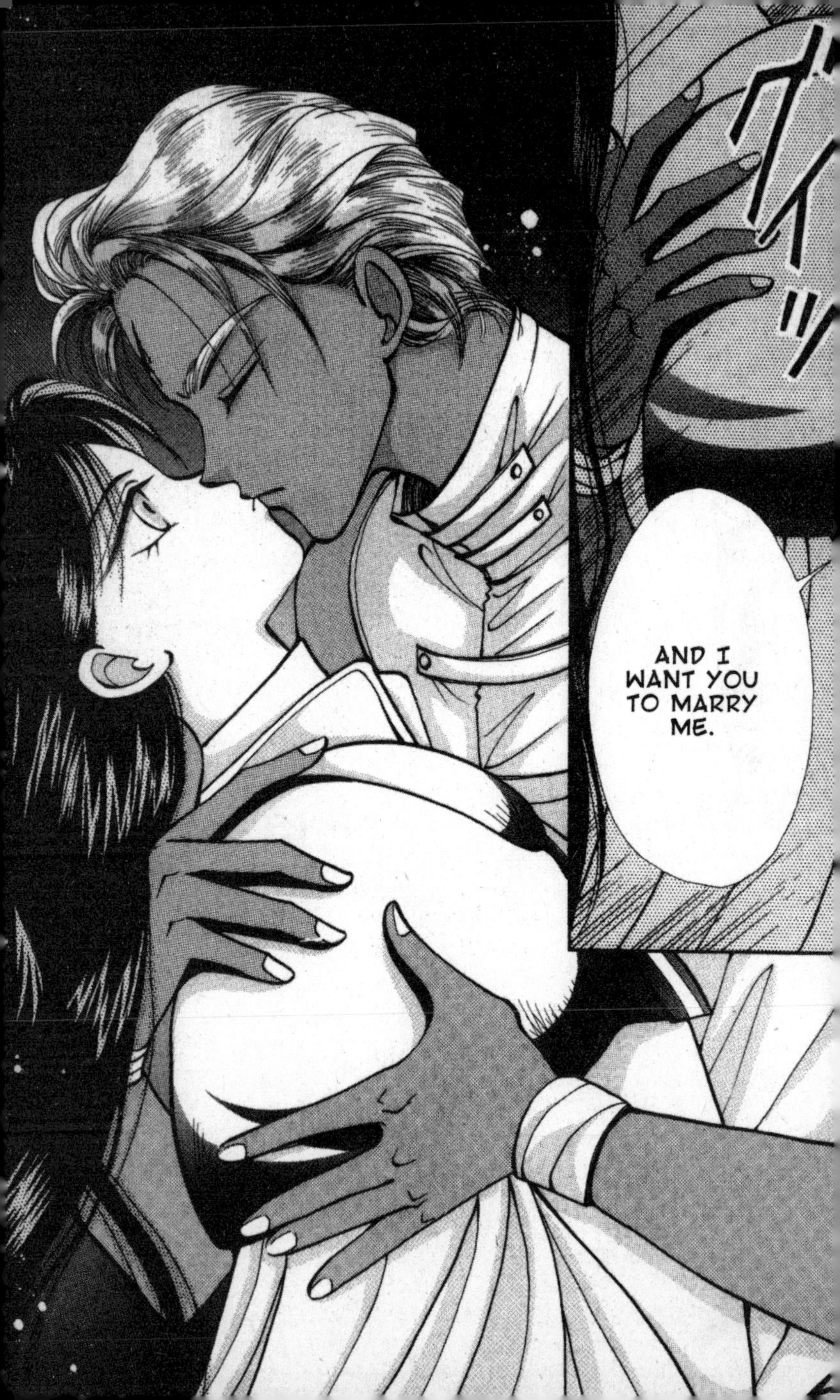
AND I WANT YOU TO MARRY ME.

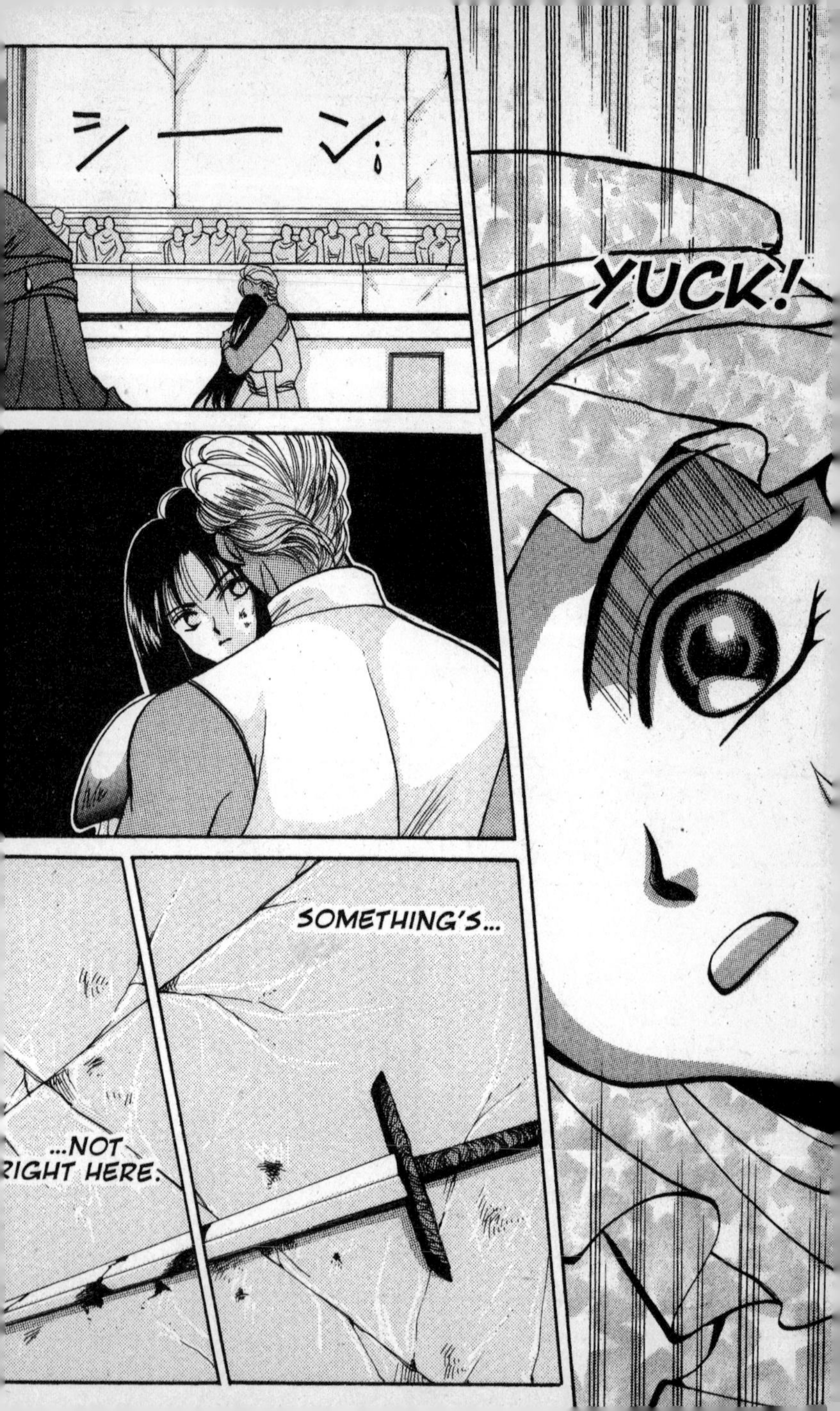
YUCK!
シーーン
SOMETHING'S...
...NOT RIGHT HERE.

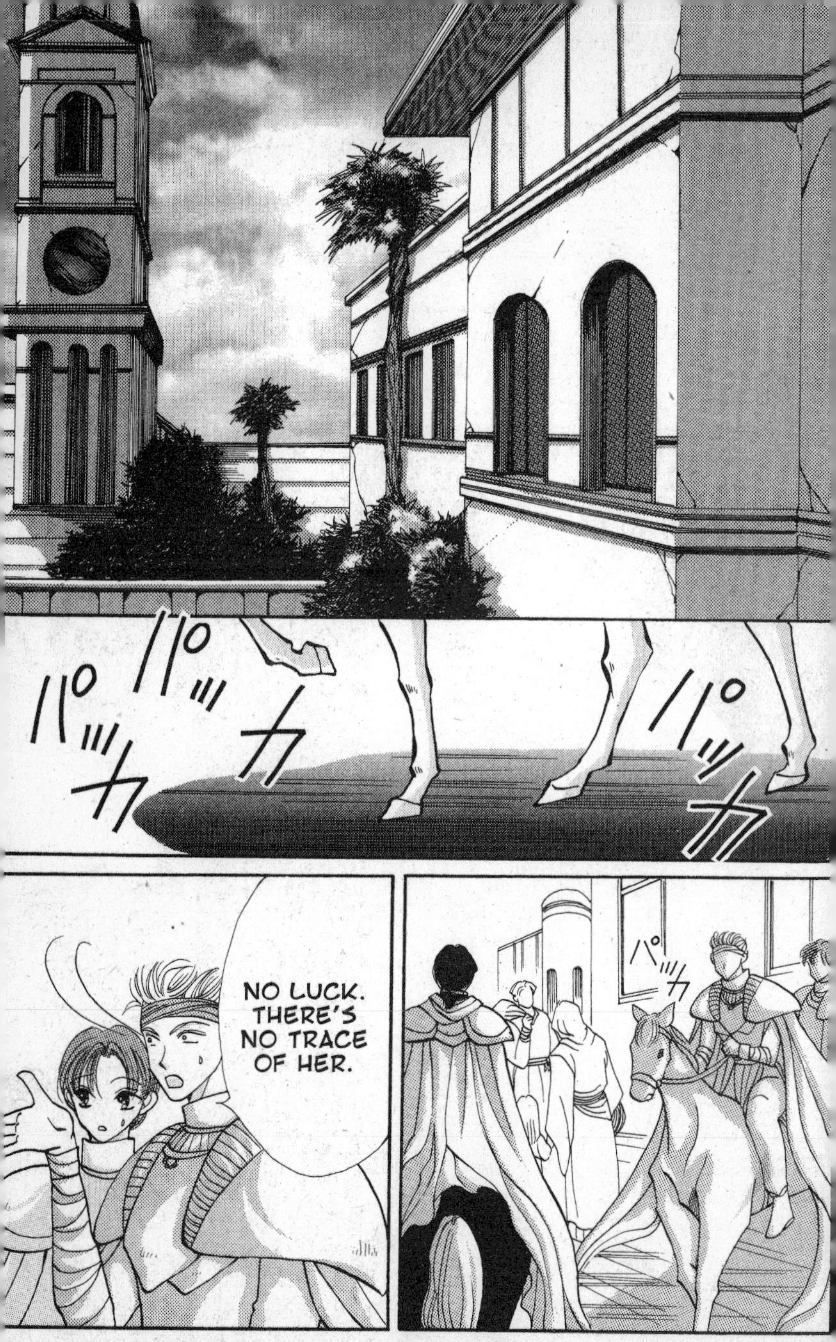
パッカ
パッカ
パッカ
パッカ
NO LUCK. THERE'S NO TRACE OF HER.

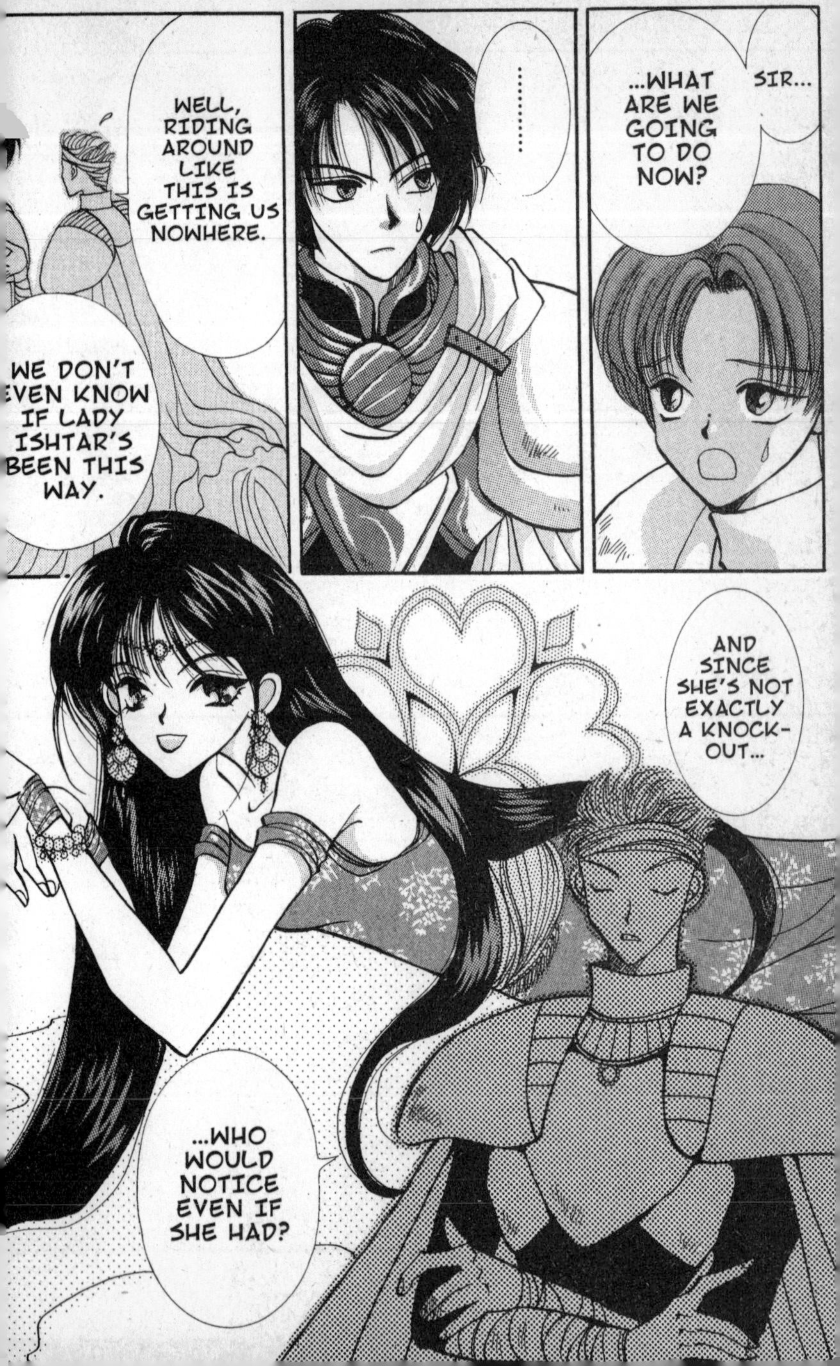
SIR...
...WHAT ARE WE GOING TO DO NOW?
......
WELL, RIDING AROUND LIKE THIS IS GETTING US NOWHERE.
WE DON'T EVEN KNOW IF LADY ISHTAR'S BEEN THIS WAY.
AND SINCE SHE'S NOT EXACTLY A KNOCK-OUT...
...WHO WOULD NOTICE EVEN IF SHE HAD?

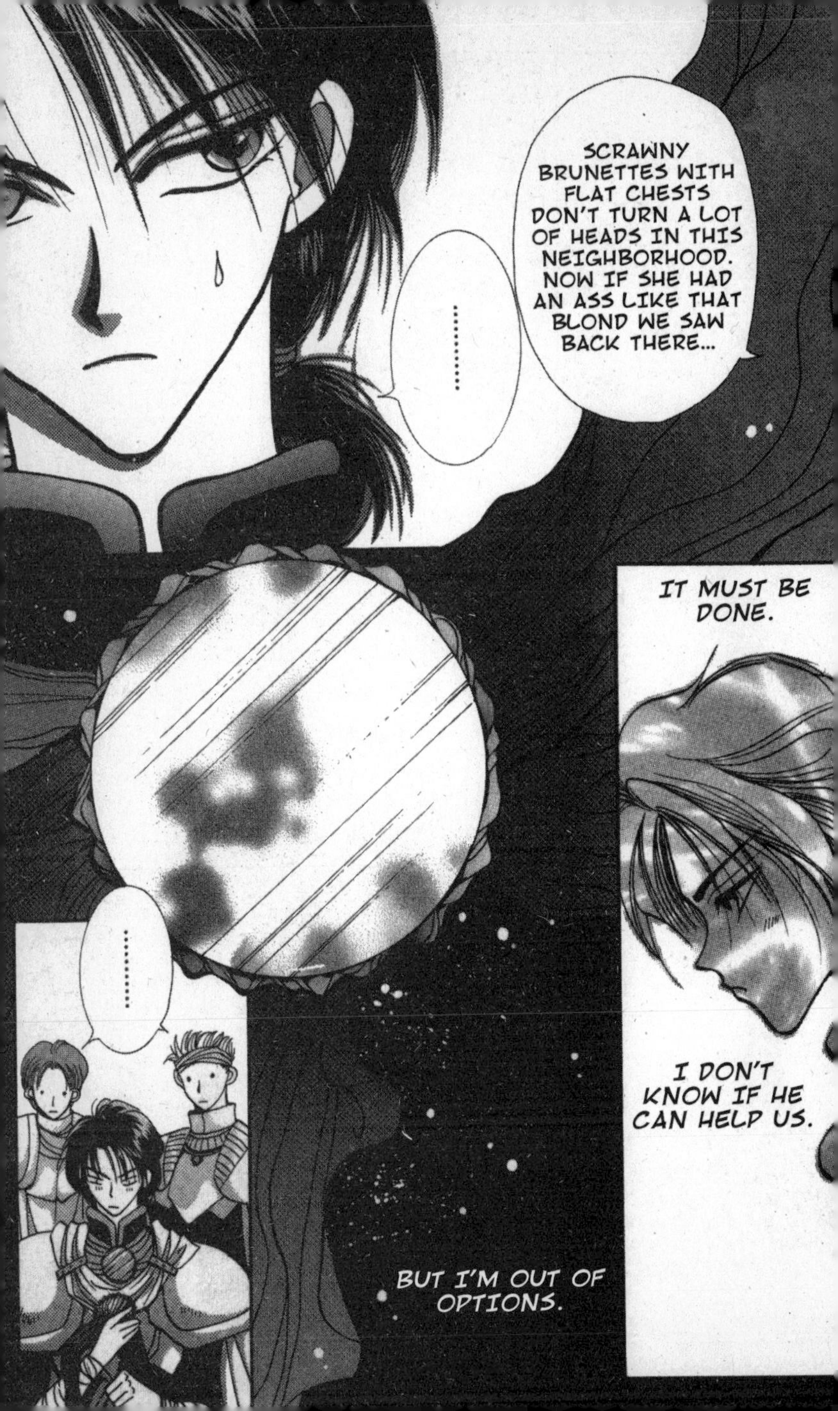
SCRAWNY BRUNETTES WITH FLAT CHESTS DON'T TURN A LOT OF HEADS IN THIS NEIGHBORHOOD. NOW IF SHE HAD AN ASS LIKE THAT BLOND WE SAW BACK THERE...
......
IT MUST BE DONE.
I DON'T KNOW IF HE CAN HELP US.
......
BUT I'M OUT OF OPTIONS.

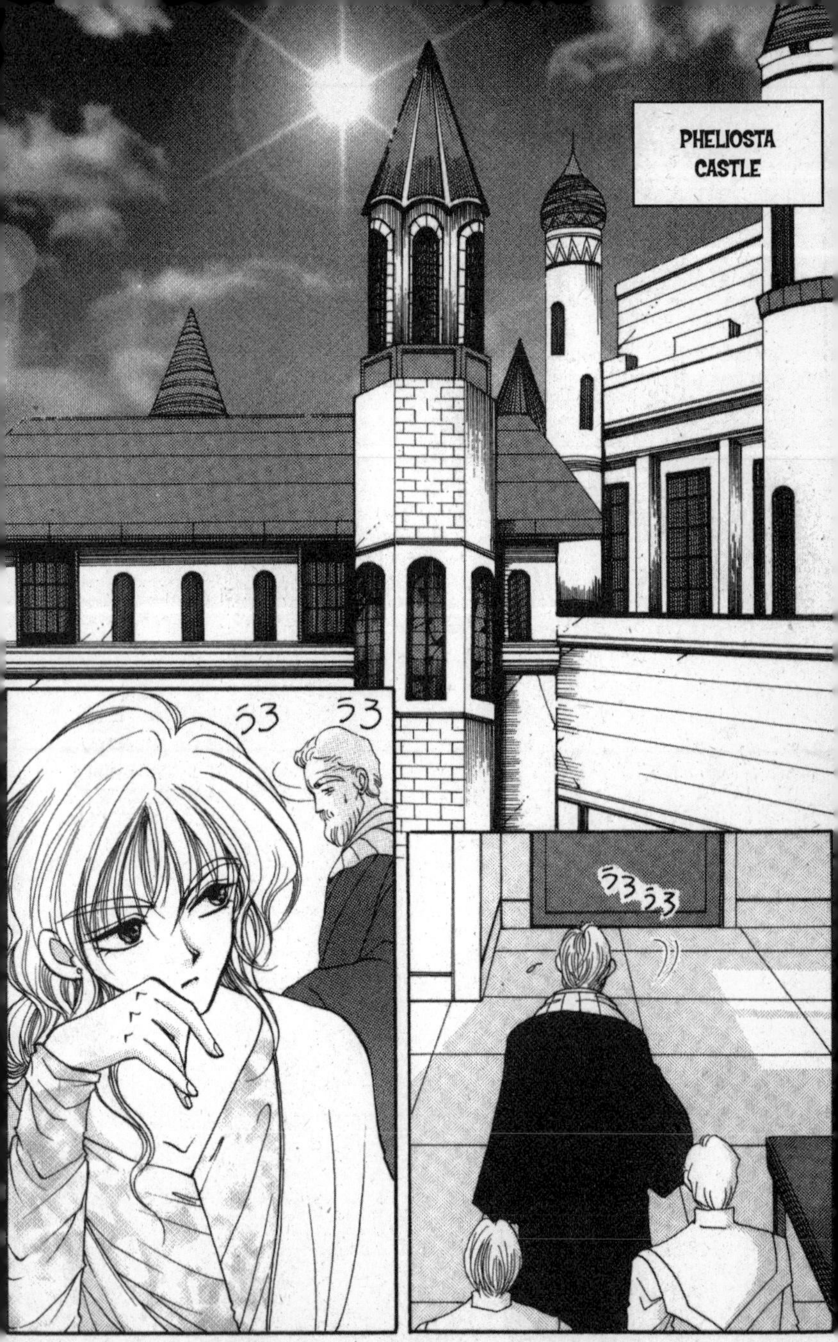
PHELIOSTA CASTLE
うろうろ
うろ うろ

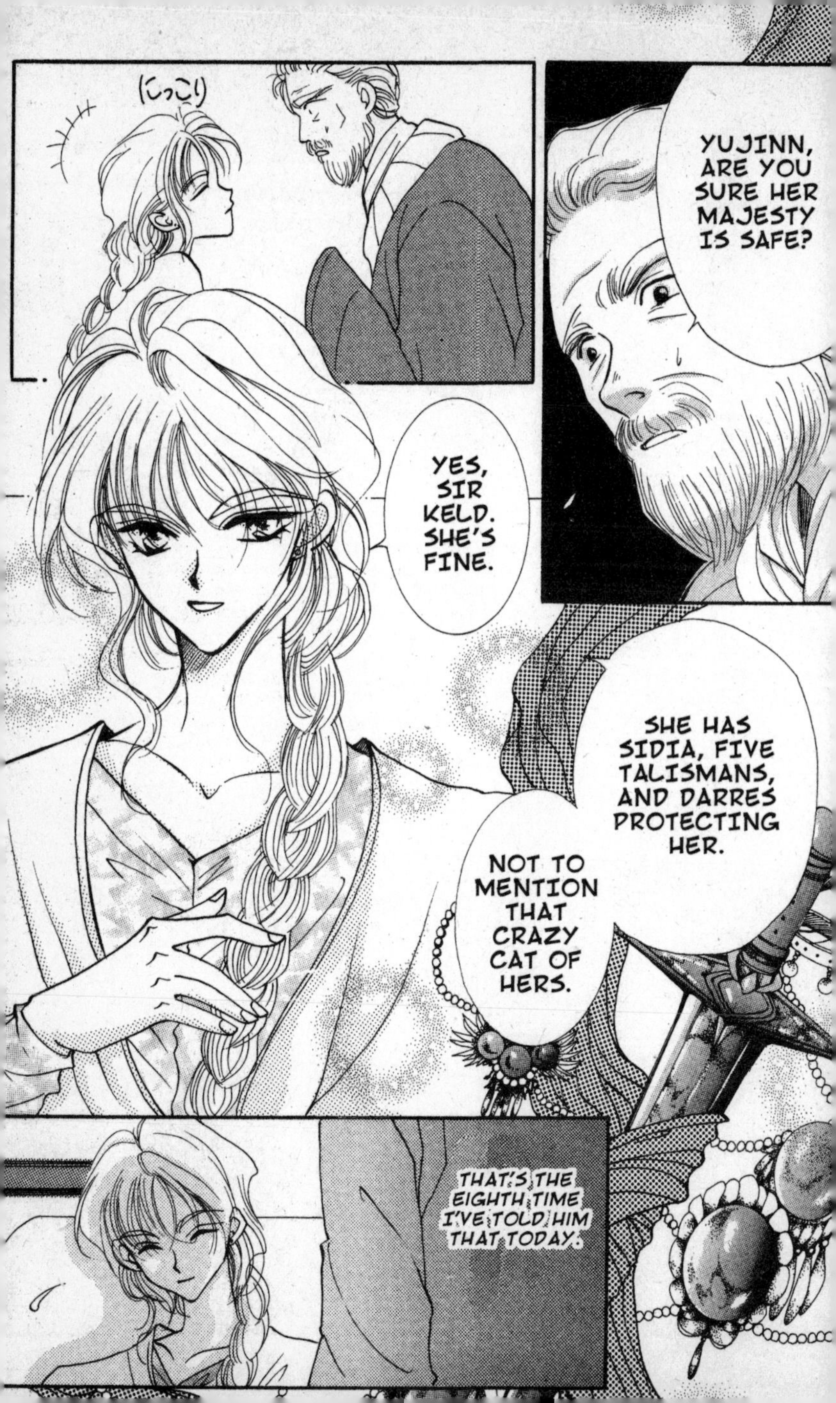
YUJINN, ARE YOU SURE HER MAJESTY IS SAFE?
にっこり
YES, SIR KELD. SHE'S FINE.
SHE HAS SIDIA, FIVE TALISMANS, AND DARRES PROTECTING HER.
NOT TO MENTION THAT CRAZY CAT OF HERS.
THAT'S THE EIGHTH TIME I'VE TOLD HIM THAT TODAY.

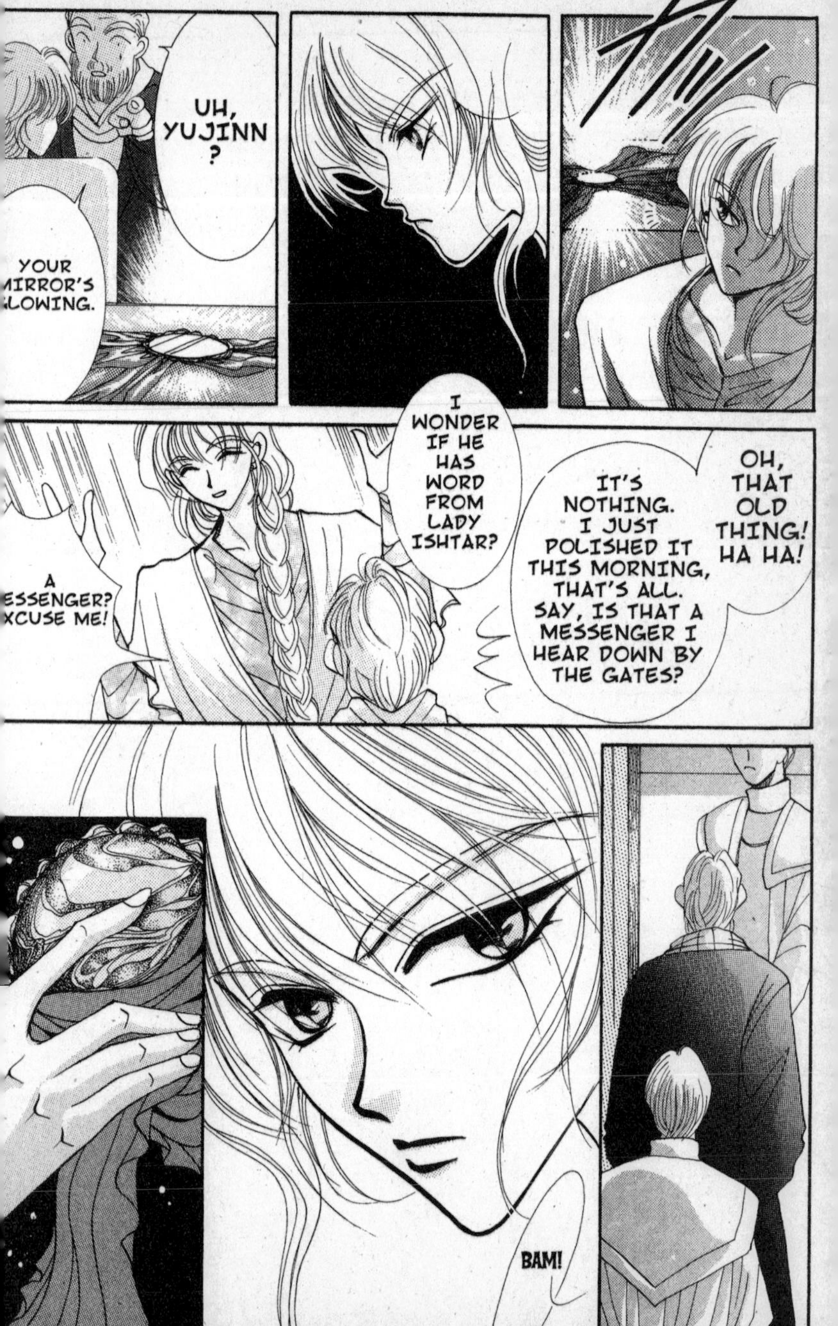
UH, YUJINN?
YOUR MIRROR'S LOWING.
OH, THAT OLD THING! HA HA!
IT'S NOTHING. I JUST POLISHED IT THIS MORNING, THAT'S ALL. SAY, IS THAT A MESSENGER I HEAR DOWN BY THE GATES?
I WONDER IF HE HAS WORD FROM LADY ISHTAR?
A ESSENGER? XCUSE ME!
BAM!

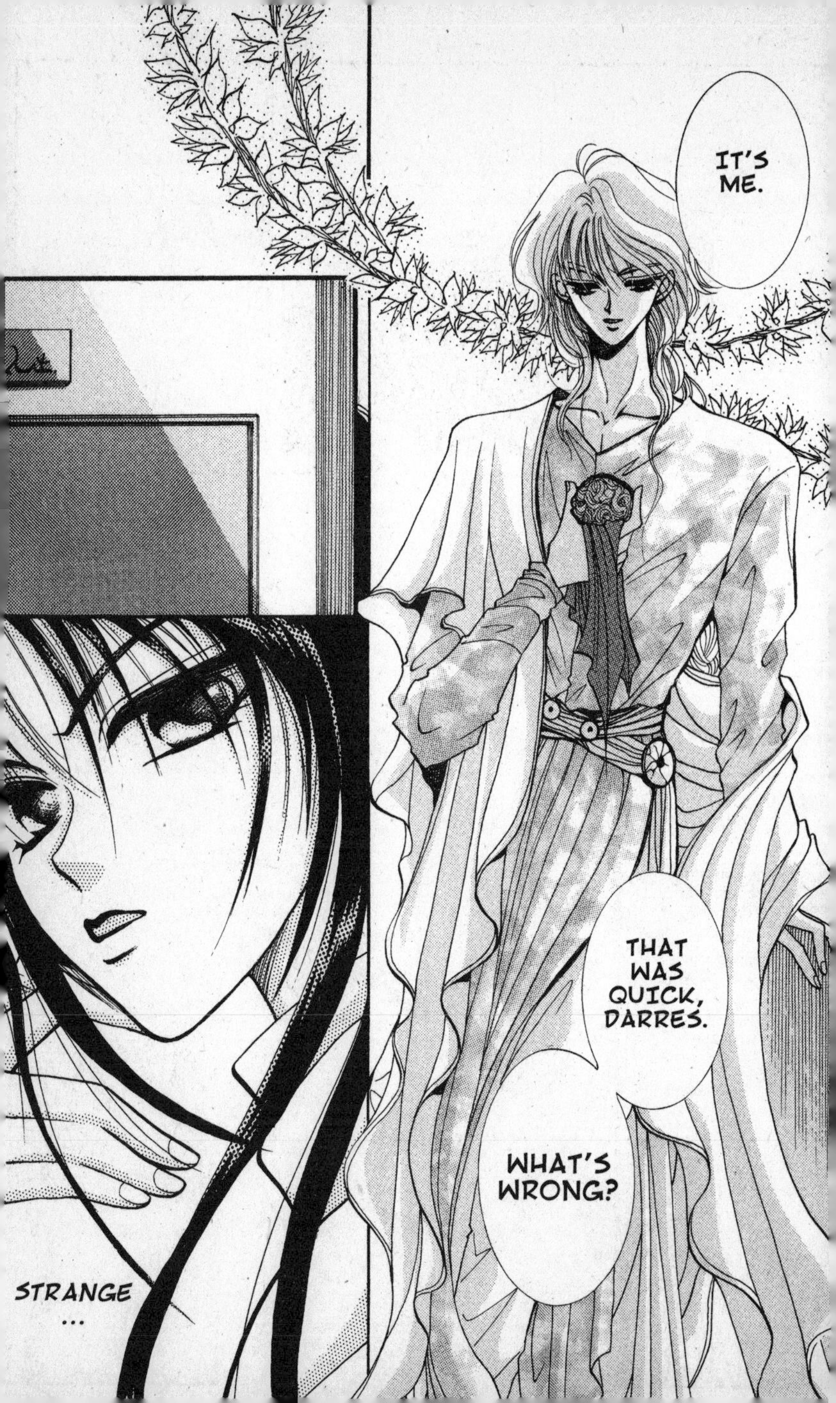

IT'S ME.
THAT WAS QUICK, DARRES.
WHAT'S WRONG?
STRANGE ...

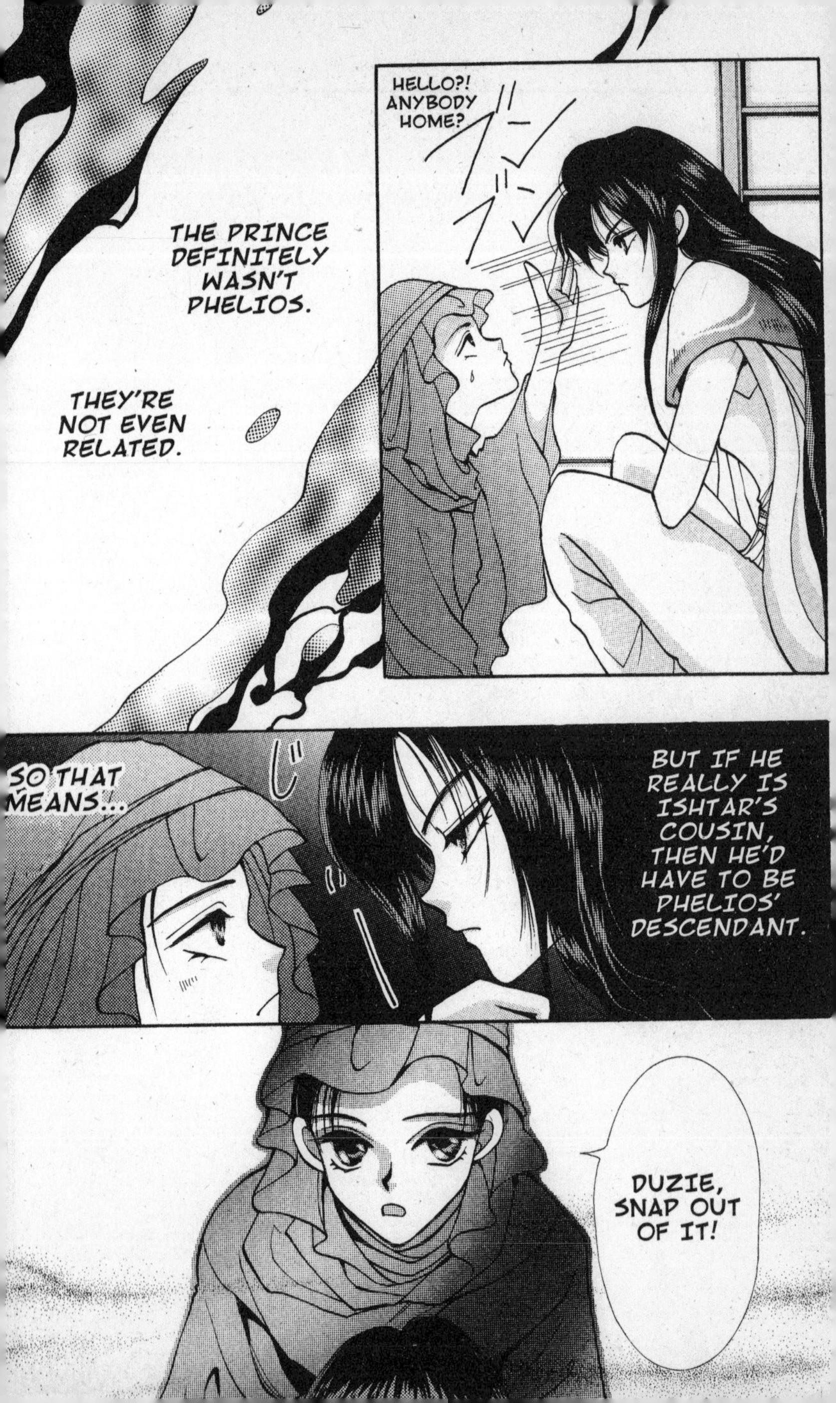
HELLO?! ANYBODY HOME?
THE PRINCE DEFINITELY WASN'T PHELIOS.
THEY'RE NOT EVEN RELATED.
BUT IF HE REALLY IS ISHTAR'S COUSIN, THEN HE'D HAVE TO BE PHELIOS' DESCENDANT.
SO THAT MEANS...
DUZIE, SNAP OUT OF IT!

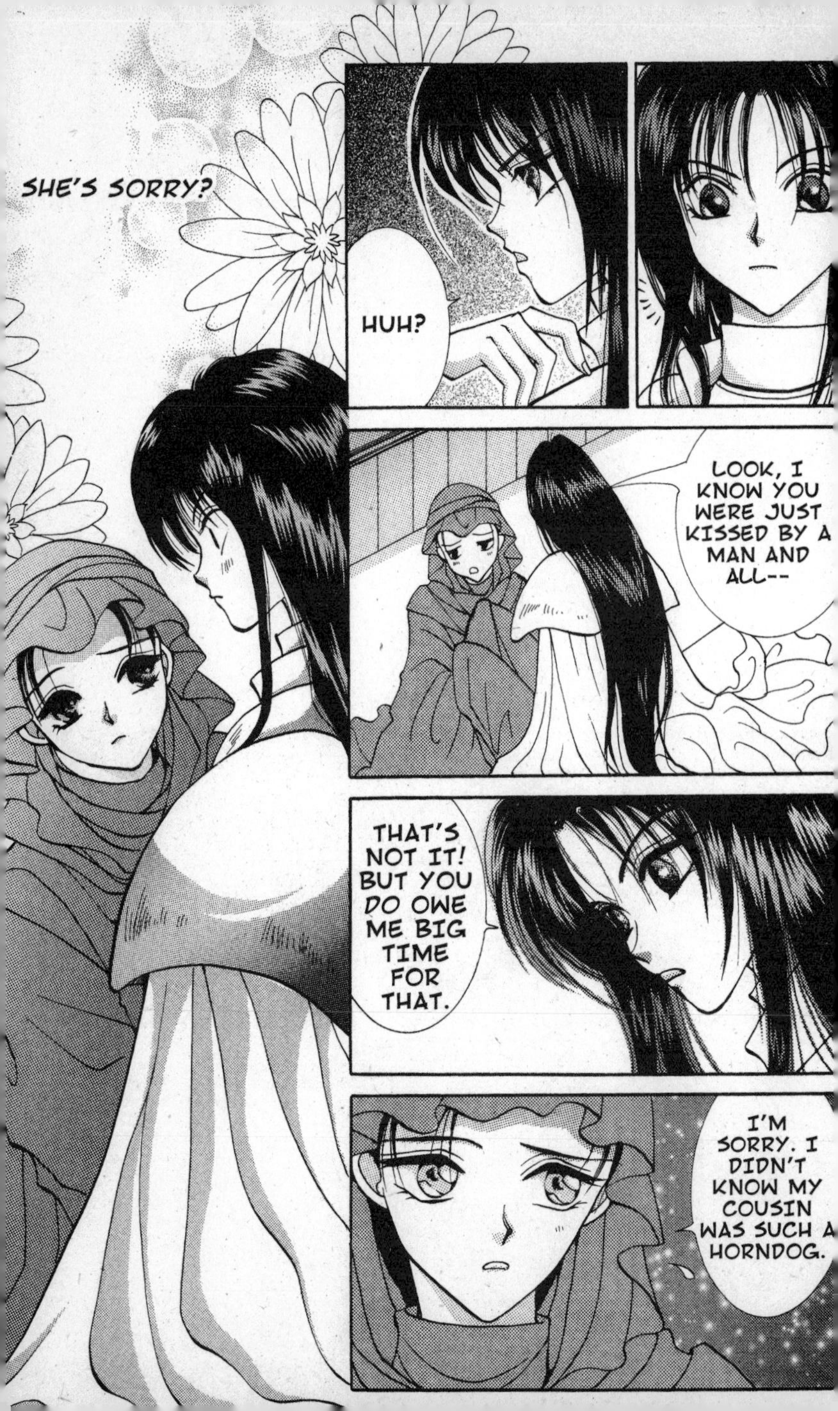
HUH?
LOOK, I KNOW YOU WERE JUST KISSED BY A MAN AND ALL--
THAT'S NOT IT! BUT YOU *DO* OWE ME BIG TIME FOR THAT.
I'M SORRY. I DIDN'T KNOW MY COUSIN WAS SUCH A HORNDOG.
SHE'S SORRY?

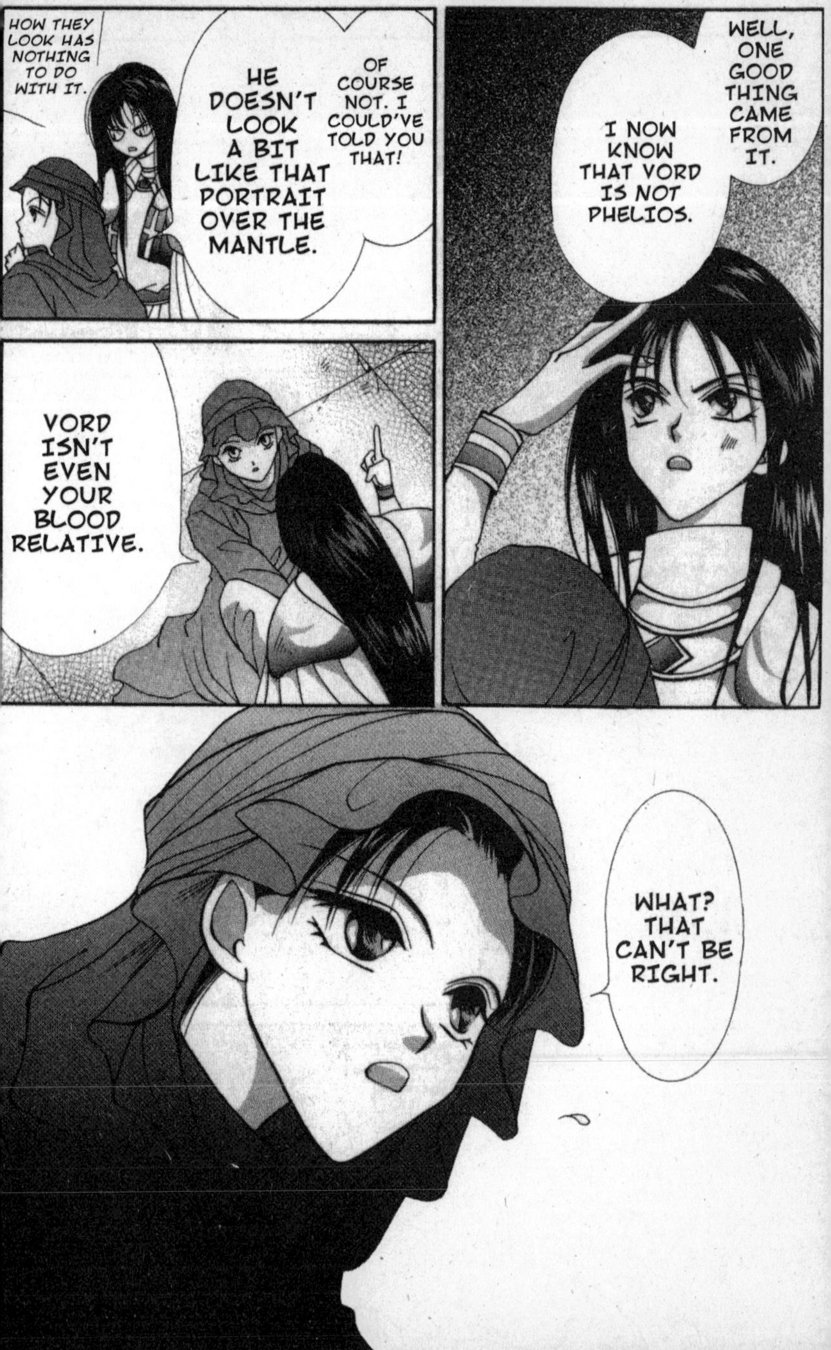
WELL, ONE GOOD THING CAME FROM IT.
I NOW KNOW THAT VORD IS *NOT* PHELIOS.
OF COURSE NOT. I COULD'VE TOLD YOU THAT!
HE DOESN'T LOOK A BIT LIKE THAT PORTRAIT OVER THE MANTLE.
HOW THEY LOOK HAS NOTHING TO DO WITH IT.
VORD ISN'T EVEN YOUR BLOOD RELATIVE.
WHAT? THAT CAN'T BE RIGHT.

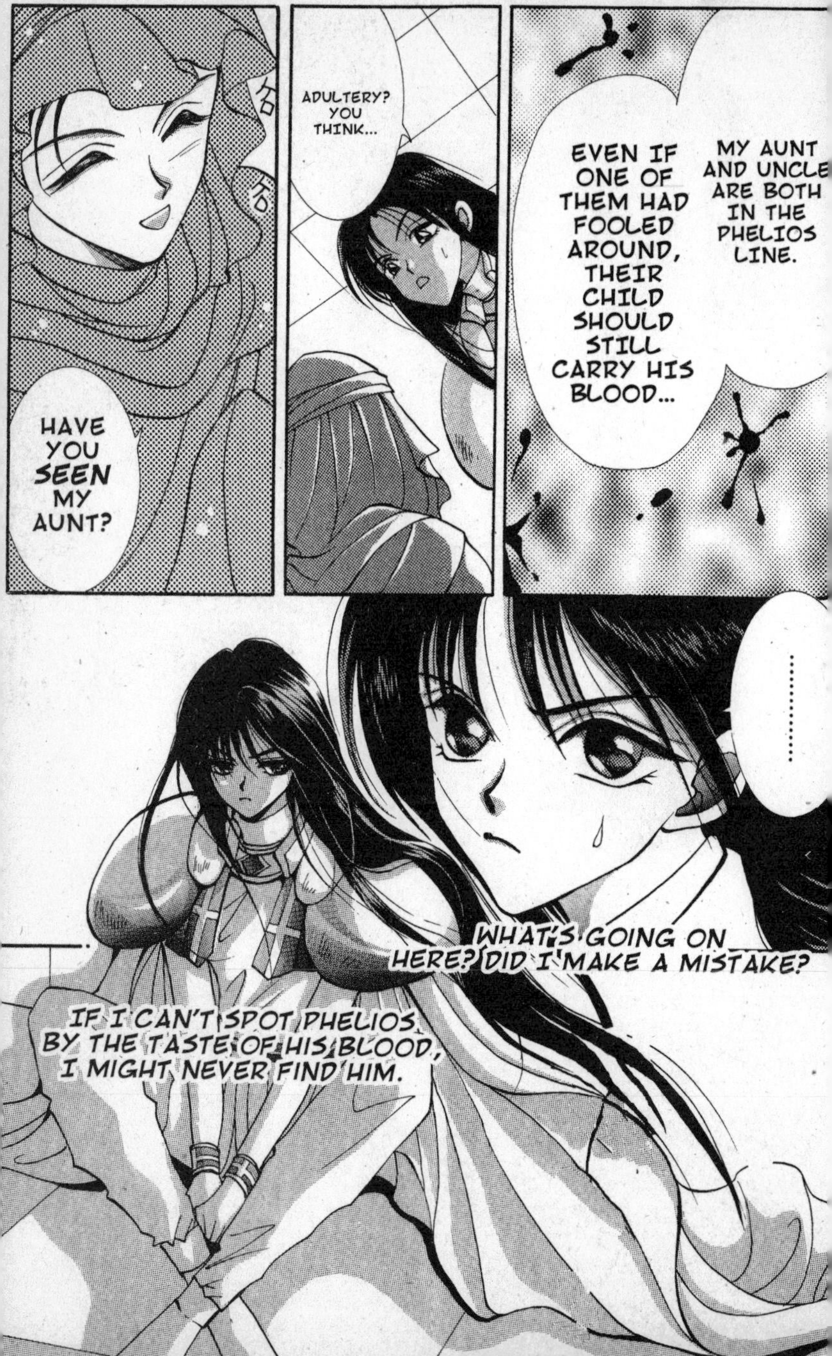
MY AUNT AND UNCLE ARE BOTH IN THE PHELIOS LINE.
EVEN IF ONE OF THEM HAD FOOLED AROUND, THEIR CHILD SHOULD STILL CARRY HIS BLOOD...
ADULTERY? YOU THINK...
HAVE YOU SEEN MY AUNT?
......
WHAT'S GOING ON HERE? DID I MAKE A MISTAKE?
IF I CAN'T SPOT PHELIOS BY THE TASTE OF HIS BLOOD, I MIGHT NEVER FIND HIM.

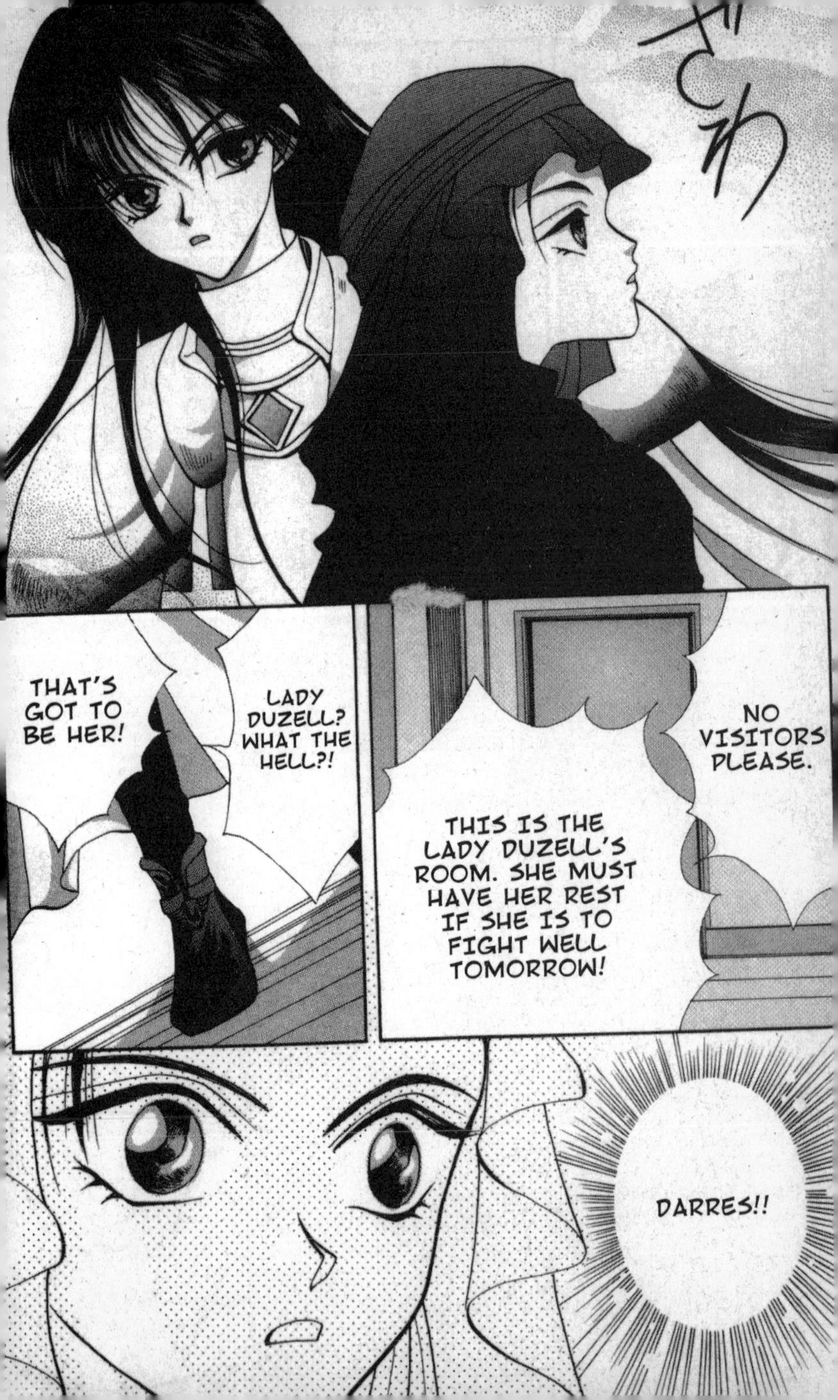
だれ
NO VISITORS PLEASE.
THIS IS THE LADY DUZELL'S ROOM. SHE MUST HAVE HER REST IF SHE IS TO FIGHT WELL TOMORROW!
LADY DUZELL? WHAT THE HELL?!
THAT'S GOT TO BE HER!
DARRES!!

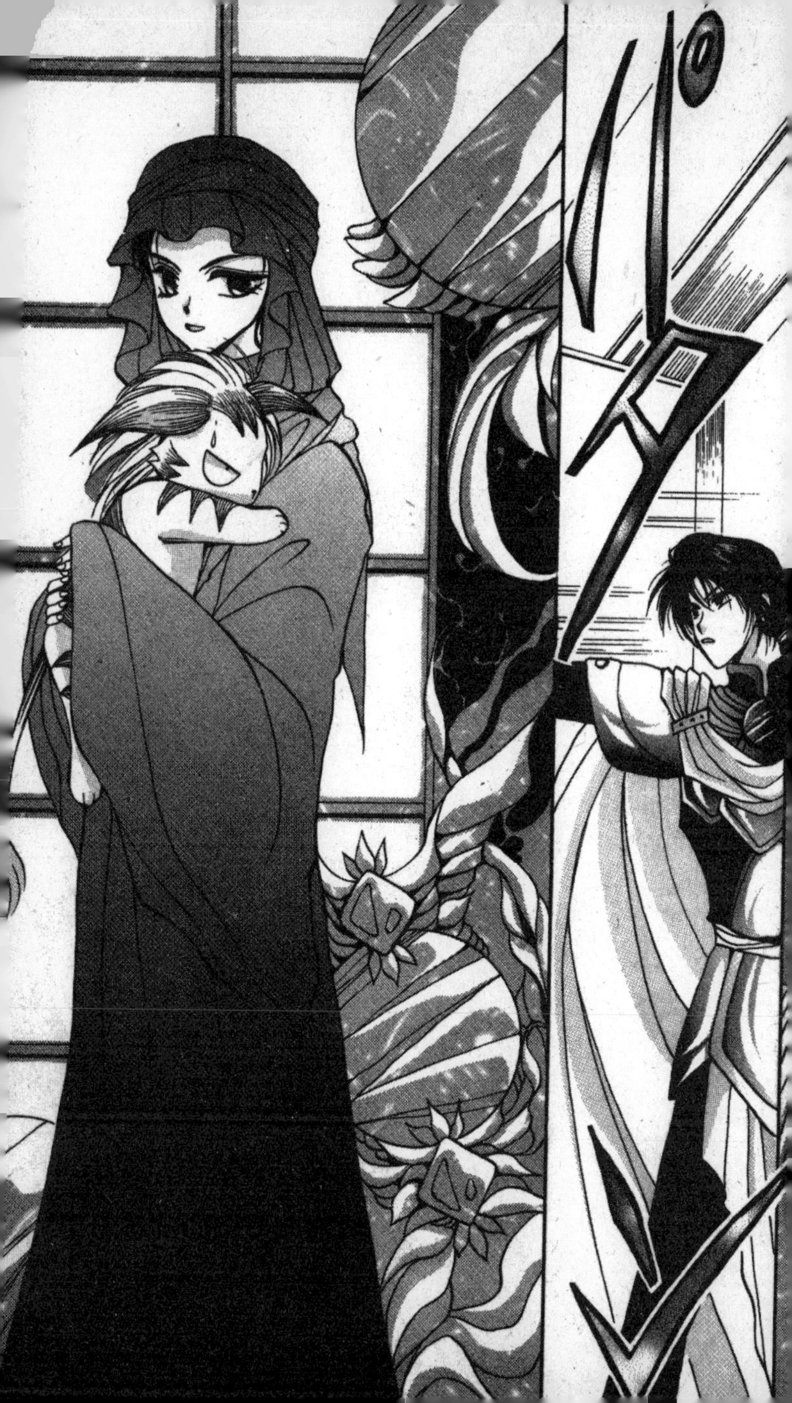

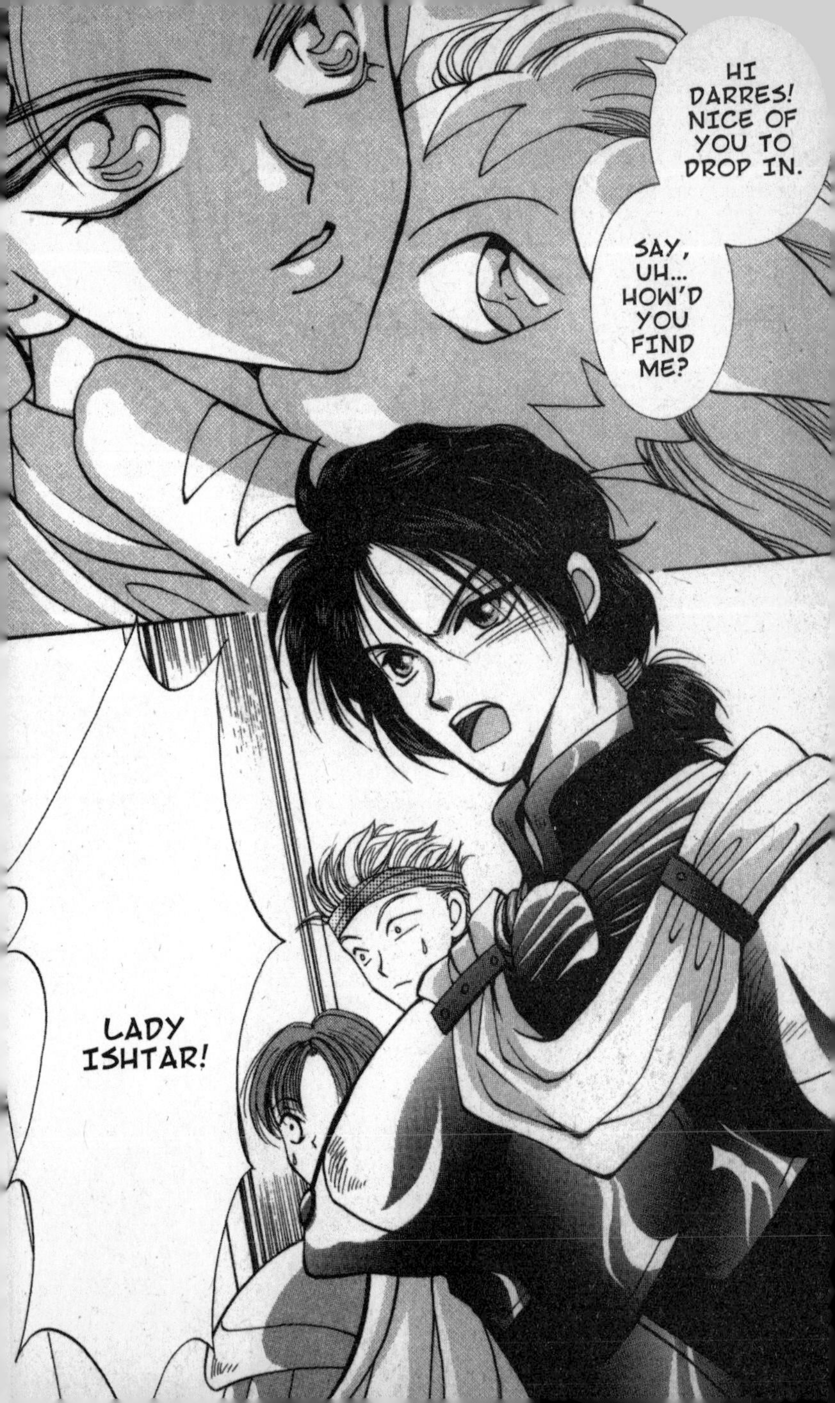
HI DARRES! NICE OF YOU TO DROP IN.
SAY, UH... HOW'D YOU FIND ME?
LADY ISHTAR!

LA NAAN
CASTLE

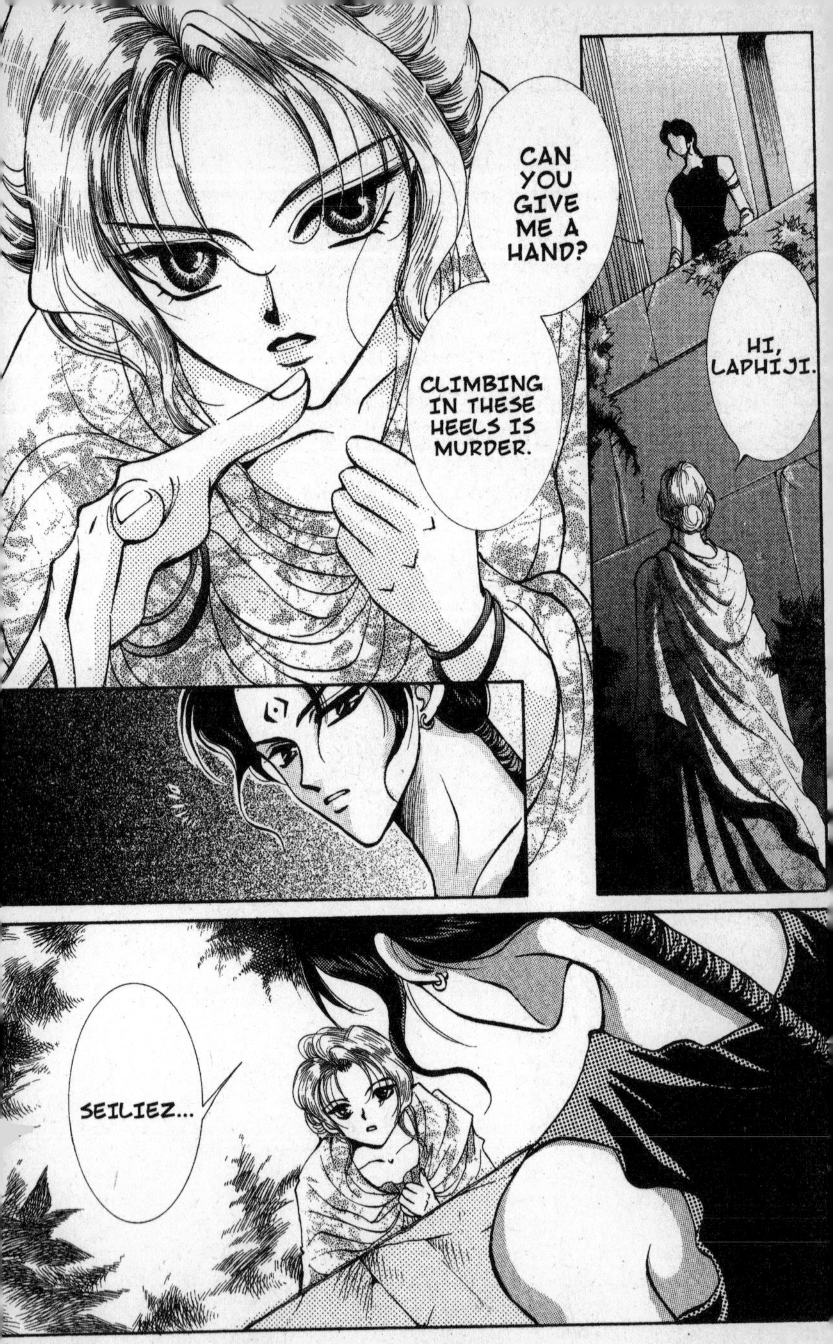
HI, LAPHIJI.
CAN YOU GIVE ME A HAND?
CLIMBING IN THESE HEELS IS MURDER.
SEILIEZ...

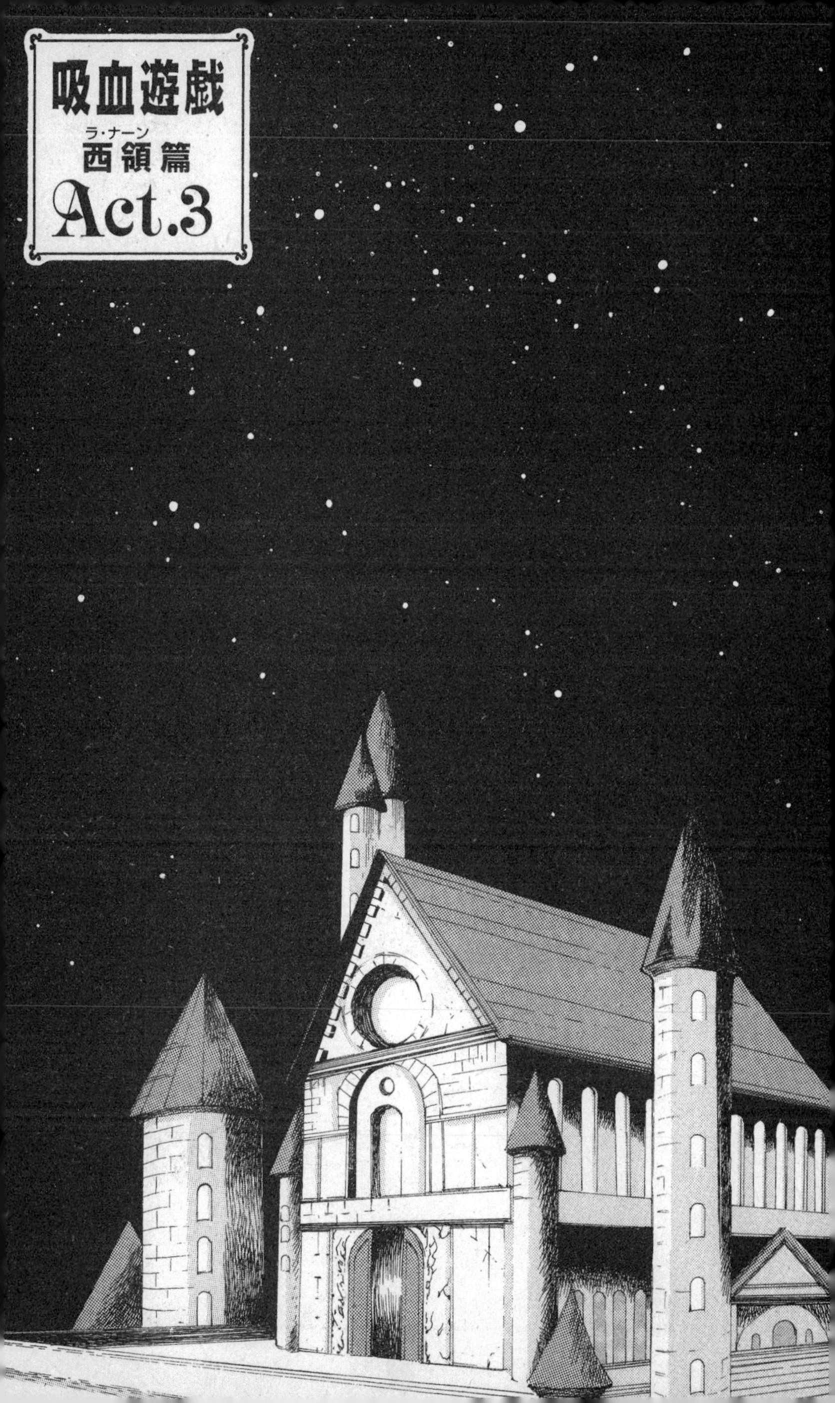
吸血遊戯
ラ・ナーン
西領篇
Act.3

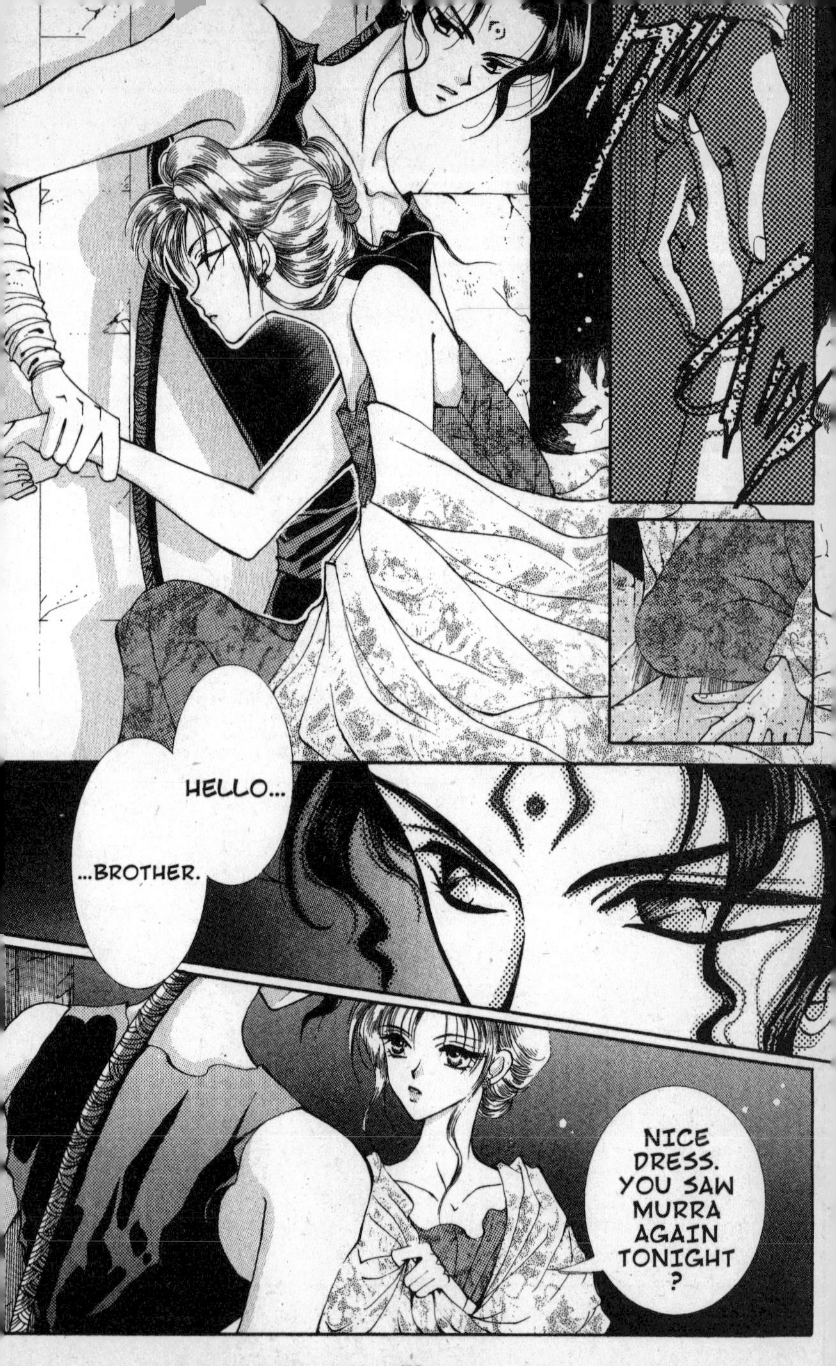
HELLO...
...BROTHER.
NICE DRESS. YOU SAW MURRA AGAIN TONIGHT?

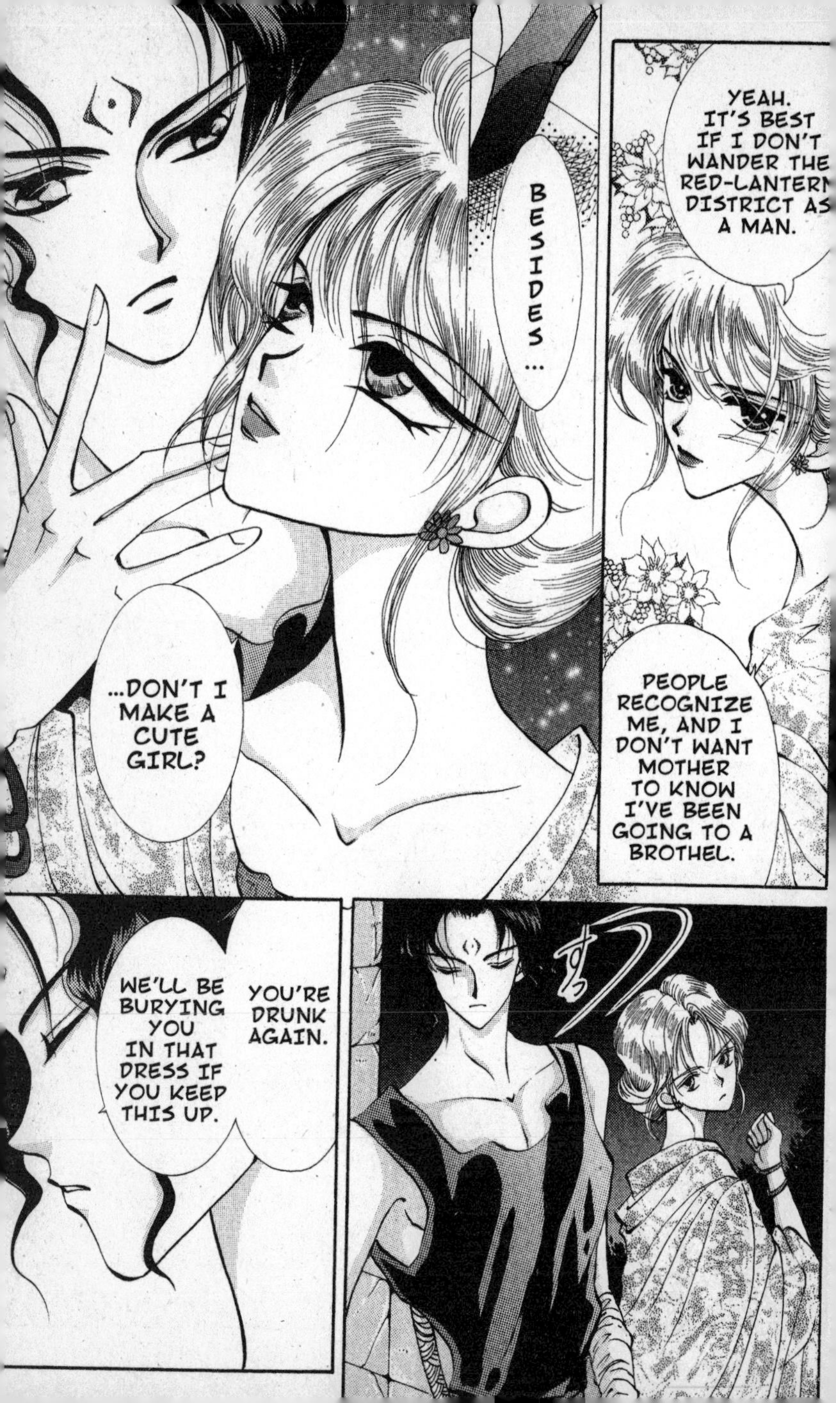
YEAH. IT'S BEST IF I DON'T WANDER THE RED-LANTERN DISTRICT AS A MAN.
PEOPLE RECOGNIZE ME, AND I DON'T WANT MOTHER TO KNOW I'VE BEEN GOING TO A BROTHEL.
BESIDES...
...DON'T I MAKE A CUTE GIRL?
YOU'RE DRUNK AGAIN.
WE'LL BE BURYING YOU IN THAT DRESS IF YOU KEEP THIS UP.

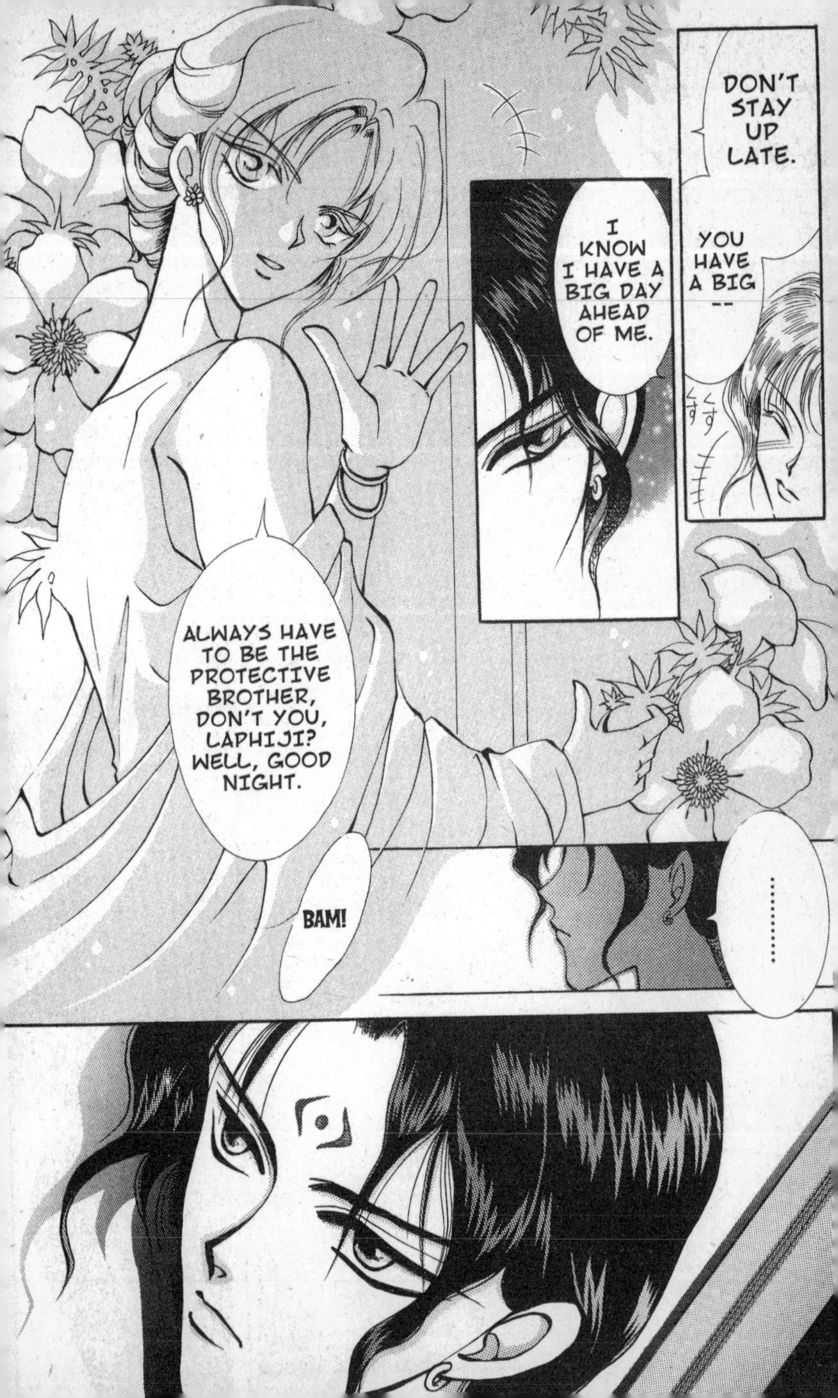
DON'T STAY UP LATE.
YOU HAVE A BIG --
くすくす
I KNOW I HAVE A BIG DAY AHEAD OF ME.
ALWAYS HAVE TO BE THE PROTECTIVE BROTHER, DON'T YOU, LAPHIJI? WELL, GOOD NIGHT.
......
BAM!

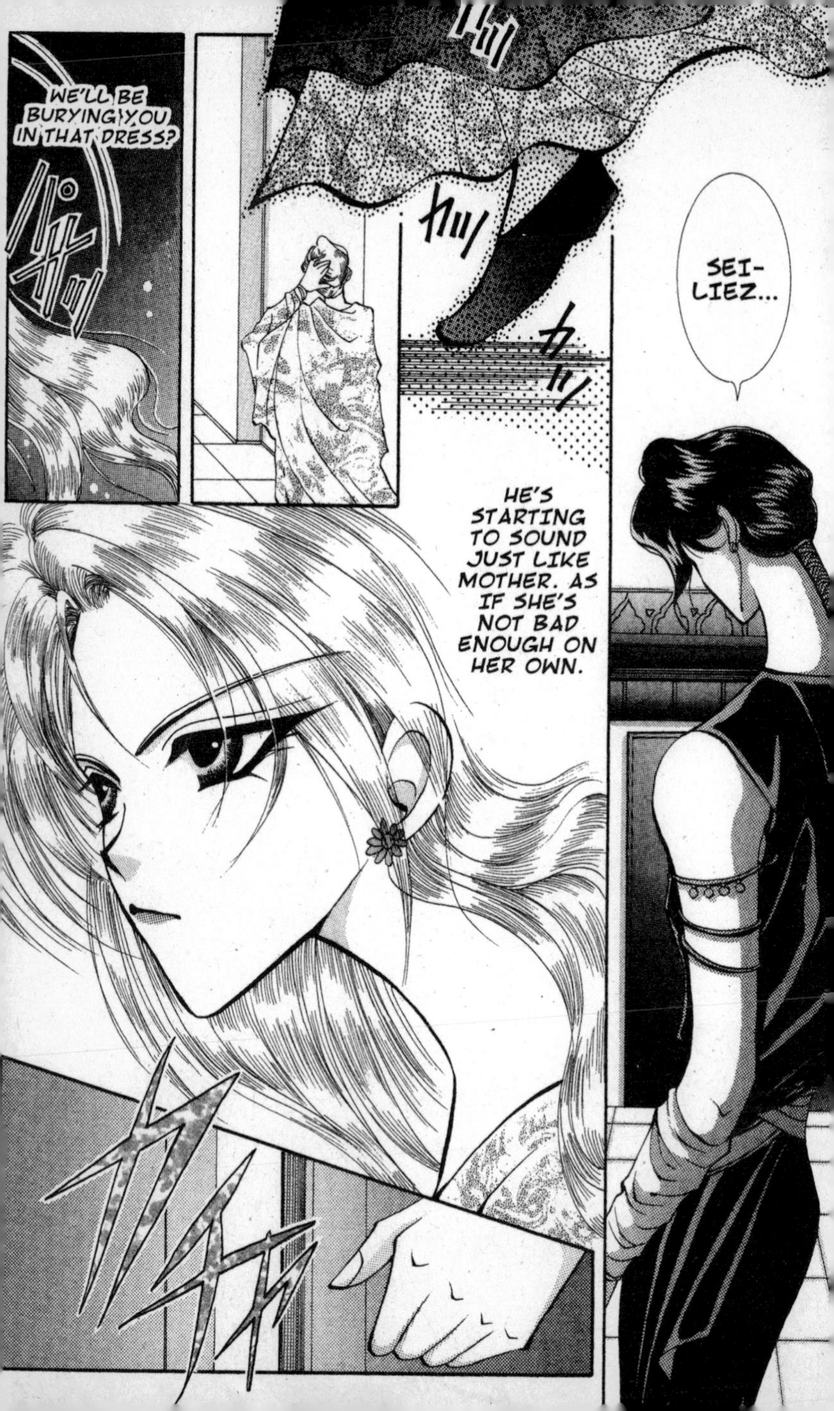
SEI-LIEZ...
WE'LL BE BURYING YOU IN THAT DRESS?
HE'S STARTING TO SOUND JUST LIKE MOTHER. AS IF SHE'S NOT BAD ENOUGH ON HER OWN.

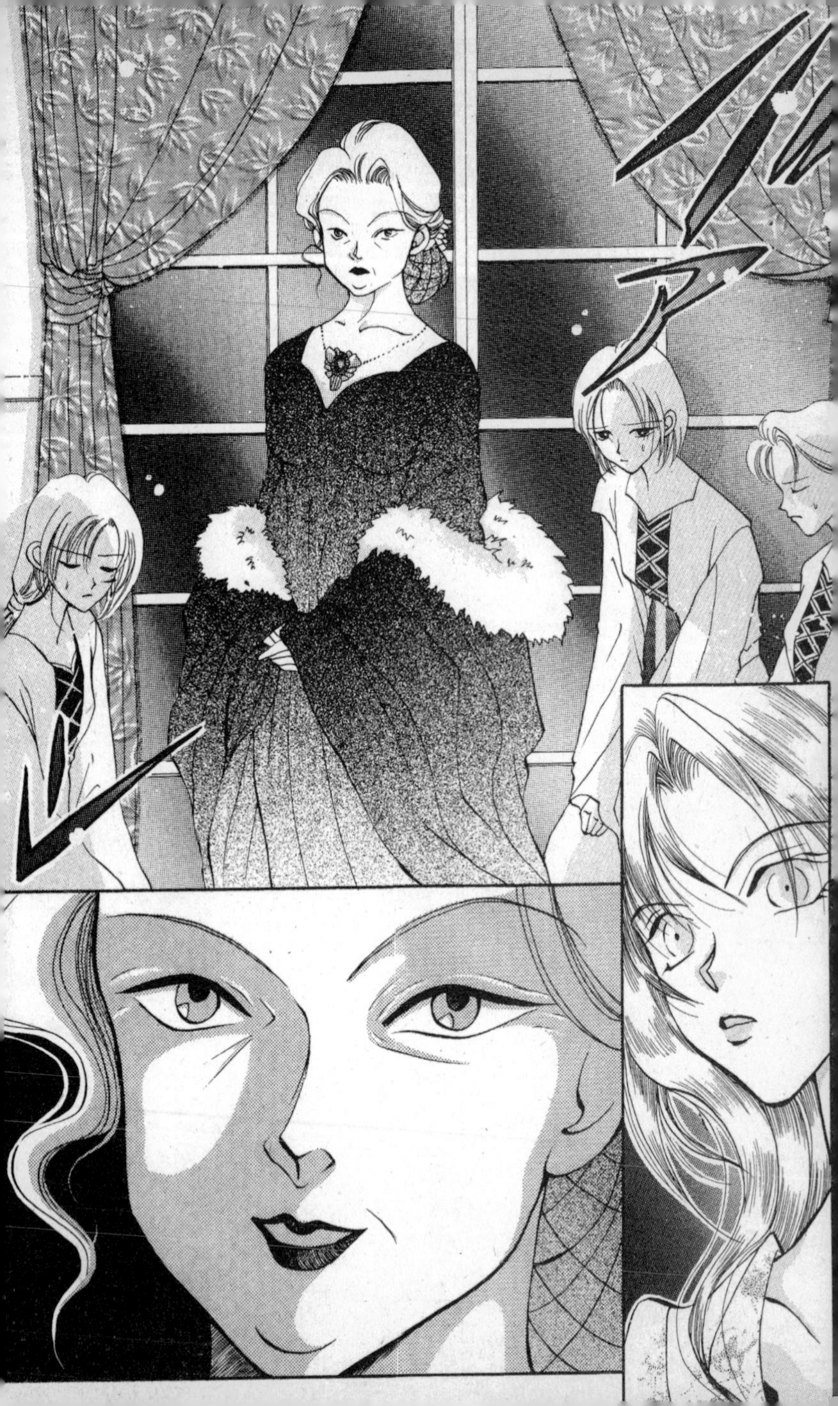

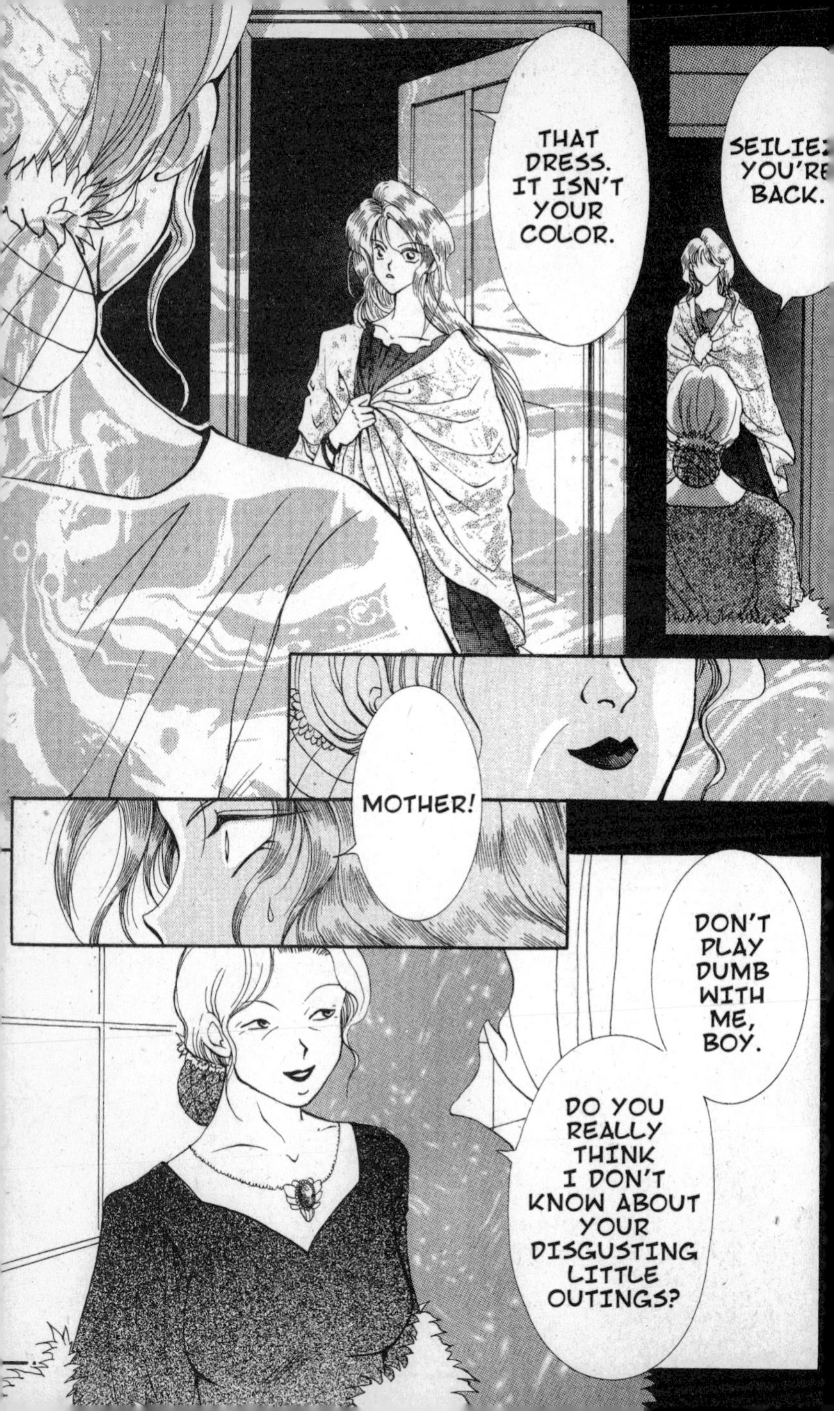
SEILIE! YOU'RE BACK.
THAT DRESS. IT ISN'T YOUR COLOR.
MOTHER!
DON'T PLAY DUMB WITH ME, BOY.
DO YOU REALLY THINK I DON'T KNOW ABOUT YOUR DISGUSTING LITTLE OUTINGS?

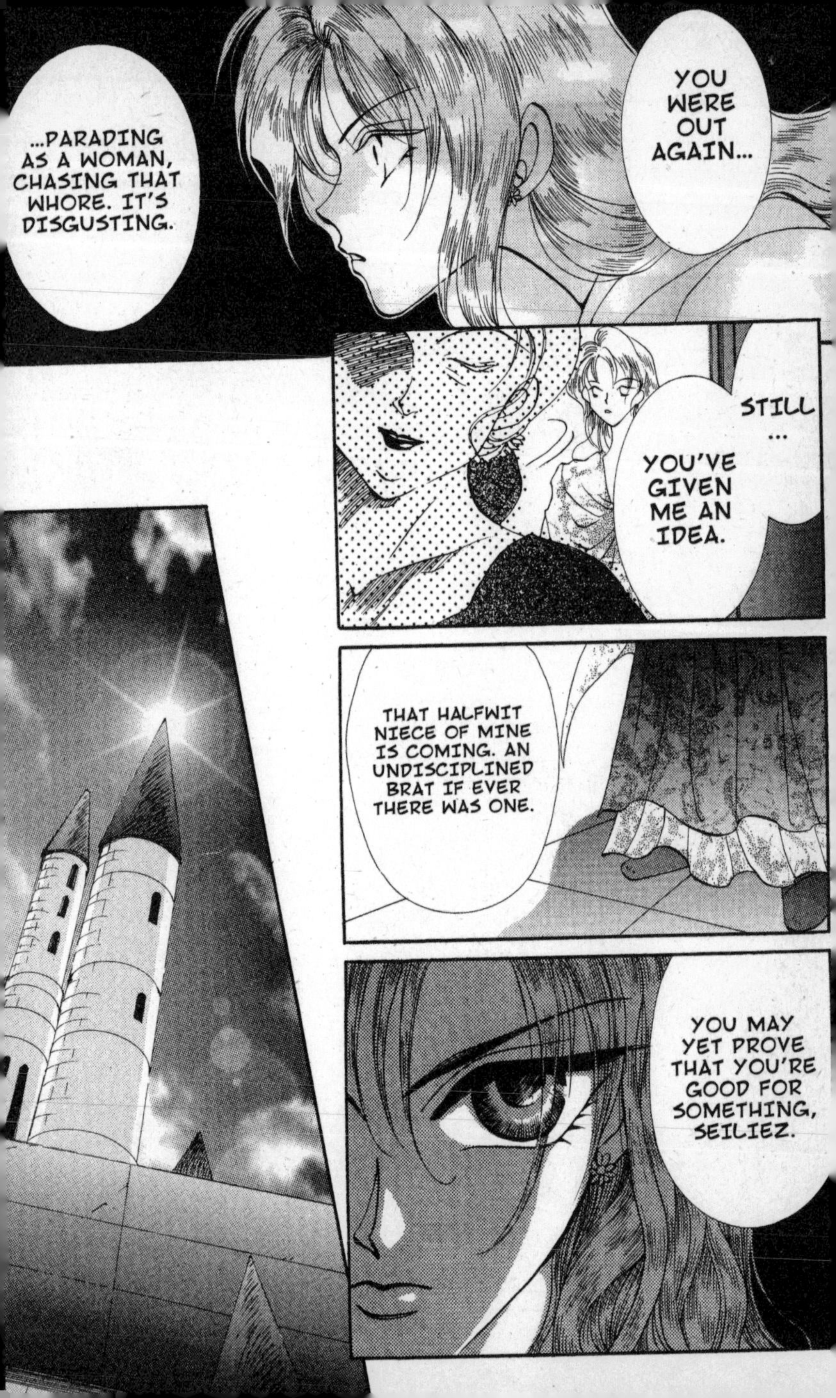
YOU WERE OUT AGAIN...
...PARADING AS A WOMAN, CHASING THAT WHORE. IT'S DISGUSTING.
STILL ...
YOU'VE GIVEN ME AN IDEA.
THAT HALFWIT NIECE OF MINE IS COMING. AN UNDISCIPLINED BRAT IF EVER THERE WAS ONE.
YOU MAY YET PROVE THAT YOU'RE GOOD FOR SOMETHING, SEILIEZ.

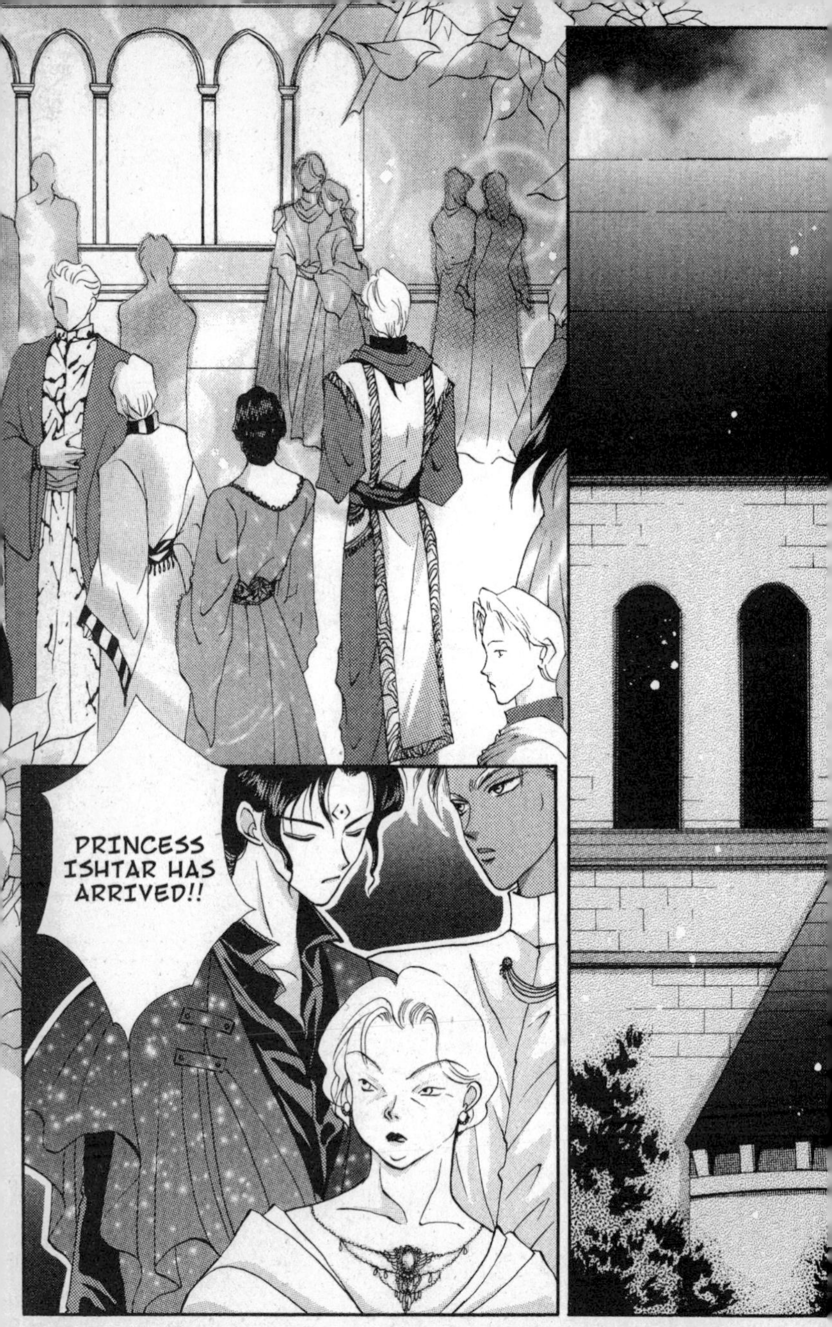
PRINCESS ISHTAR HAS ARRIVED!!

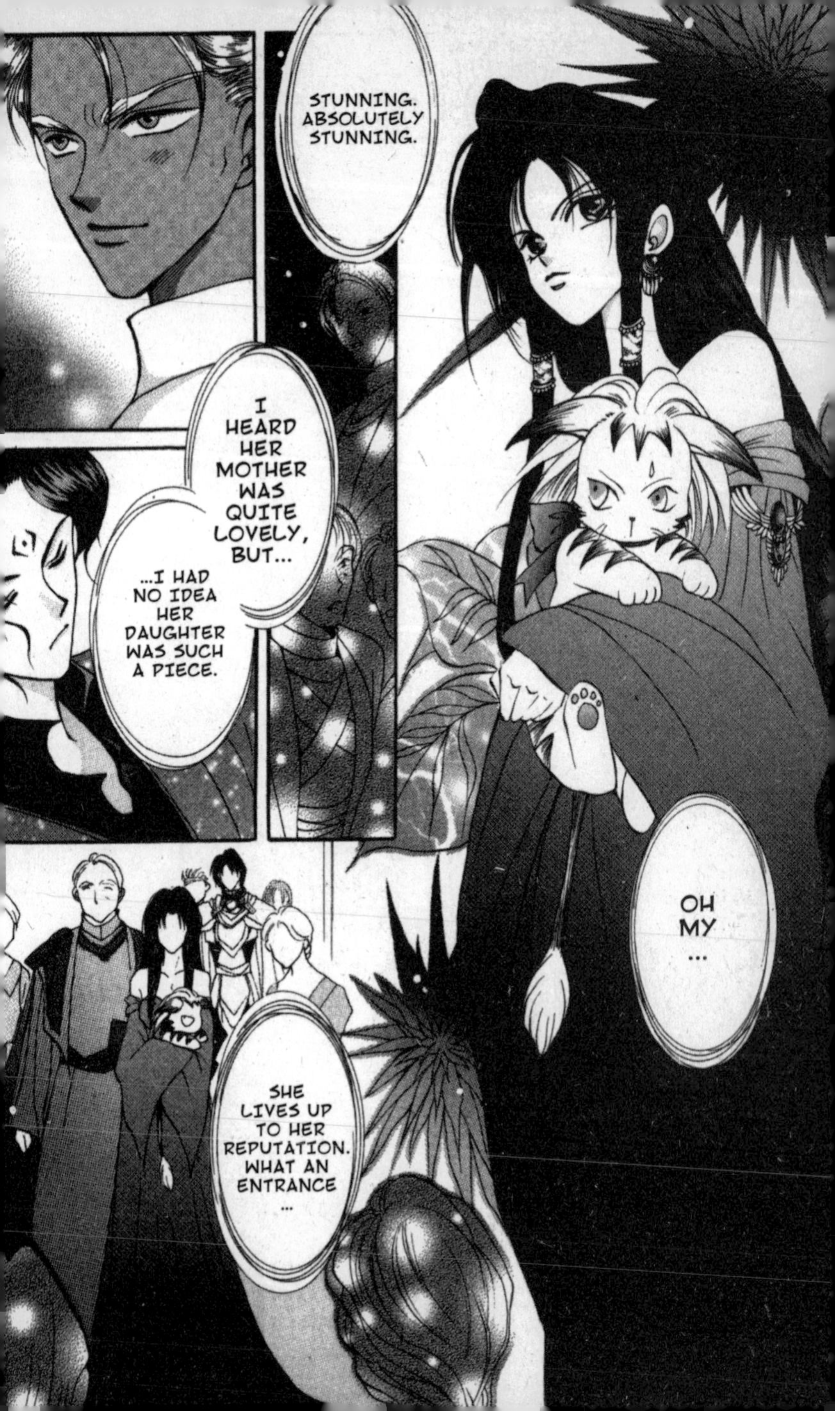
OH MY ...
STUNNING. ABSOLUTELY STUNNING.
I HEARD HER MOTHER WAS QUITE LOVELY, BUT...
...I HAD NO IDEA HER DAUGHTER WAS SUCH A PIECE.
SHE LIVES UP TO HER REPUTATION. WHAT AN ENTRANCE ...

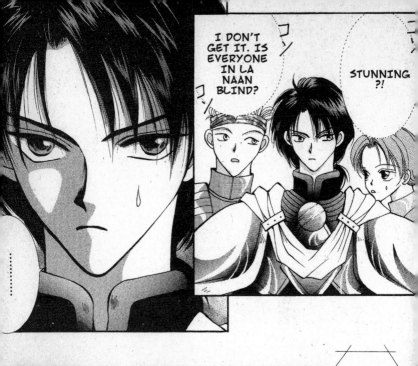

I DON'T GET IT. IS EVERYONE IN LA NAAN BLIND?

STUNNING?!

HER MAJESTY'S MISSING? AGAIN?

HMM... SHE'S NEVER BEEN TO LA NAAN BEFORE.

AND SHE SAID SHE WANTED TO GO TO THE MARTIAL ARTS COMPETITION. I'D CHECK THE COLISEUM FIRST.

ASK PEOPLE IF THEY'VE SEEN THE "BEAUTIFUL KNIGHT."

ODDS ARE YOU'LL FIND HER THERE. IF NOT--

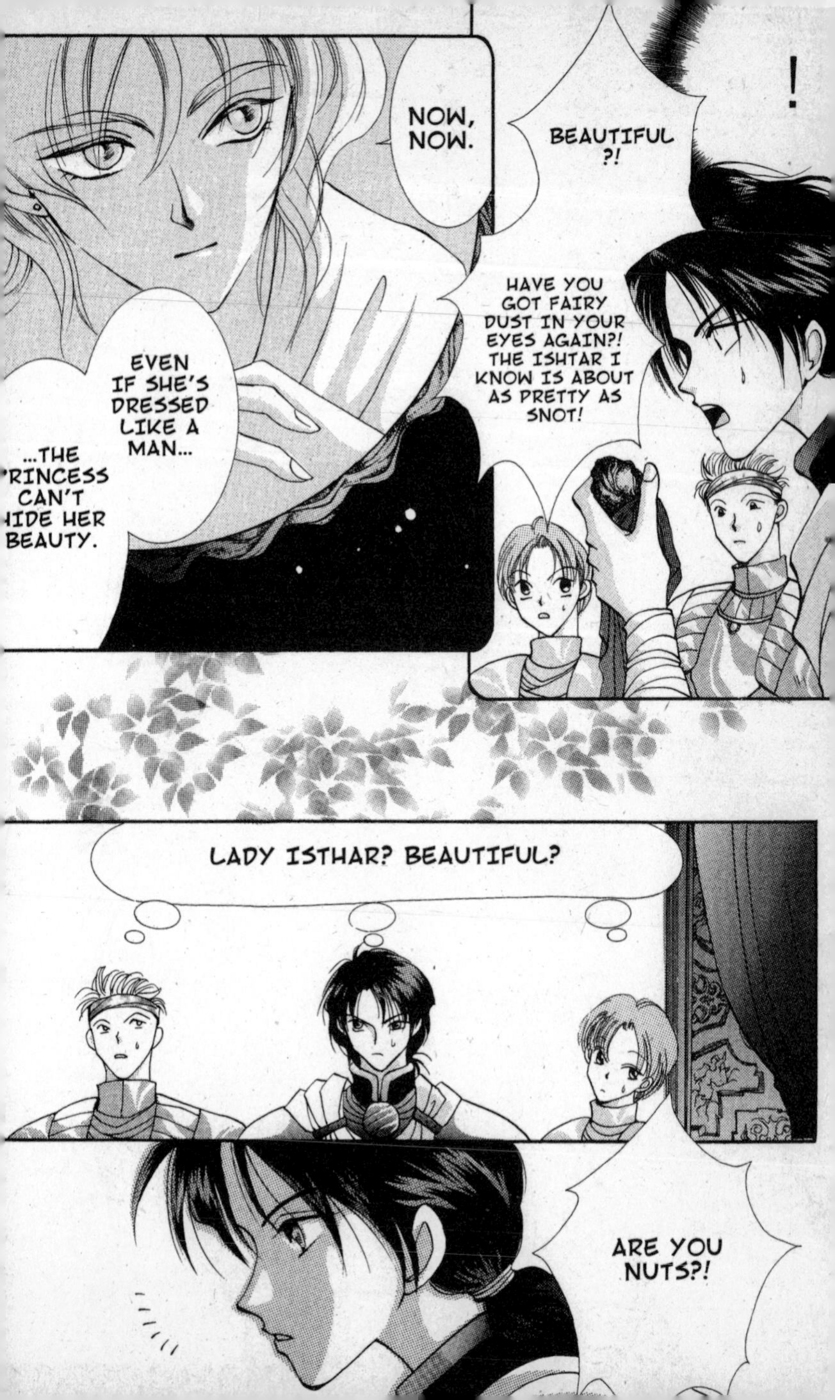
!
BEAUTIFUL ?!
HAVE YOU GOT FAIRY DUST IN YOUR EYES AGAIN?! THE ISHTAR I KNOW IS ABOUT AS PRETTY AS SNOT!
NOW, NOW.
EVEN IF SHE'S DRESSED LIKE A MAN...
...THE PRINCESS CAN'T HIDE HER BEAUTY.
LADY ISTHAR? BEAUTIFUL?
ARE YOU NUTS?!

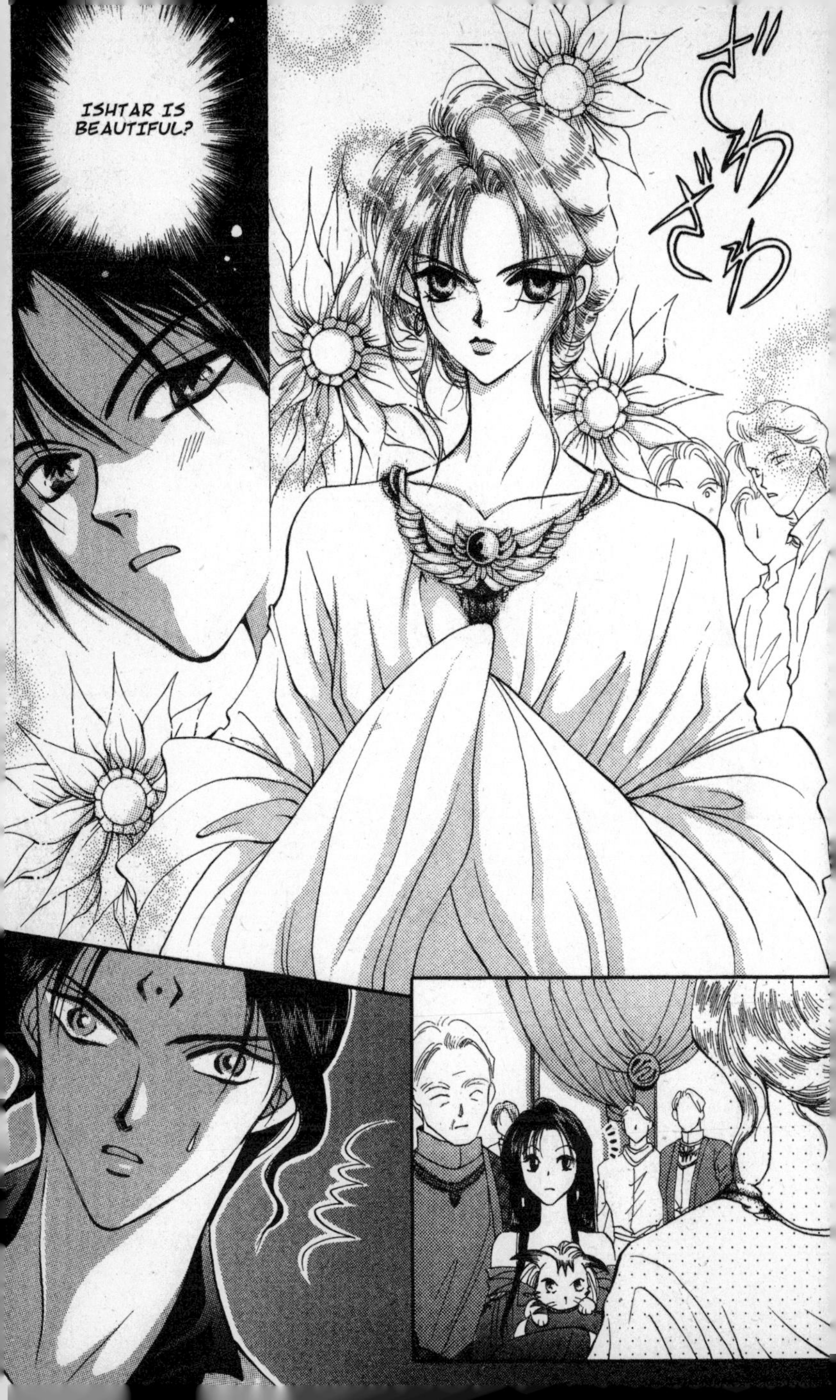
ISHTAR IS BEAUTIFUL?
ざわざわ

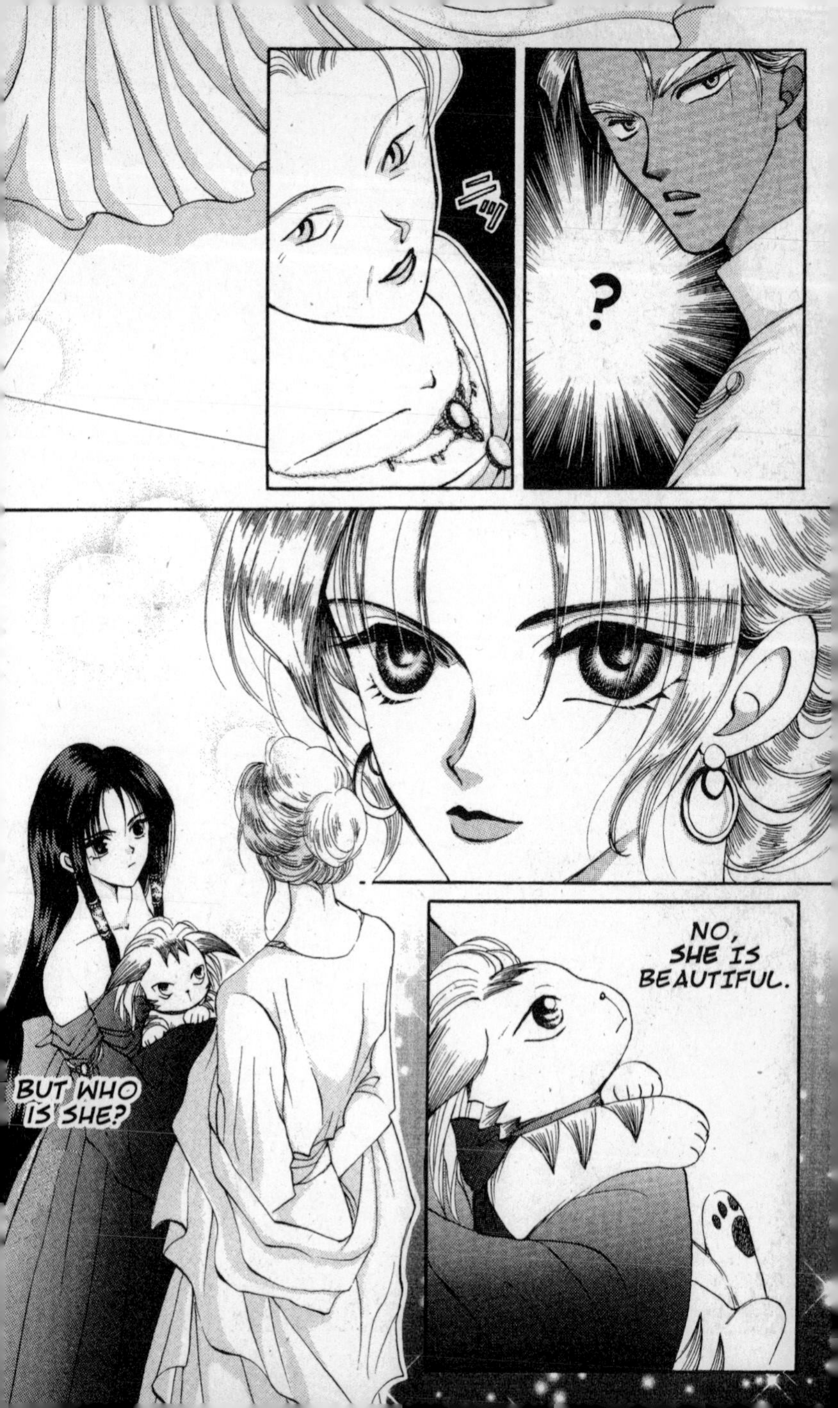
?
NO, SHE IS BEAUTIFUL.
BUT WHO IS SHE?

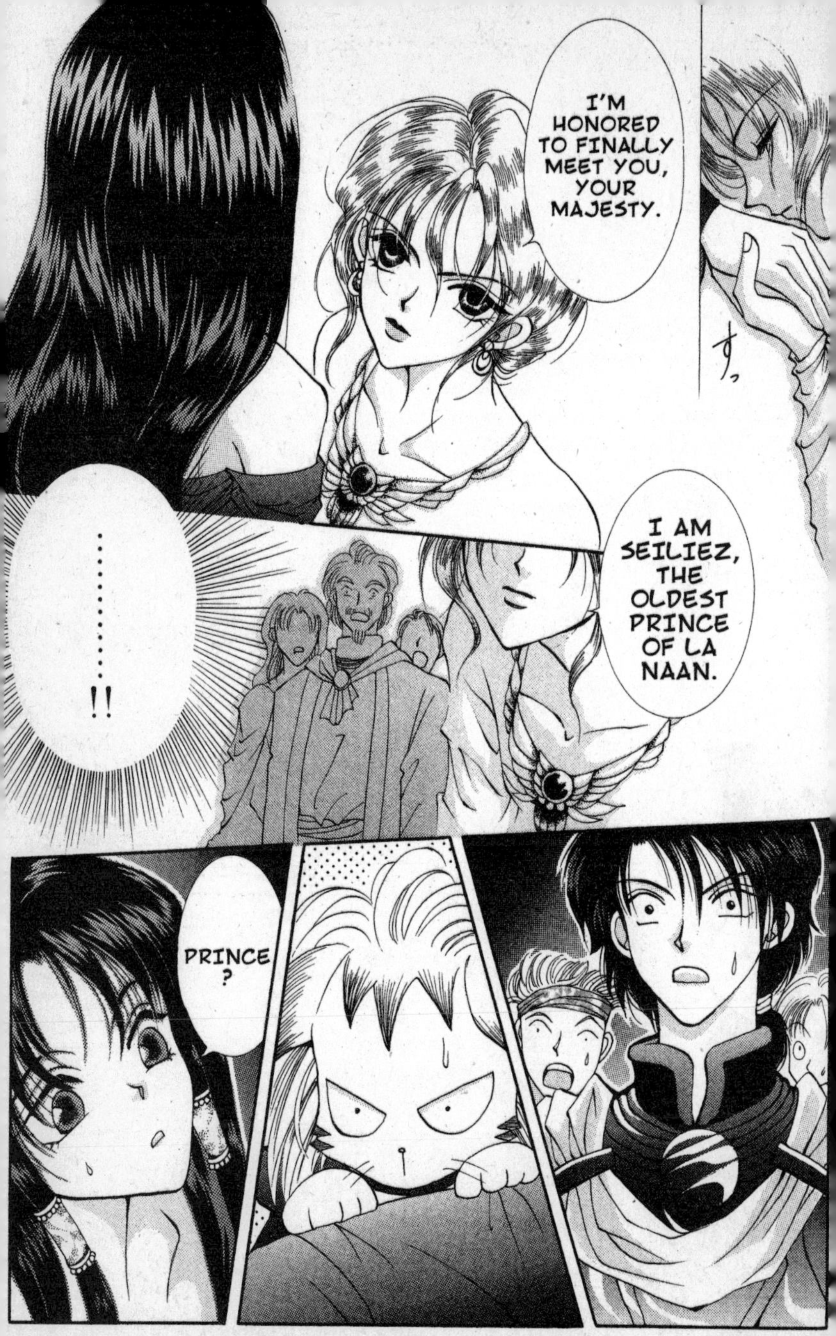
すっ
I'M HONORED TO FINALLY MEET YOU, YOUR MAJESTY.
I AM SEILIEZ, THE OLDEST PRINCE OF LA NAAN.
......!!
PRINCE?

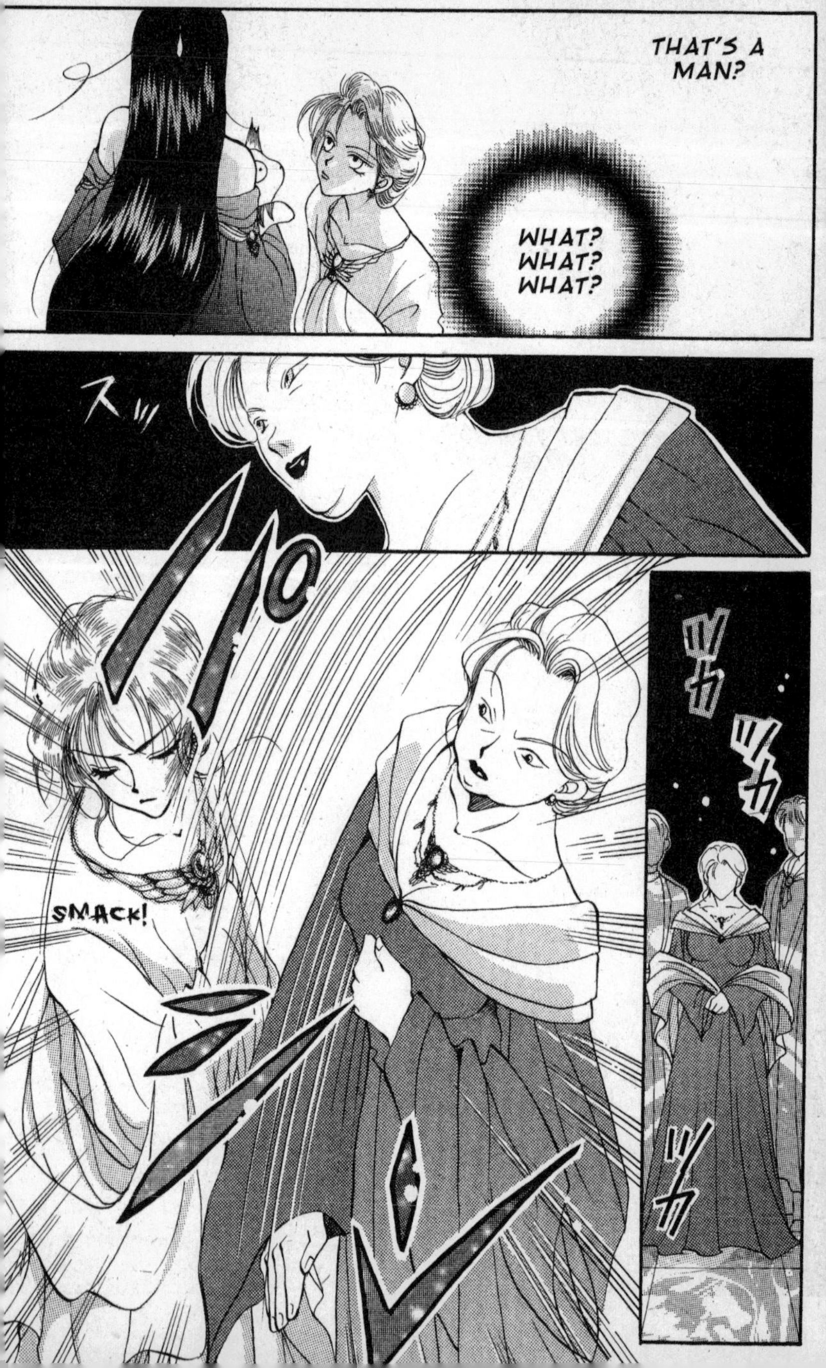
THAT'S A MAN?
WHAT? WHAT? WHAT?
スッ
ヅカ
ヅカ
ヅカ
SMACK!

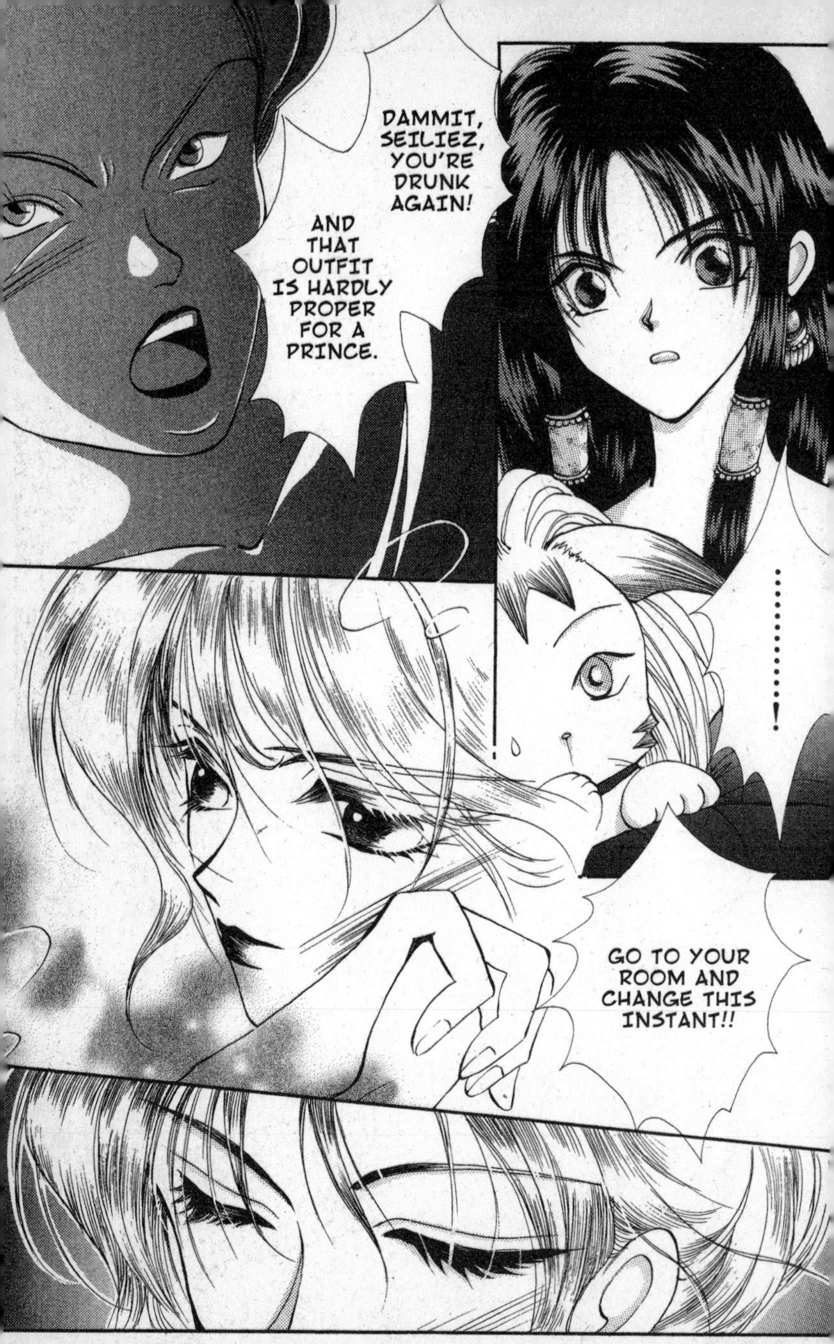
DAMMIT, SEILIEZ, YOU'RE DRUNK AGAIN!
AND THAT OUTFIT IS HARDLY PROPER FOR A PRINCE.
......!
GO TO YOUR ROOM AND CHANGE THIS INSTANT!!

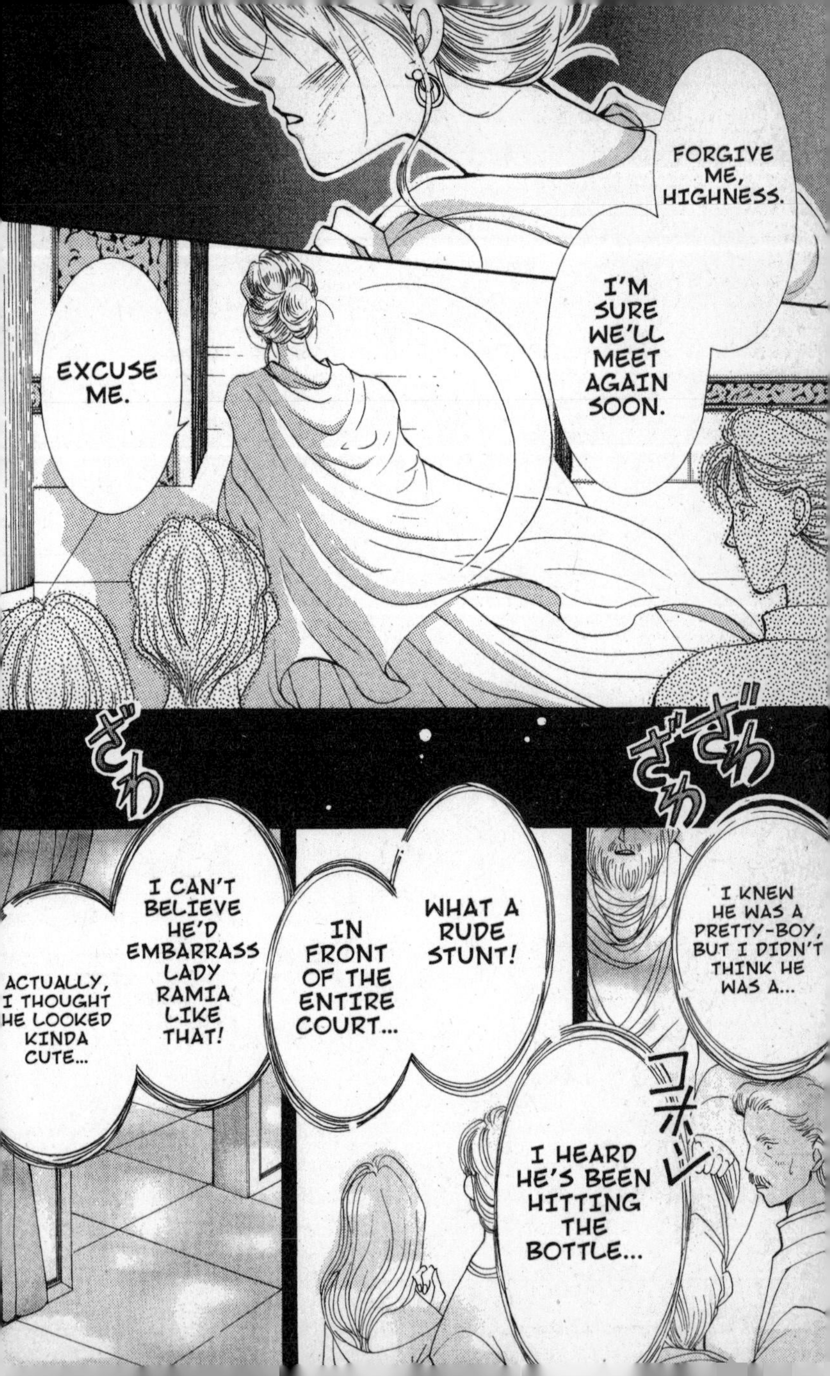
FORGIVE ME, HIGHNESS.
I'M SURE WE'LL MEET AGAIN SOON.
EXCUSE ME.
ざわ ざわ
ざわ
I KNEW HE WAS A PRETTY-BOY, BUT I DIDN'T THINK HE WAS A...
コホン
I HEARD HE'S BEEN HITTING THE BOTTLE...
WHAT A RUDE STUNT!
IN FRONT OF THE ENTIRE COURT...
I CAN'T BELIEVE HE'D EMBARRASS LADY RAMIA LIKE THAT!
ACTUALLY, I THOUGHT HE LOOKED KINDA CUTE...

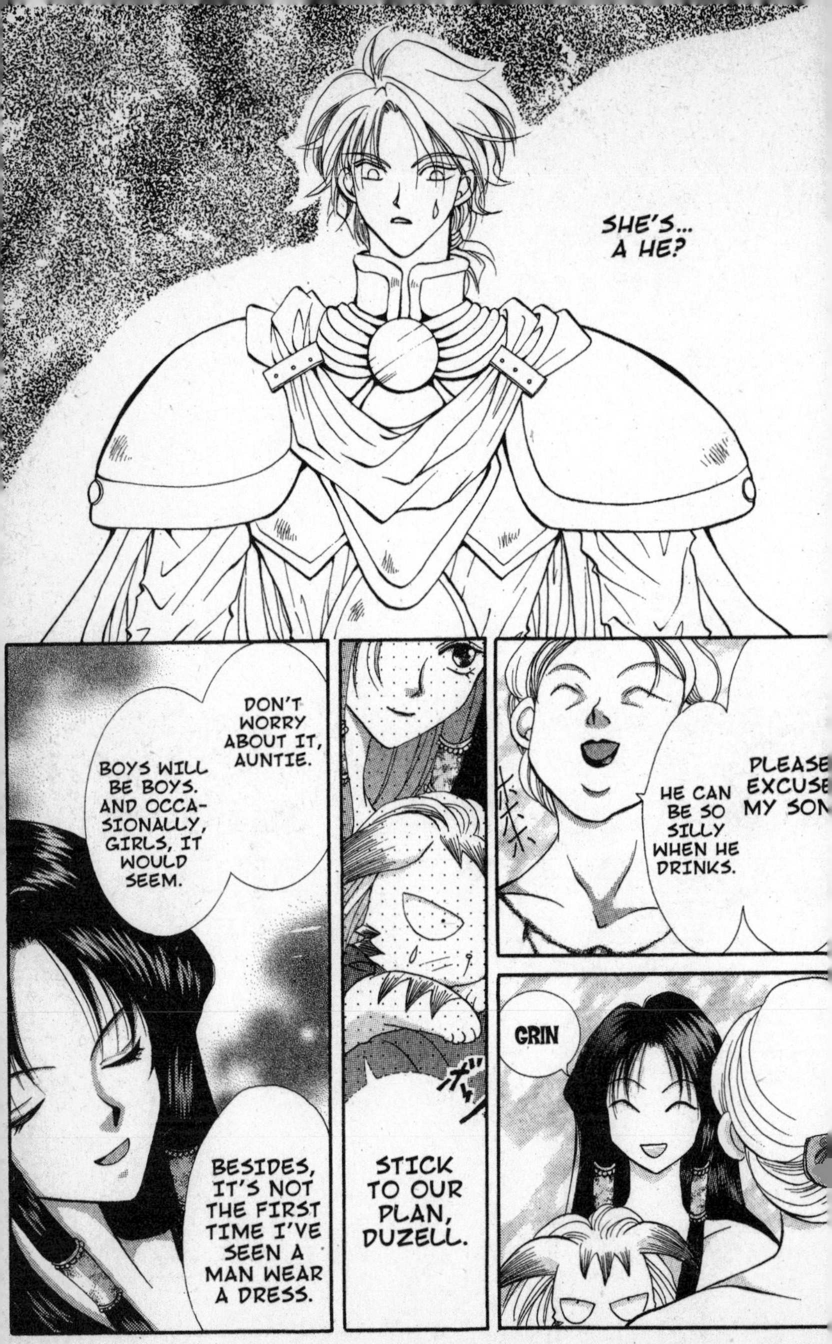
SHE'S... A HE?
PLEASE EXCUSE MY SON
HE CAN BE SO SILLY WHEN HE DRINKS.
GRIN
STICK TO OUR PLAN, DUZELL.
DON'T WORRY ABOUT IT, AUNTIE.
BOYS WILL BE BOYS. AND OCCASIONALLY, GIRLS, IT WOULD SEEM.
BESIDES, IT'S NOT THE FIRST TIME I'VE SEEN A MAN WEAR A DRESS.

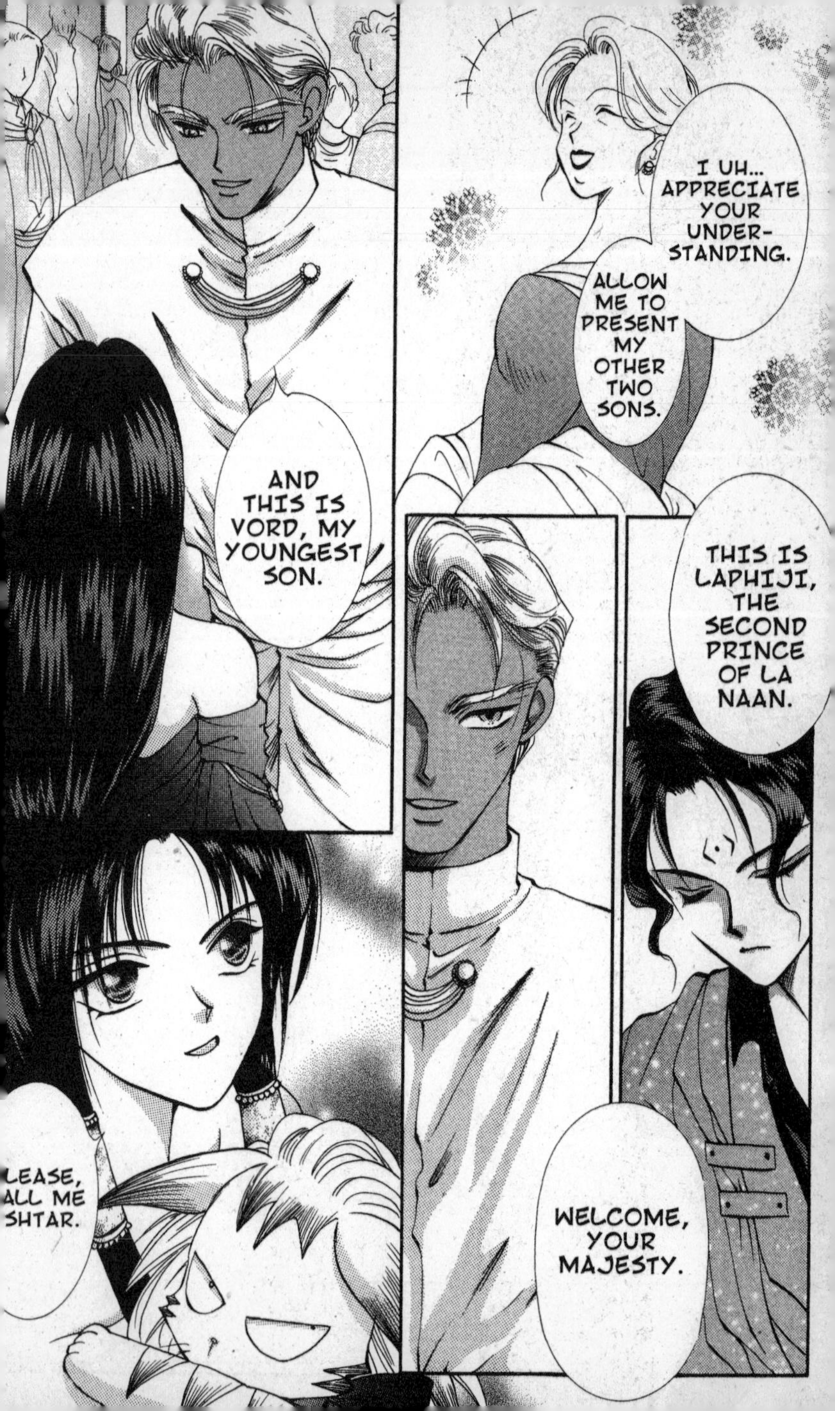
I UH... APPRECIATE YOUR UNDER-STANDING.
ALLOW ME TO PRESENT MY OTHER TWO SONS.
THIS IS LAPHIJI, THE SECOND PRINCE OF LA NAAN.
WELCOME, YOUR MAJESTY.
AND THIS IS VORD, MY YOUNGEST SON.
LEASE, ALL ME SHTAR.

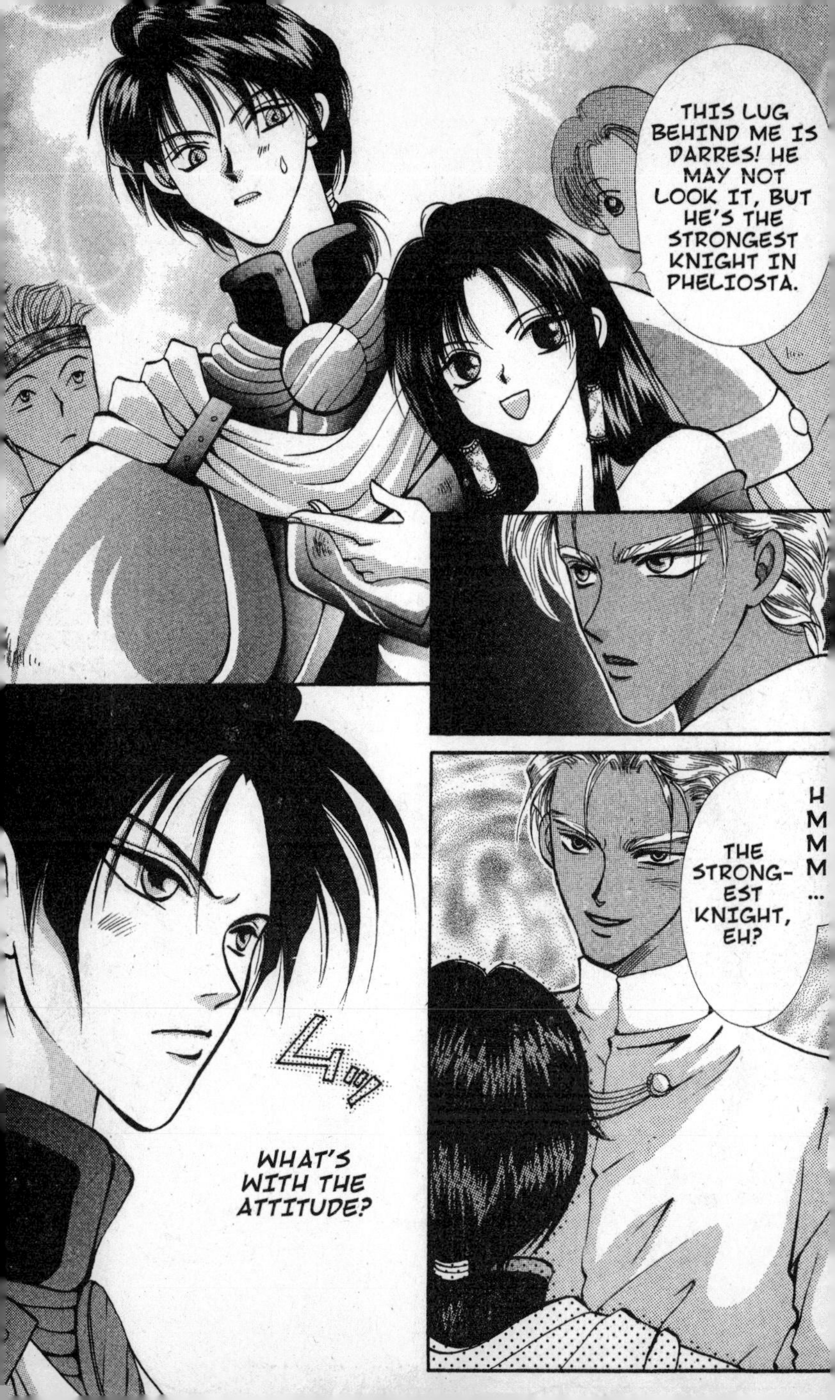
THIS LUG BEHIND ME IS DARRES! HE MAY NOT LOOK IT, BUT HE'S THE STRONGEST KNIGHT IN PHELIOSTA.
HMMM...
THE STRONG-EST KNIGHT, EH?
WHAT'S WITH THE ATTITUDE?

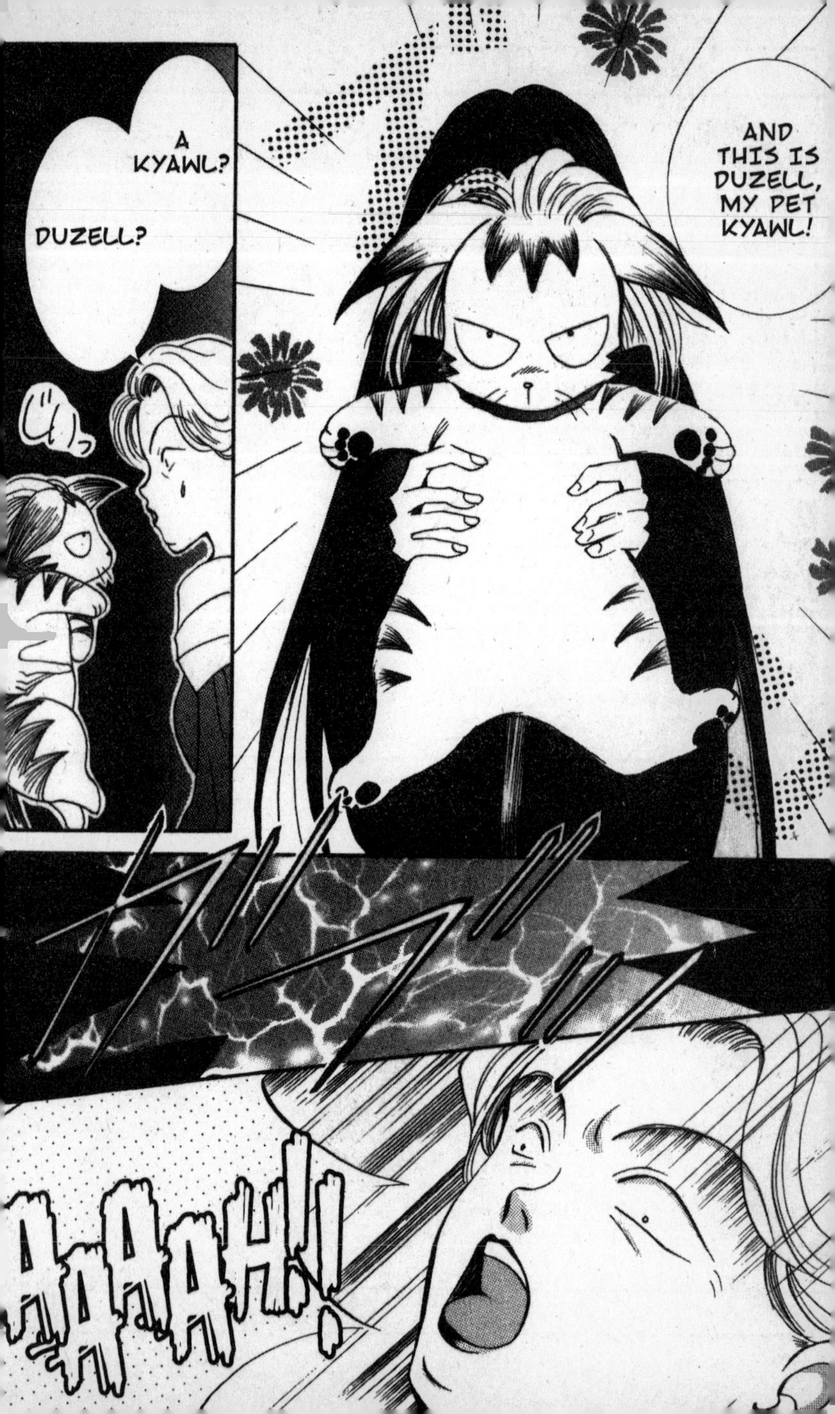
AND THIS IS DUZELL, MY PET KYAWL!
A KYAWL?
DUZELL?
AAAH!!

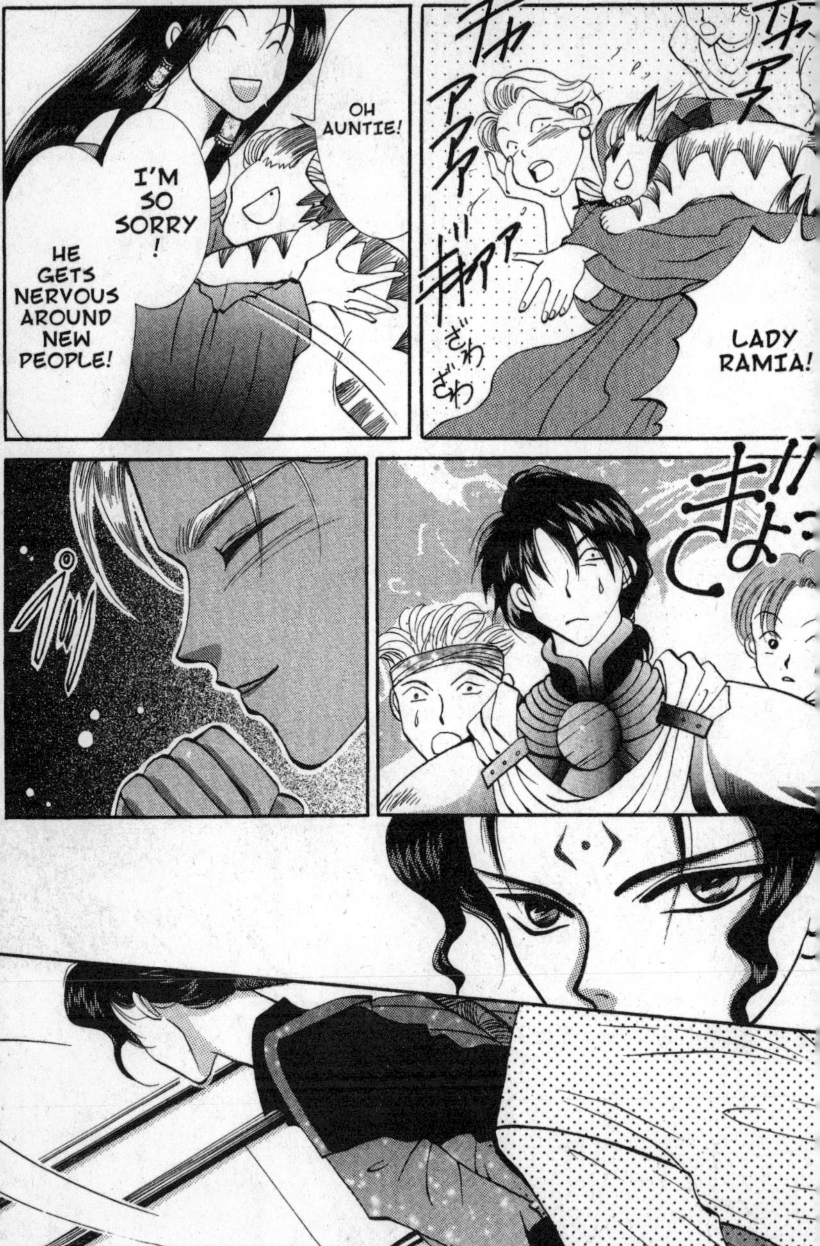
ギャアア
ギャアア
ギャアア
ざわざわ
LADY RAMIA!
OH AUNTIE!
I'M SO SORRY!
HE GETS NERVOUS AROUND NEW PEOPLE!

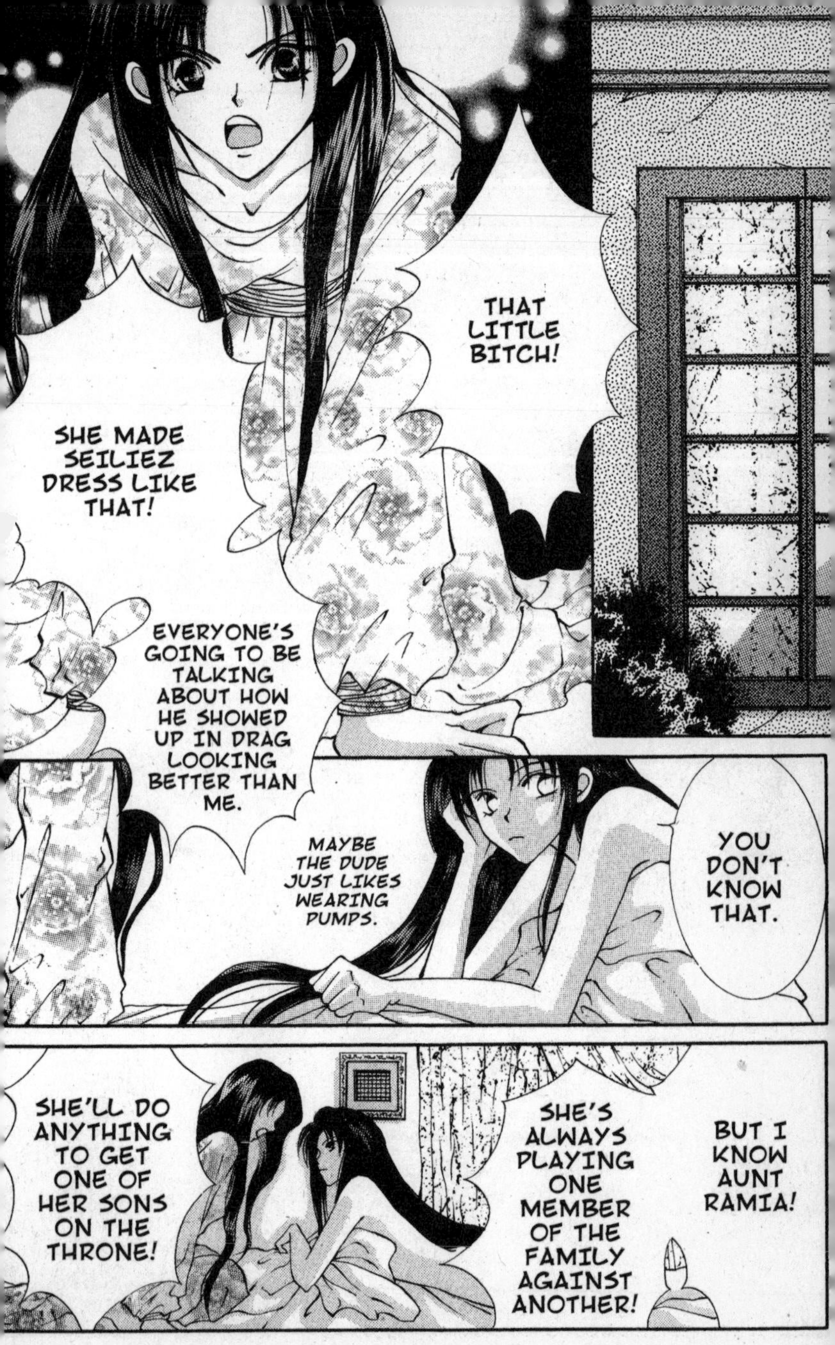
THAT LITTLE BITCH!
SHE MADE SEILIEZ DRESS LIKE THAT!
EVERYONE'S GOING TO BE TALKING ABOUT HOW HE SHOWED UP IN DRAG LOOKING BETTER THAN ME.
YOU DON'T KNOW THAT.
MAYBE THE DUDE JUST LIKES WEARING PUMPS.
BUT I KNOW AUNT RAMIA!
SHE'S ALWAYS PLAYING ONE MEMBER OF THE FAMILY AGAINST ANOTHER!
SHE'LL DO ANYTHING TO GET ONE OF HER SONS ON THE THRONE!

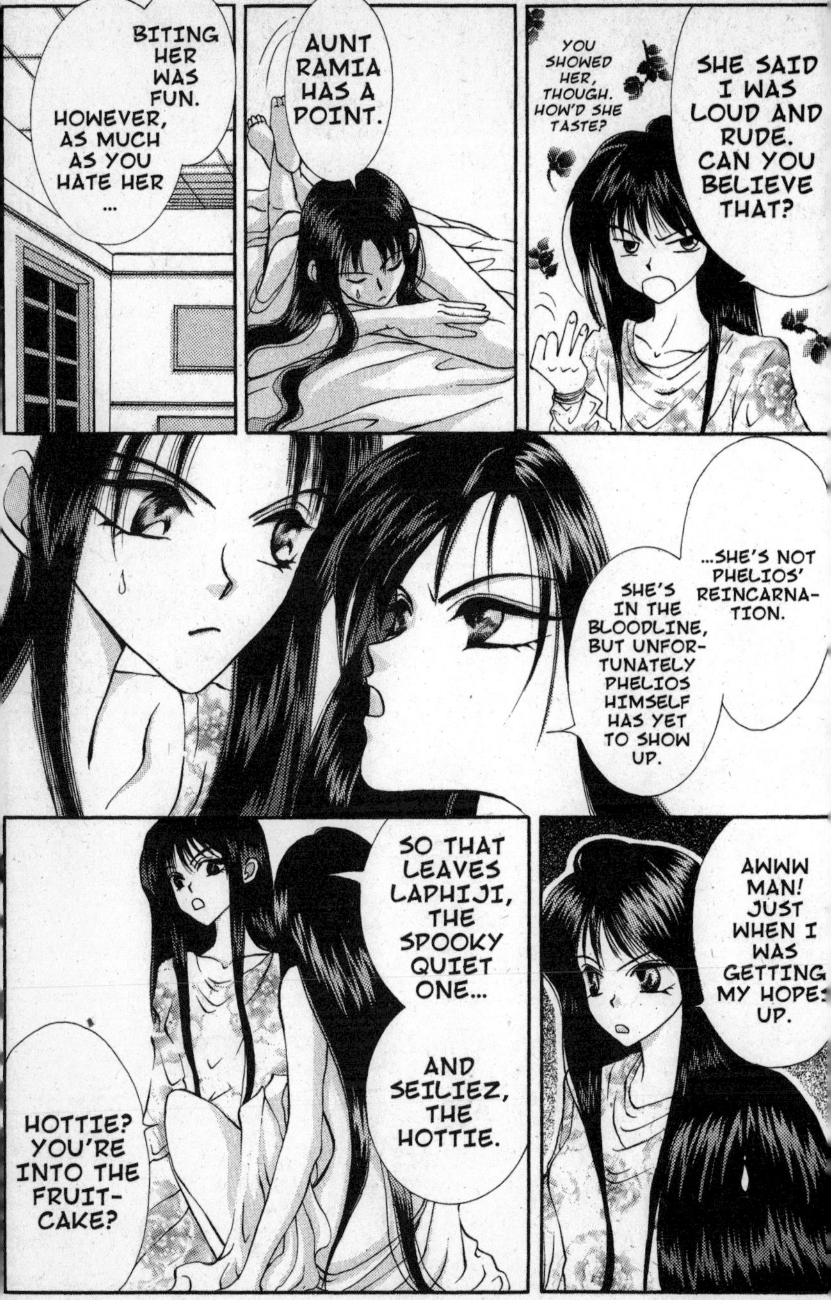
SHE SAID I WAS LOUD AND RUDE. CAN YOU BELIEVE THAT?
YOU SHOWED HER, THOUGH. HOW'D SHE TASTE?
AUNT RAMIA HAS A POINT.
BITING HER WAS FUN. HOWEVER, AS MUCH AS YOU HATE HER ...
...SHE'S NOT PHELIOS' REINCARNATION.
SHE'S IN THE BLOODLINE, BUT UNFORTUNATELY PHELIOS HIMSELF HAS YET TO SHOW UP.
AWWW MAN! JUST WHEN I WAS GETTING MY HOPES UP.
SO THAT LEAVES LAPHIJI, THE SPOOKY QUIET ONE...
AND SEILIEZ, THE HOTTIE.
HOTTIE? YOU'RE INTO THE FRUIT-CAKE?

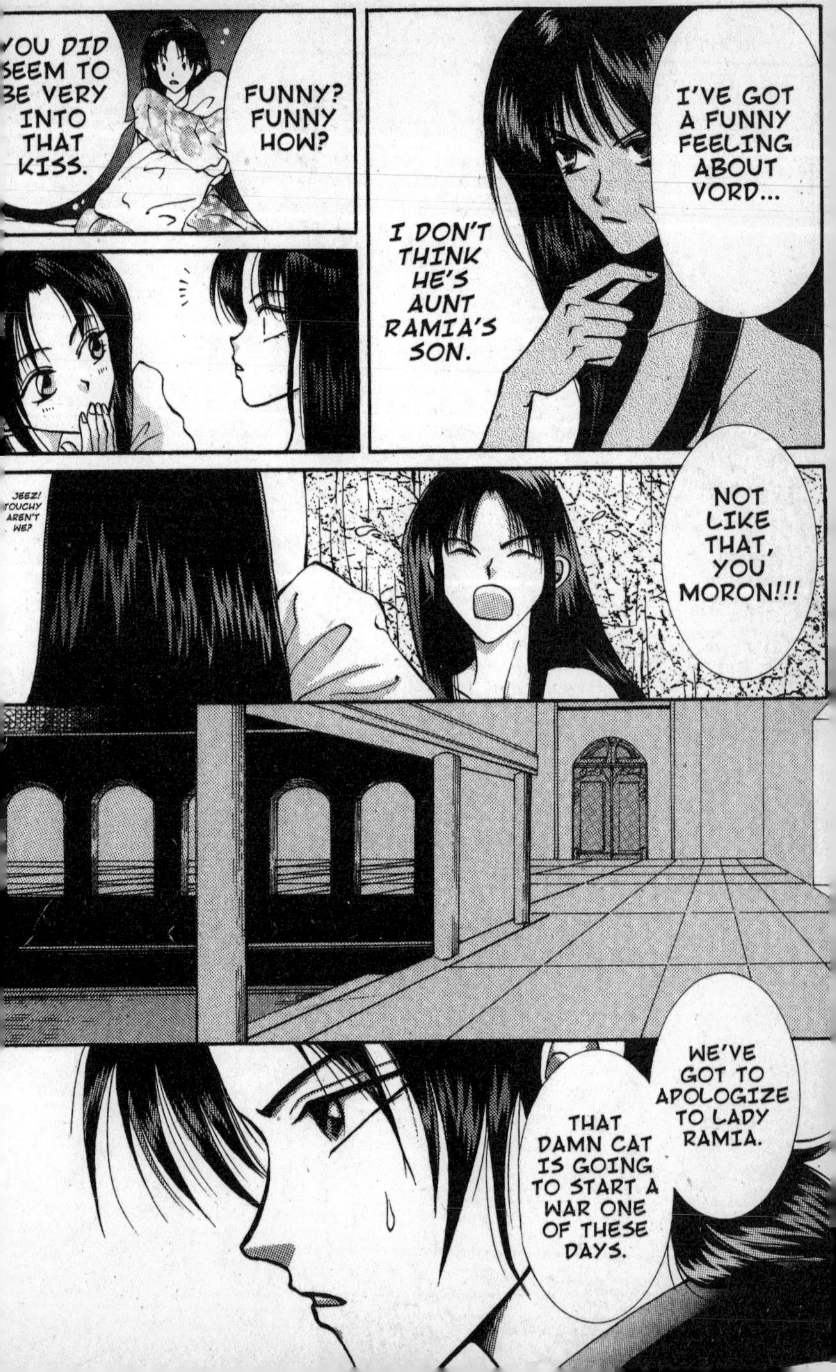
I'VE GOT A FUNNY FEELING ABOUT VORD...
I DON'T THINK HE'S AUNT RAMIA'S SON.
FUNNY? FUNNY HOW?
YOU DID SEEM TO BE VERY INTO THAT KISS.
NOT LIKE THAT, YOU MORON!!!
JEEZ! TOUCHY AREN'T WE?
WE'VE GOT TO APOLOGIZE TO LADY RAMIA.
THAT DAMN CAT IS GOING TO START A WAR ONE OF THESE DAYS.

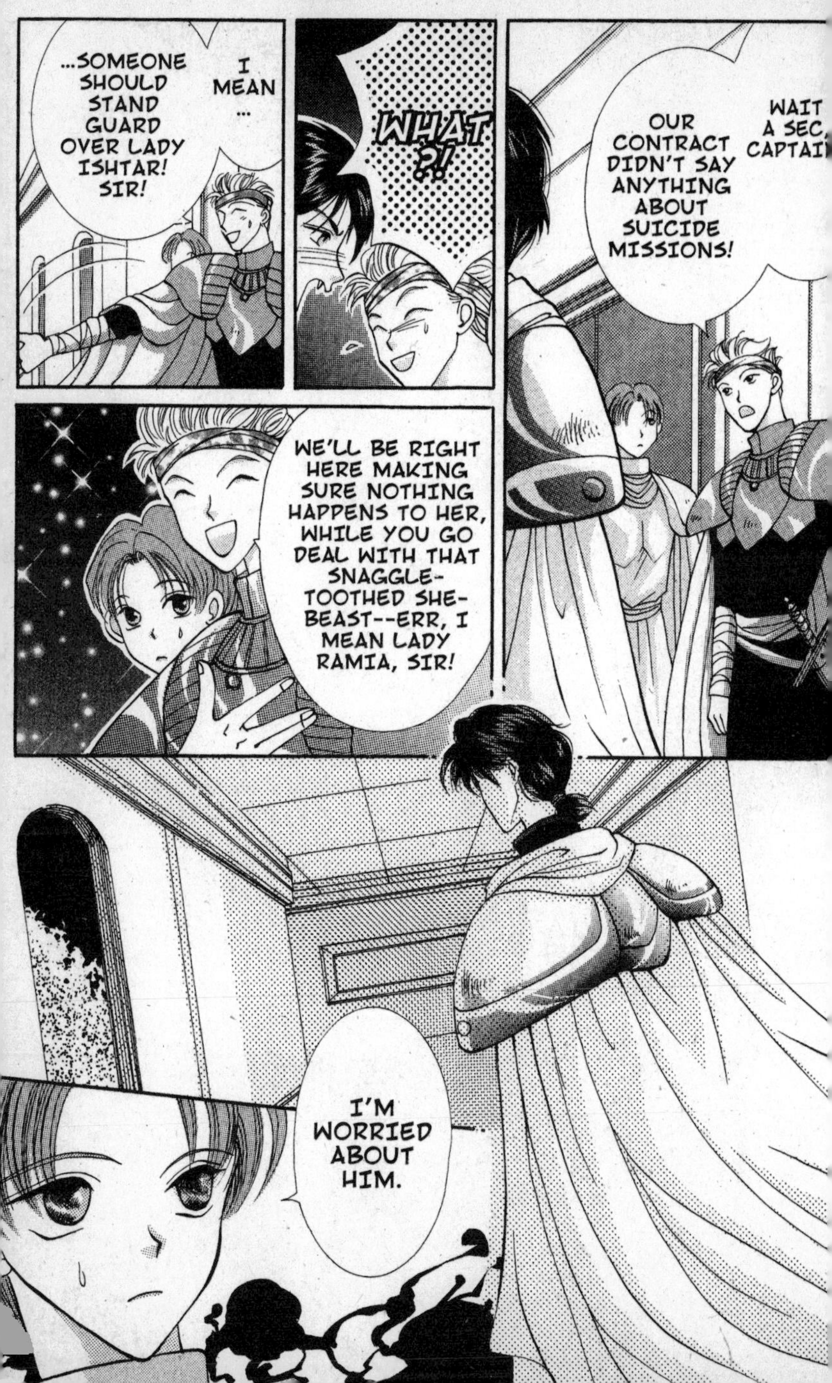
WAIT A SEC, CAPTAI
OUR CONTRACT DIDN'T SAY ANYTHING ABOUT SUICIDE MISSIONS!
WHAT?!
I MEAN ...
...SOMEONE SHOULD STAND GUARD OVER LADY ISHTAR! SIR!
WE'LL BE RIGHT HERE MAKING SURE NOTHING HAPPENS TO HER, WHILE YOU GO DEAL WITH THAT SNAGGLE-TOOTHED SHE-BEAST--ERR, I MEAN LADY RAMIA, SIR!
I'M WORRIED ABOUT HIM.

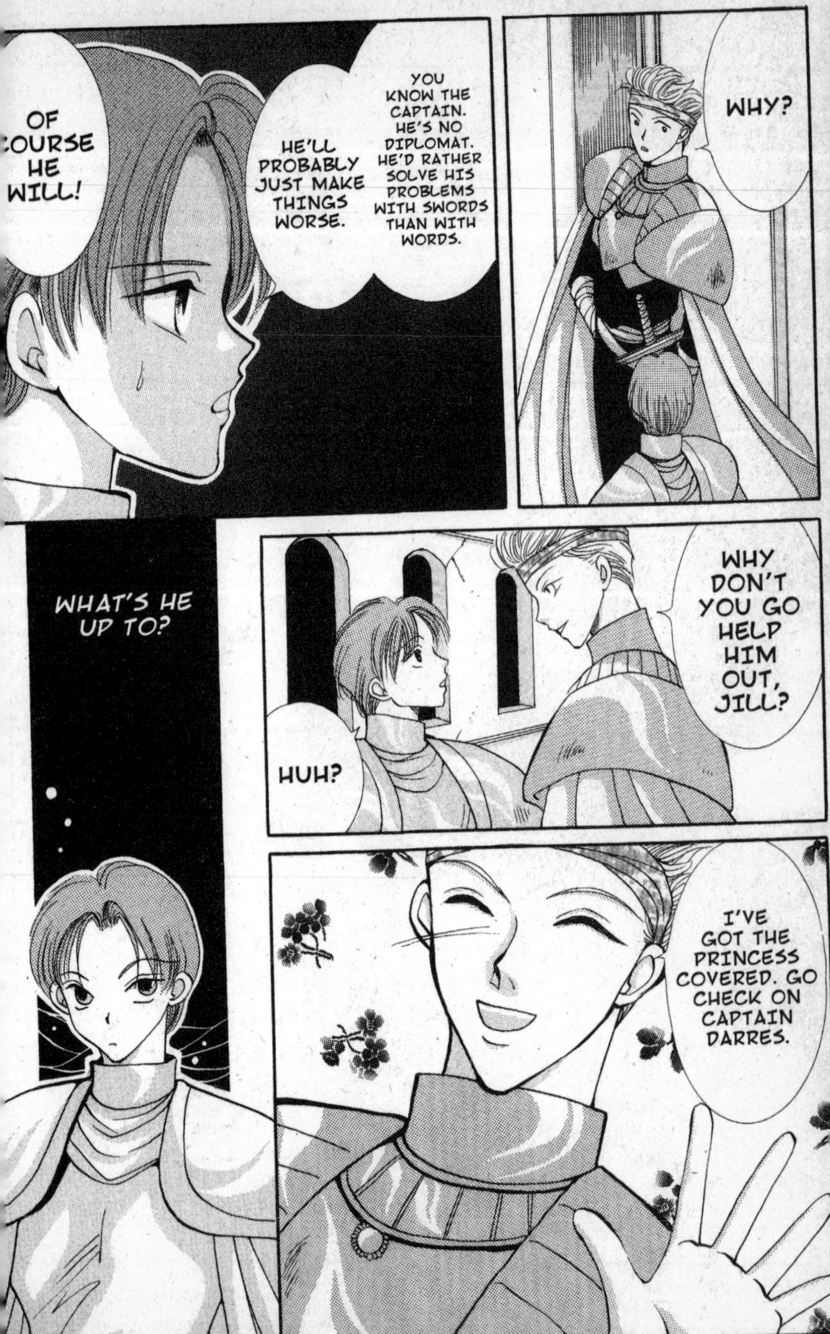
WHY?
YOU KNOW THE CAPTAIN. HE'S NO DIPLOMAT. HE'D RATHER SOLVE HIS PROBLEMS WITH SWORDS THAN WITH WORDS.
HE'LL PROBABLY JUST MAKE THINGS WORSE.
OF COURSE HE WILL!
WHY DON'T YOU GO HELP HIM OUT, JILL?
HUH?
I'VE GOT THE PRINCESS COVERED. GO CHECK ON CAPTAIN DARRES.
WHAT'S HE UP TO?

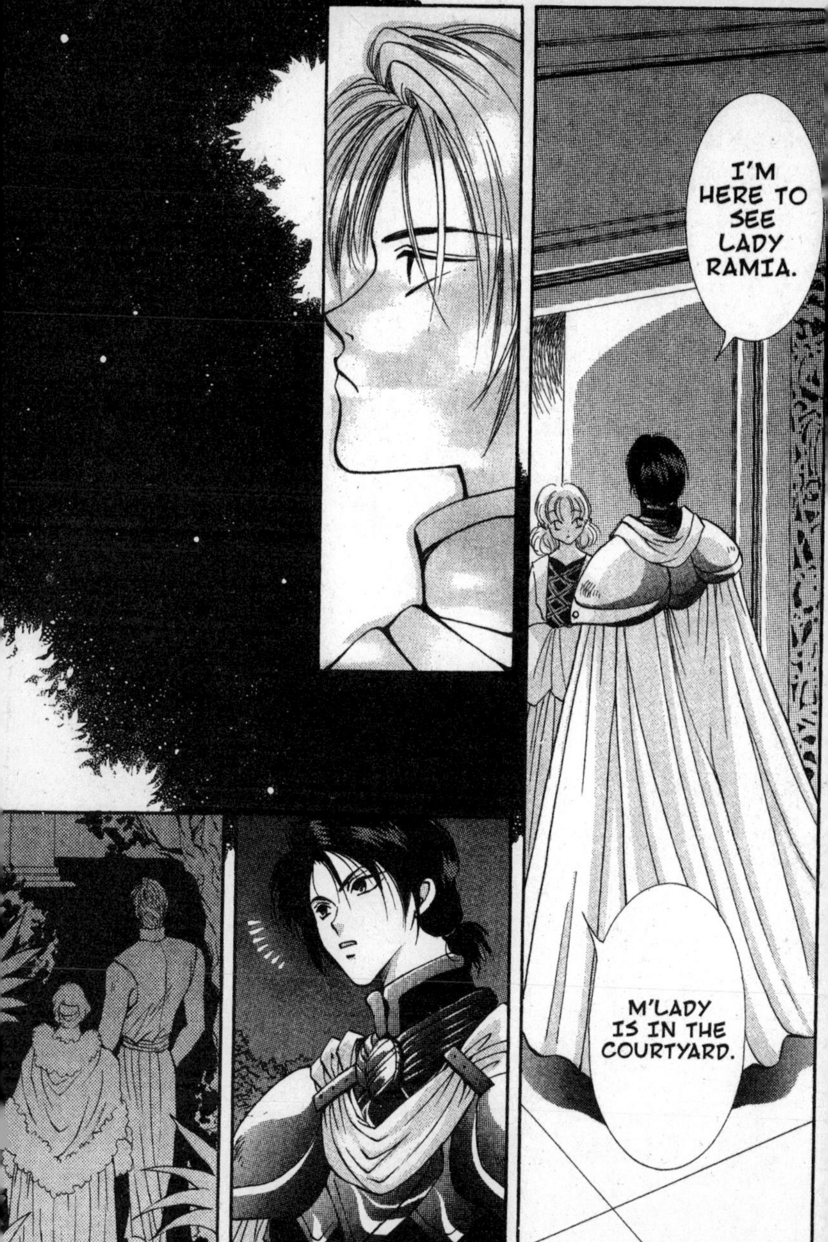
I'M HERE TO SEE LADY RAMIA.
M'LADY IS IN THE COURTYARD.

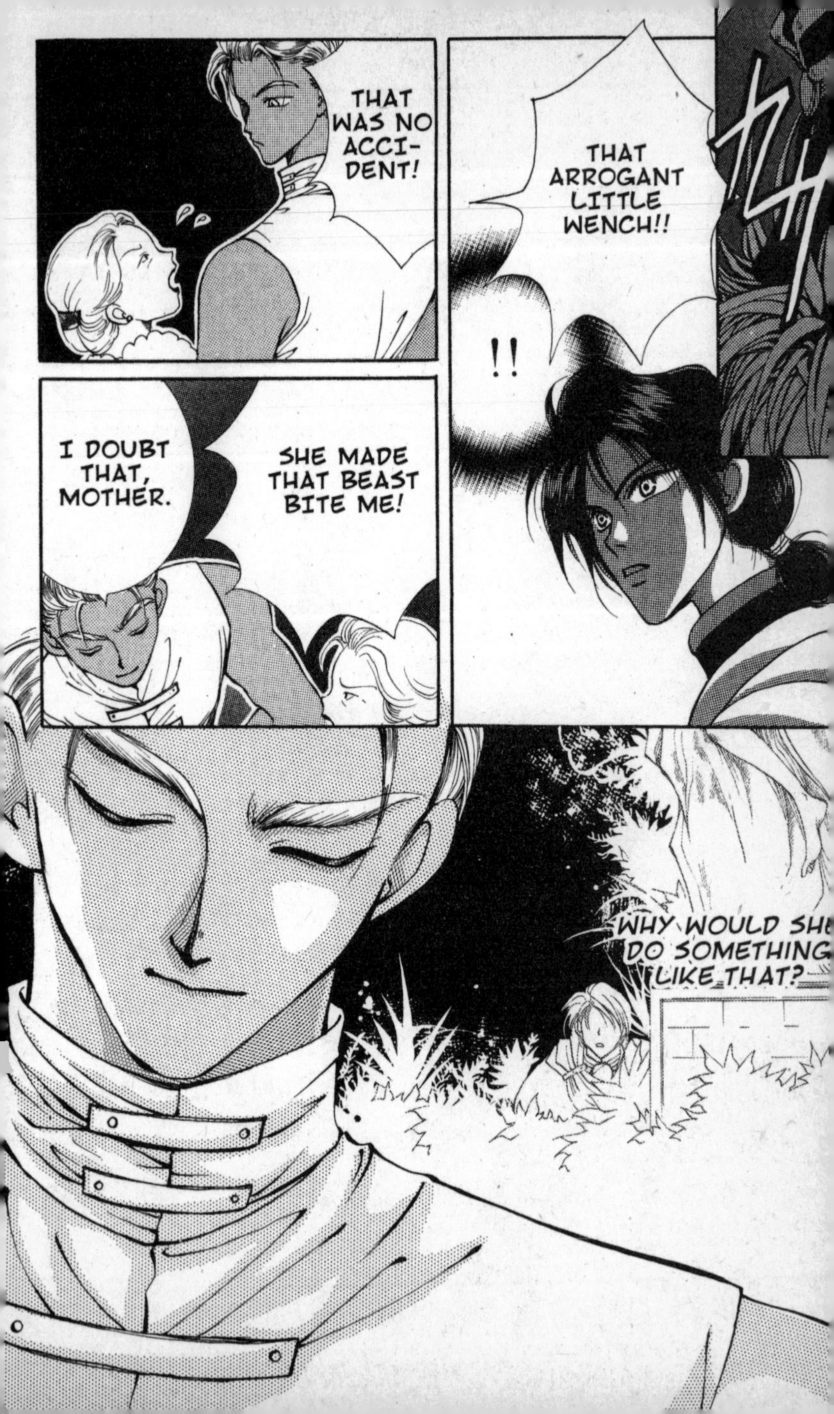
THAT ARROGANT LITTLE WENCH!!
!!
THAT WAS NO ACCI-DENT!
SHE MADE THAT BEAST BITE ME!
I DOUBT THAT, MOTHER.
WHY WOULD SHE DO SOMETHING LIKE THAT?

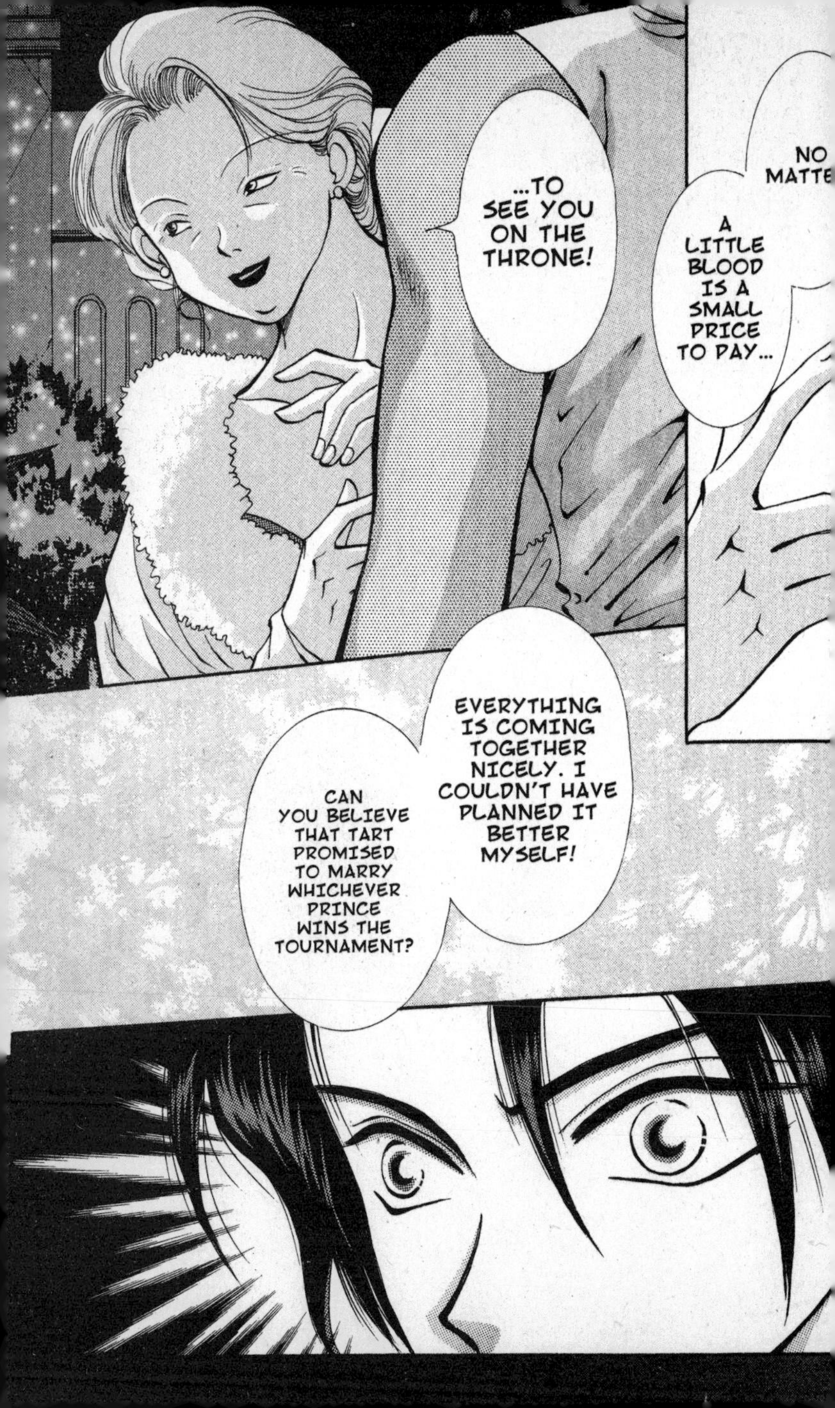
NO MATTE
A LITTLE BLOOD IS A SMALL PRICE TO PAY...
...TO SEE YOU ON THE THRONE!
EVERYTHING IS COMING TOGETHER NICELY. I COULDN'T HAVE PLANNED IT BETTER MYSELF!
CAN YOU BELIEVE THAT TART PROMISED TO MARRY WHICHEVER PRINCE WINS THE TOURNAMENT?

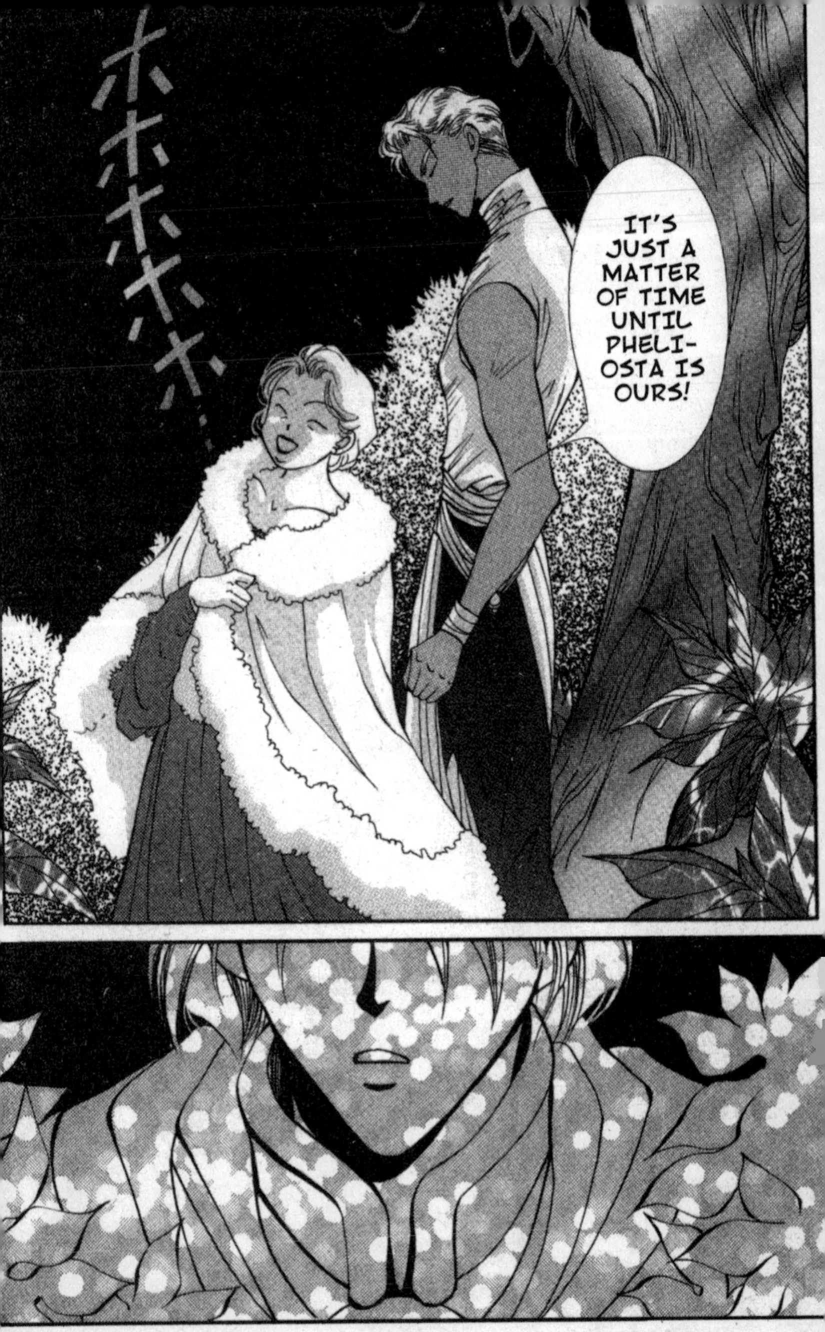
ホホホホホ
IT'S JUST A MATTER OF TIME UNTIL PHELI-OSTA IS OURS!

吸血遊戯
西領篇（ラ・ナーン）
Act.4

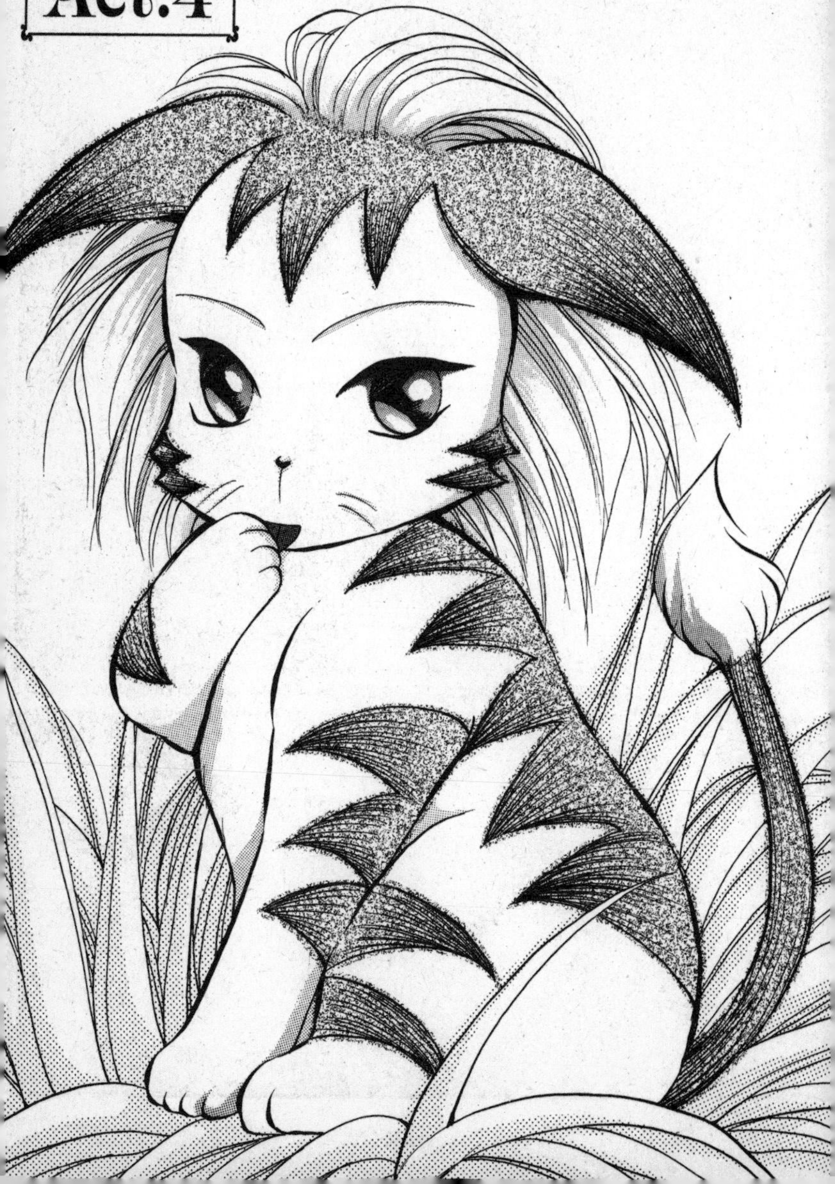

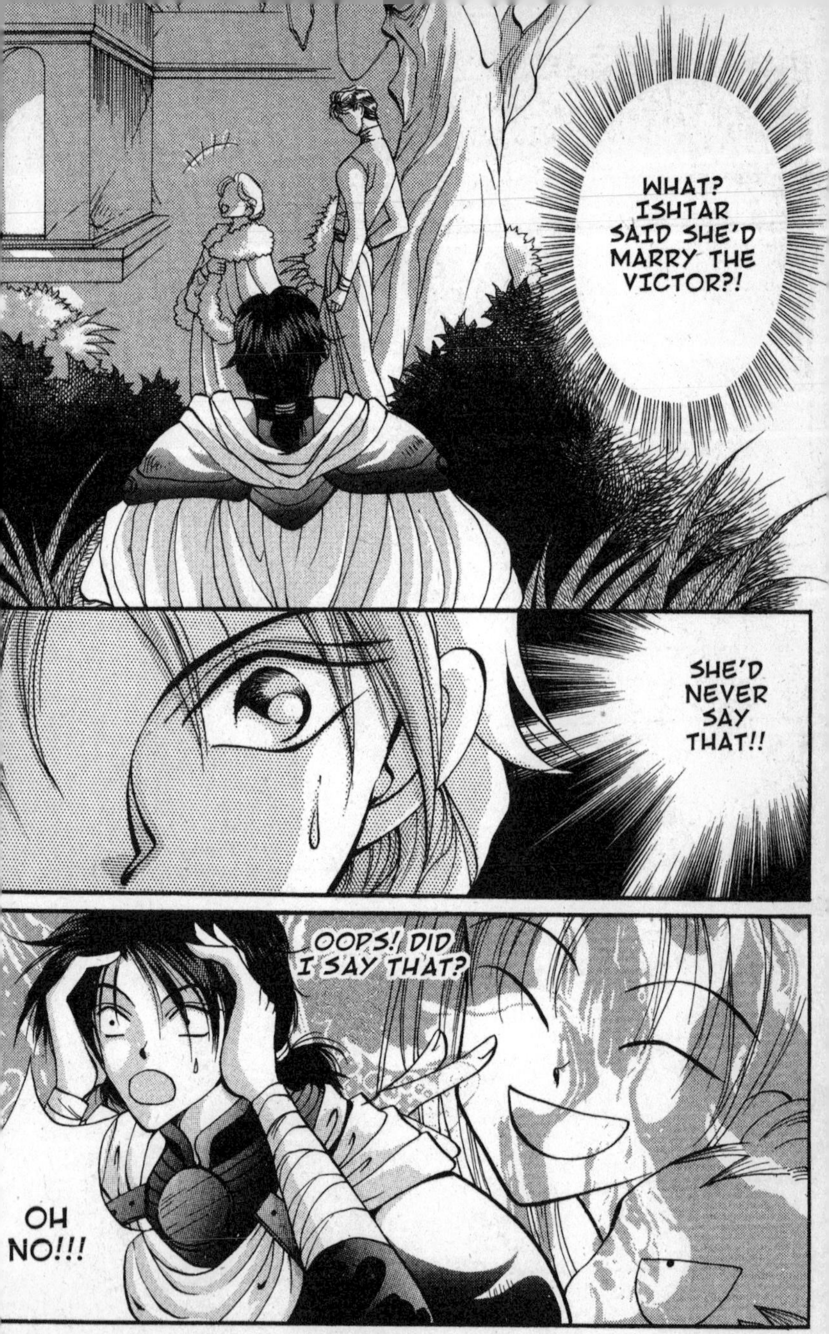
WHAT? ISHTAR SAID SHE'D MARRY THE VICTOR?!
SHE'D NEVER SAY THAT!!
OOPS! DID I SAY THAT?
OH NO!!!

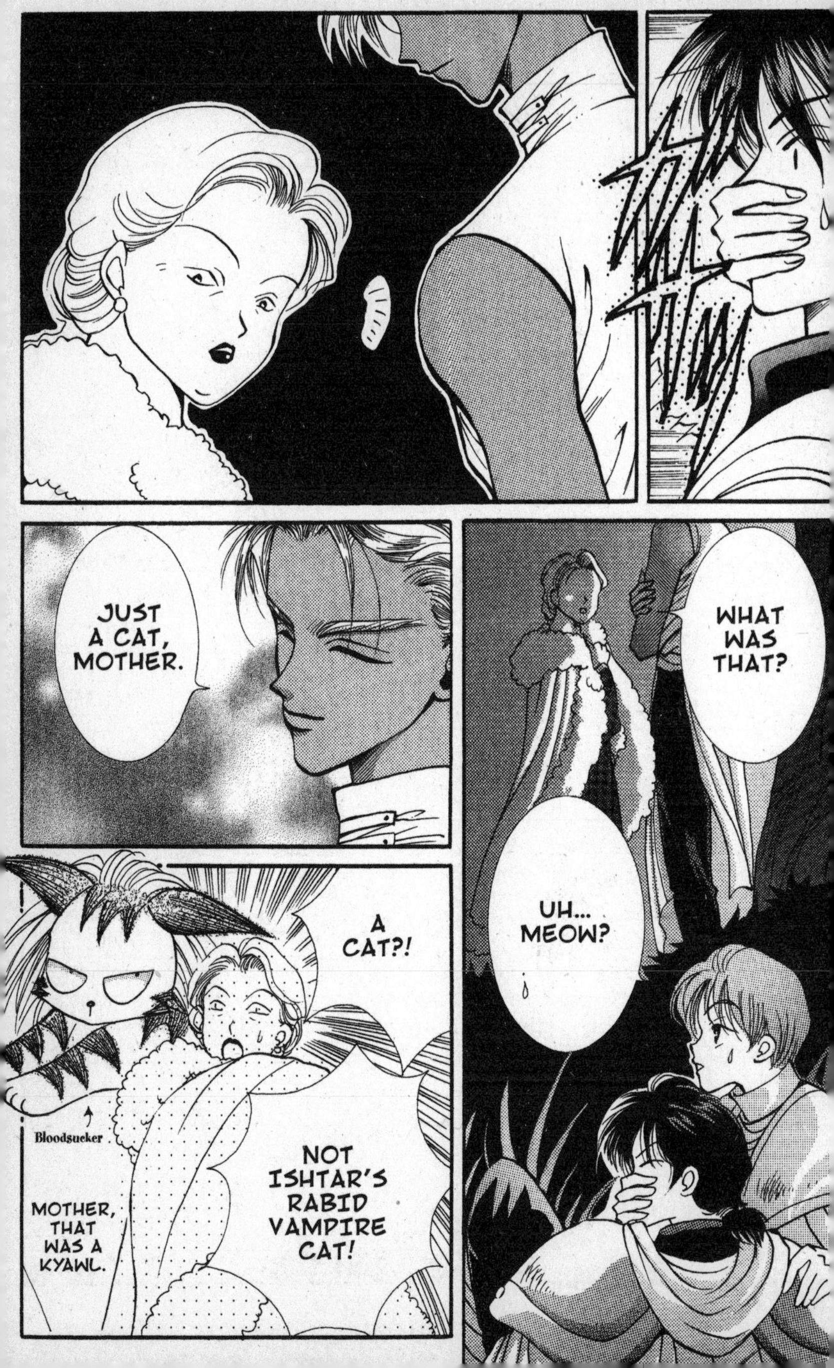
WHAT WAS THAT?
UH... MEOW?
JUST A CAT, MOTHER.
A CAT?!
NOT ISHTAR'S RABID VAMPIRE CAT!
Bloodsucker
MOTHER, THAT WAS A KYAWL.

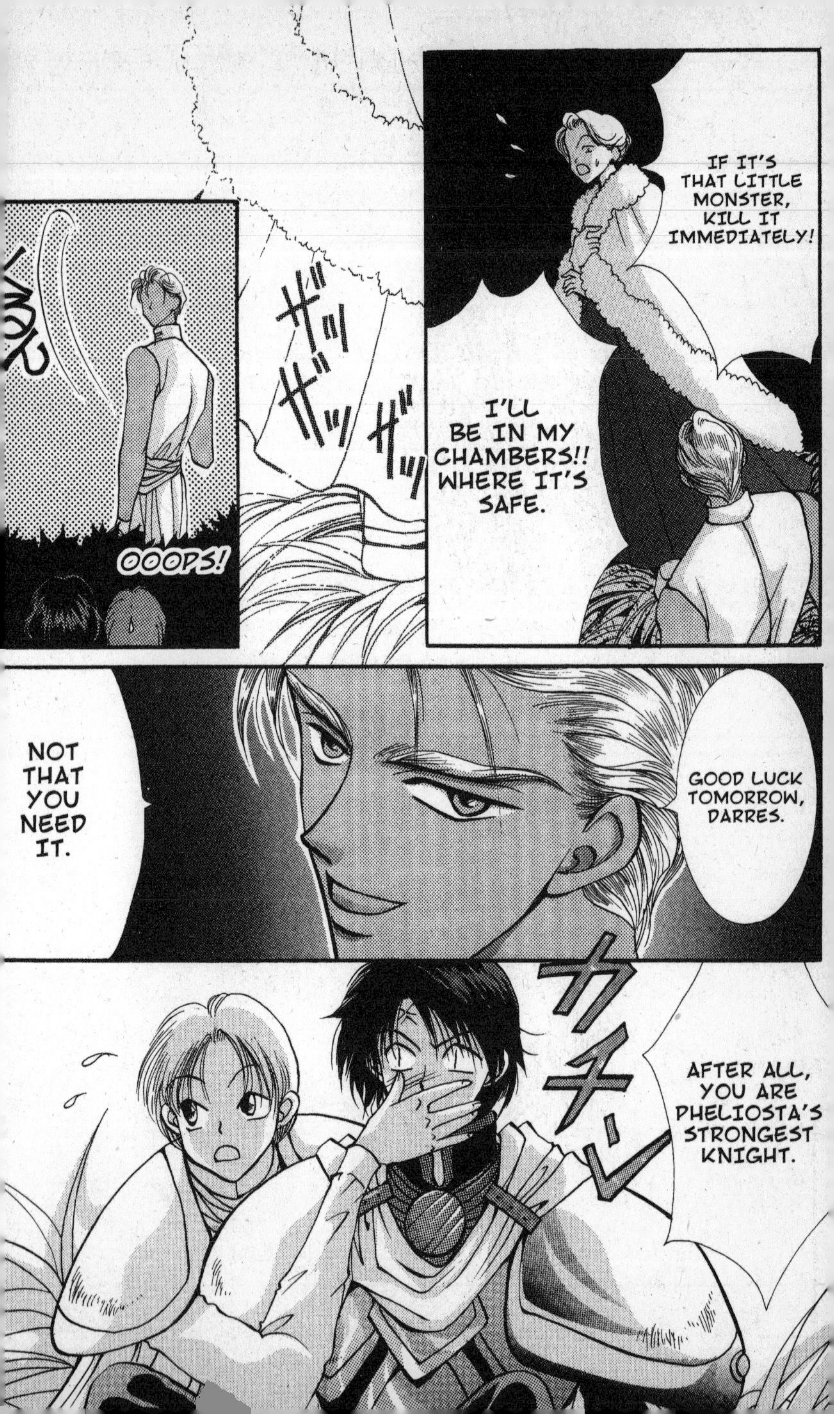
IF IT'S THAT LITTLE MONSTER, KILL IT IMMEDIATELY!
I'LL BE IN MY CHAMBERS!! WHERE IT'S SAFE.
ザッザッ ザッザッ
OOOPS!
GOOD LUCK TOMORROW, DARRES.
NOT THAT YOU NEED IT.
カチン
AFTER ALL, YOU ARE PHELIOSTA'S STRONGEST KNIGHT.

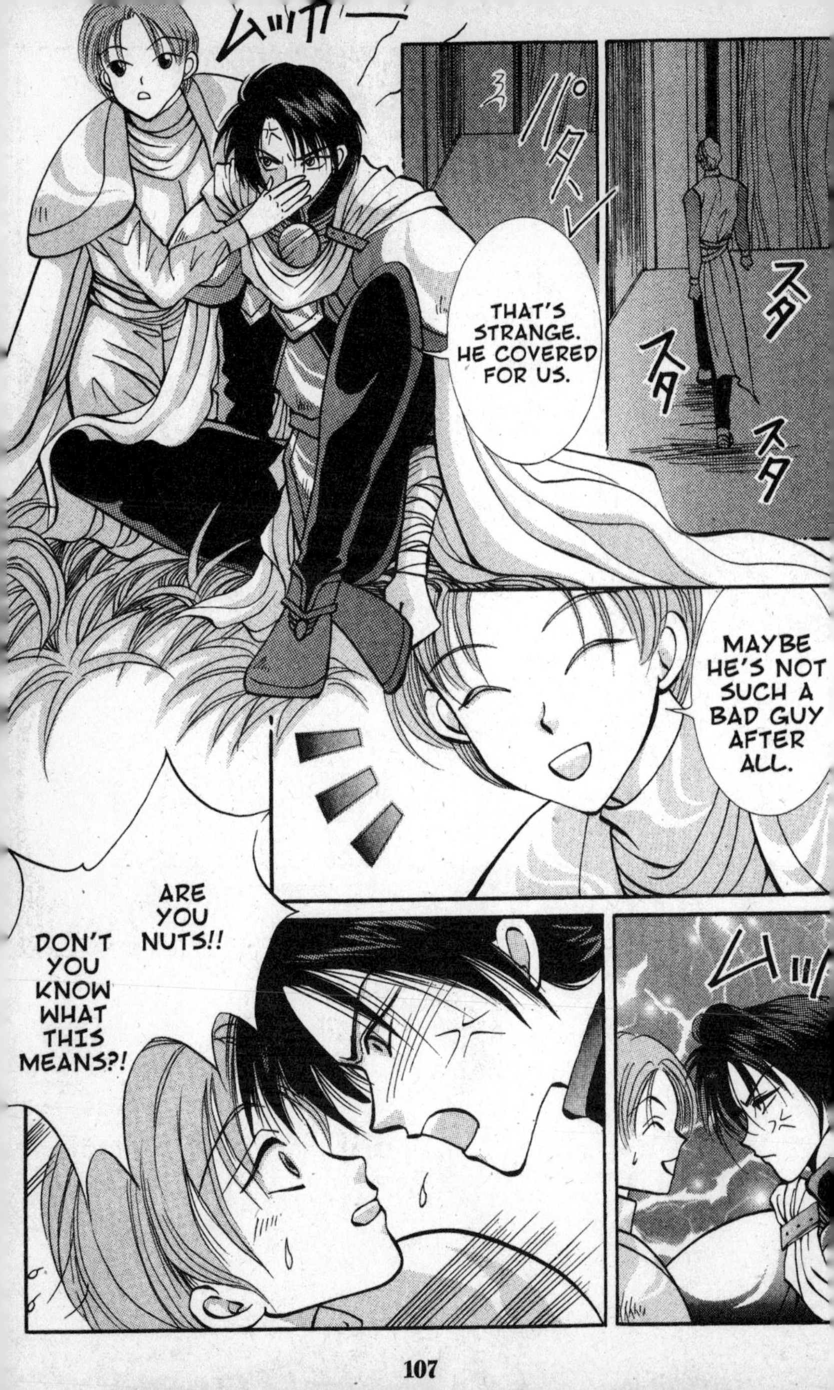
スタ スタ スタ
パタン
ムッカー
THAT'S STRANGE. HE COVERED FOR US.
MAYBE HE'S NOT SUCH A BAD GUY AFTER ALL.
ムッ
ARE YOU NUTS!!
DON'T YOU KNOW WHAT THIS MEANS?!

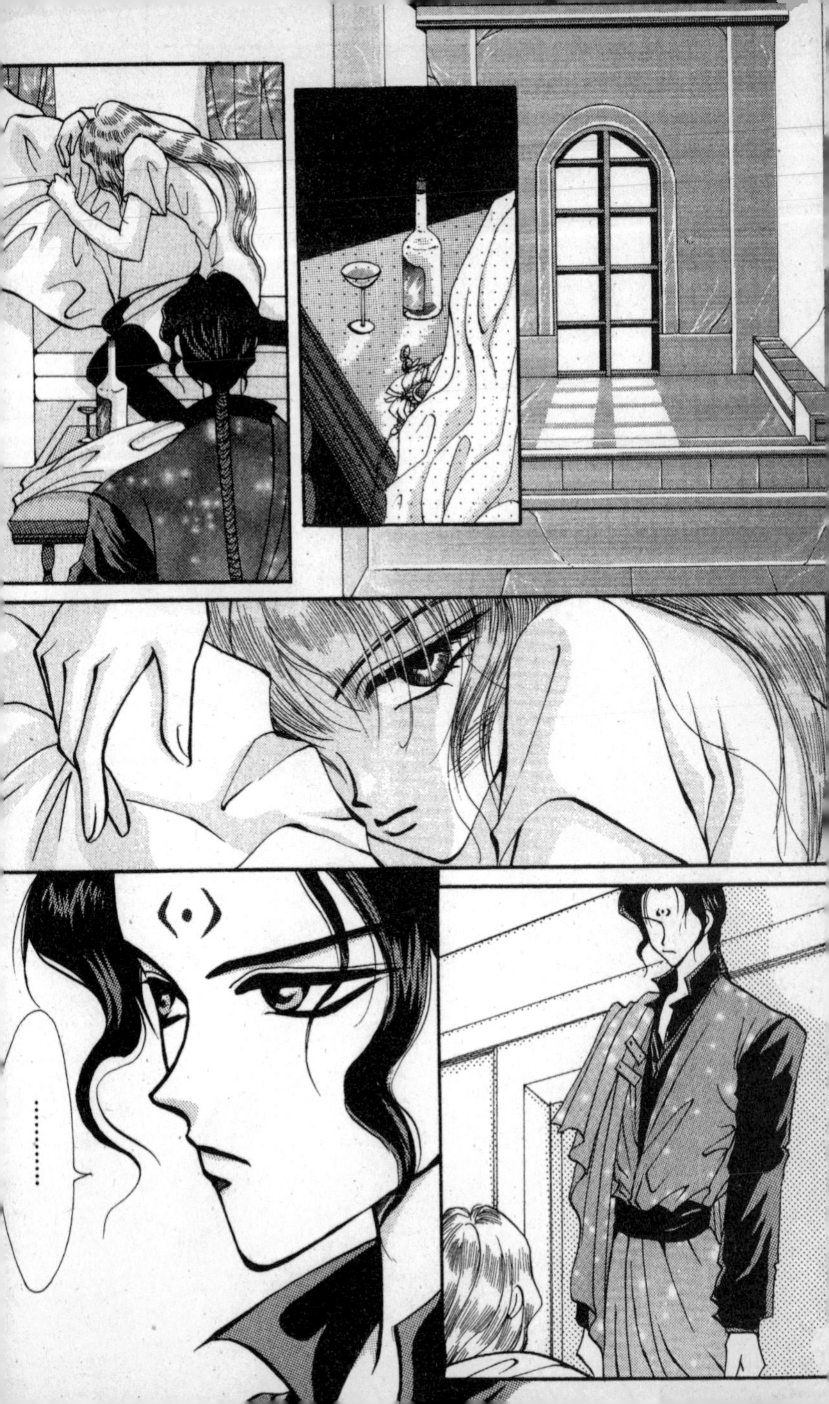

……

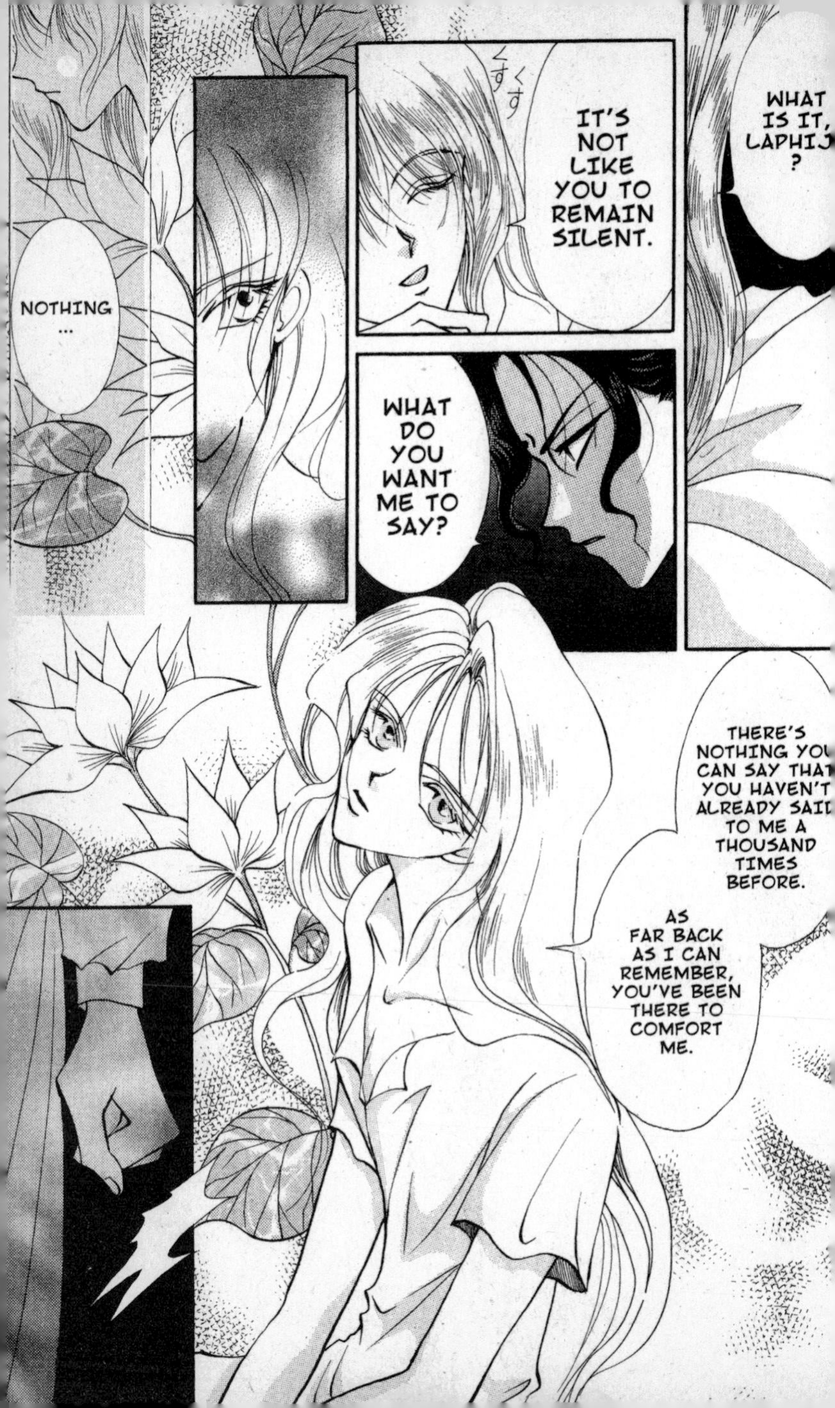
WHAT IS IT, LAPHI ?
くすくす
IT'S NOT LIKE YOU TO REMAIN SILENT.
WHAT DO YOU WANT ME TO SAY?
NOTHING ...
THERE'S NOTHING YOU CAN SAY THAT YOU HAVEN'T ALREADY SAID TO ME A THOUSAND TIMES BEFORE.
AS FAR BACK AS I CAN REMEMBER, YOU'VE BEEN THERE TO COMFORT ME.

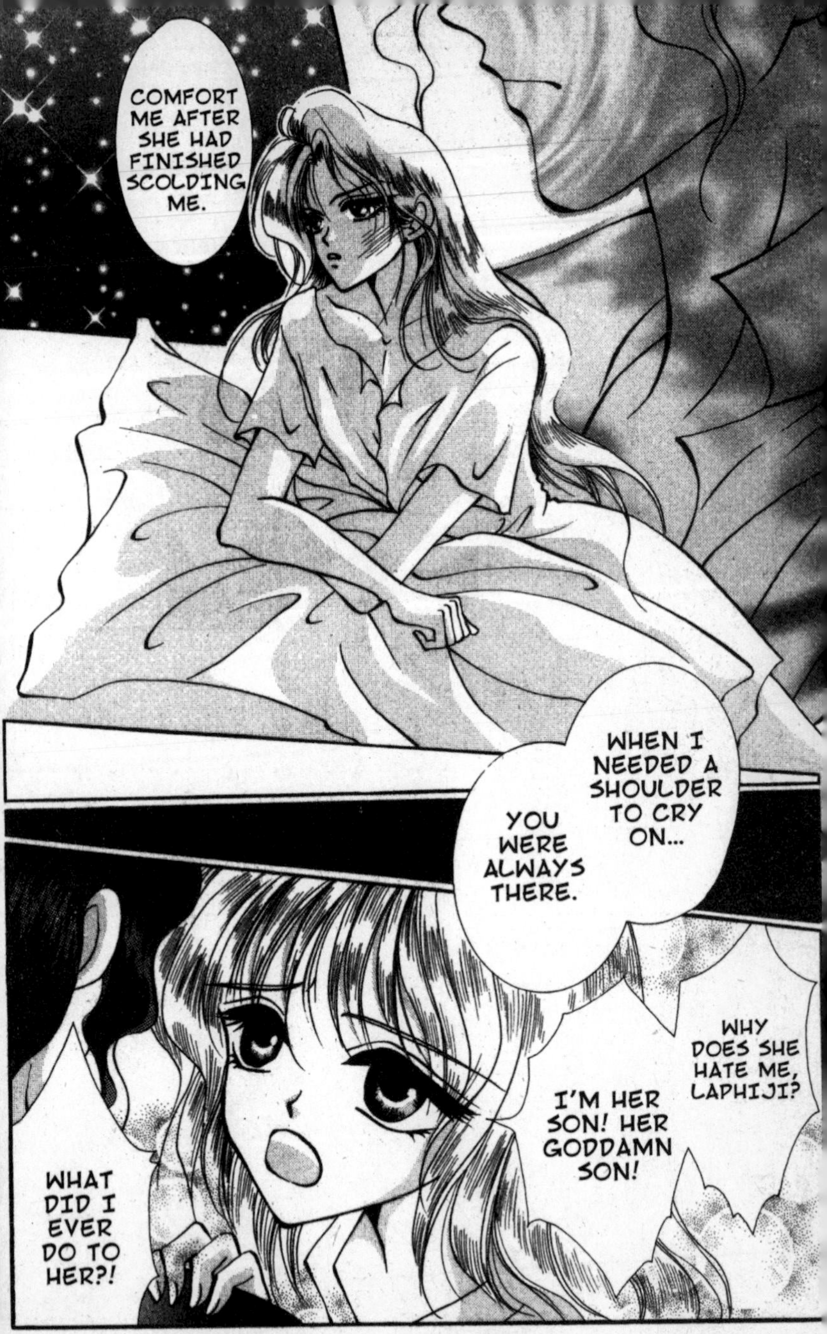
COMFORT ME AFTER SHE HAD FINISHED SCOLDING ME.
WHEN I NEEDED A SHOULDER TO CRY ON...
YOU WERE ALWAYS THERE.
WHY DOES SHE HATE ME, LAPHIJI?
I'M HER SON! HER GODDAMN SON!
WHAT DID I EVER DO TO HER?!

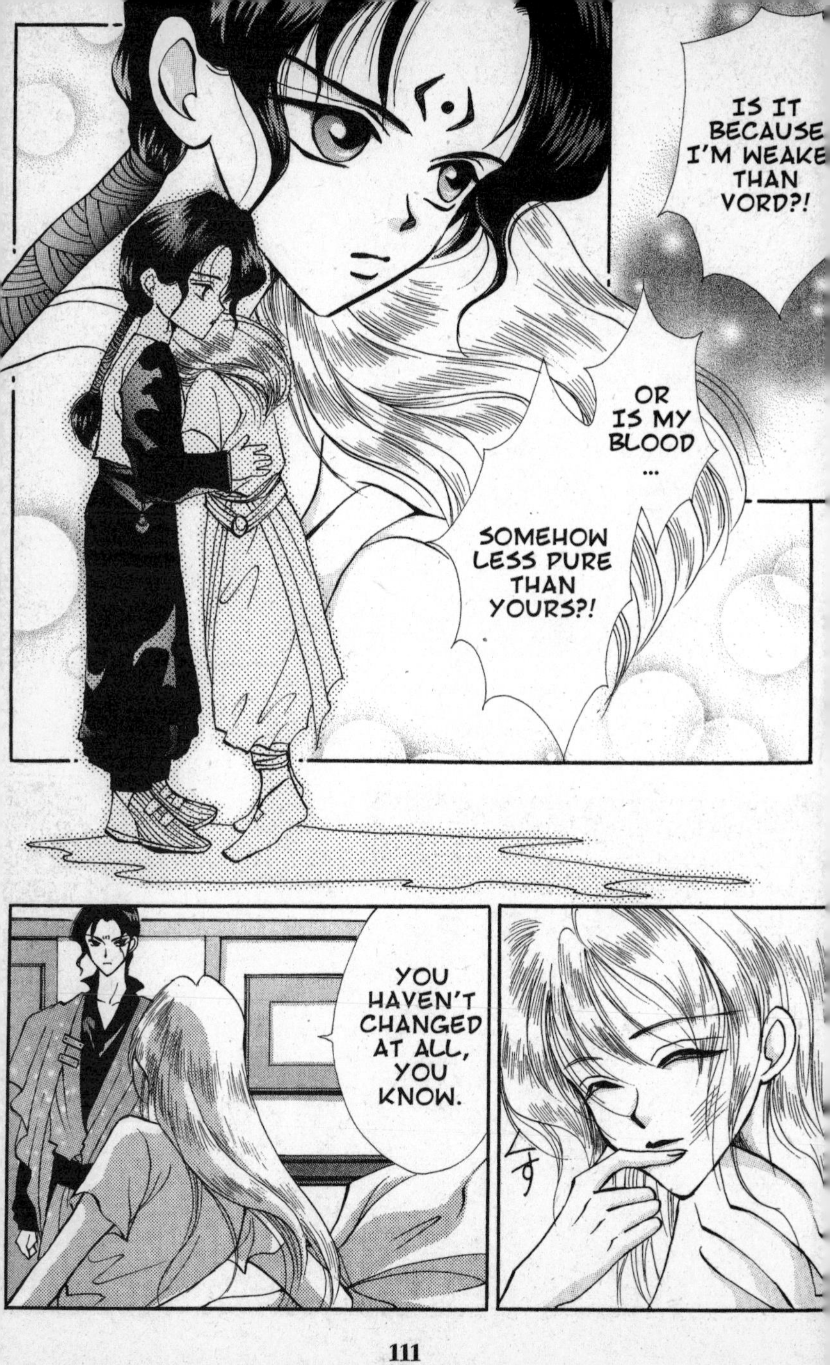
IS IT BECAUSE I'M WEAKE THAN VORD?!
OR IS MY BLOOD ...
SOMEHOW LESS PURE THAN YOURS?!
す
YOU HAVEN'T CHANGED AT ALL, YOU KNOW.

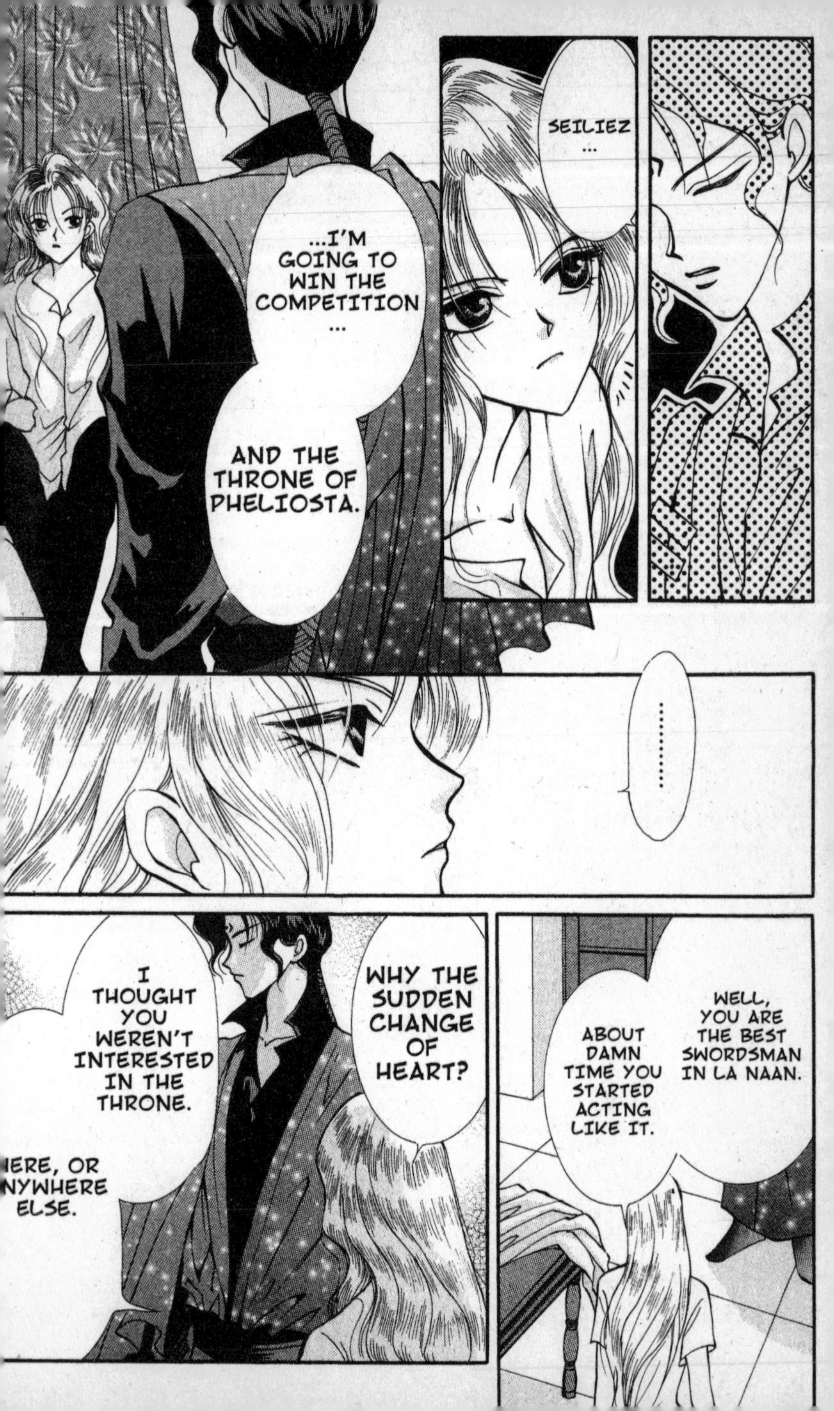
SEILIEZ ...
...I'M GOING TO WIN THE COMPETITION ...
AND THE THRONE OF PHELIOSTA.
......
WELL, YOU ARE THE BEST SWORDSMAN IN LA NAAN.
ABOUT DAMN TIME YOU STARTED ACTING LIKE IT.
WHY THE SUDDEN CHANGE OF HEART?
I THOUGHT YOU WEREN'T INTERESTED IN THE THRONE.
ERE, OR NYWHERE ELSE.

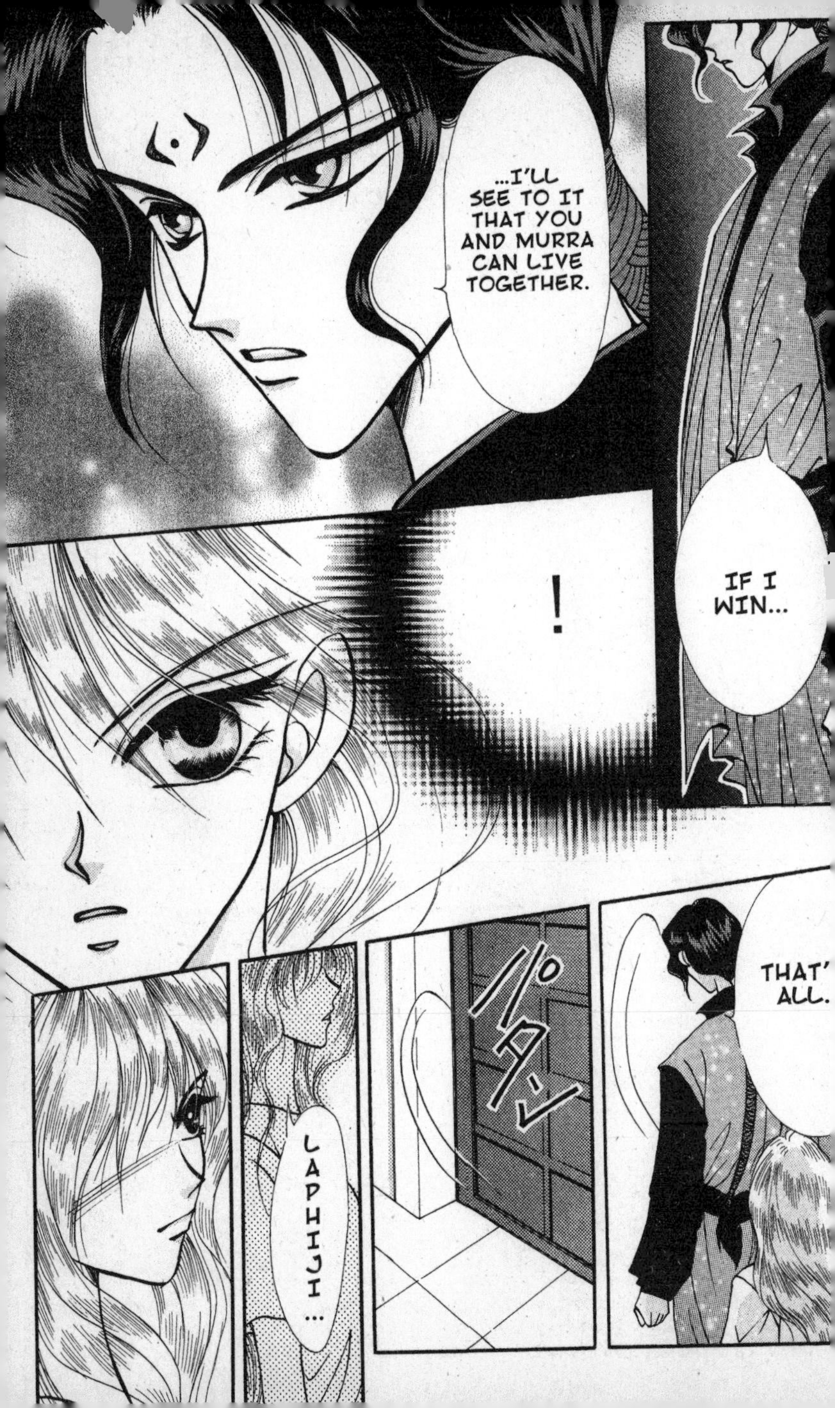
IF I WIN...
...I'LL SEE TO IT THAT YOU AND MURRA CAN LIVE TOGETHER.
!
THAT' ALL.
パタン
LAPHIJI...

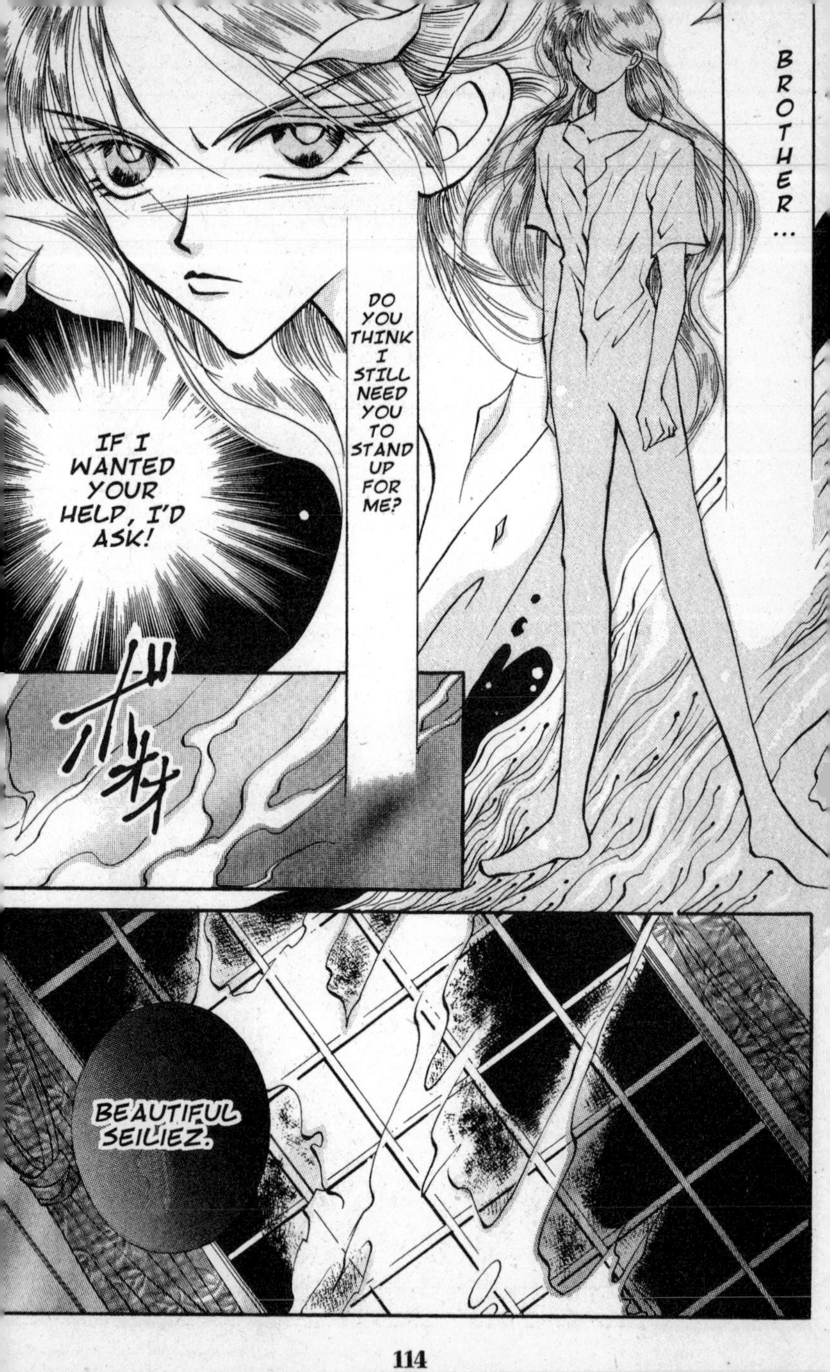
BROTHER...
DO YOU THINK I STILL NEED YOU TO STAND UP FOR ME?
IF I WANTED YOUR HELP, I'D ASK!
BEAUTIFUL SEILIEZ.

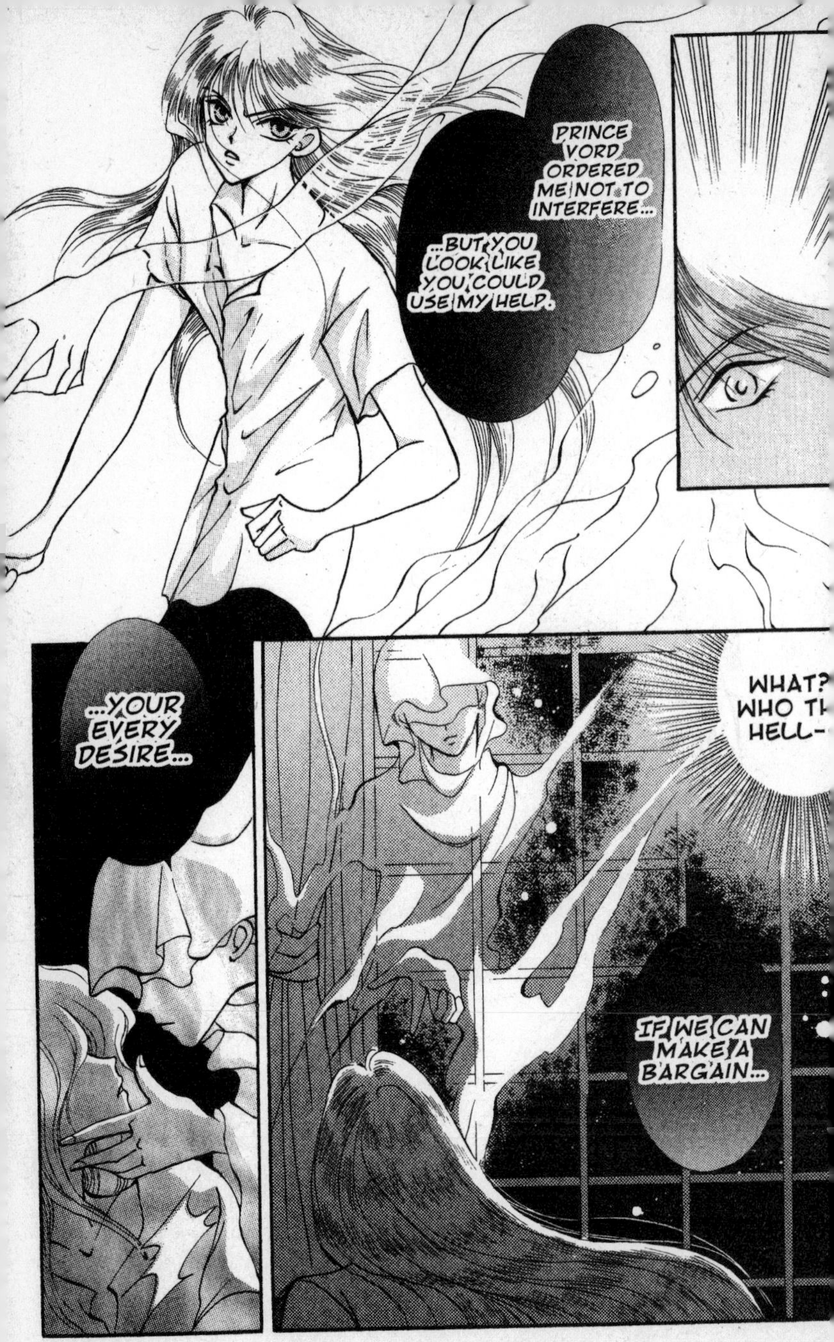
PRINCE VORD ORDERED ME NOT TO INTERFERE...
...BUT YOU LOOK LIKE YOU COULD USE MY HELP.
WHAT? WHO TH HELL-
IF WE CAN MAKE A BARGAIN...
...YOUR EVERY DESIRE...

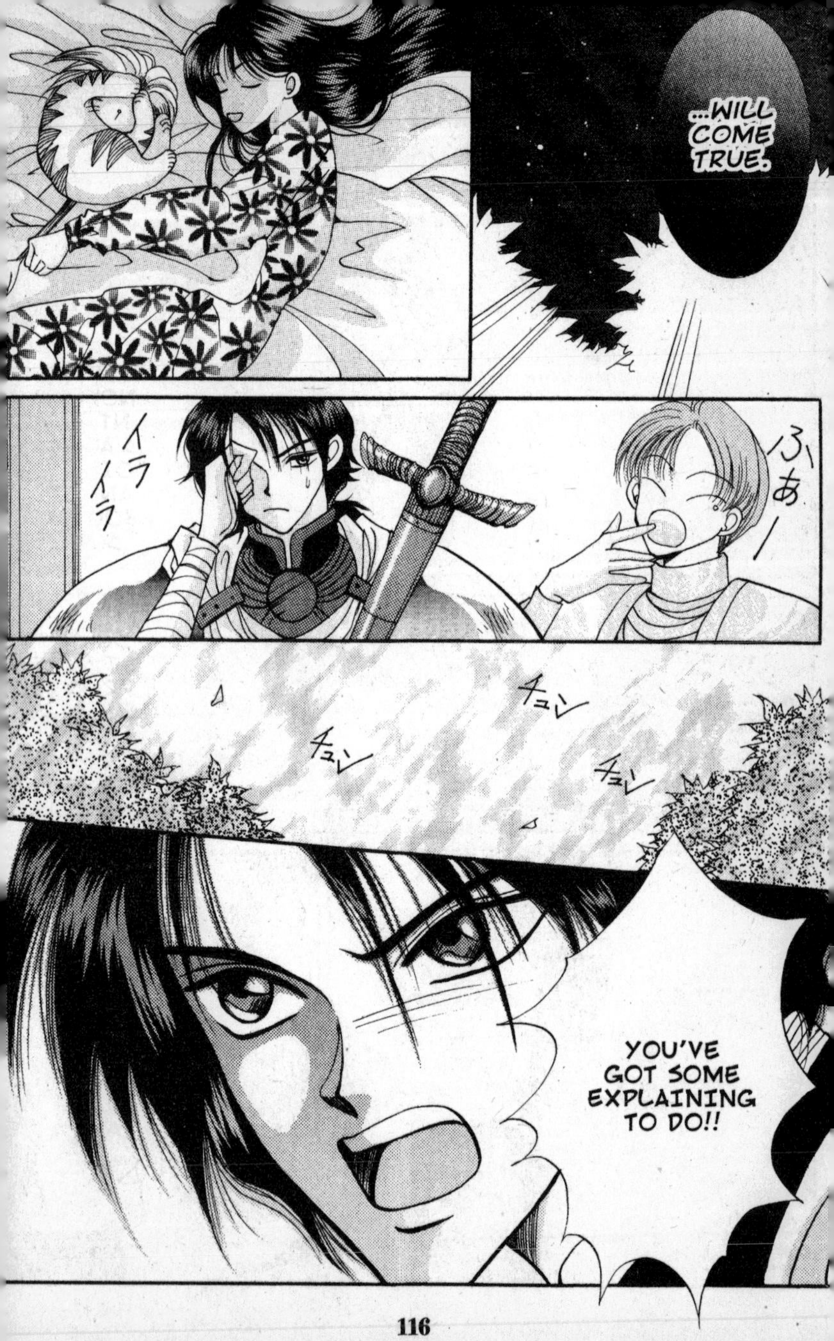
...WILL COME TRUE.
ふあー
イライラ
チュン
チュン
チュン
YOU'VE GOT SOME EXPLAINING TO DO!!

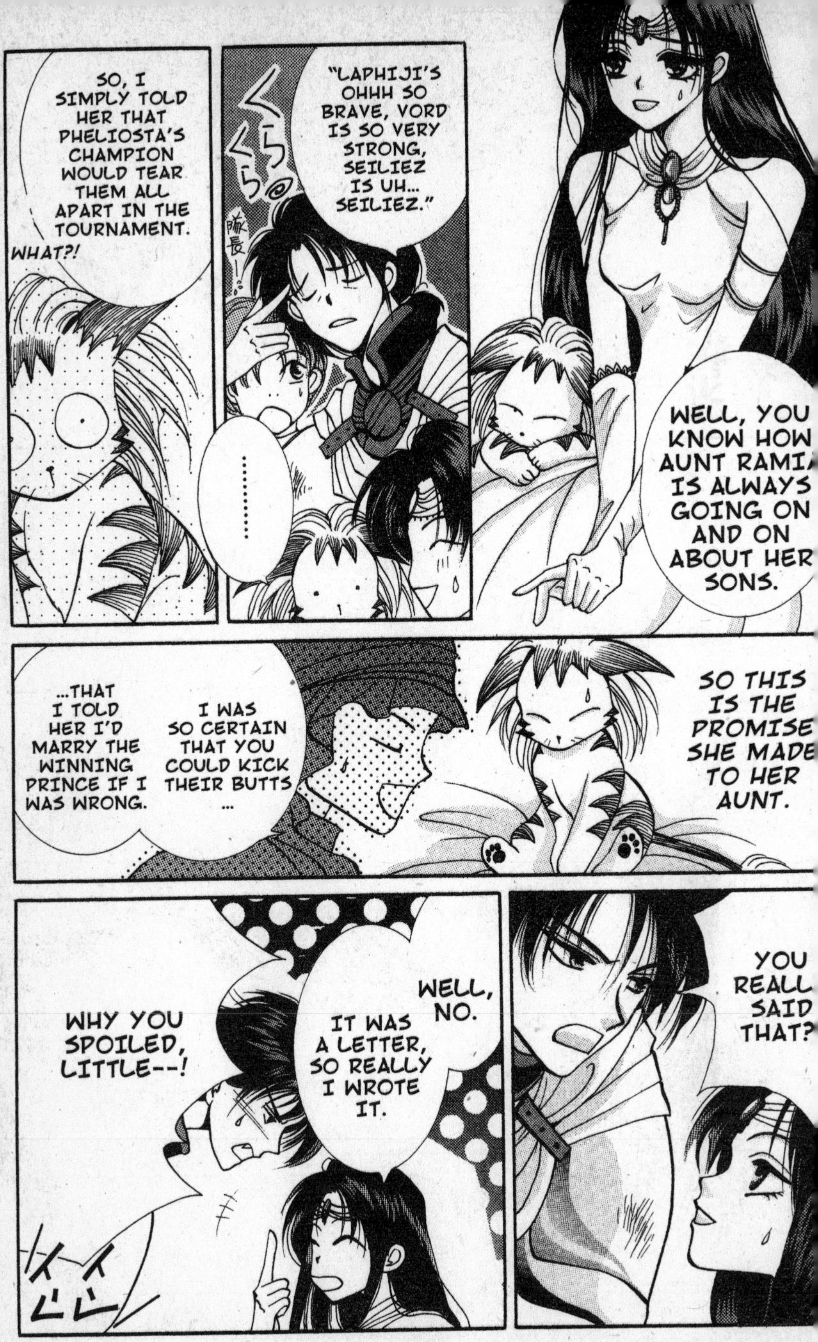
WELL, YOU KNOW HOW AUNT RAMIA IS ALWAYS GOING ON AND ON ABOUT HER SONS.
"LAPHIJI'S OHHH SO BRAVE, VORD IS SO VERY STRONG, SEILIEZ IS UH... SEILIEZ."
くらくら
隊長…!
......
SO, I SIMPLY TOLD HER THAT PHELIOSTA'S CHAMPION WOULD TEAR THEM ALL APART IN THE TOURNAMENT.
WHAT?!
SO THIS IS THE PROMISE SHE MADE TO HER AUNT.
I WAS SO CERTAIN THAT YOU COULD KICK THEIR BUTTS...
...THAT I TOLD HER I'D MARRY THE WINNING PRINCE IF I WAS WRONG.
YOU REALL SAID THAT?
WELL, NO.
IT WAS A LETTER, SO REALLY I WROTE IT.
WHY YOU SPOILED, LITTLE--!

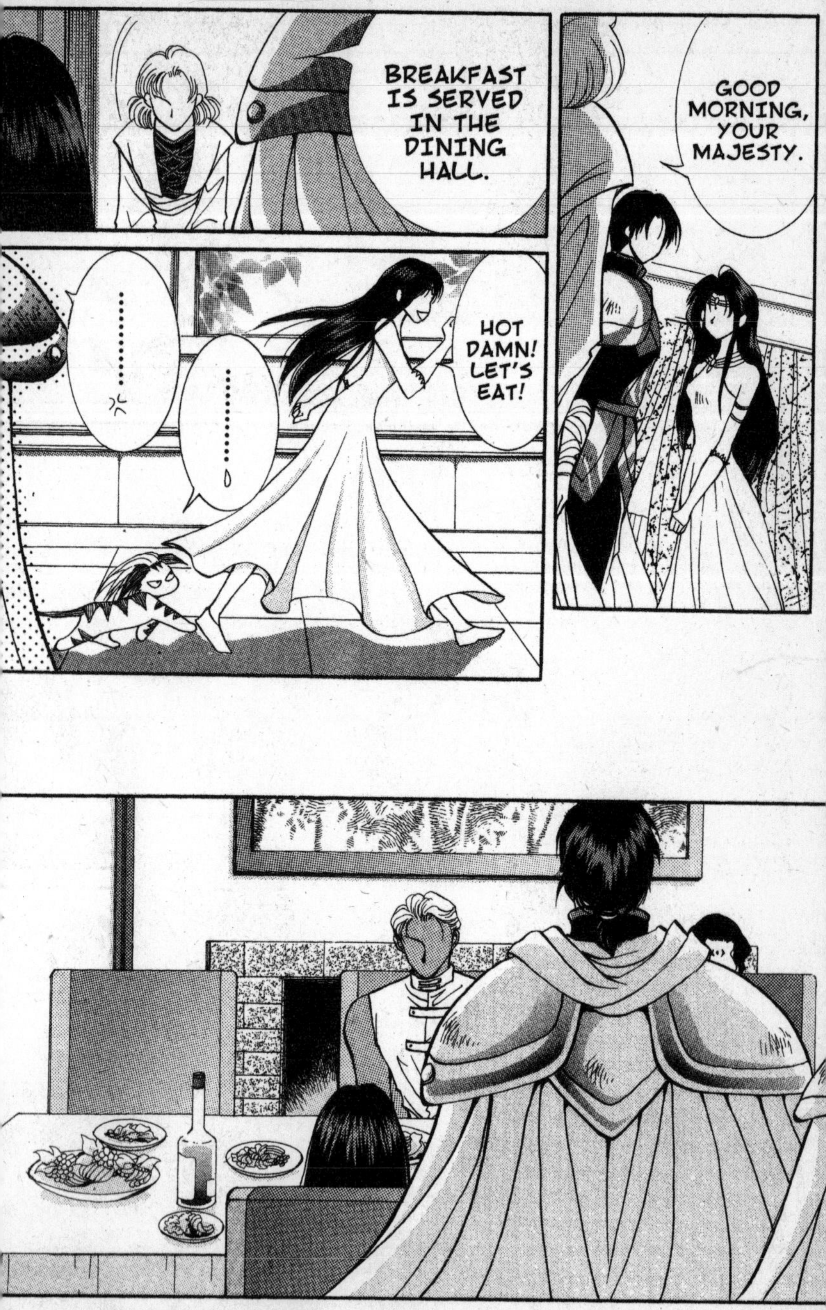
GOOD MORNING, YOUR MAJESTY.
BREAKFAST IS SERVED IN THE DINING HALL.
HOT DAMN! LET'S EAT!
....
....

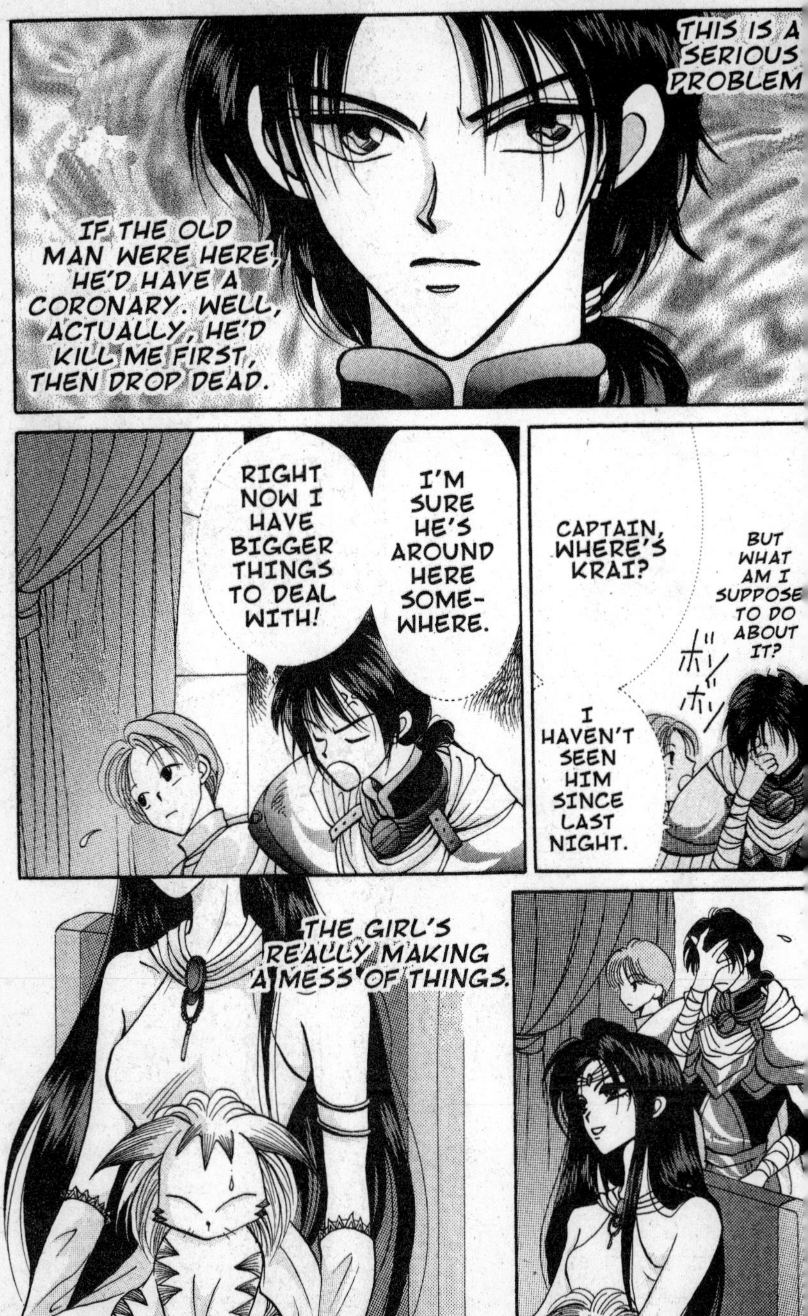
THIS IS A SERIOUS PROBLEM
IF THE OLD MAN WERE HERE, HE'D HAVE A CORONARY. WELL, ACTUALLY, HE'D KILL ME FIRST, THEN DROP DEAD.
CAPTAIN, WHERE'S KRAI?
I HAVEN'T SEEN HIM SINCE LAST NIGHT.
ボソ ボソ
BUT WHAT AM I SUPPOSE TO DO ABOUT IT?
I'M SURE HE'S AROUND HERE SOME-WHERE.
RIGHT NOW I HAVE BIGGER THINGS TO DEAL WITH!
THE GIRL'S REALLY MAKING A MESS OF THINGS.

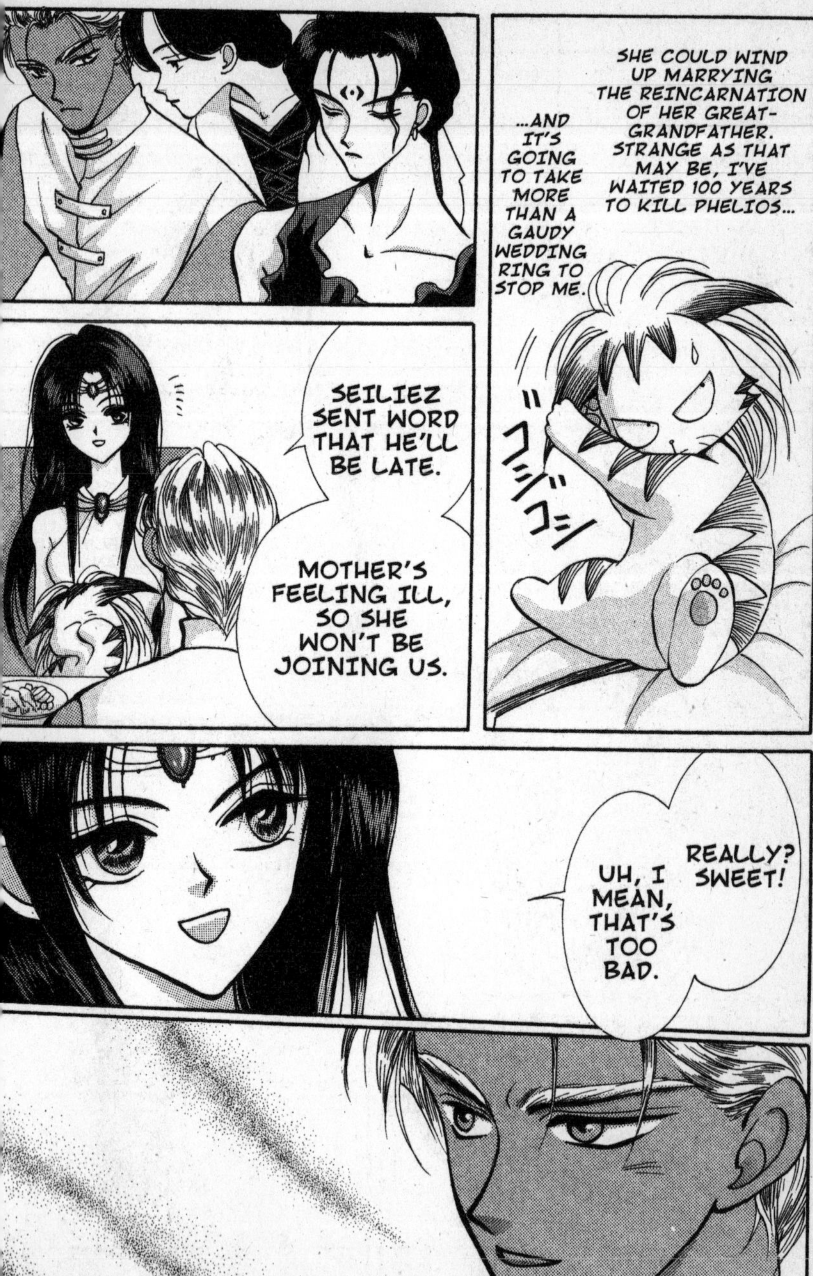
SHE COULD WIND UP MARRYING THE REINCARNATION OF HER GREAT-GRANDFATHER. STRANGE AS THAT MAY BE, I'VE WAITED 100 YEARS TO KILL PHELIOS...
...AND IT'S GOING TO TAKE MORE THAN A GAUDY WEDDING RING TO STOP ME.
ゴシゴシ
SEILIEZ SENT WORD THAT HE'LL BE LATE.
MOTHER'S FEELING ILL, SO SHE WON'T BE JOINING US.
REALLY? SWEET!
UH, I MEAN, THAT'S TOO BAD.

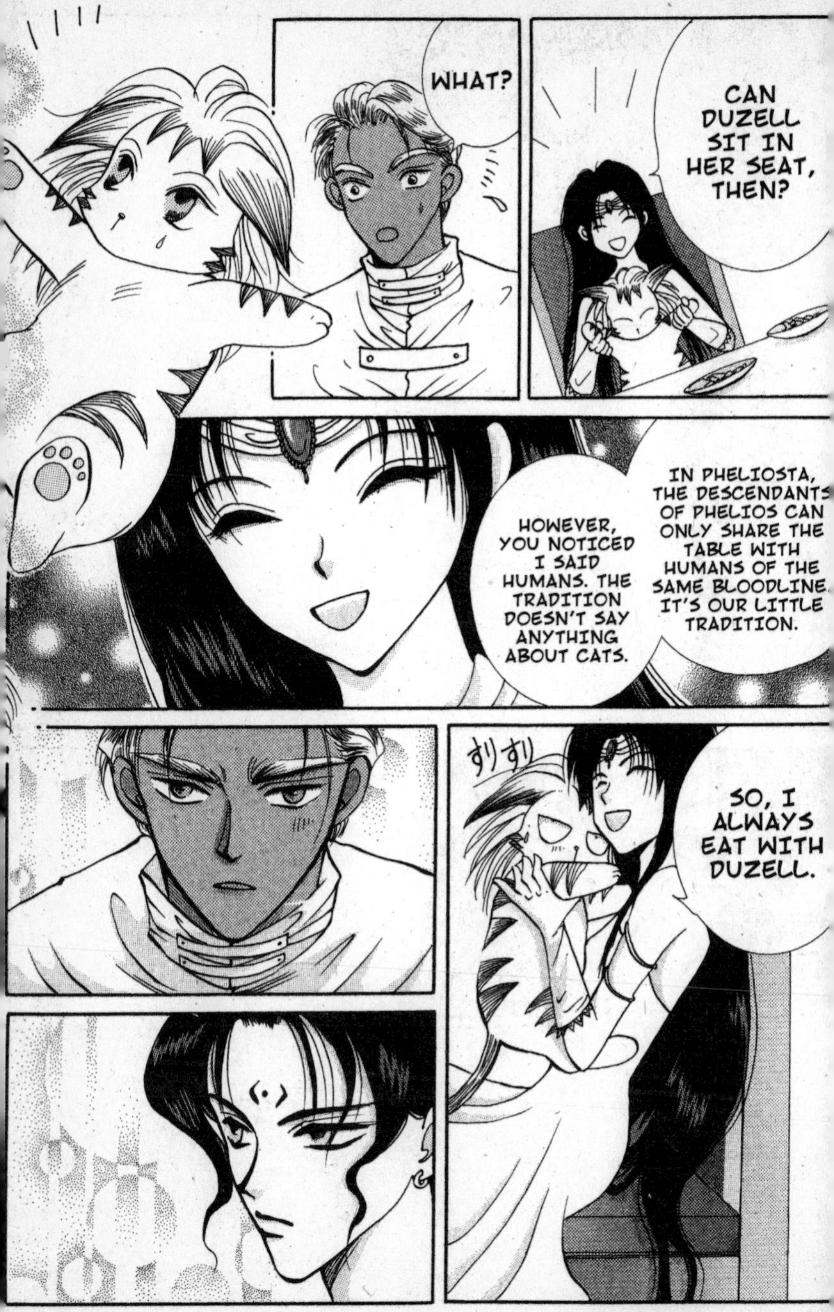
CAN DUZELL SIT IN HER SEAT, THEN?
WHAT?
IN PHELIOSTA, THE DESCENDANTS OF PHELIOS CAN ONLY SHARE THE TABLE WITH HUMANS OF THE SAME BLOODLINE. IT'S OUR LITTLE TRADITION.
HOWEVER, YOU NOTICED I SAID HUMANS. THE TRADITION DOESN'T SAY ANYTHING ABOUT CATS.
SO, I ALWAYS EAT WITH DUZELL.
すりすり

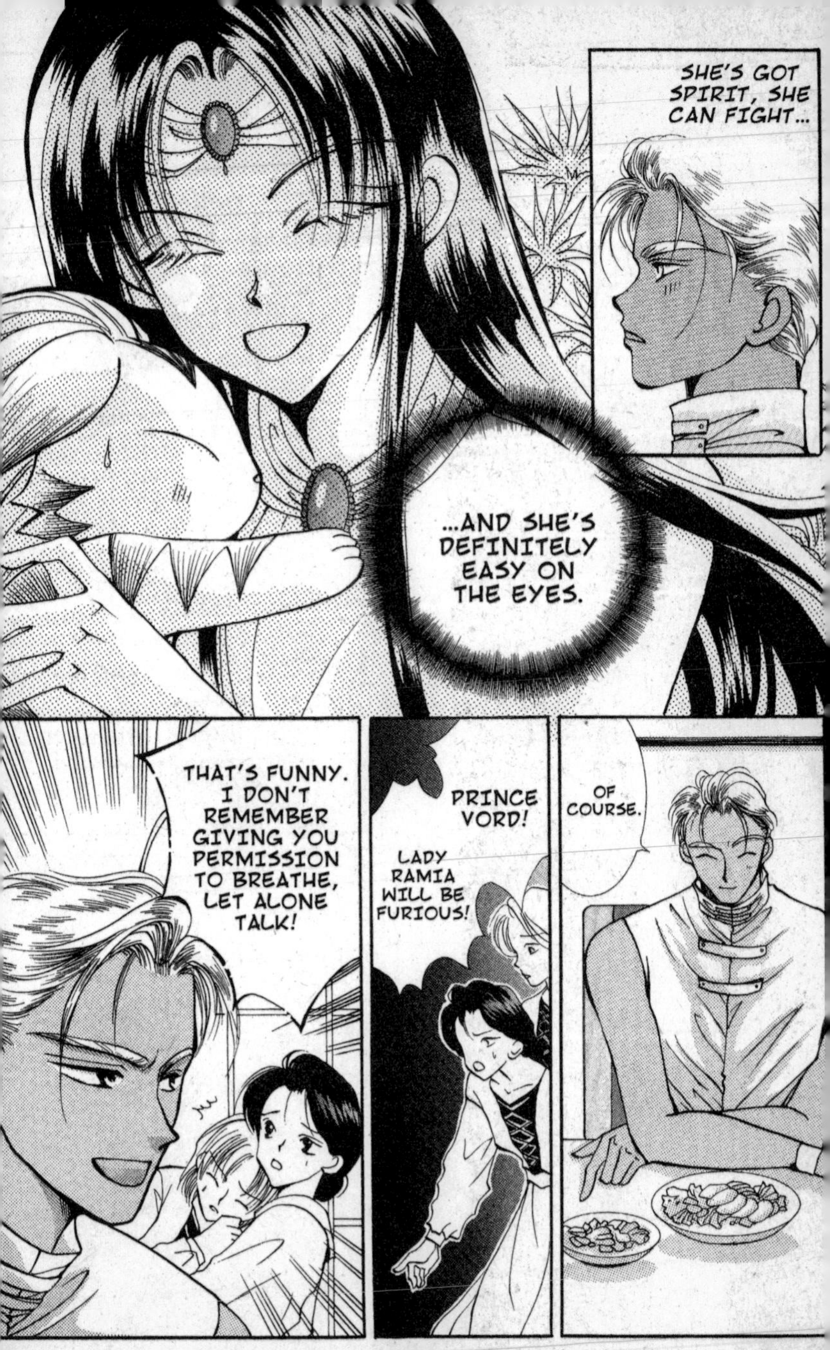
SHE'S GOT SPIRIT, SHE CAN FIGHT...
...AND SHE'S DEFINITELY EASY ON THE EYES.
OF COURSE.
PRINCE VORD!
LADY RAMIA WILL BE FURIOUS!
THAT'S FUNNY. I DON'T REMEMBER GIVING YOU PERMISSION TO BREATHE, LET ALONE TALK!

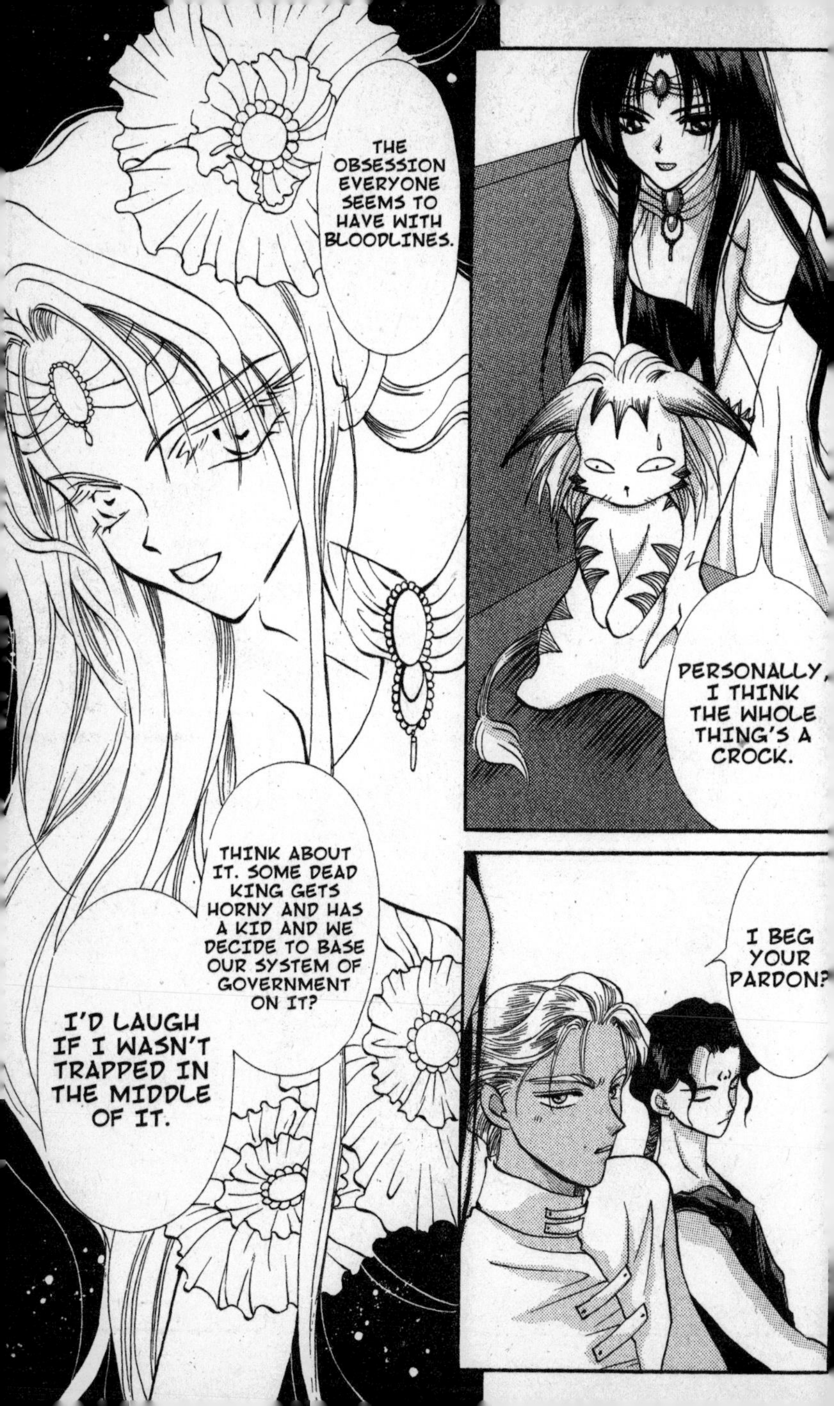
PERSONALLY, I THINK THE WHOLE THING'S A CROCK.
I BEG YOUR PARDON?
THE OBSESSION EVERYONE SEEMS TO HAVE WITH BLOODLINES.
THINK ABOUT IT. SOME DEAD KING GETS HORNY AND HAS A KID AND WE DECIDE TO BASE OUR SYSTEM OF GOVERNMENT ON IT?
I'D LAUGH IF I WASN'T TRAPPED IN THE MIDDLE OF IT.

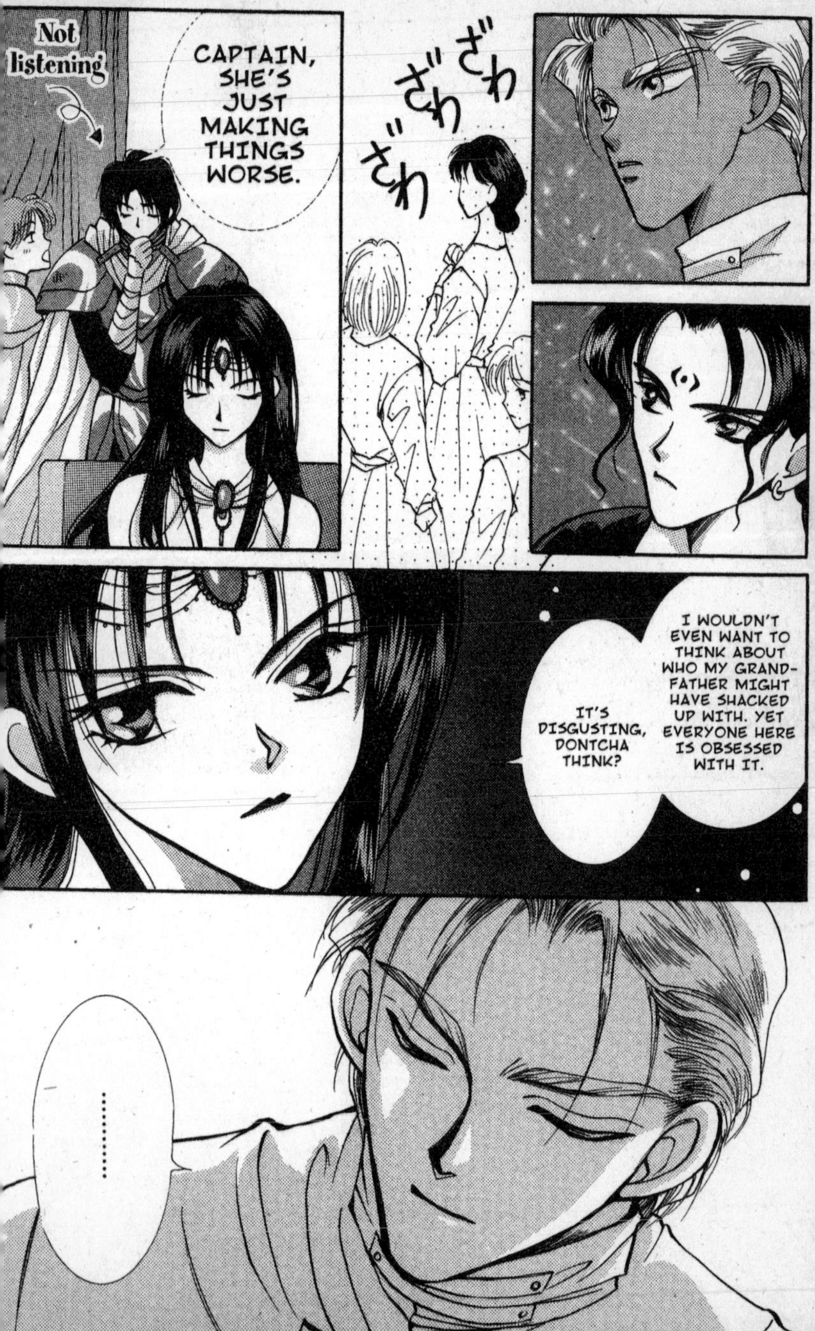

ざわ ざわ ざわ
Not listening
CAPTAIN, SHE'S JUST MAKING THINGS WORSE.
I WOULDN'T EVEN WANT TO THINK ABOUT WHO MY GRAND-FATHER MIGHT HAVE SHACKED UP WITH. YET EVERYONE HERE IS OBSESSED WITH IT.
IT'S DISGUSTING, DONTCHA THINK?
......

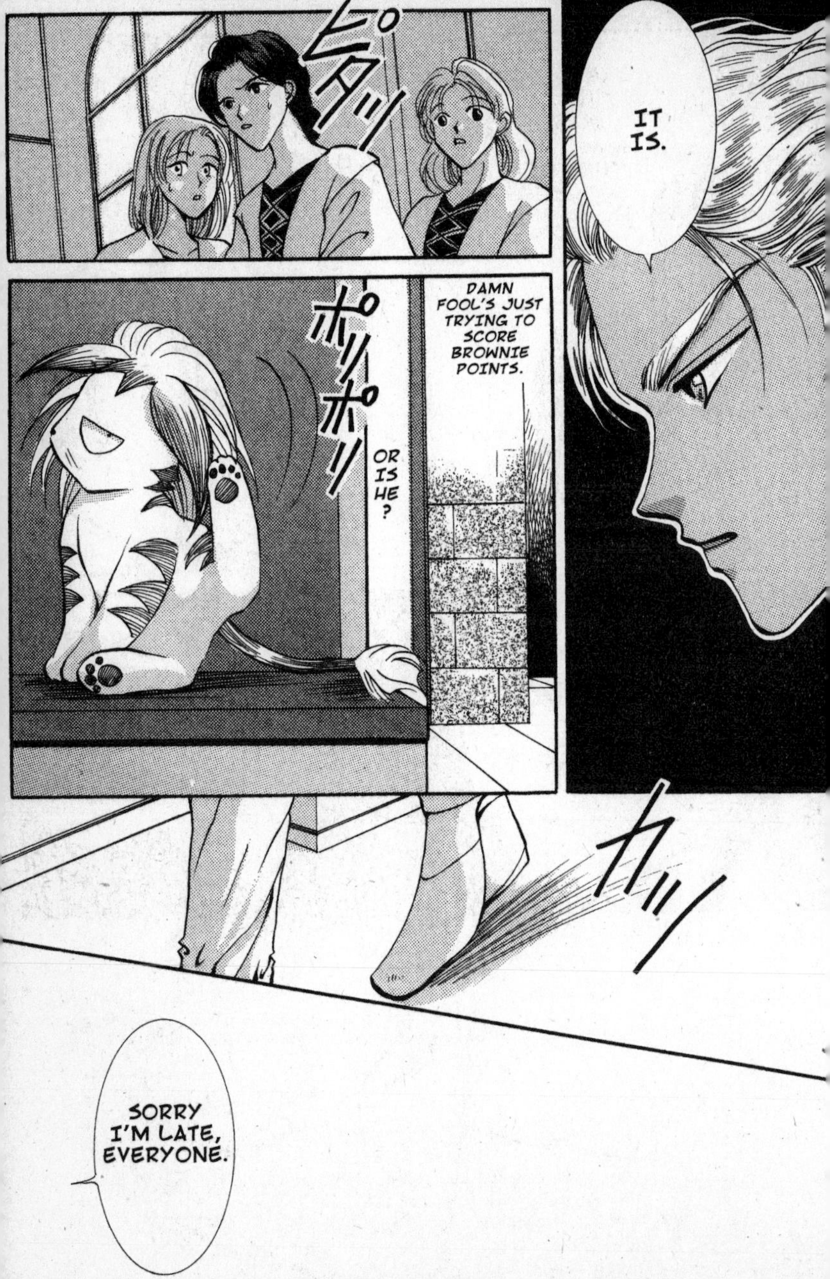
IT IS.
ピタッ
DAMN FOOL'S JUST TRYING TO SCORE BROWNIE POINTS.
ポリポリ
OR IS HE?
カッ
SORRY I'M LATE, EVERYONE.

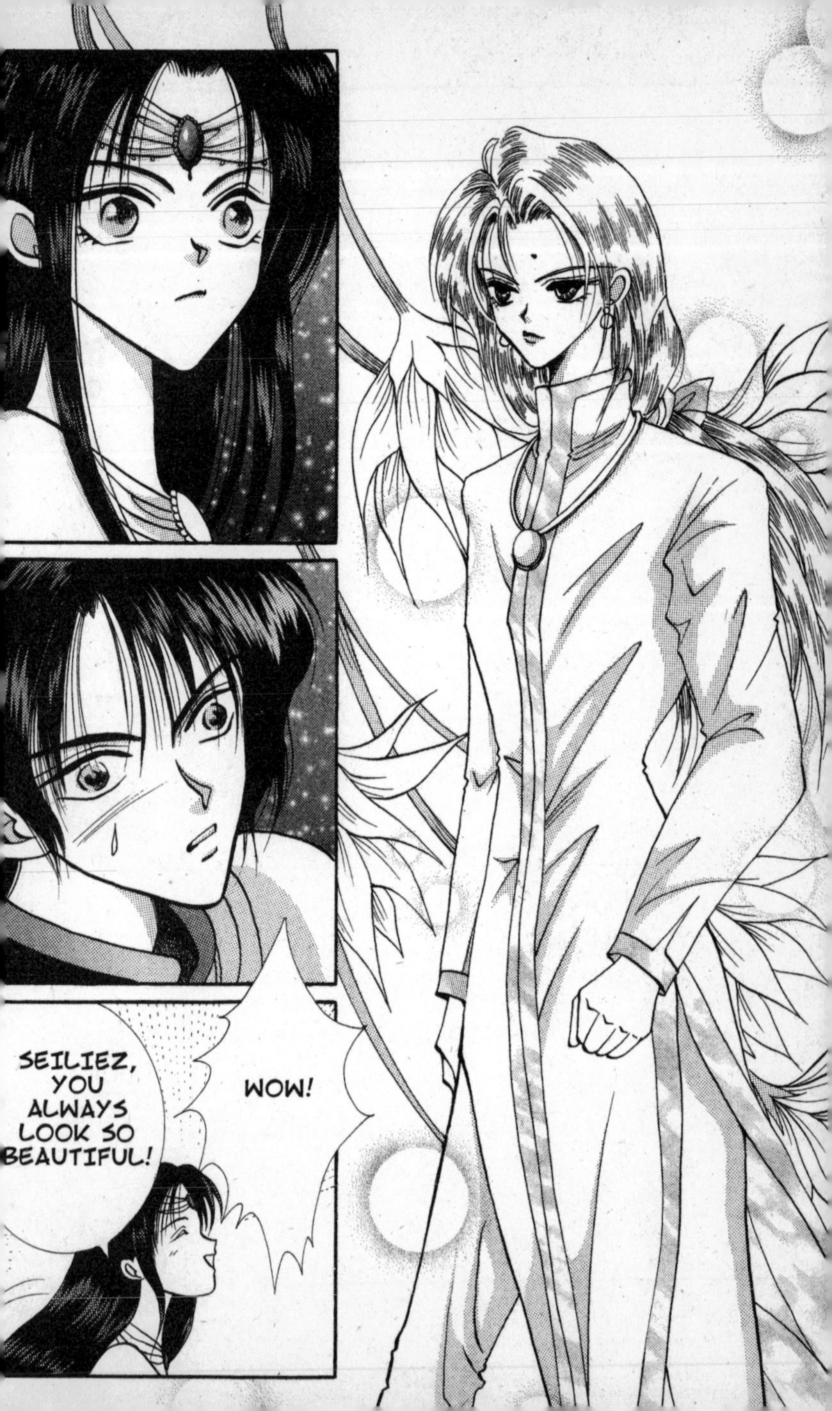
WOW!
SEILIEZ, YOU ALWAYS LOOK SO BEAUTIFUL!

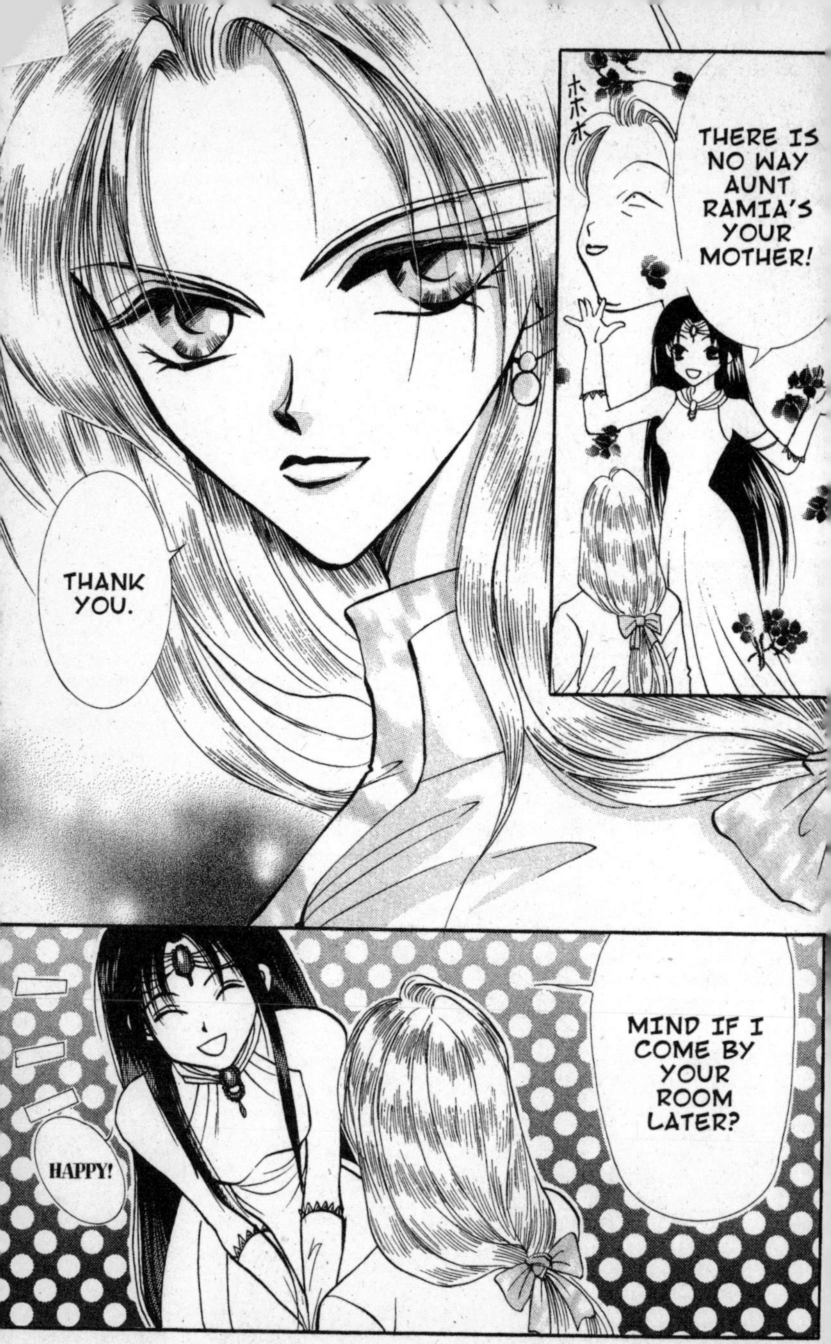
ホホホ
THERE IS NO WAY AUNT RAMIA'S YOUR MOTHER!
THANK YOU.
MIND IF I COME BY YOUR ROOM LATER?
HAPPY!

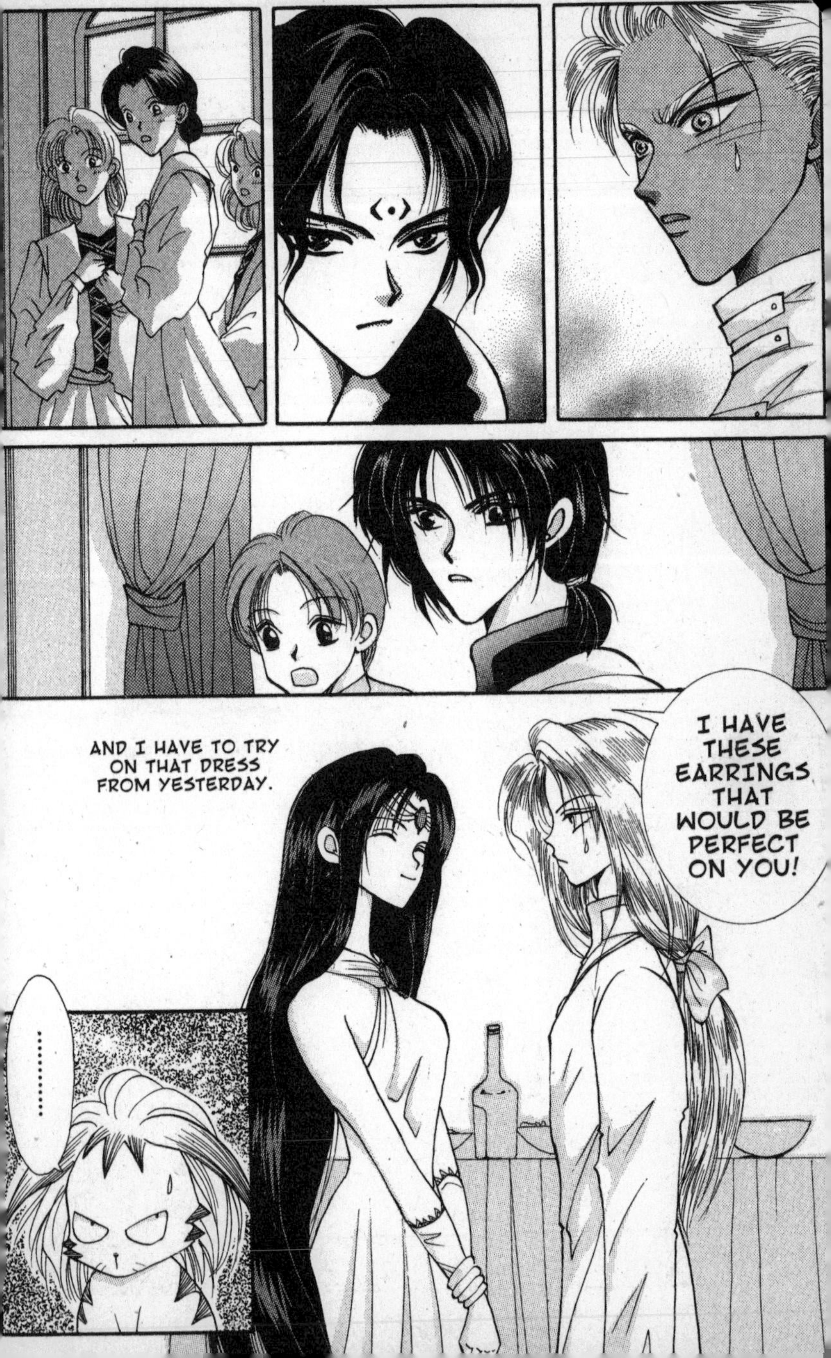
I HAVE THESE EARRINGS THAT WOULD BE PERFECT ON YOU!
AND I HAVE TO TRY ON THAT DRESS FROM YESTERDAY.
......

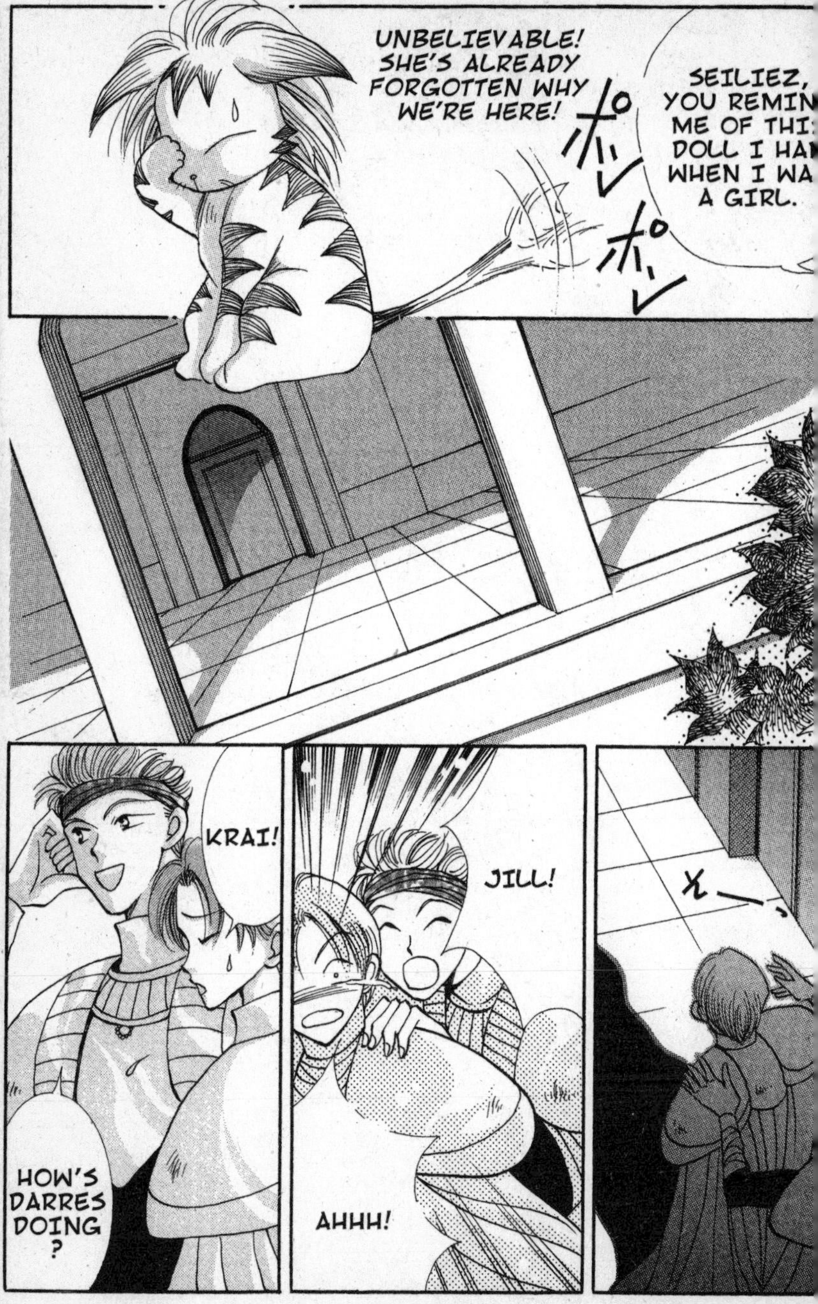
SEILIEZ, YOU REMIN ME OF THI DOLL I HA WHEN I WA A GIRL.
ポン ポン
UNBELIEVABLE! SHE'S ALREADY FORGOTTEN WHY WE'RE HERE!
JILL!
AHHH!
KRAI!
HOW'S DARRES DOING?

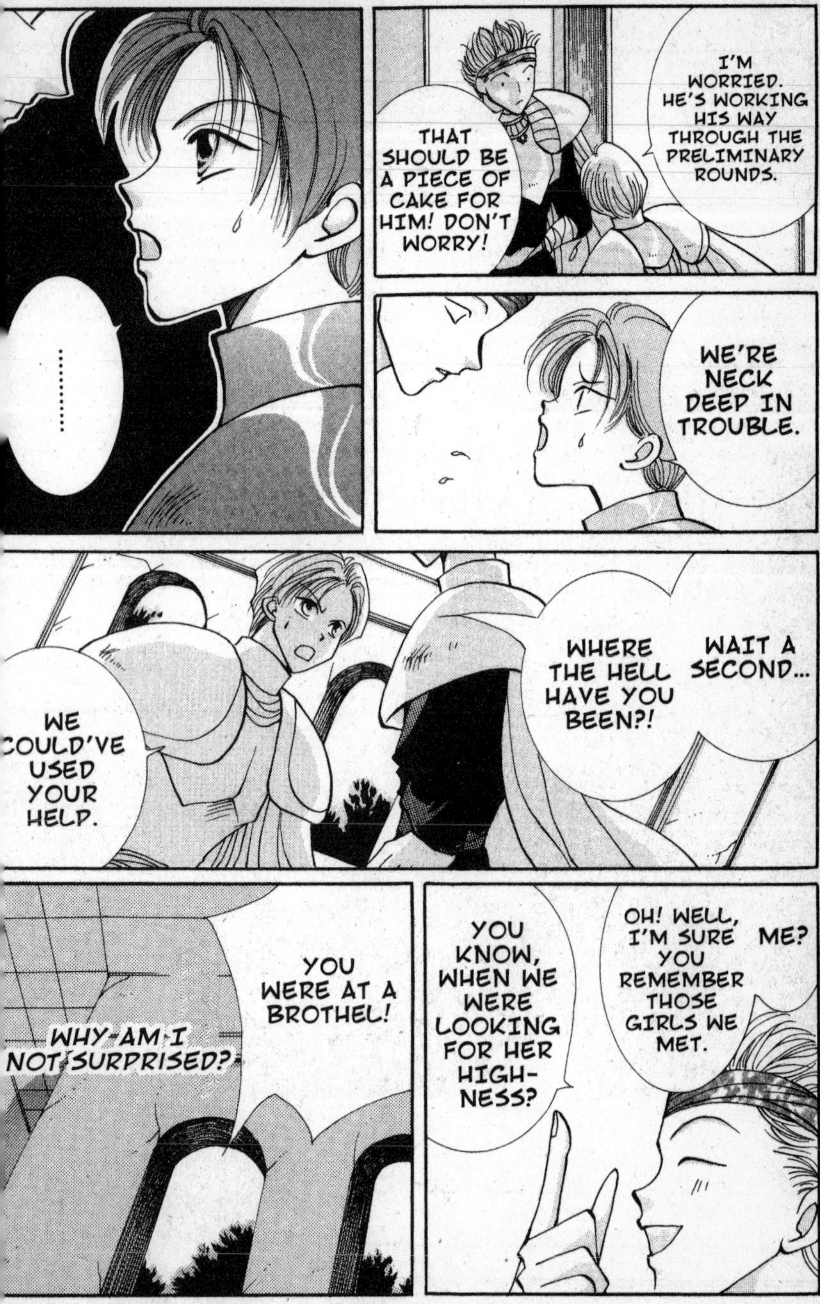

I'M WORRIED. HE'S WORKING HIS WAY THROUGH THE PRELIMINARY ROUNDS.
THAT SHOULD BE A PIECE OF CAKE FOR HIM! DON'T WORRY!
WE'RE NECK DEEP IN TROUBLE.
……
WAIT A SECOND...
WHERE THE HELL HAVE YOU BEEN?!
WE COULD'VE USED YOUR HELP.
ME?
OH! WELL, I'M SURE YOU REMEMBER THOSE GIRLS WE MET.
YOU KNOW, WHEN WE WERE LOOKING FOR HER HIGHNESS?
YOU WERE AT A BROTHEL!
WHY AM I NOT SURPRISED?

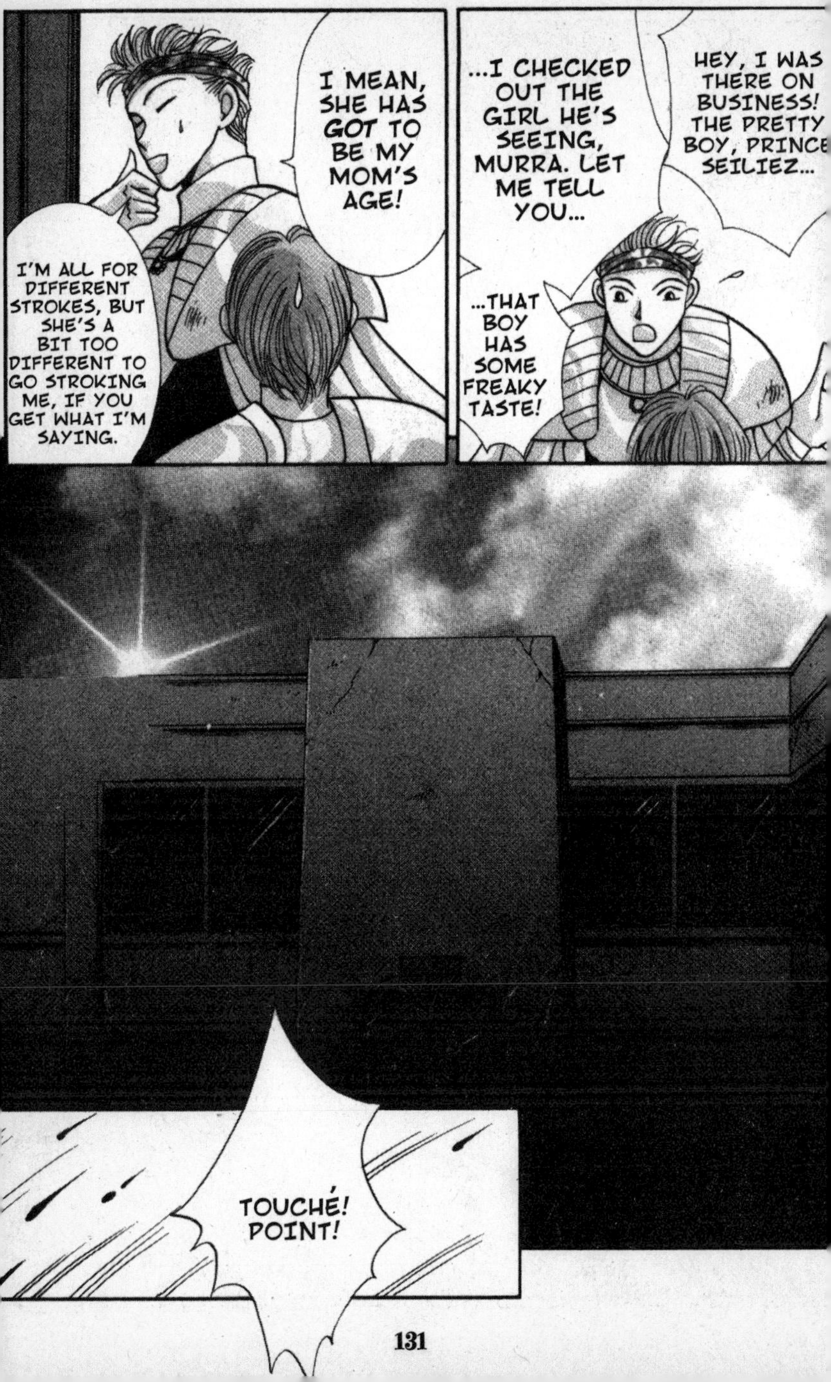
HEY, I WAS THERE ON BUSINESS! THE PRETTY BOY, PRINCE SEILIEZ...
...I CHECKED OUT THE GIRL HE'S SEEING, MURRA. LET ME TELL YOU...
...THAT BOY HAS SOME FREAKY TASTE!
I MEAN, SHE HAS *GOT* TO BE MY MOM'S AGE!
I'M ALL FOR DIFFERENT STROKES, BUT SHE'S A BIT TOO DIFFERENT TO GO STROKING ME, IF YOU GET WHAT I'M SAYING.
TOUCHÉ! POINT!

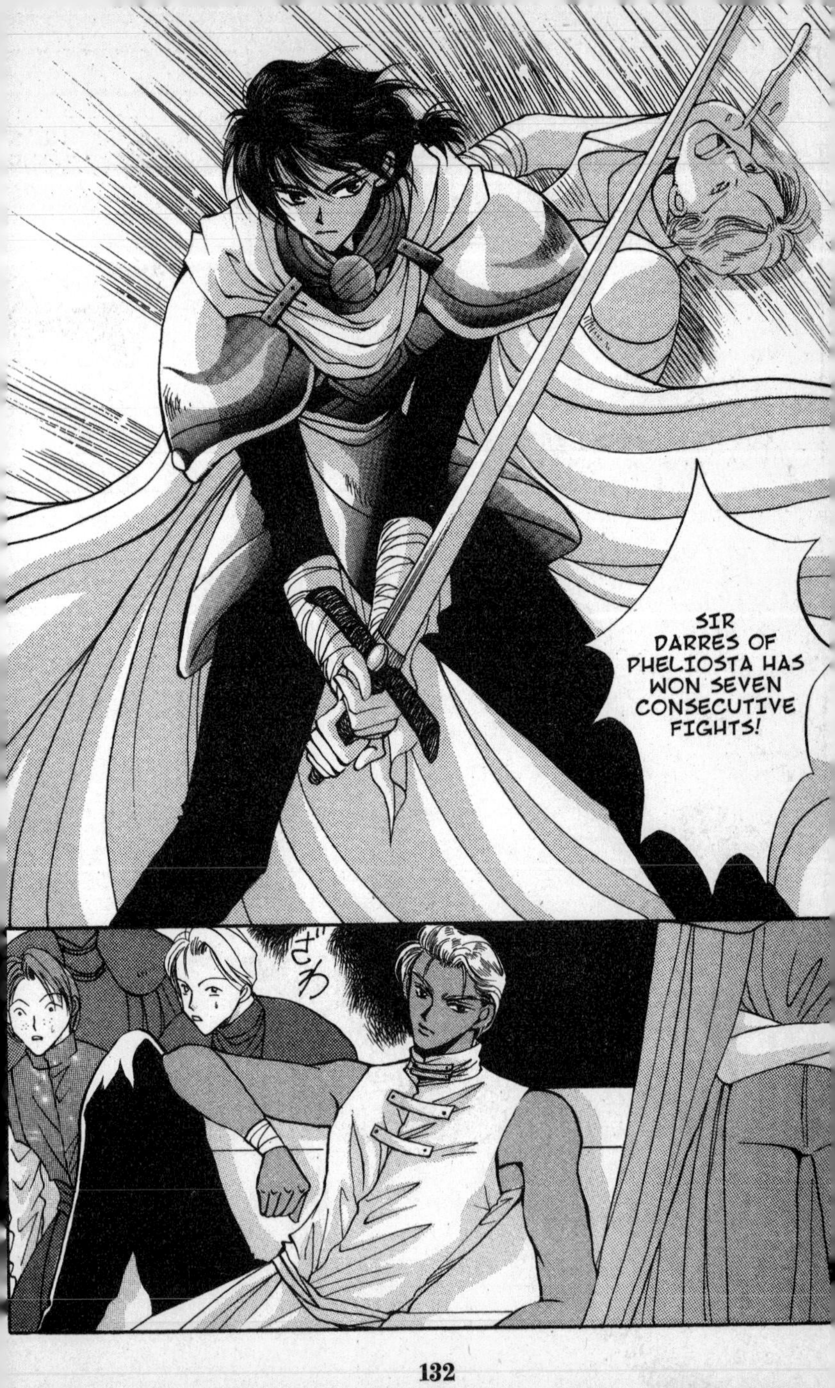
SIR DARRES OF PHELIOSTA HAS WON SEVEN CONSECUTIVE FIGHTS!
ざわ

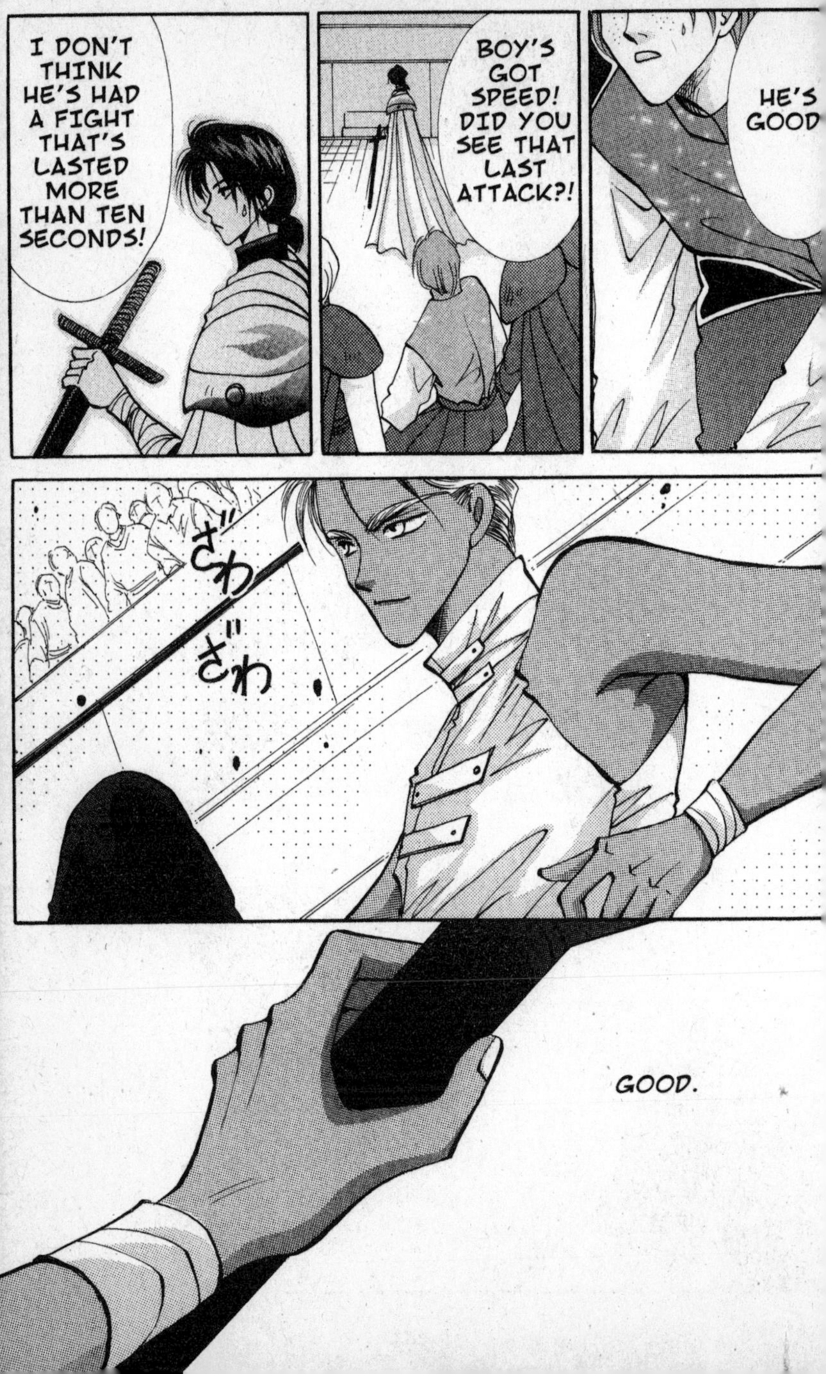
HE'S GOOD
BOY'S GOT SPEED! DID YOU SEE THAT LAST ATTACK?!
I DON'T THINK HE'S HAD A FIGHT THAT'S LASTED MORE THAN TEN SECONDS!
ざわ ざわ
GOOD.

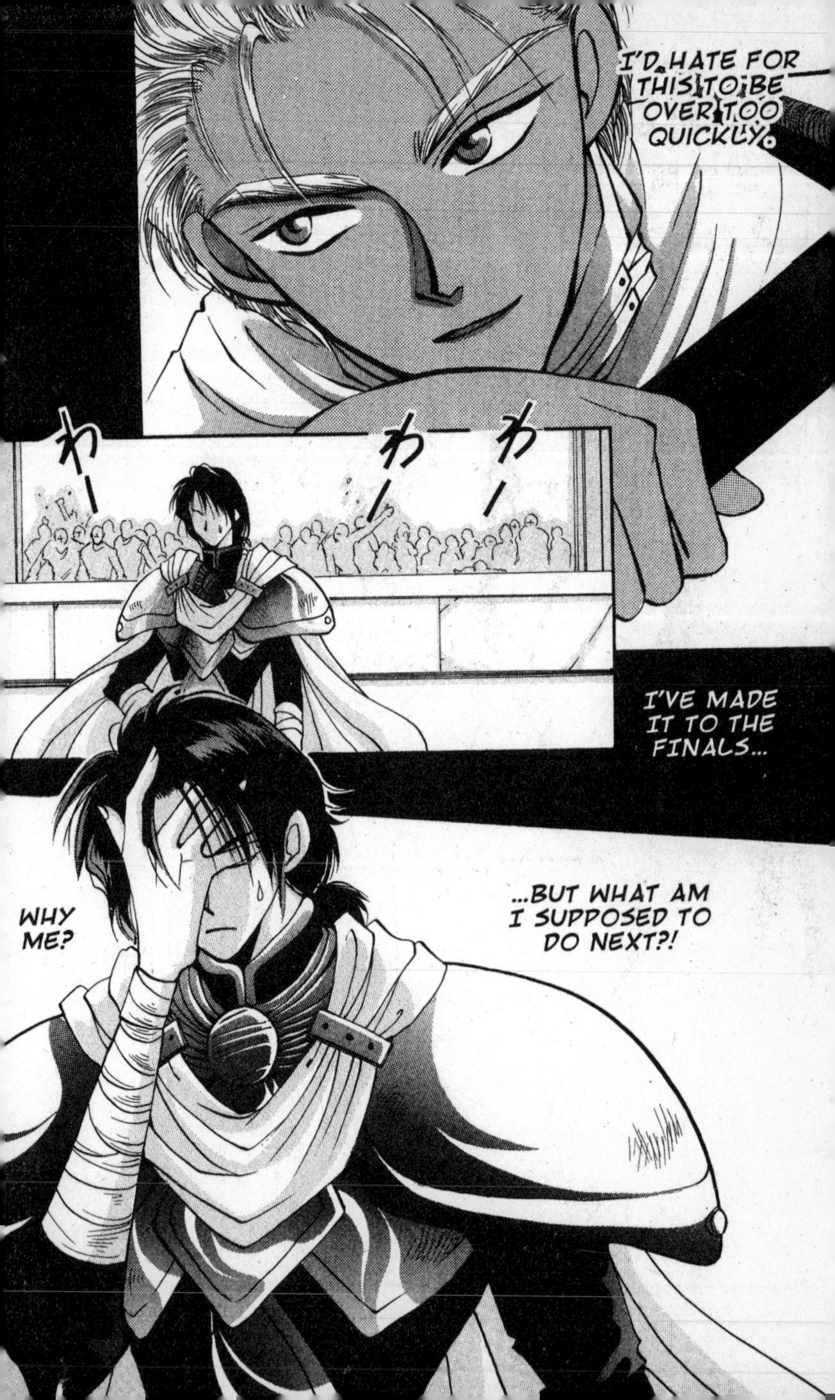
I'D HATE FOR THIS TO BE OVER TOO QUICKLY.
わー
わー
わー
I'VE MADE IT TO THE FINALS...
...BUT WHAT AM I SUPPOSED TO DO NEXT?!
WHY ME?

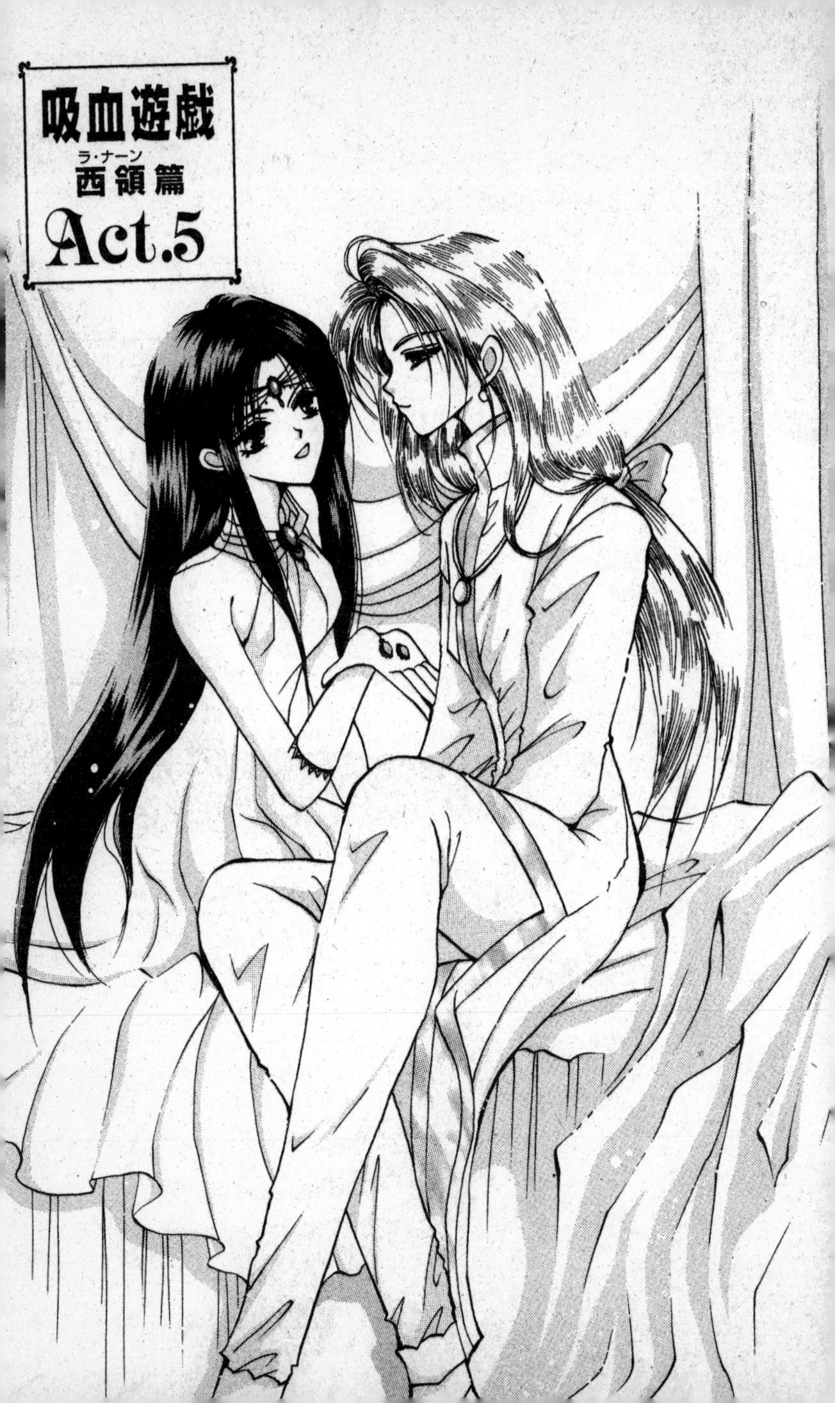
吸血遊戯
ラ・ナーン
西領篇
Act.5

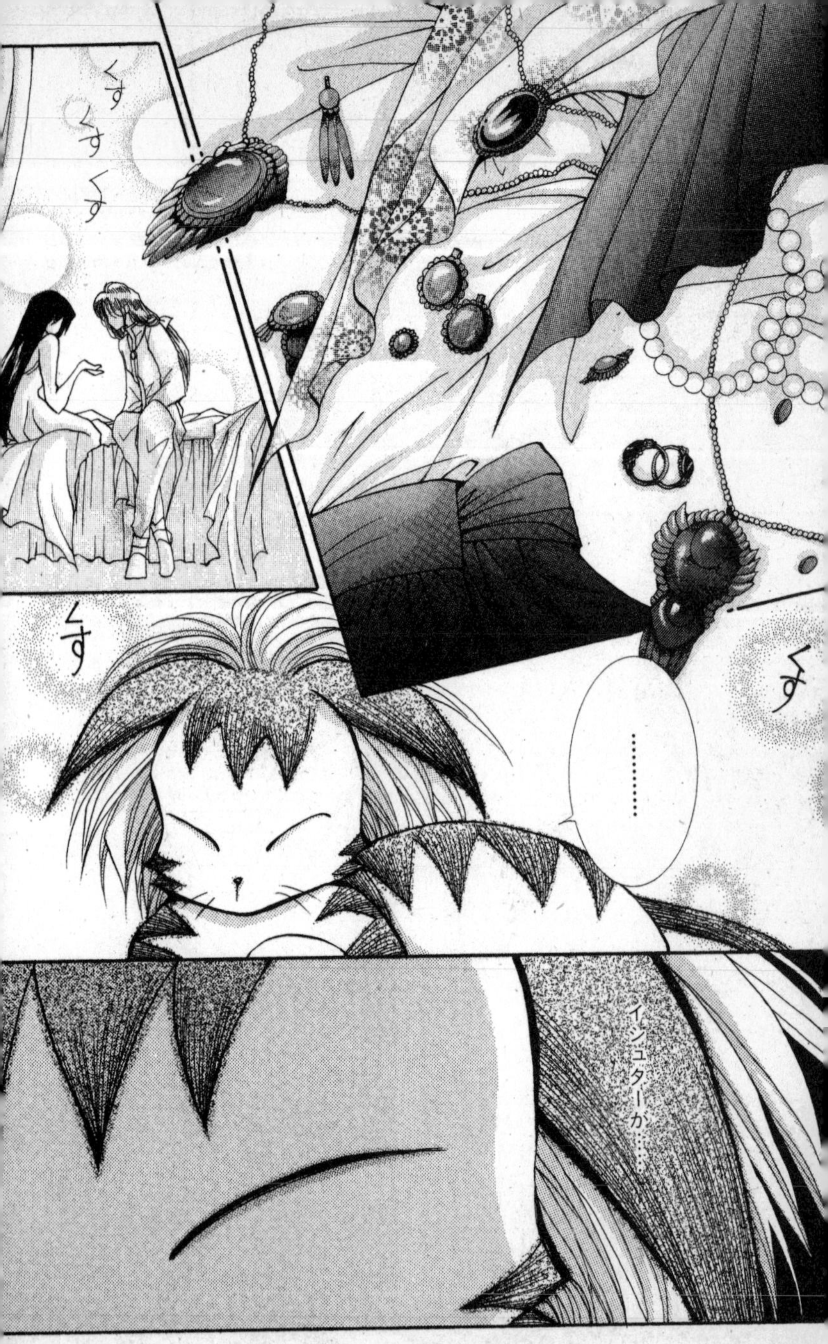
くすくすくす
くす
……
くす
イシュターか……

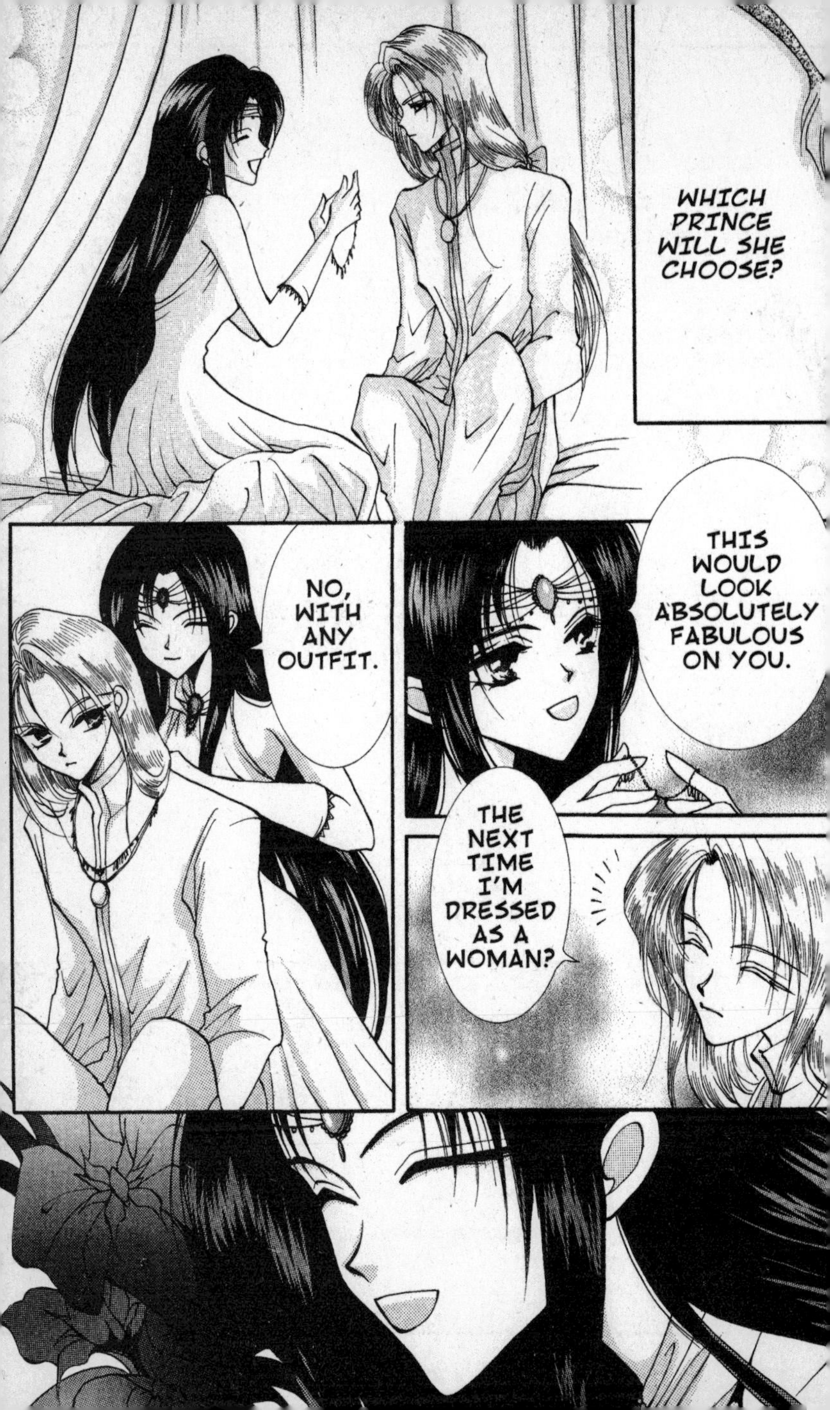
WHICH PRINCE WILL SHE CHOOSE?
THIS WOULD LOOK ABSOLUTELY FABULOUS ON YOU.
THE NEXT TIME I'M DRESSED AS A WOMAN?
NO, WITH ANY OUTFIT.

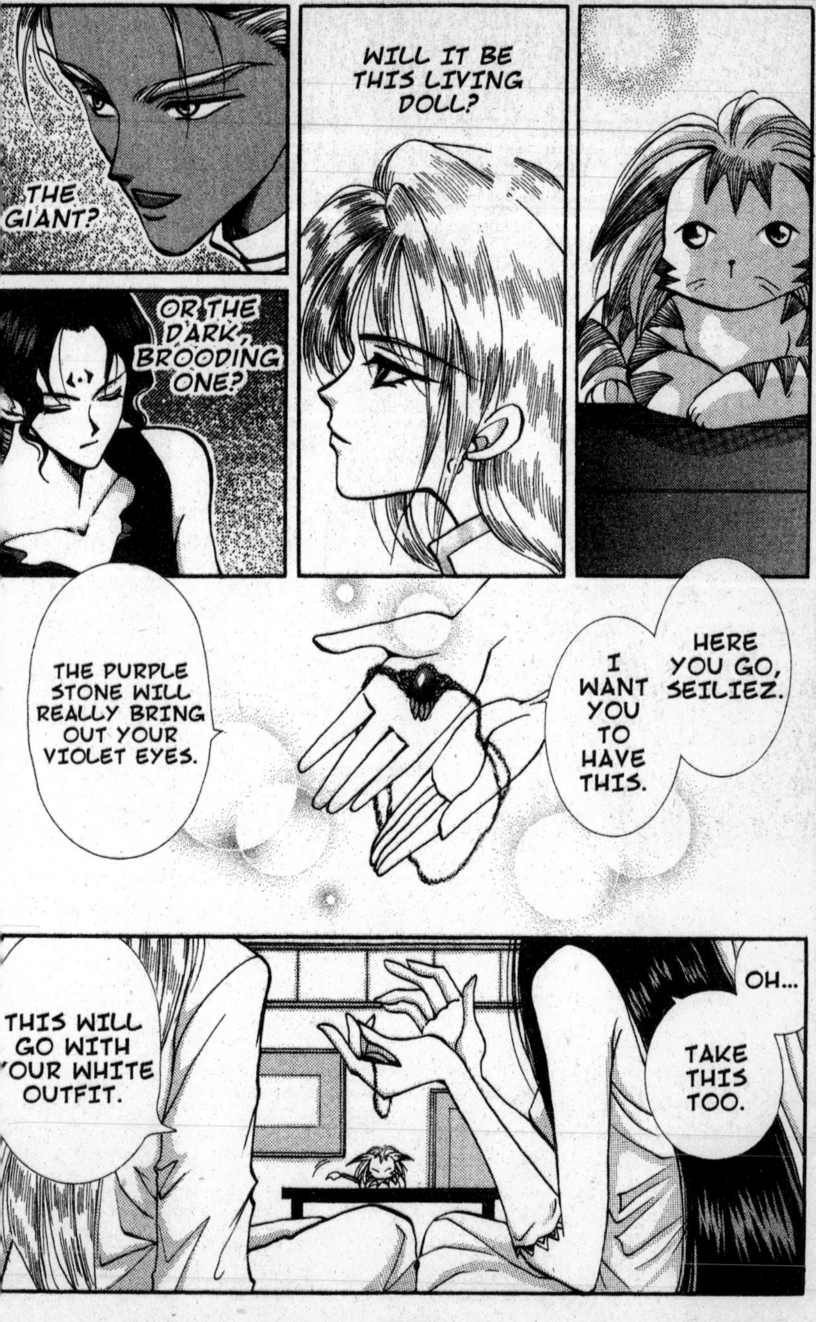
WILL IT BE THIS LIVING DOLL?
THE GIANT?
OR THE DARK, BROODING ONE?
HERE YOU GO, SEILIEZ.
I WANT YOU TO HAVE THIS.
THE PURPLE STONE WILL REALLY BRING OUT YOUR VIOLET EYES.
OH...
TAKE THIS TOO.
THIS WILL GO WITH OUR WHITE OUTFIT.

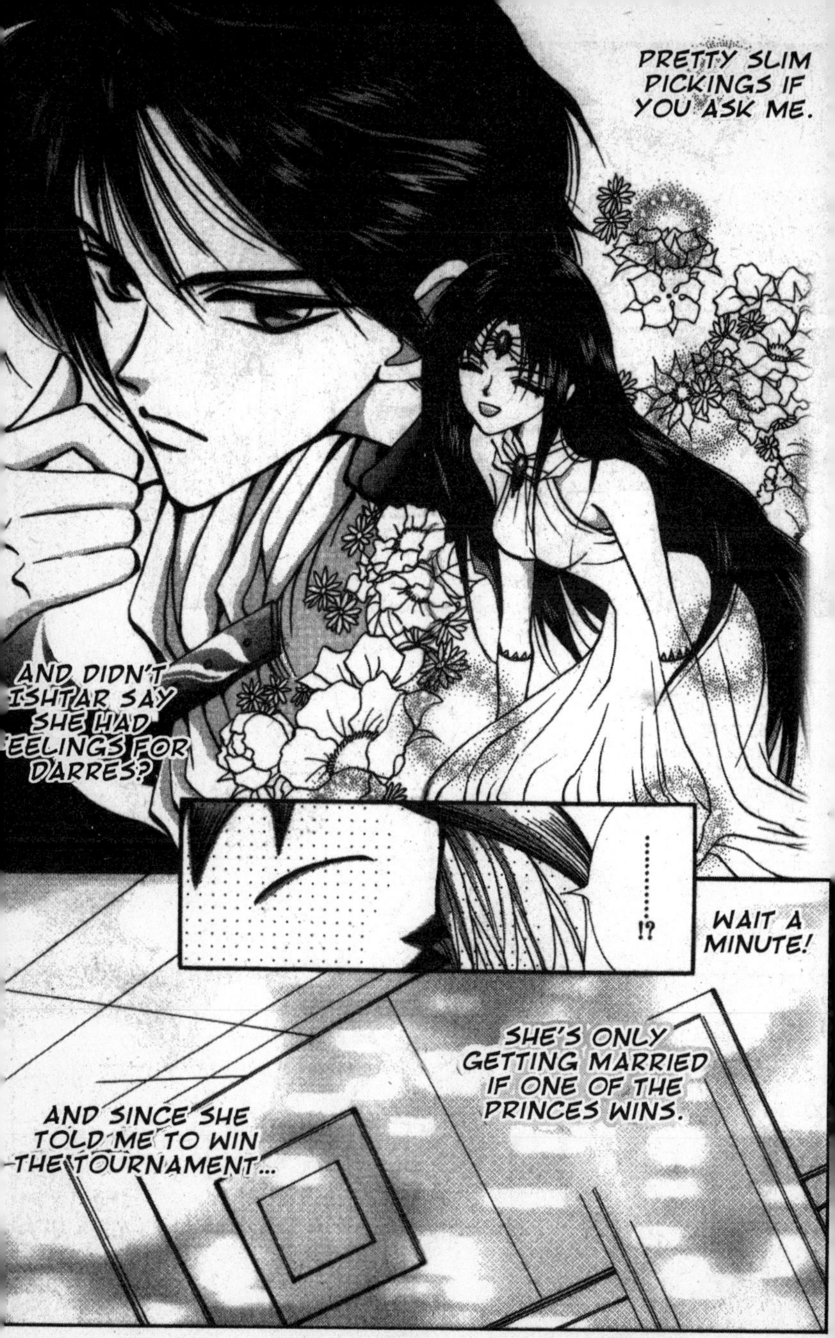
PRETTY SLIM PICKINGS IF YOU ASK ME.
AND DIDN'T ISHTAR SAY SHE HAD EELINGS FOR DARRES?
WAIT A MINUTE!
......!?
SHE'S ONLY GETTING MARRIED IF ONE OF THE PRINCES WINS.
AND SINCE SHE TOLD ME TO WIN THE TOURNAMENT...

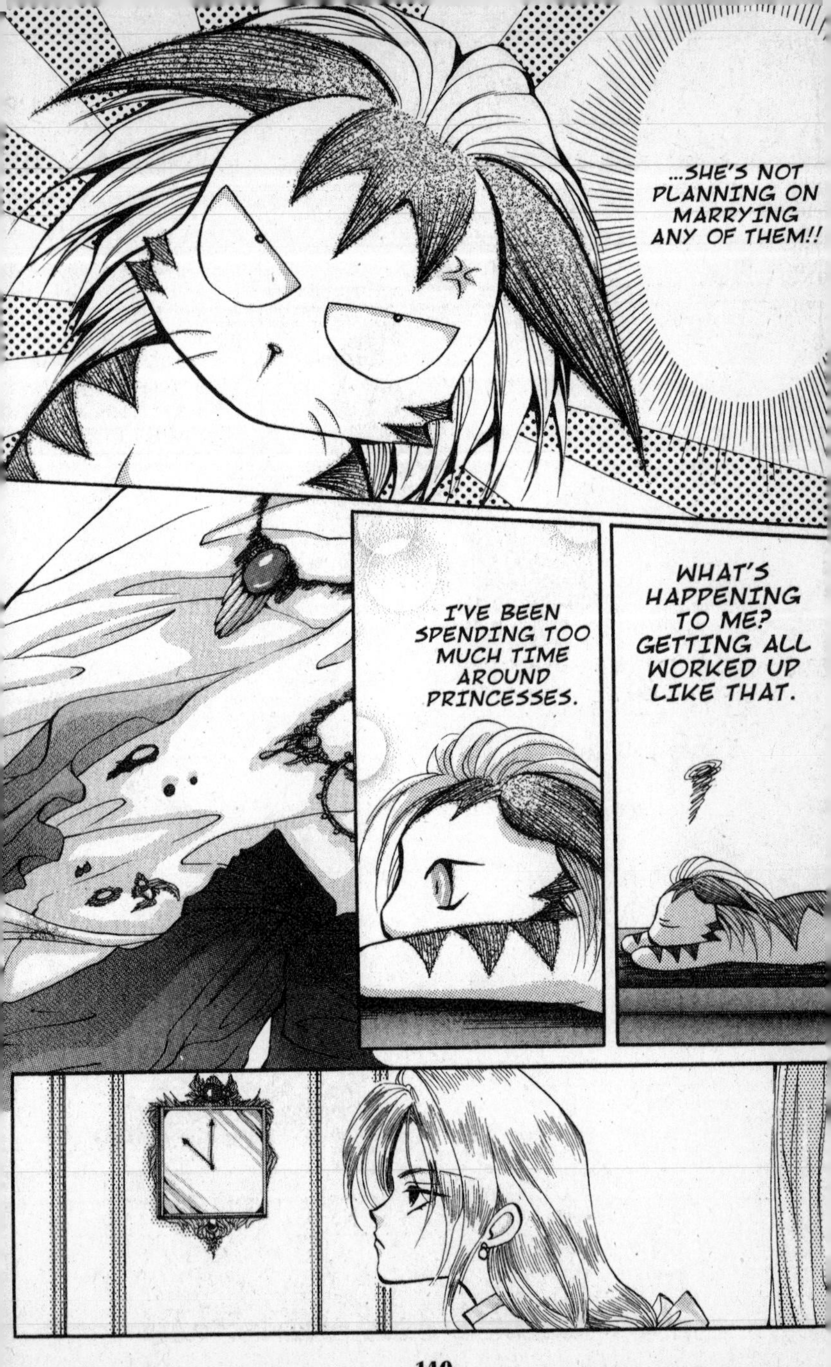
...SHE'S NOT PLANNING ON MARRYING ANY OF THEM!!
WHAT'S HAPPENING TO ME? GETTING ALL WORKED UP LIKE THAT.
I'VE BEEN SPENDING TOO MUCH TIME AROUND PRINCESSES.

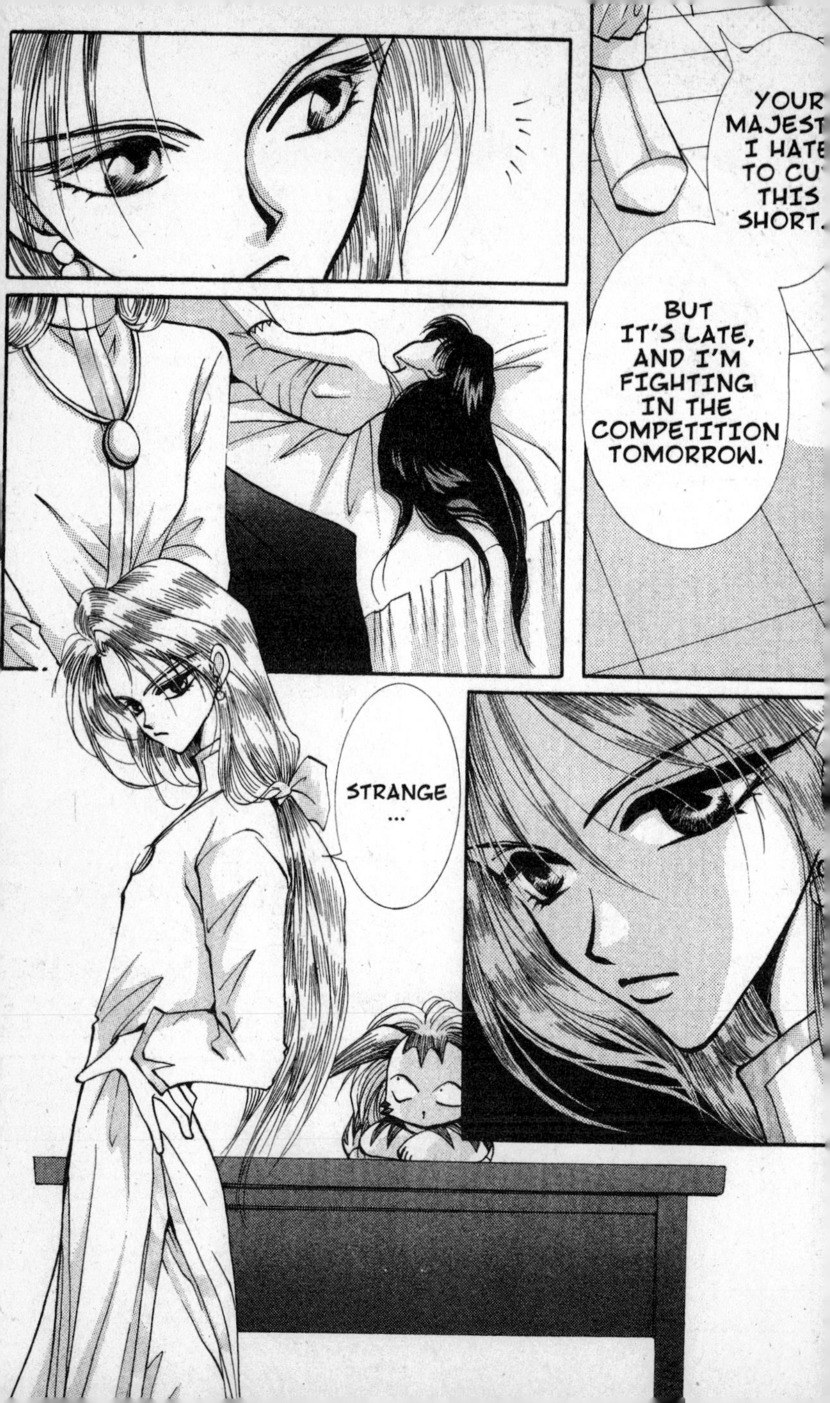
YOUR MAJEST I HATE TO CU THIS SHORT.
BUT IT'S LATE, AND I'M FIGHTING IN THE COMPETITION TOMORROW.
STRANGE ...

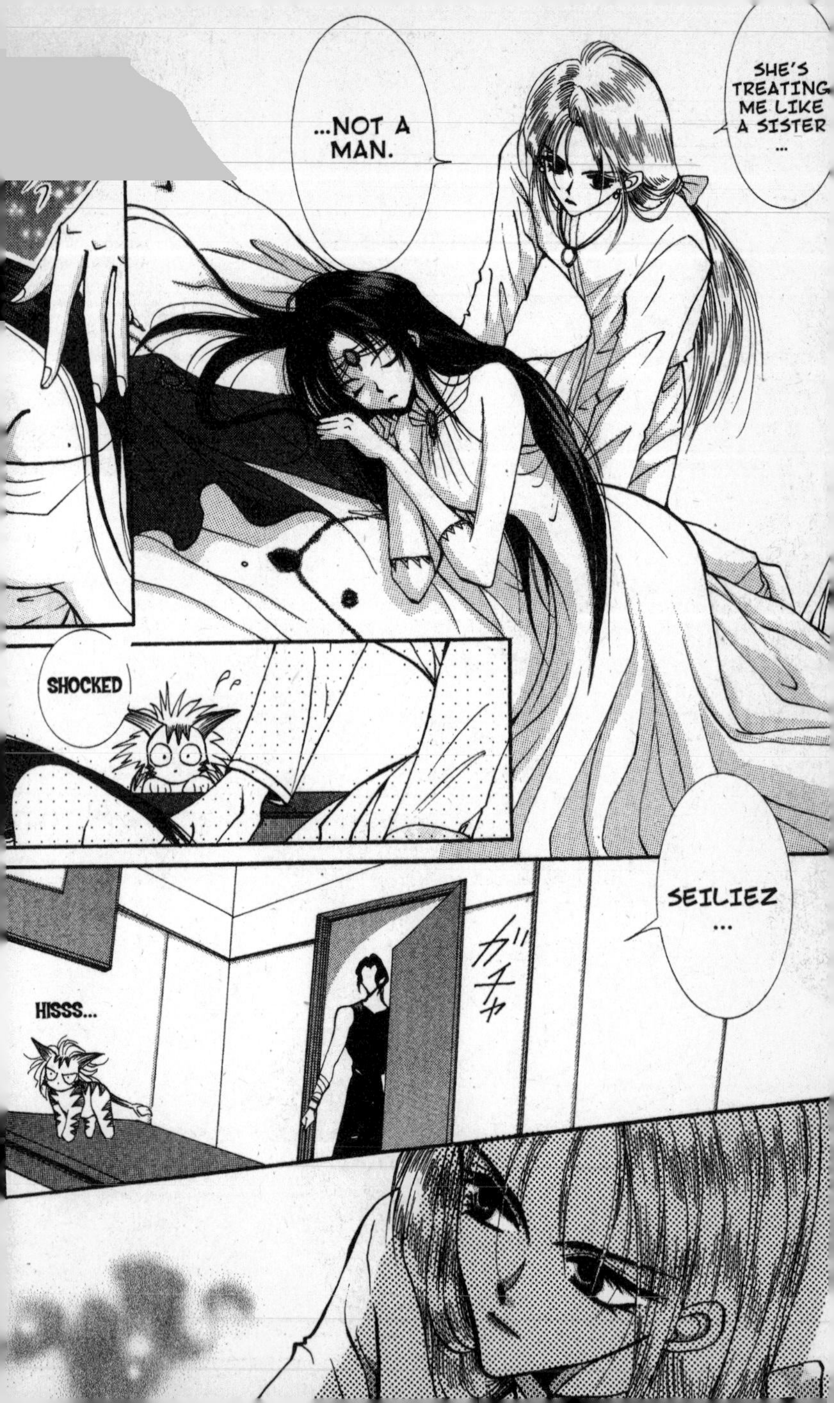
SHE'S TREATING ME LIKE A SISTER ...
...NOT A MAN.
SHOCKED
SEILIEZ ...
ガチャ
HISSS...

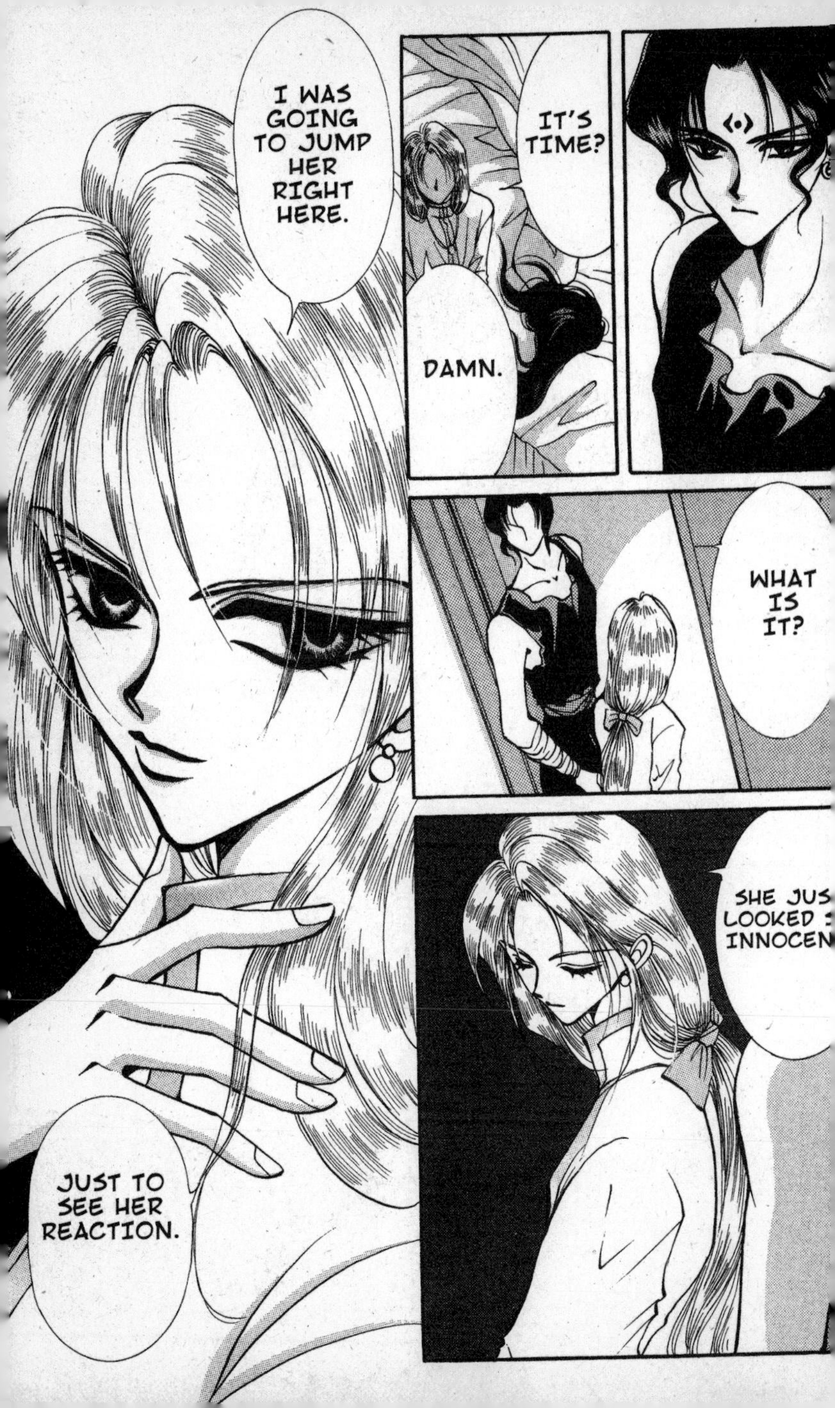
IT'S TIME?
DAMN.
WHAT IS IT?
SHE JUS LOOKED INNOCEN
I WAS GOING TO JUMP HER RIGHT HERE.
JUST TO SEE HER REACTION.

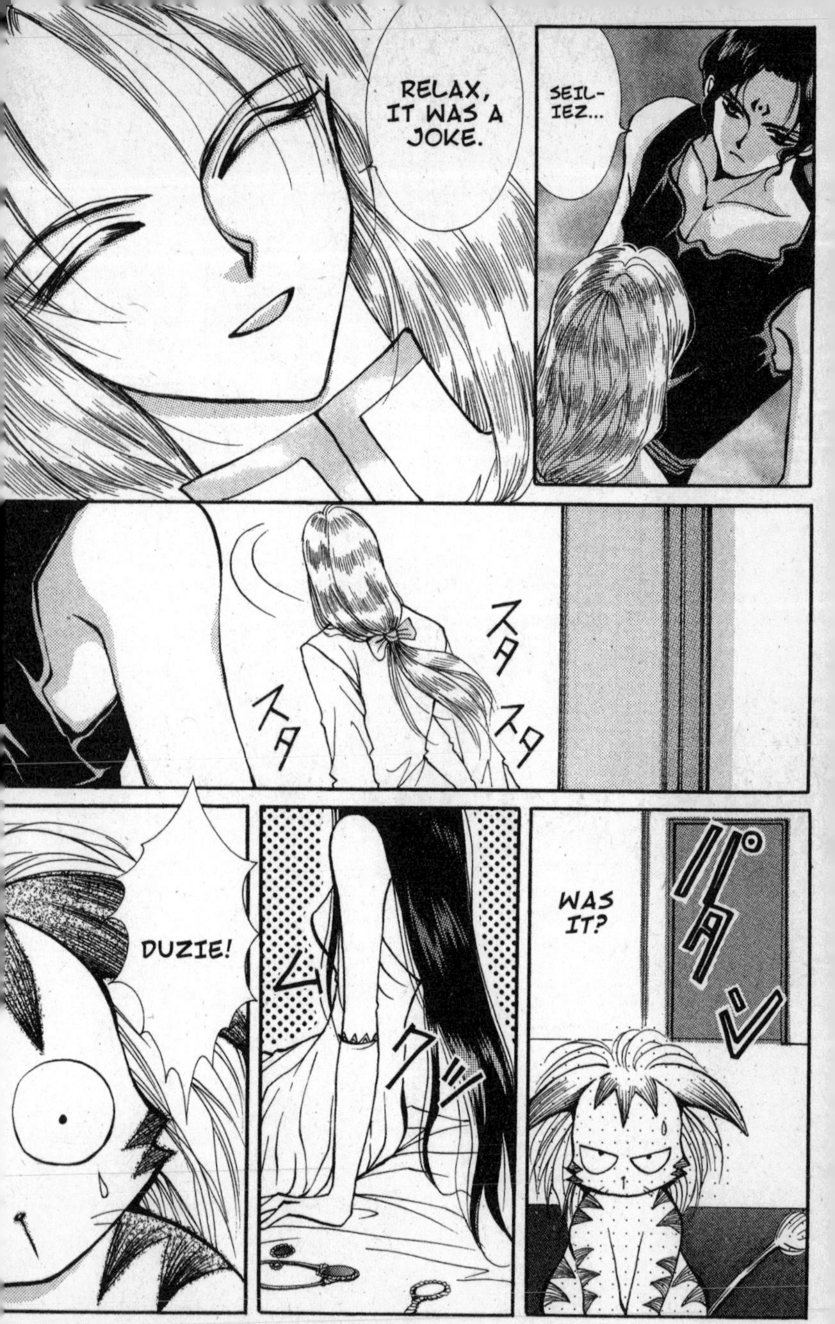
SEIL-
IEZ...
RELAX, IT WAS A JOKE.
スタ
スタ
スタ
パタン
WAS IT?
ムクッ
DUZIE!

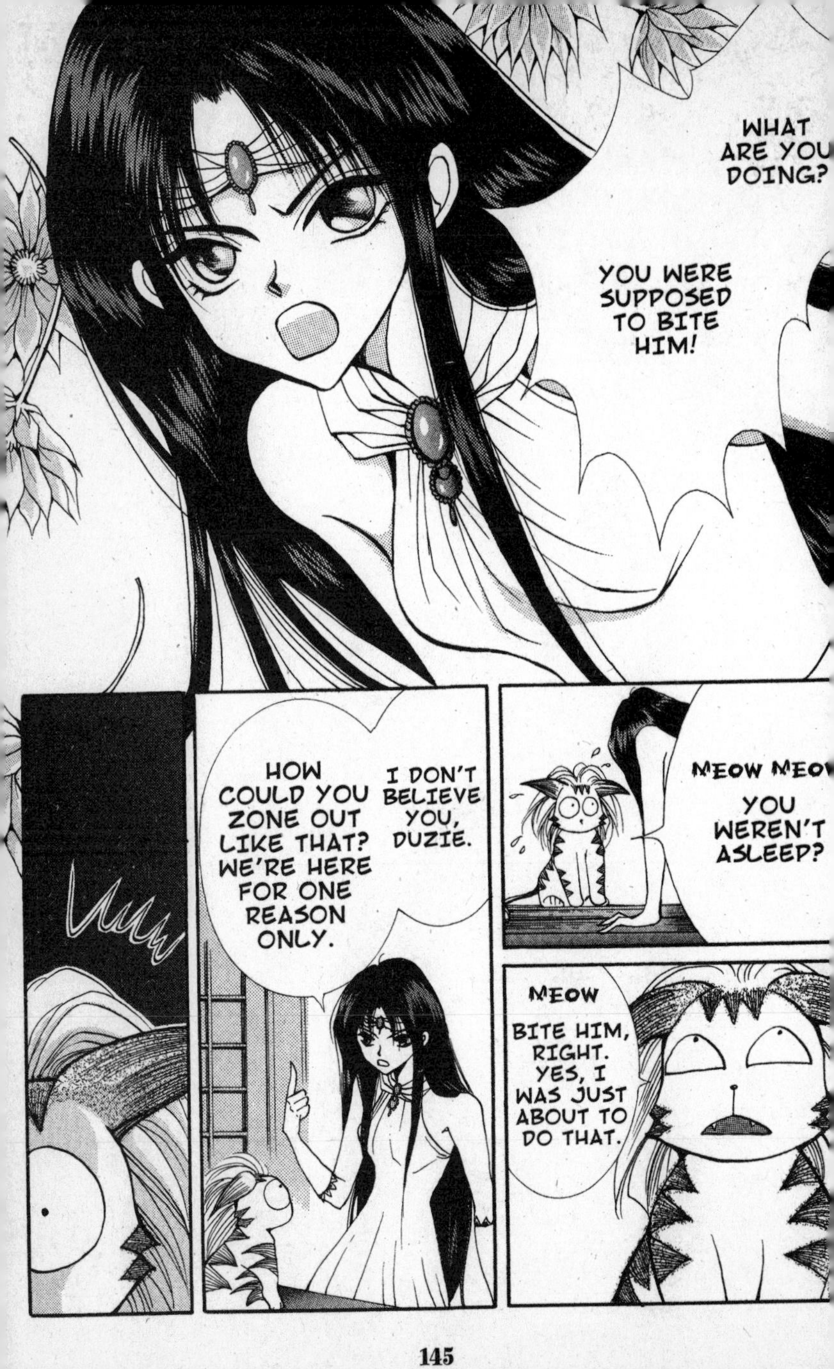
WHAT ARE YOU DOING?
YOU WERE SUPPOSED TO BITE HIM!
MEOW MEO
YOU WEREN'T ASLEEP?
MEOW
BITE HIM, RIGHT. YES, I WAS JUST ABOUT TO DO THAT.
I DON'T BELIEVE YOU, DUZIE.
HOW COULD YOU ZONE OUT LIKE THAT? WE'RE HERE FOR ONE REASON ONLY.

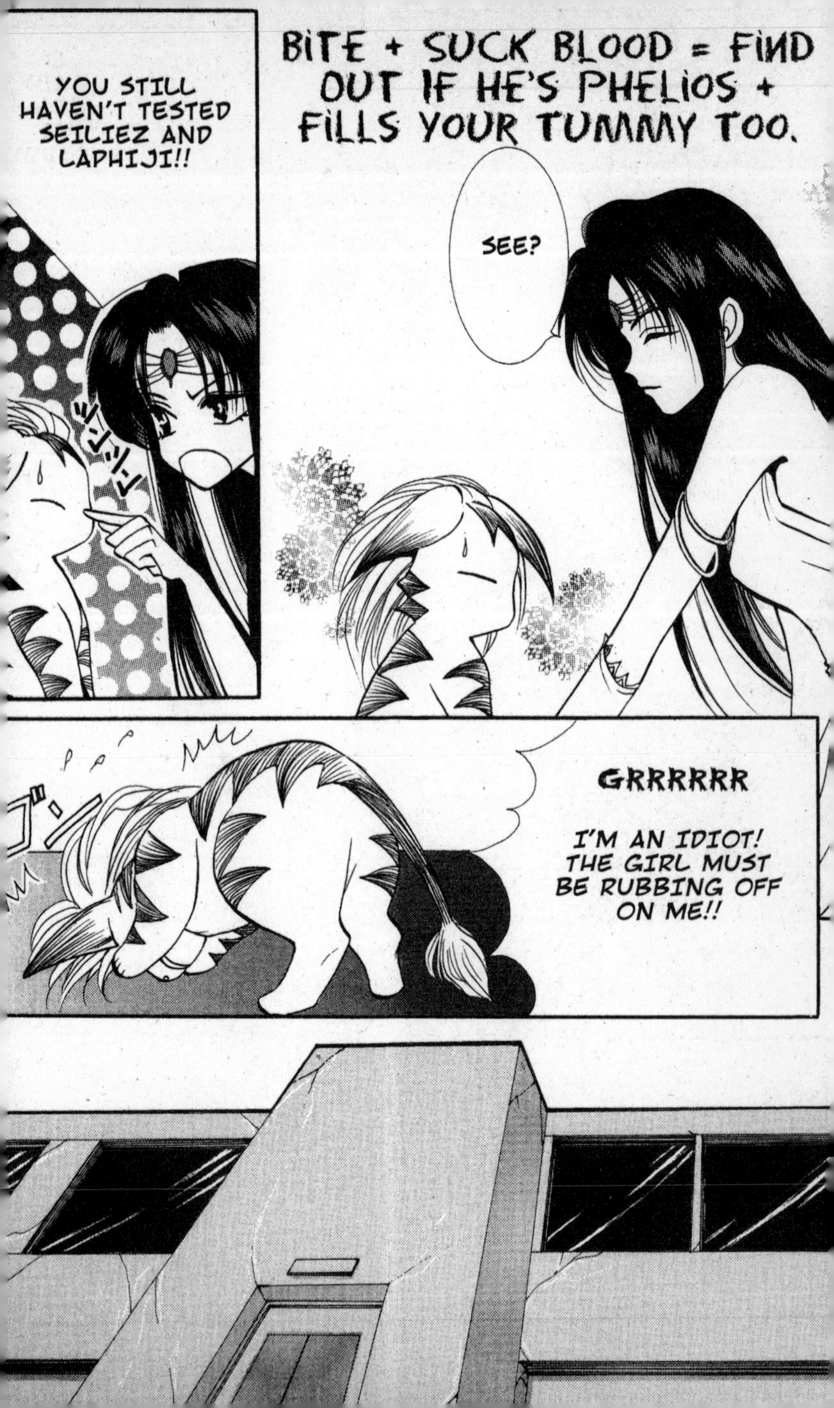
BITE + SUCK BLOOD = FIND OUT IF HE'S PHELIOS + FILLS YOUR TUMMY TOO.
SEE?
YOU STILL HAVEN'T TESTED SEILIEZ AND LAPHIJI!!
GRRRRRR
I'M AN IDIOT! THE GIRL MUST BE RUBBING OFF ON ME!!

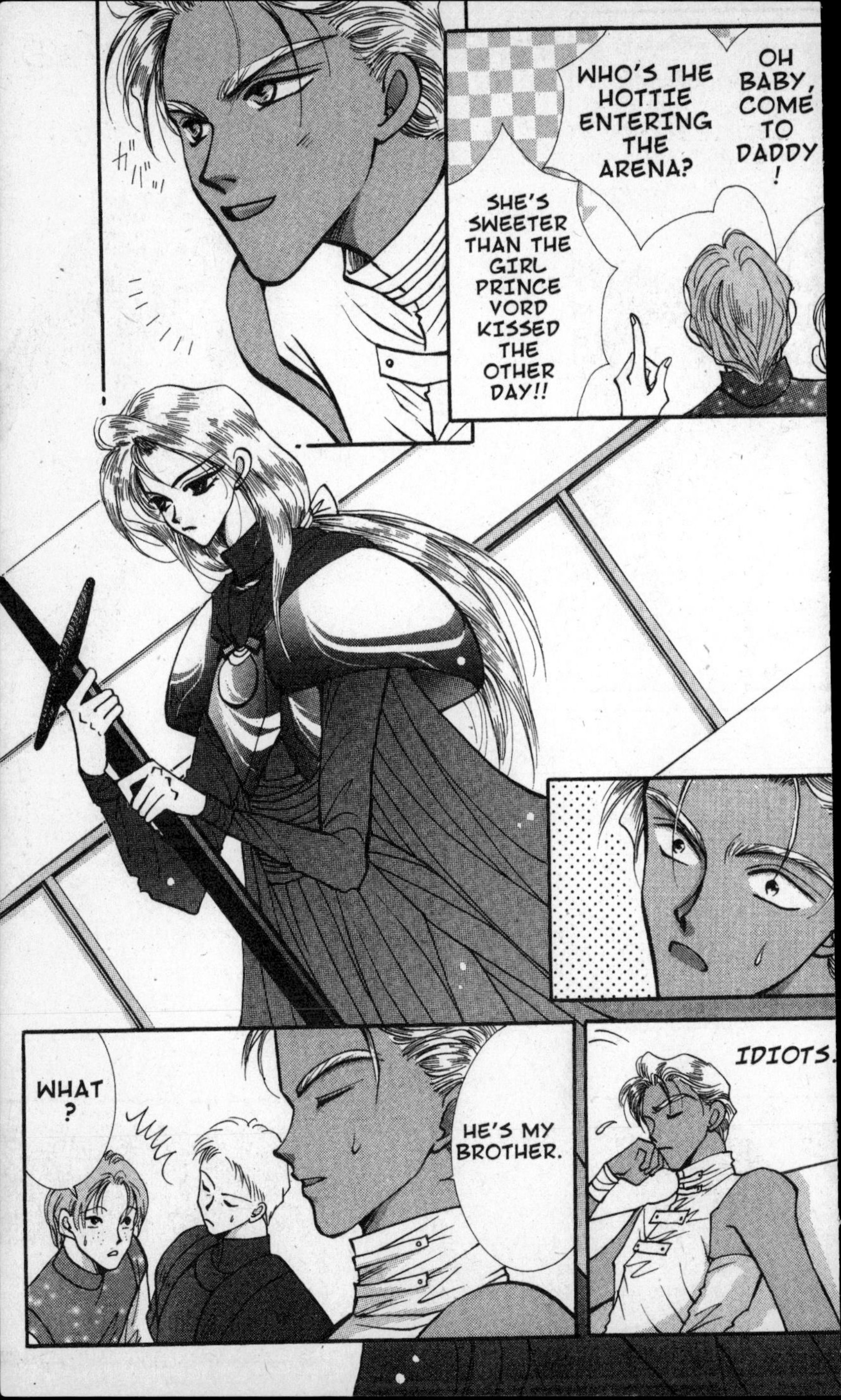
OH BABY, COME TO DADDY!
WHO'S THE HOTTIE ENTERING THE ARENA?
SHE'S SWEETER THAN THE GIRL PRINCE VORD KISSED THE OTHER DAY!!
IDIOTS.
HE'S MY BROTHER.
WHAT?

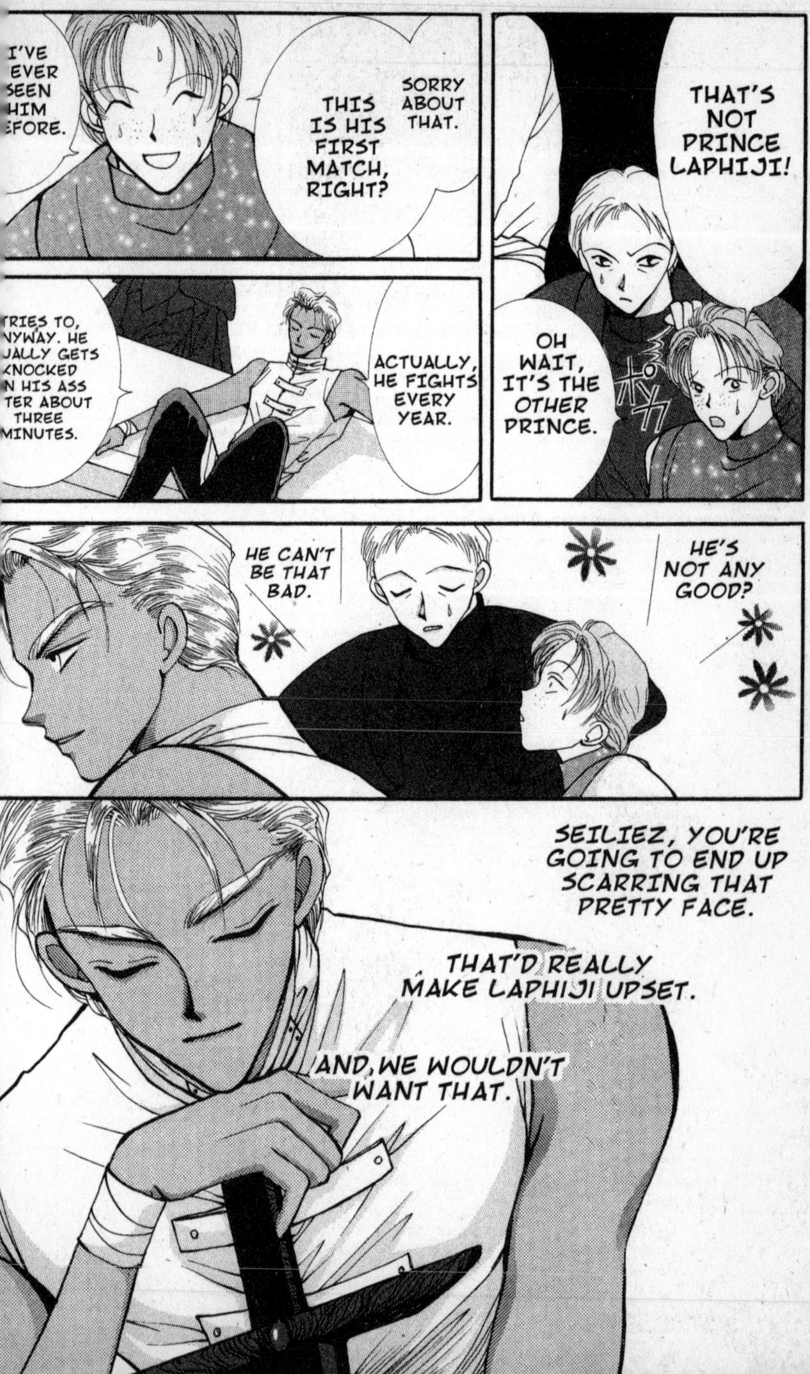
THAT'S NOT PRINCE LAPHIJI!
OH WAIT, IT'S THE OTHER PRINCE.
SORRY ABOUT THAT.
THIS IS HIS FIRST MATCH, RIGHT?
I'VE EVER SEEN HIM EFORE.
ACTUALLY, HE FIGHTS EVERY YEAR.
TRIES TO, NYWAY. HE JALLY GETS KNOCKED N HIS ASS TER ABOUT THREE MINUTES.
HE'S NOT ANY GOOD?
HE CAN'T BE THAT BAD.
SEILIEZ, YOU'RE GOING TO END UP SCARRING THAT PRETTY FACE.
THAT'D REALLY MAKE LAPHIJI UPSET.
AND, WE WOULDN'T WANT THAT.

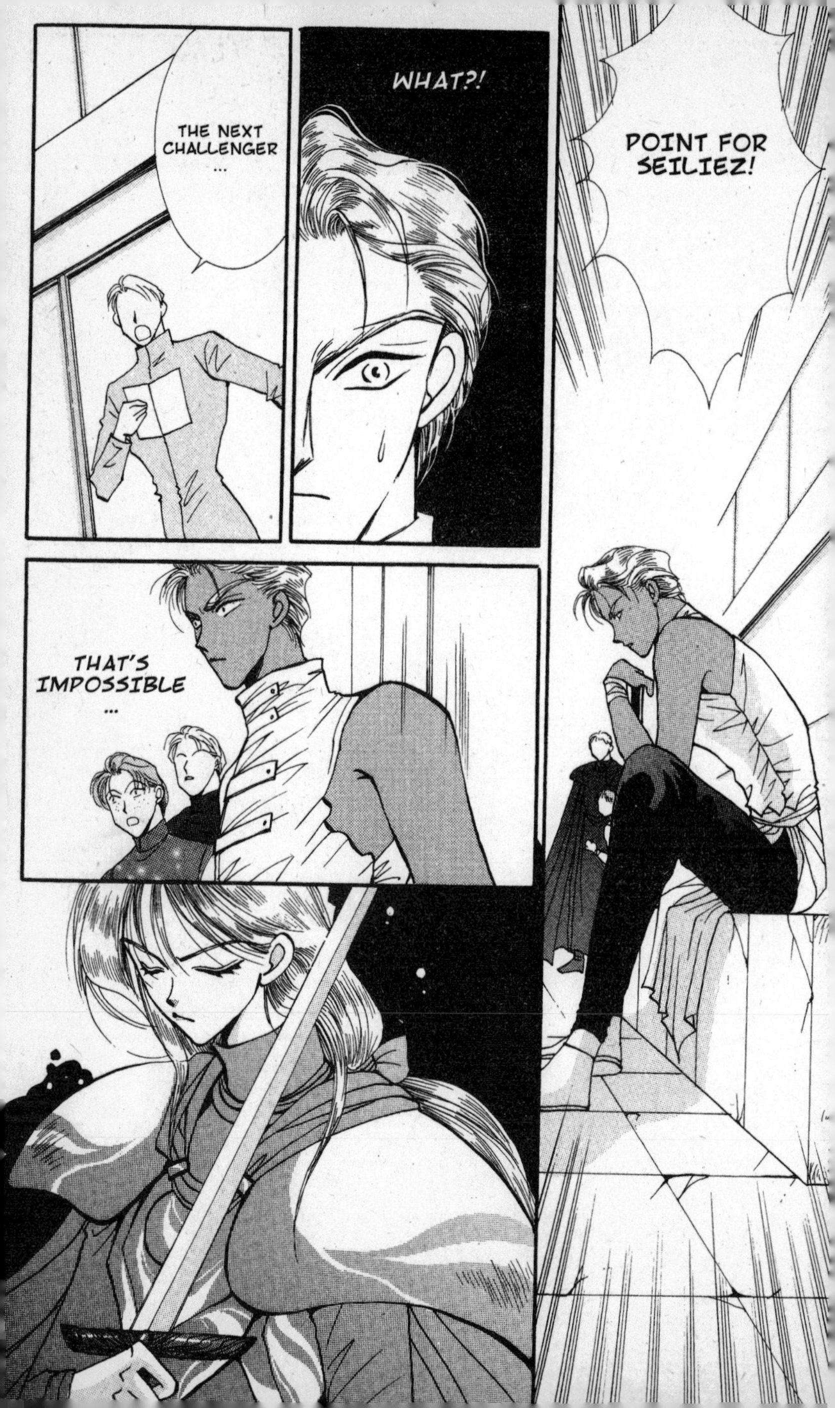
POINT FOR SEILIEZ!
WHAT?!
THE NEXT CHALLENGER ...
THAT'S IMPOSSIBLE ...

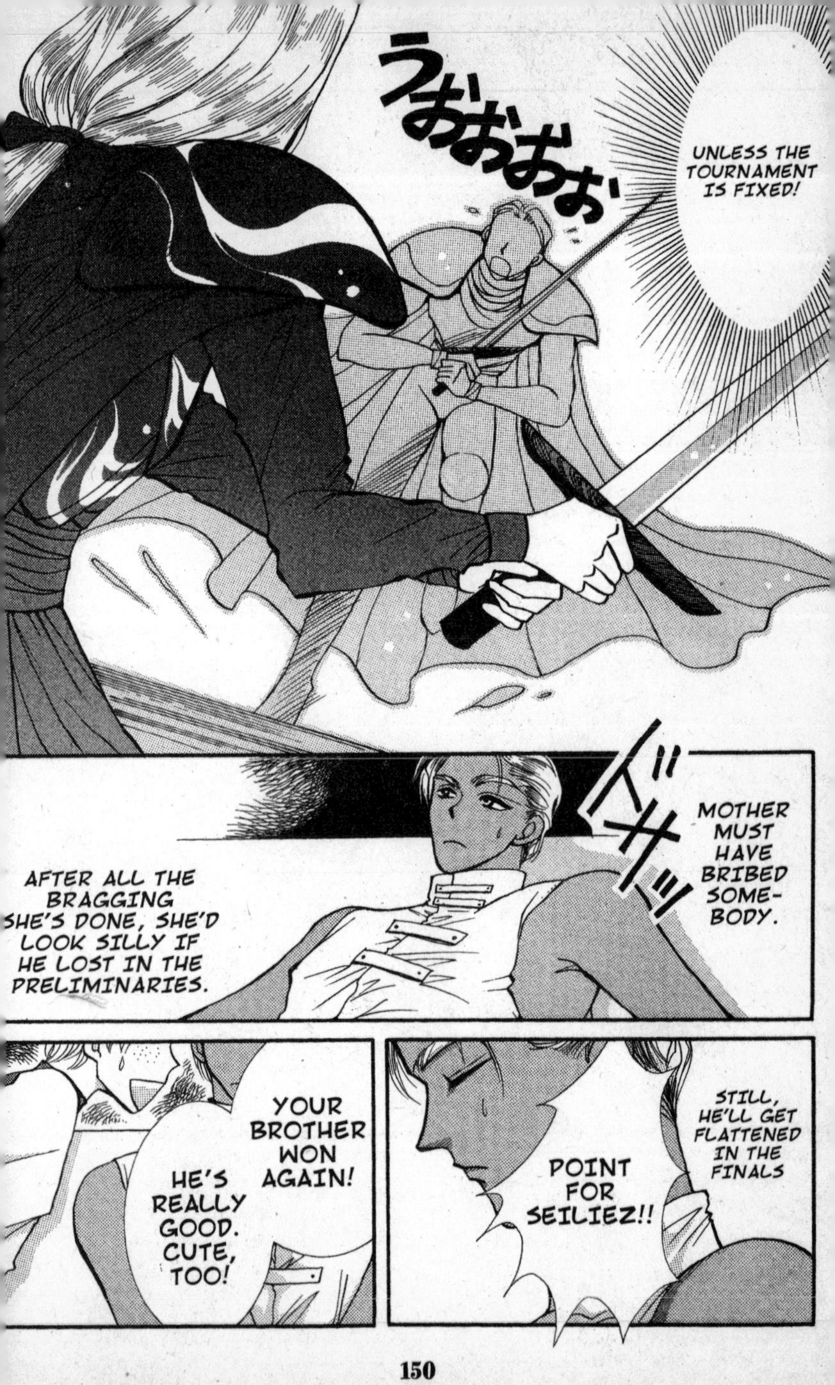
うおおおお
UNLESS THE TOURNAMENT IS FIXED!
MOTHER MUST HAVE BRIBED SOMEBODY.
ドサッ
AFTER ALL THE BRAGGING SHE'S DONE, SHE'D LOOK SILLY IF HE LOST IN THE PRELIMINARIES.
STILL, HE'LL GET FLATTENED IN THE FINALS
POINT FOR SEILIEZ!!
YOUR BROTHER WON AGAIN!
HE'S REALLY GOOD. CUTE, TOO!

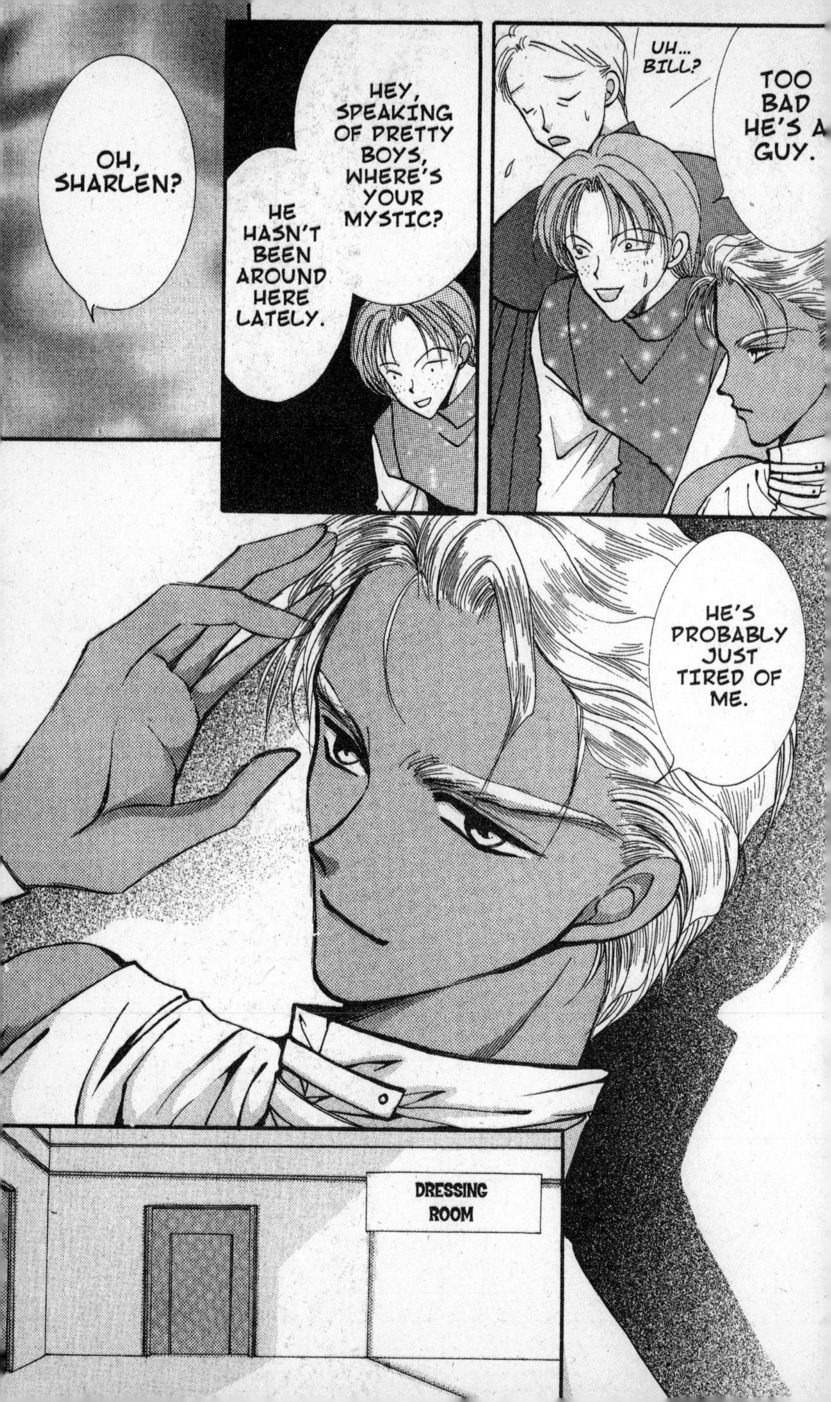
TOO BAD HE'S A GUY.
UH... BILL?
HEY, SPEAKING OF PRETTY BOYS, WHERE'S YOUR MYSTIC?
HE HASN'T BEEN AROUND HERE LATELY.
OH, SHARLEN?
HE'S PROBABLY JUST TIRED OF ME.
DRESSING ROOM

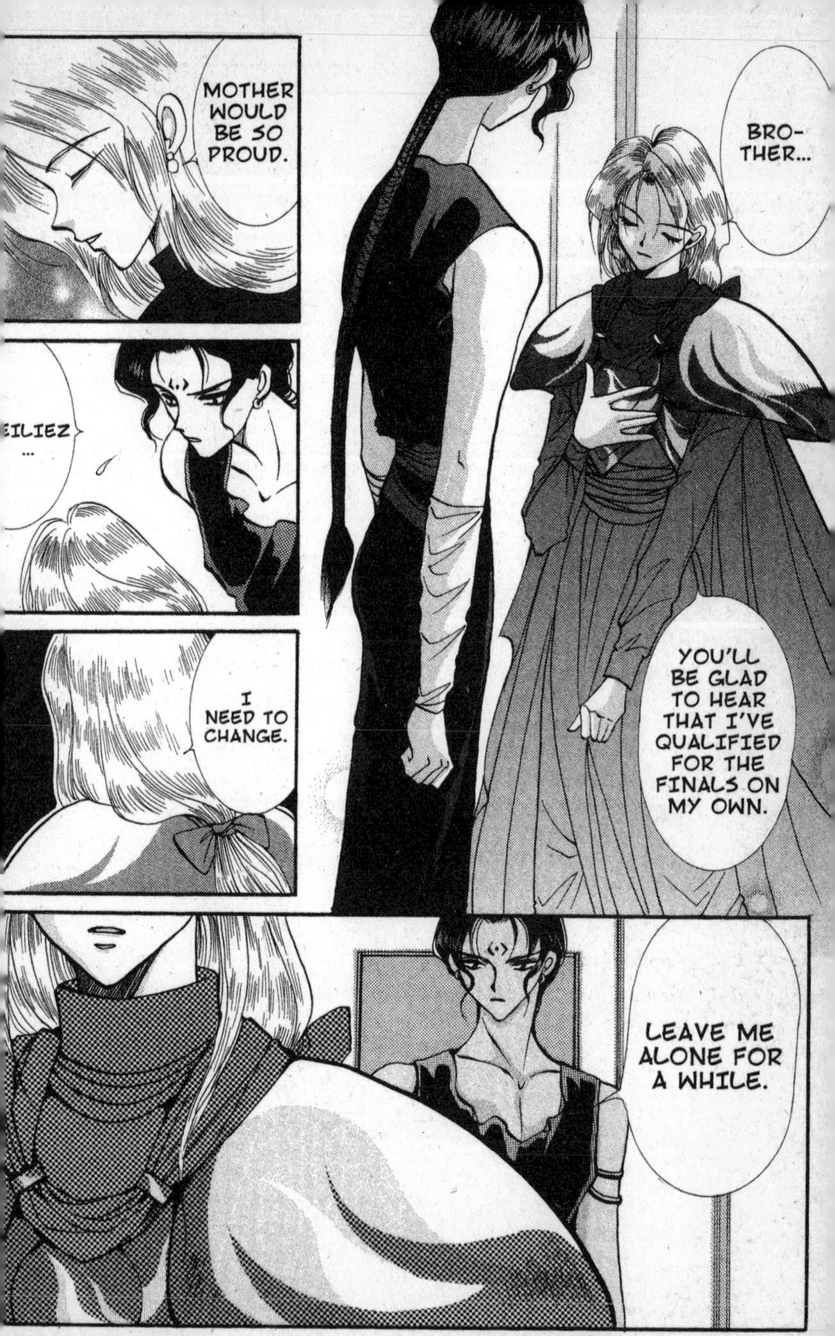

BRO-THER...
YOU'LL BE GLAD TO HEAR THAT I'VE QUALIFIED FOR THE FINALS ON MY OWN.
MOTHER WOULD BE SO PROUD.
EILIEZ ...
I NEED TO CHANGE.
LEAVE ME ALONE FOR A WHILE.

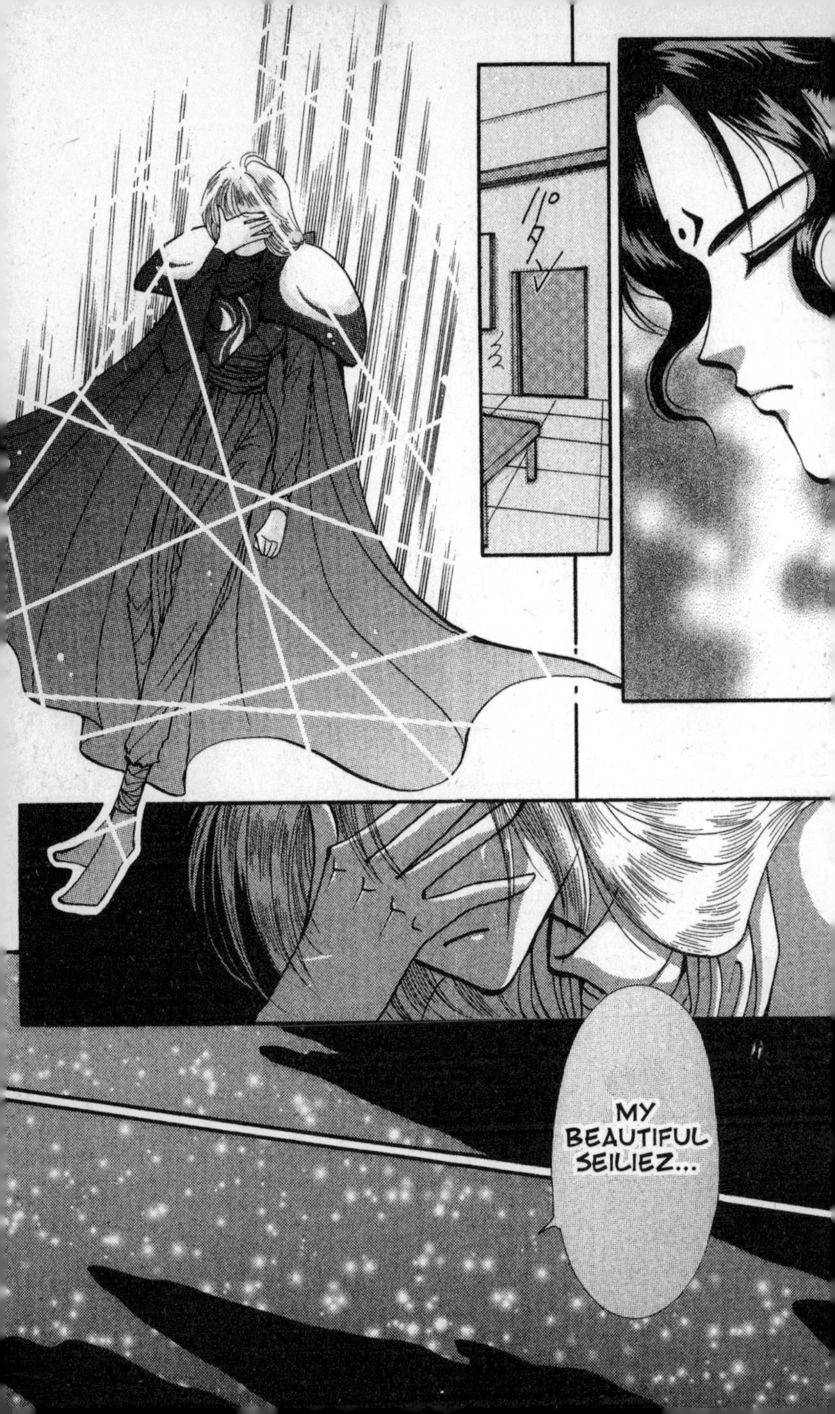
パタン
MY BEAUTIFUL SEILIEZ...

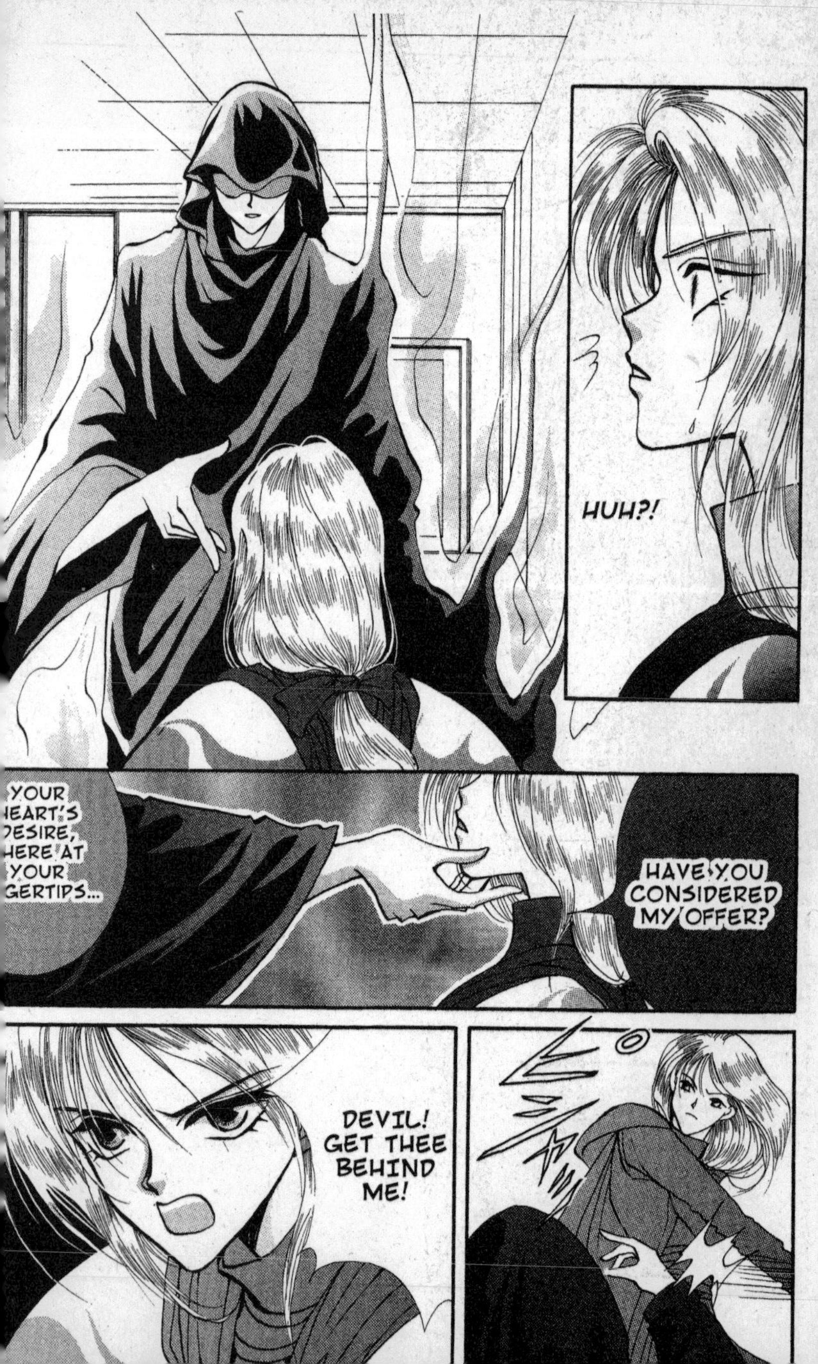
HUH?!
HAVE YOU CONSIDERED MY OFFER?
YOUR EART'S ESIRE, HERE AT YOUR GERTIPS...
DEVIL! GET THEE BEHIND ME!

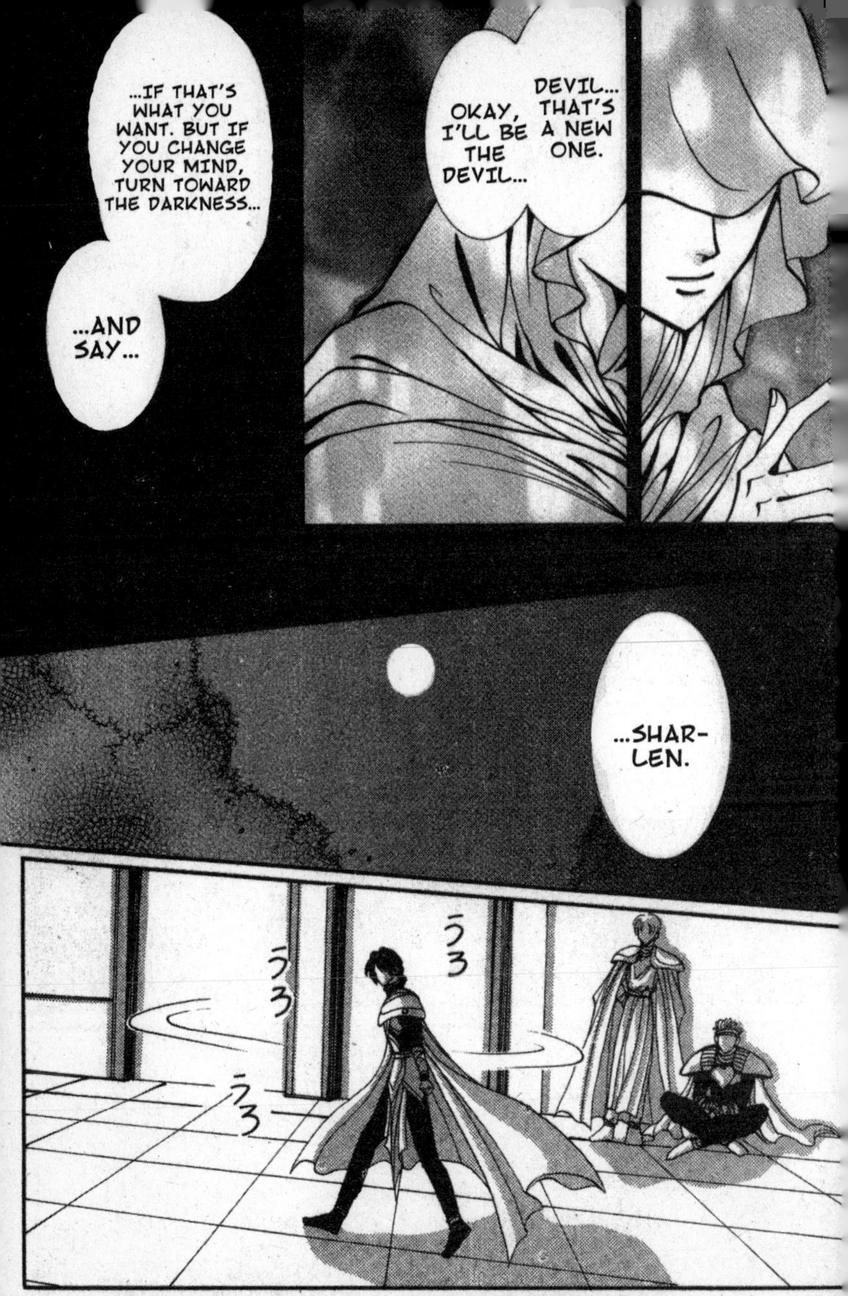
DEVIL... THAT'S A NEW ONE.
OKAY, I'LL BE THE DEVIL...
...IF THAT'S WHAT YOU WANT. BUT IF YOU CHANGE YOUR MIND, TURN TOWARD THE DARKNESS...
...AND SAY...
...SHARLEN.
うろ
うろ
うろ

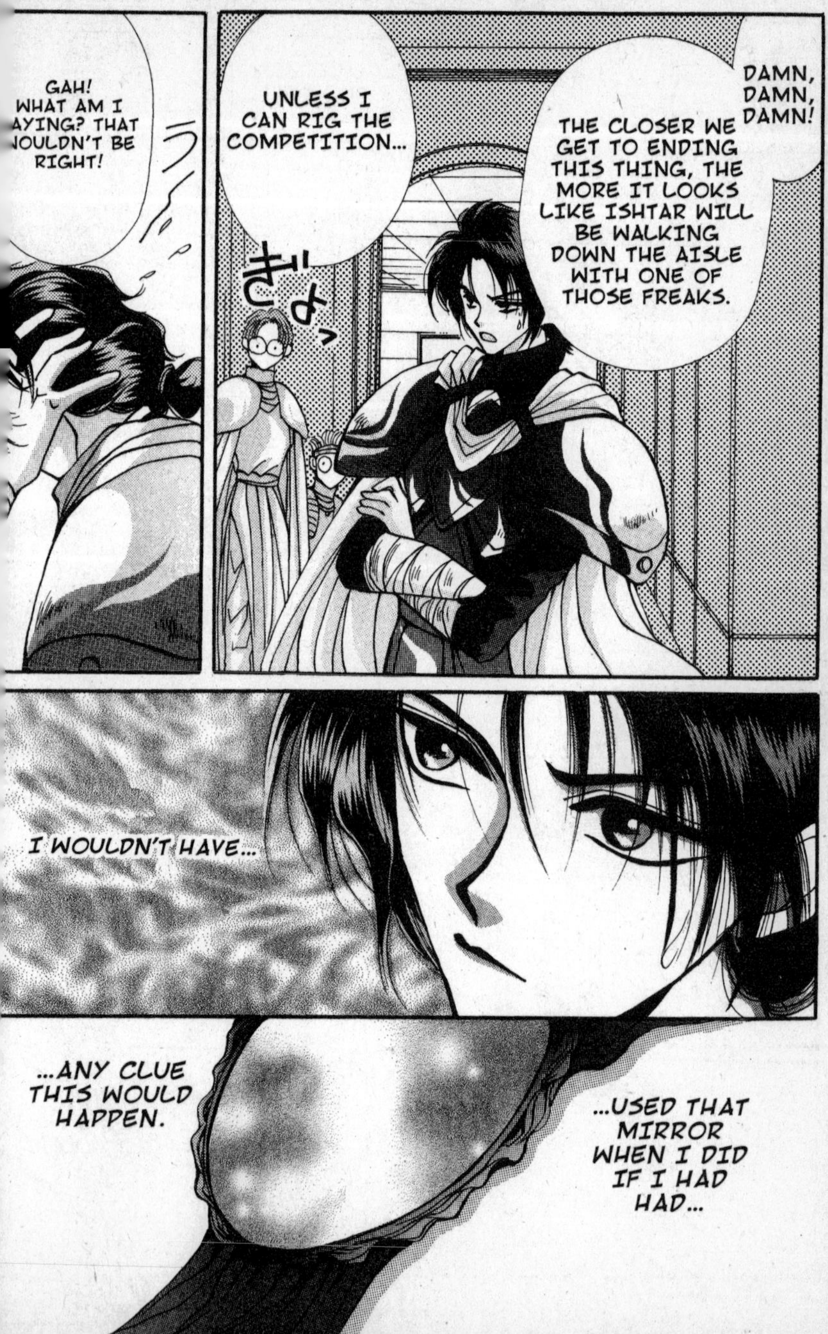
DAMN, DAMN, DAMN!
THE CLOSER WE GET TO ENDING THIS THING, THE MORE IT LOOKS LIKE ISHTAR WILL BE WALKING DOWN THE AISLE WITH ONE OF THOSE FREAKS.
UNLESS I CAN RIG THE COMPETITION...
ぎょっ
GAH! WHAT AM I AYING? THAT OULDN'T BE RIGHT!
I WOULDN'T HAVE...
...USED THAT MIRROR WHEN I DID IF I HAD HAD...
...ANY CLUE THIS WOULD HAPPEN.

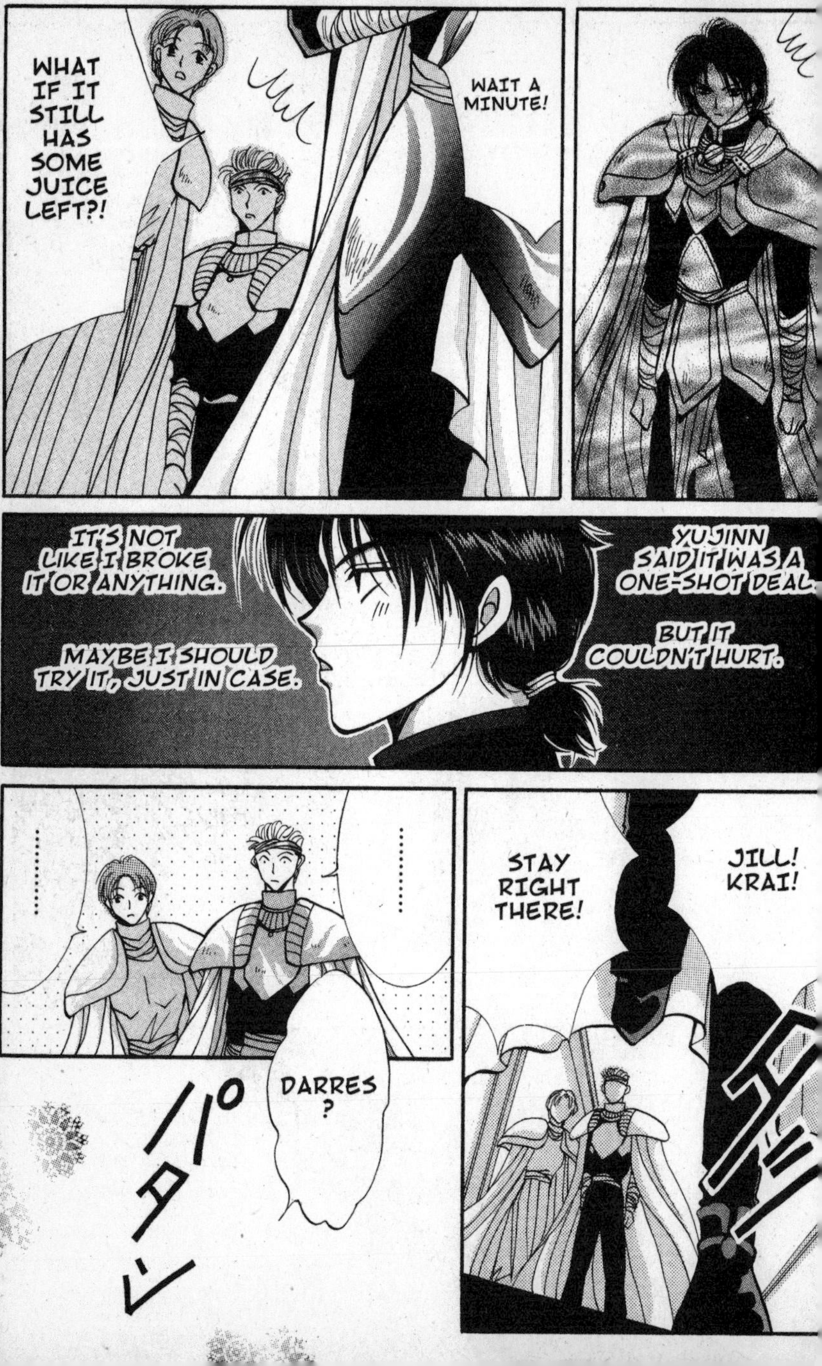
WAIT A MINUTE!
WHAT IF IT STILL HAS SOME JUICE LEFT?!
YU JINN SAID IT WAS A ONE-SHOT DEAL.
BUT IT COULDN'T HURT.
IT'S NOT LIKE I BROKE IT OR ANYTHING.
MAYBE I SHOULD TRY IT, JUST IN CASE.
JILL! KRAI!
STAY RIGHT THERE!
......
......
DARRES ?
パタン

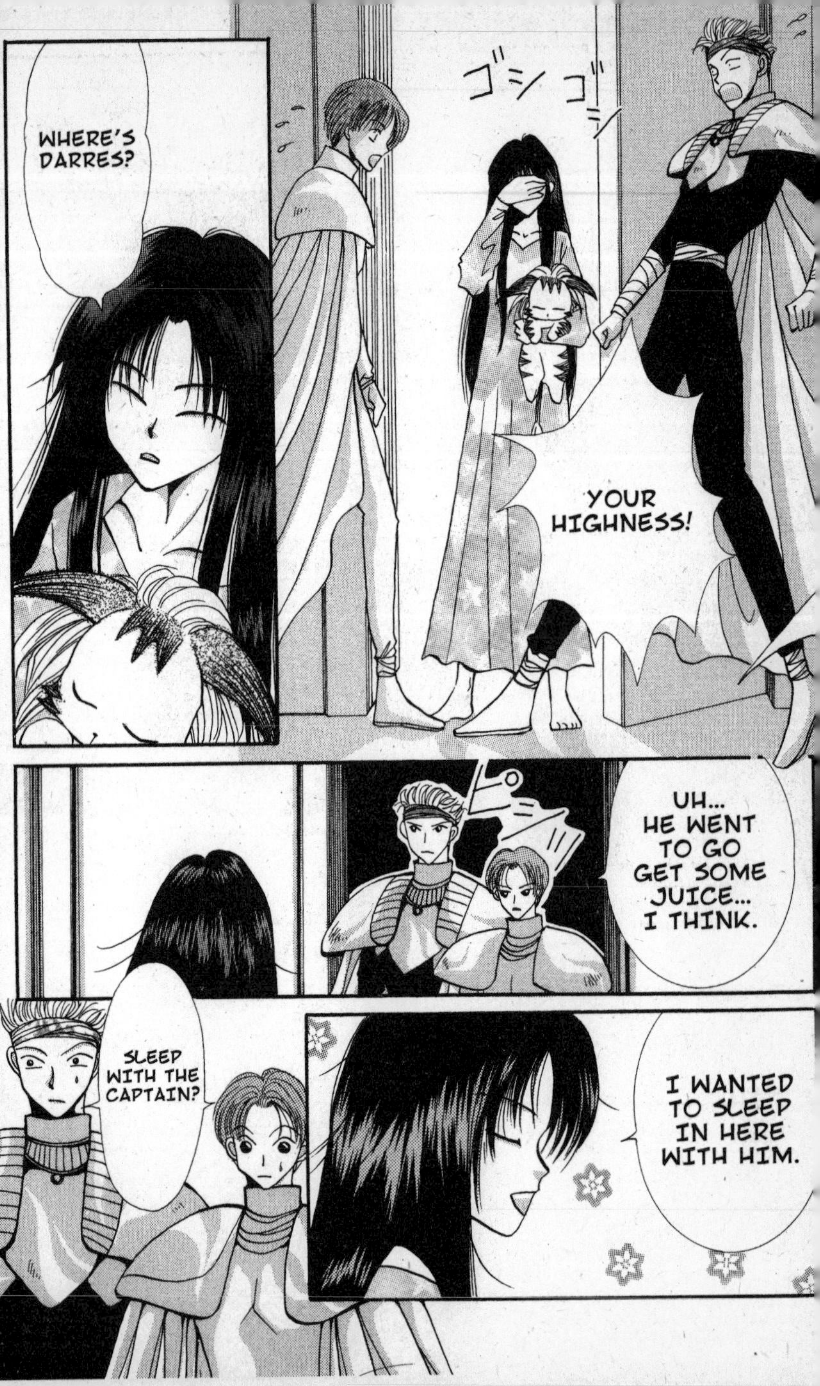
ゴシゴシ
YOUR HIGHNESS!
WHERE'S DARRES?
UH... HE WENT TO GO GET SOME JUICE... I THINK.
I WANTED TO SLEEP IN HERE WITH HIM.
SLEEP WITH THE CAPTAIN?

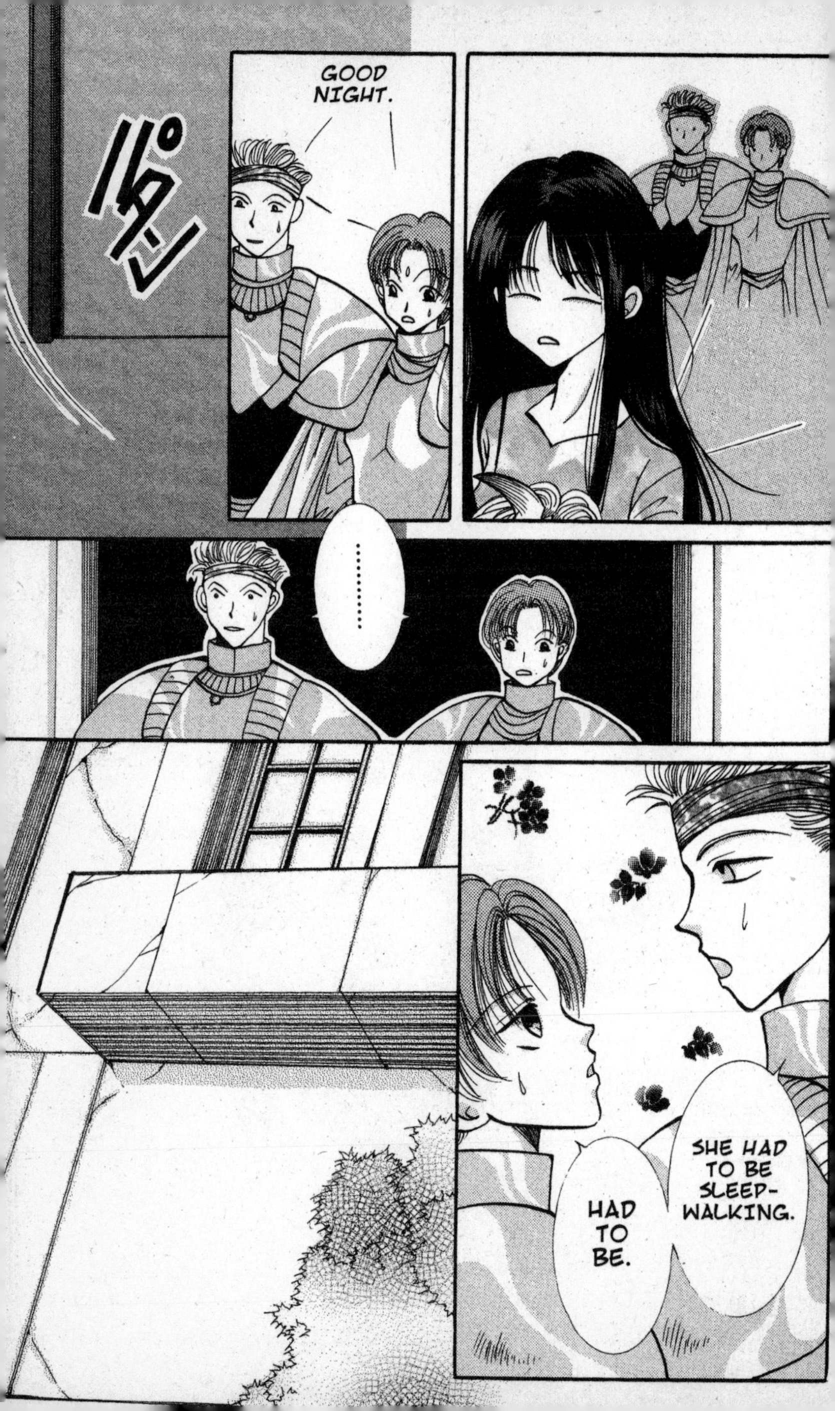
GOOD NIGHT.
パタン
......
SHE HAD TO BE SLEEP-WALKING.
HAD TO BE.

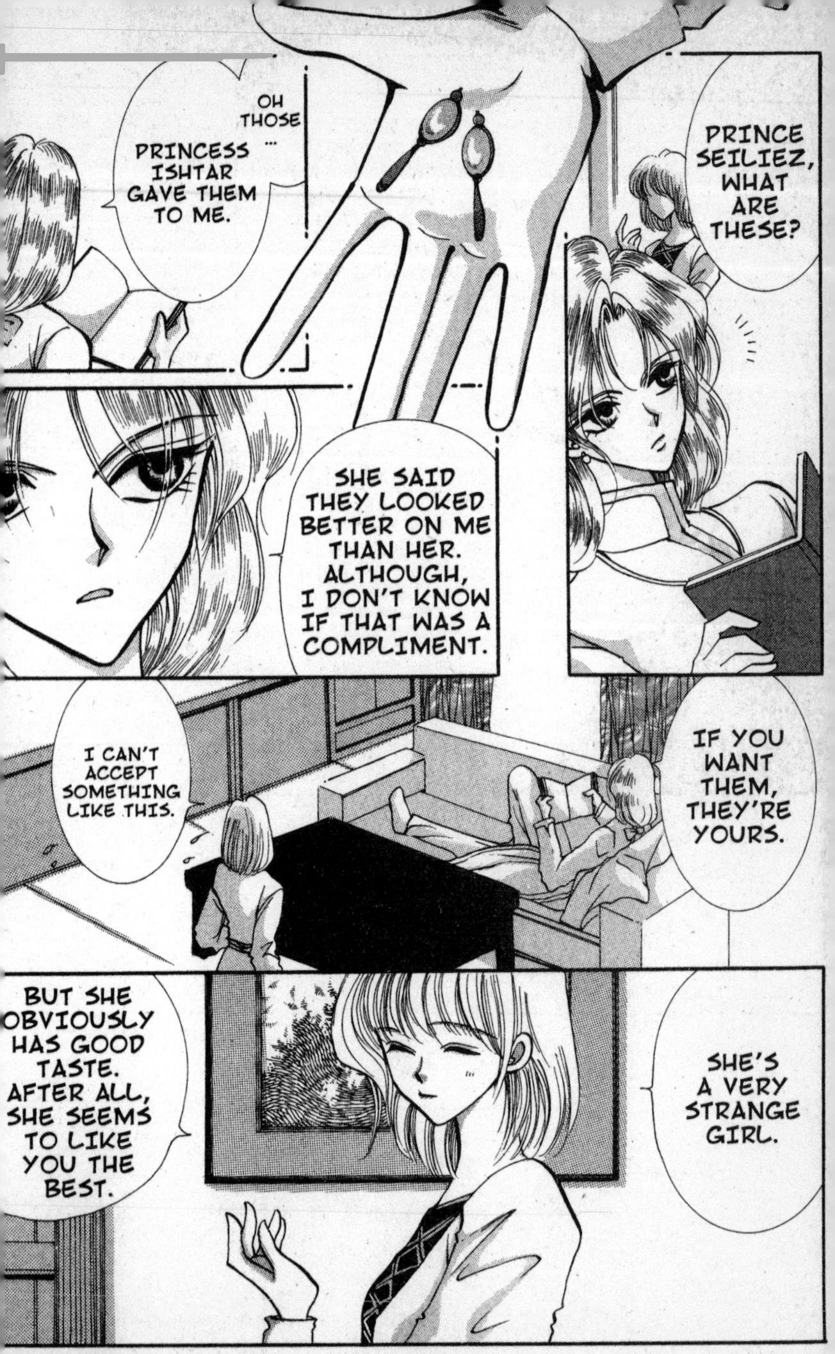
PRINCE SEILIEZ, WHAT ARE THESE?
OH THOSE ...
PRINCESS ISHTAR GAVE THEM TO ME.
SHE SAID THEY LOOKED BETTER ON ME THAN HER. ALTHOUGH, I DON'T KNOW IF THAT WAS A COMPLIMENT.
IF YOU WANT THEM, THEY'RE YOURS.
I CAN'T ACCEPT SOMETHING LIKE THIS.
SHE'S A VERY STRANGE GIRL.
BUT SHE OBVIOUSLY HAS GOOD TASTE. AFTER ALL, SHE SEEMS TO LIKE YOU THE BEST.

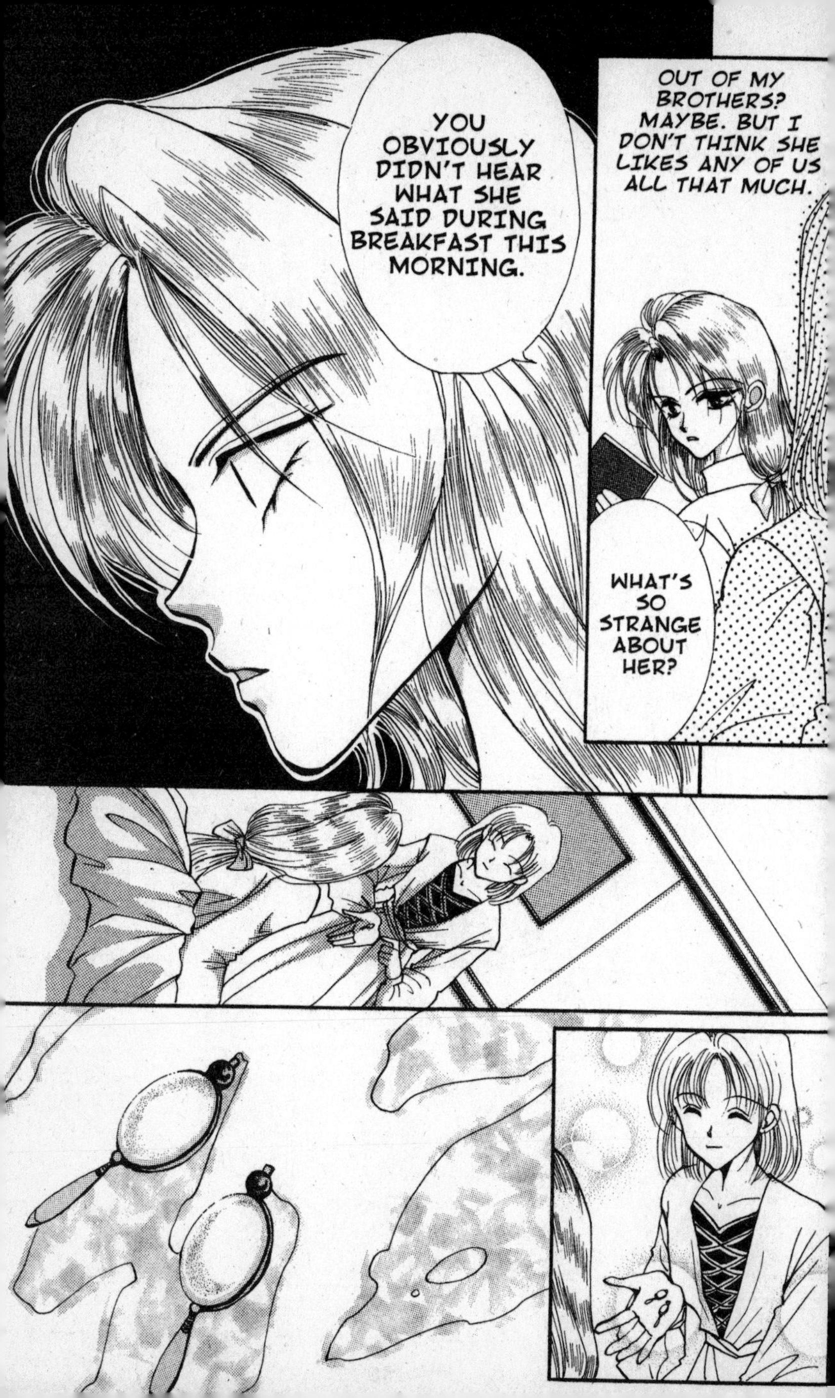
OUT OF MY BROTHERS? MAYBE. BUT I DON'T THINK SHE LIKES ANY OF US ALL THAT MUCH.
WHAT'S SO STRANGE ABOUT HER?
YOU OBVIOUSLY DIDN'T HEAR WHAT SHE SAID DURING BREAKFAST THIS MORNING.

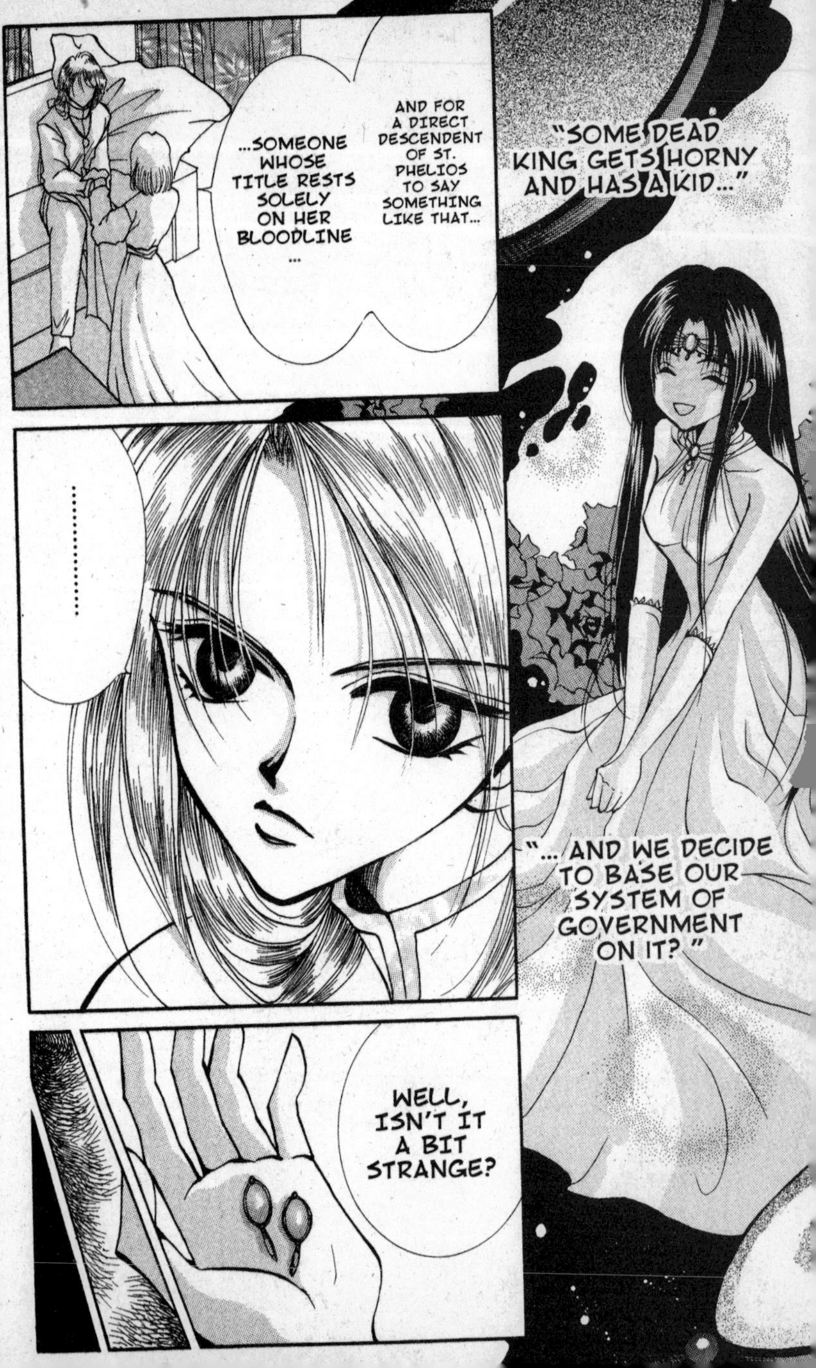
"SOME DEAD KING GETS HORNY AND HAS A KID..."
"... AND WE DECIDE TO BASE OUR SYSTEM OF GOVERNMENT ON IT?"
AND FOR A DIRECT DESCENDENT OF ST. PHELIOS TO SAY SOMETHING LIKE THAT...
...SOMEONE WHOSE TITLE RESTS SOLELY ON HER BLOODLINE ...
....
WELL, ISN'T IT A BIT STRANGE?

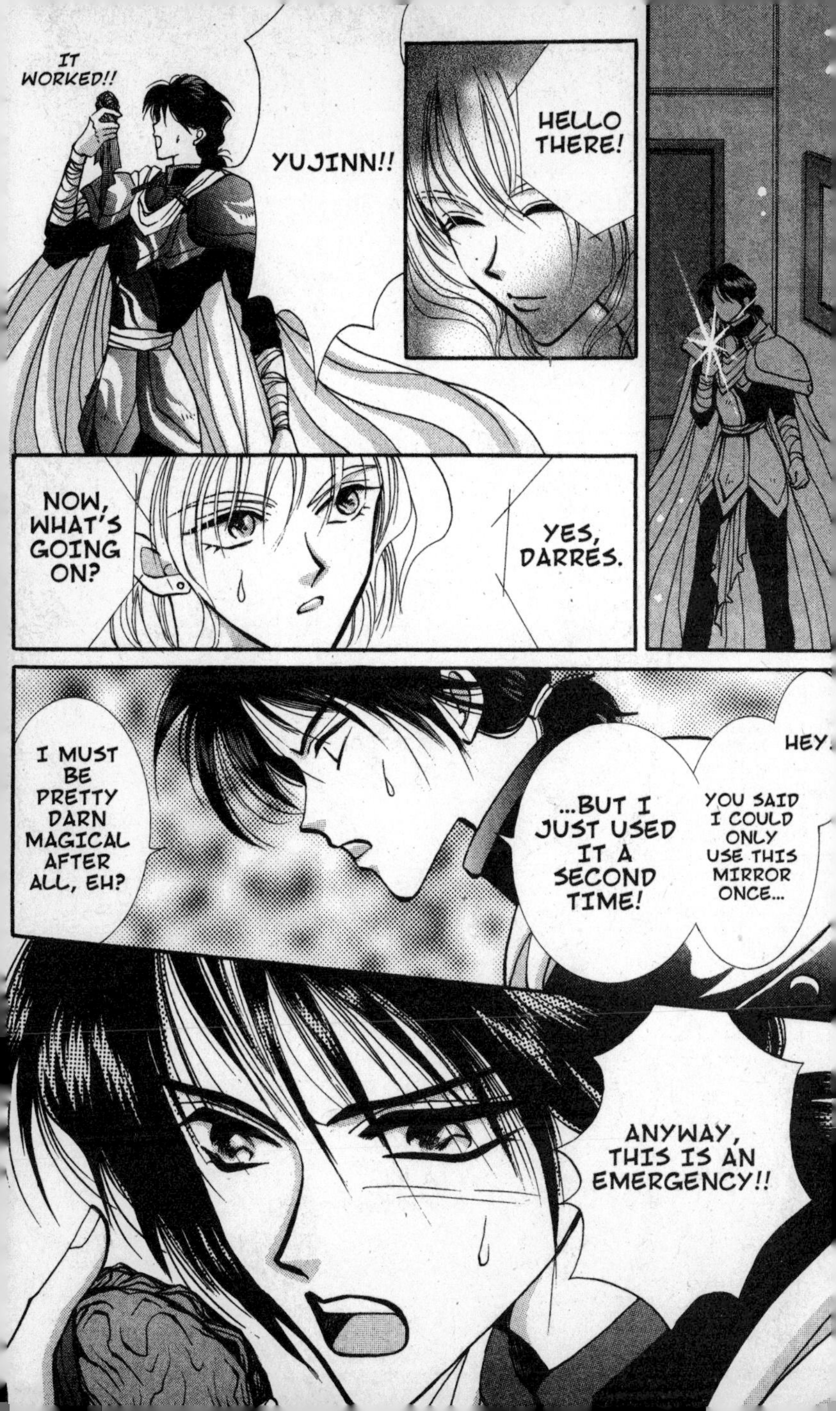
IT WORKED!!
YUJINN!!
HELLO THERE!
YES, DARRES.
NOW, WHAT'S GOING ON?
HEY.
YOU SAID I COULD ONLY USE THIS MIRROR ONCE...
...BUT I JUST USED IT A SECOND TIME!
I MUST BE PRETTY DARN MAGICAL AFTER ALL, EH?
ANYWAY, THIS IS AN EMERGENCY!!

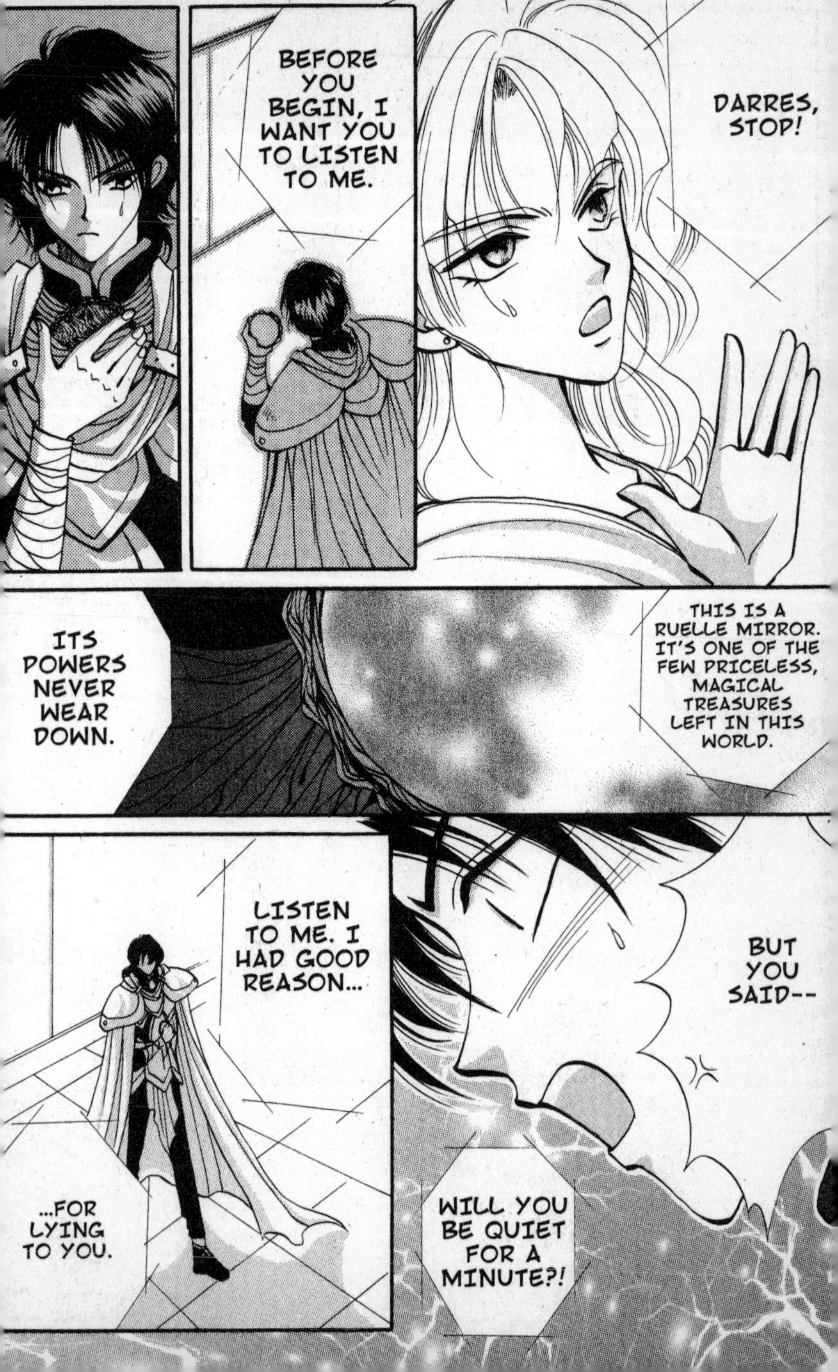
DARRES, STOP!
BEFORE YOU BEGIN, I WANT YOU TO LISTEN TO ME.
THIS IS A RUELLE MIRROR. IT'S ONE OF THE FEW PRICELESS, MAGICAL TREASURES LEFT IN THIS WORLD.
ITS POWERS NEVER WEAR DOWN.
BUT YOU SAID--
WILL YOU BE QUIET FOR A MINUTE?!
LISTEN TO ME. I HAD GOOD REASON...
...FOR LYING TO YOU.

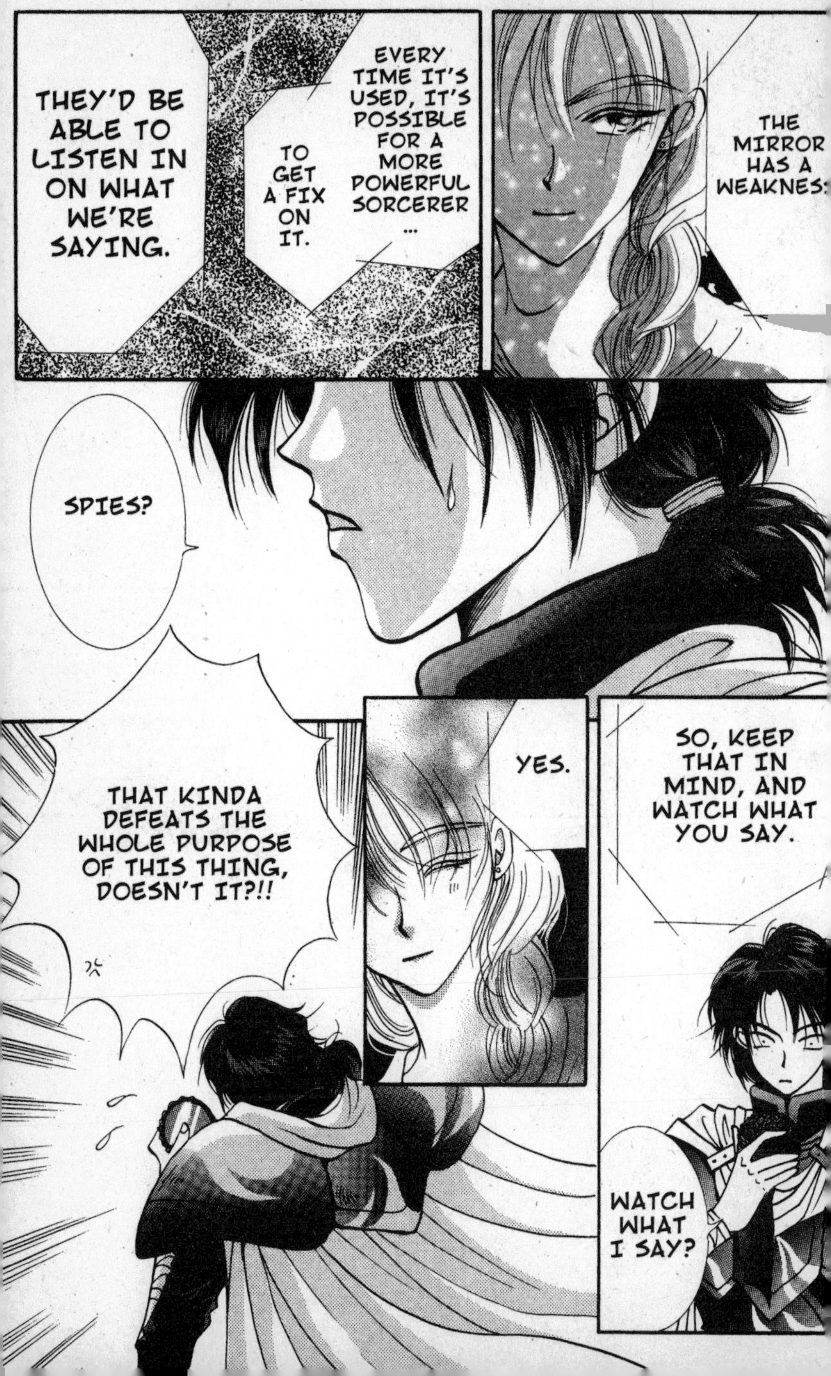
THE MIRROR HAS A WEAKNES:
EVERY TIME IT'S USED, IT'S POSSIBLE FOR A MORE POWERFUL SORCERER ...
TO GET A FIX ON IT.
THEY'D BE ABLE TO LISTEN IN ON WHAT WE'RE SAYING.
SPIES?
THAT KINDA DEFEATS THE WHOLE PURPOSE OF THIS THING, DOESN'T IT?!!
YES.
SO, KEEP THAT IN MIND, AND WATCH WHAT YOU SAY.
WATCH WHAT I SAY?

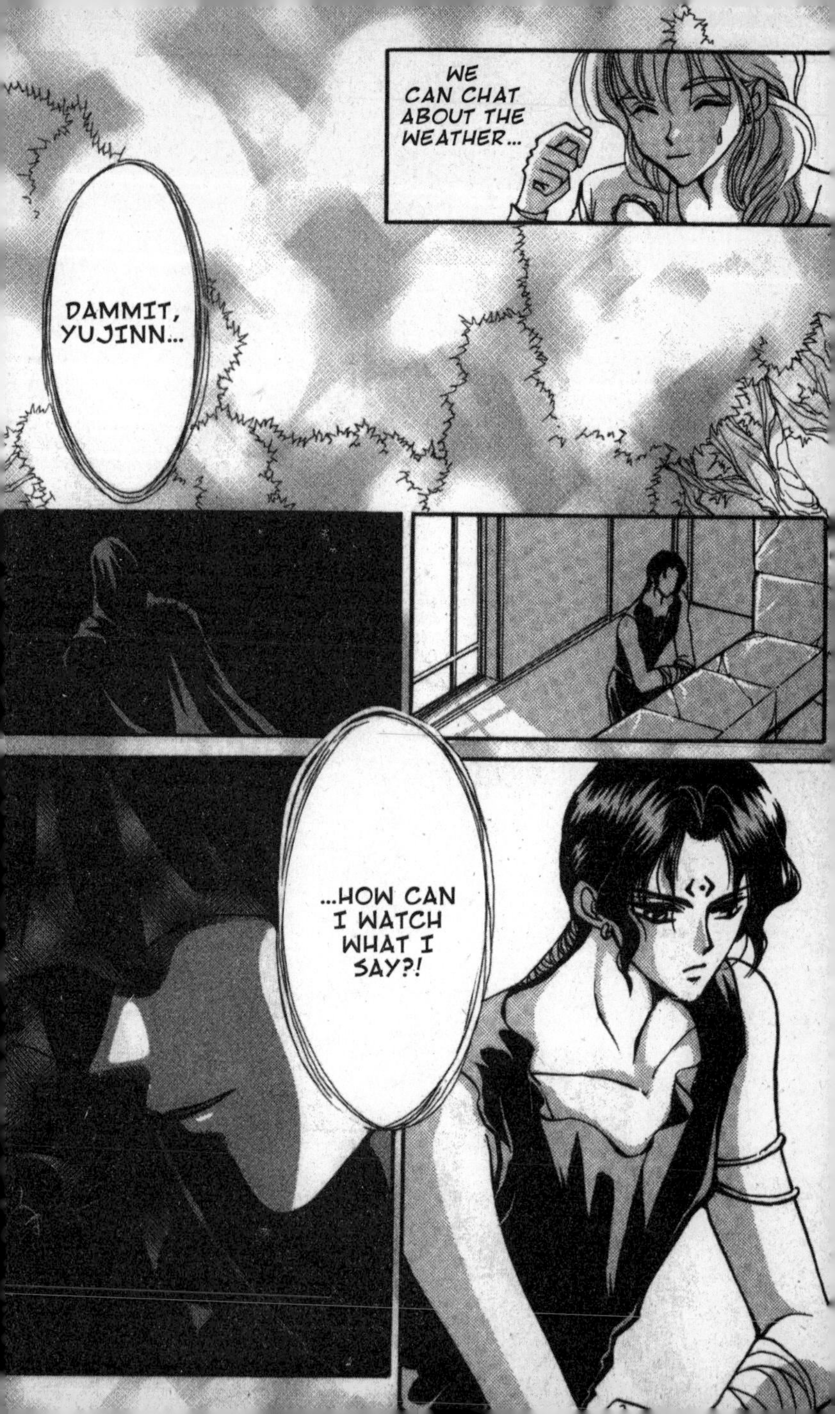
WE CAN CHAT ABOUT THE WEATHER...
DAMMIT, YUJINN...
...HOW CAN I WATCH WHAT I SAY?!

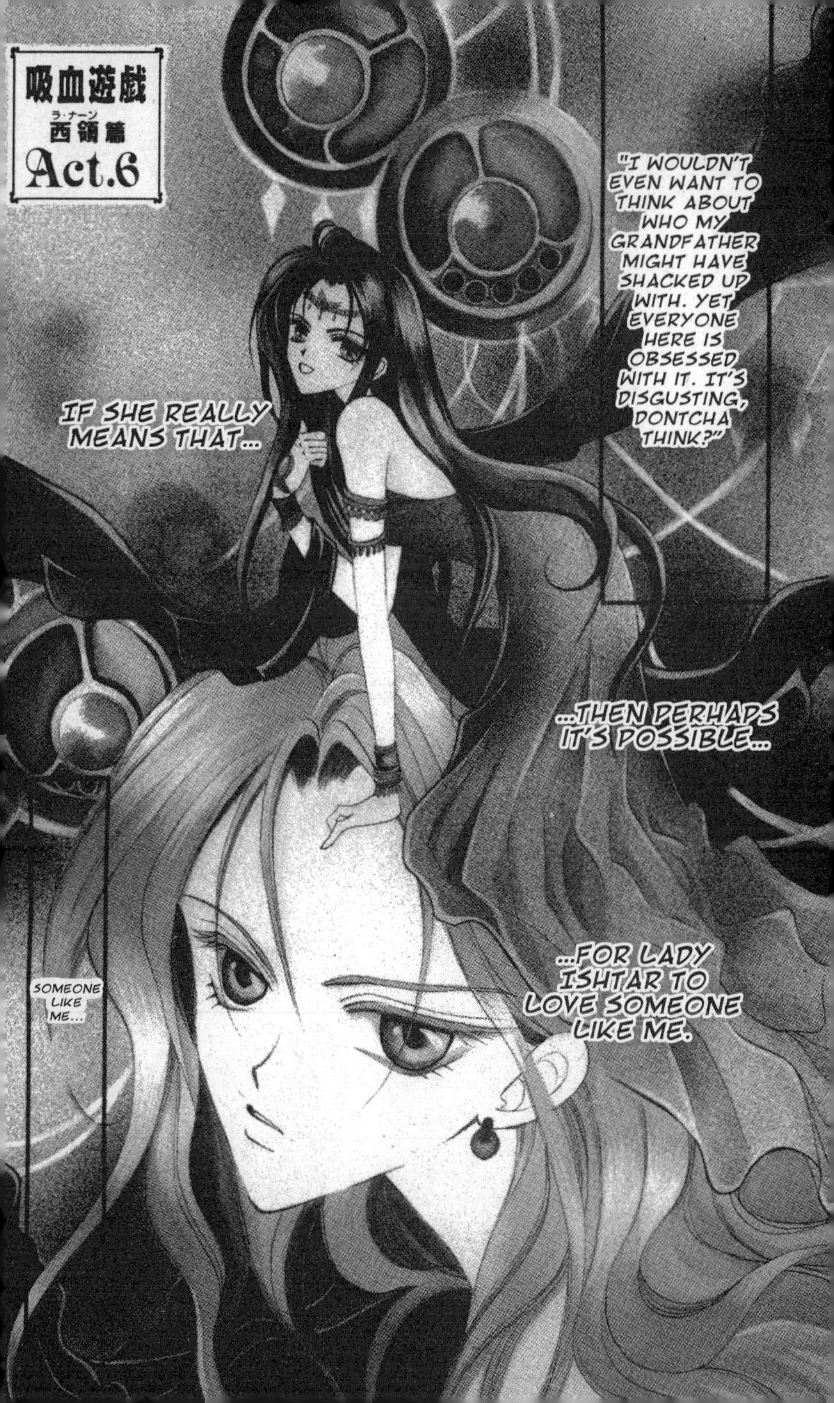
吸血遊戯
ラ・ナーン
西領篇
Act.6
"I WOULDN'T EVEN WANT TO THINK ABOUT WHO MY GRANDFATHER MIGHT HAVE SHACKED UP WITH. YET EVERYONE HERE IS OBSESSED WITH IT. IT'S DISGUSTING, DONTCHA THINK?"
IF SHE REALLY MEANS THAT...
...THEN PERHAPS IT'S POSSIBLE...
...FOR LADY ISHTAR TO LOVE SOMEONE LIKE ME.
SOMEONE LIKE ME...

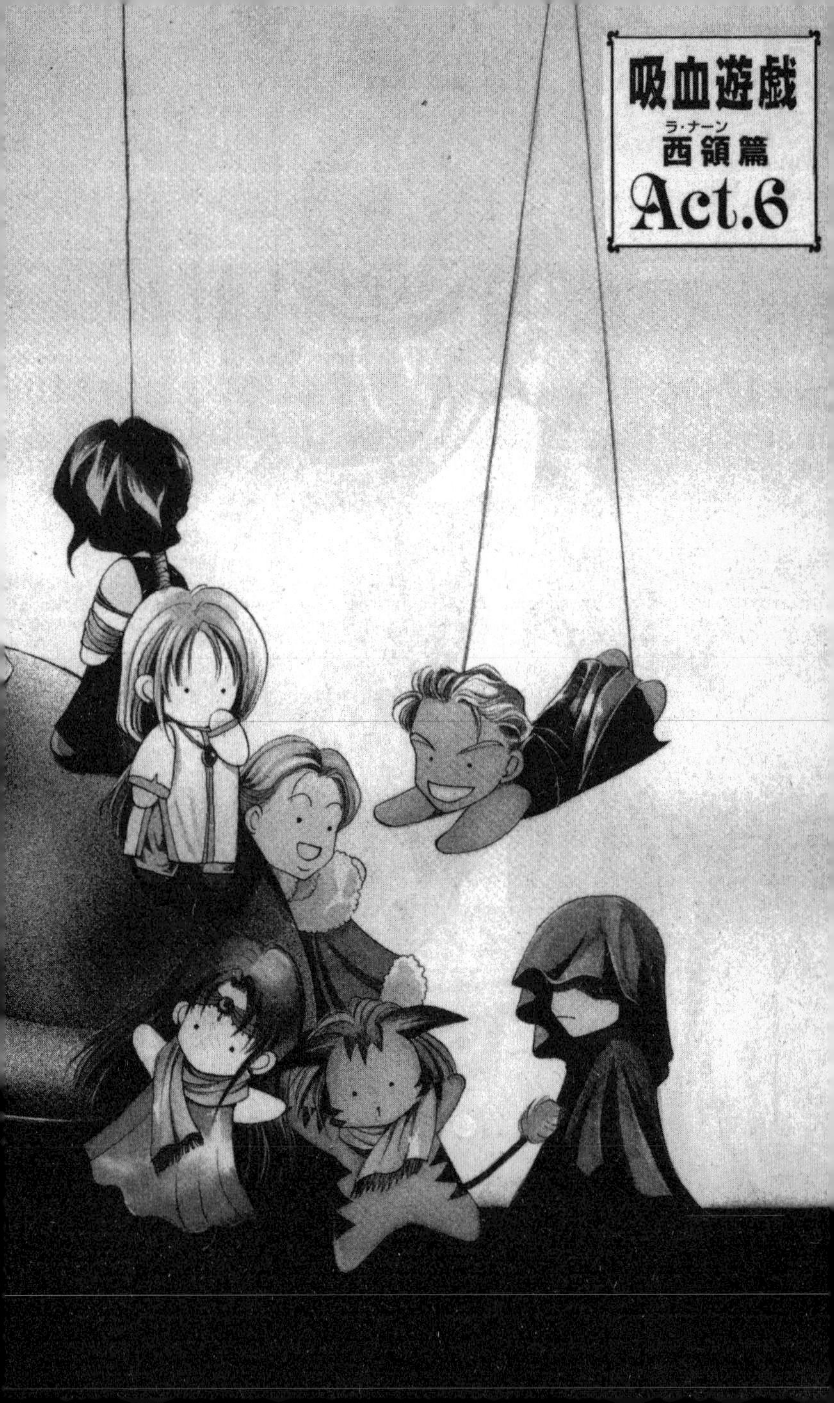
吸血遊戯
ラ・ナーン
西領篇
Act.6

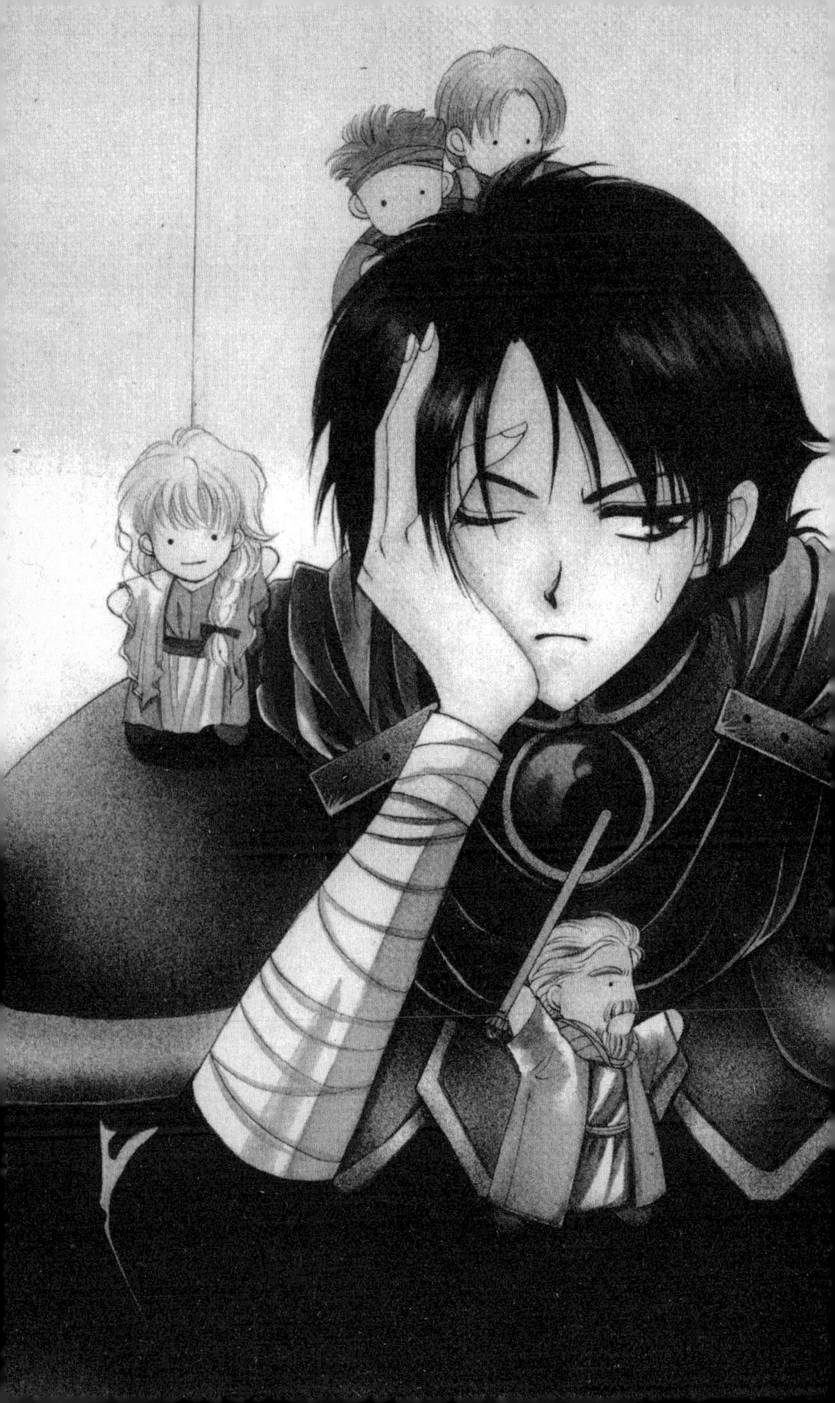

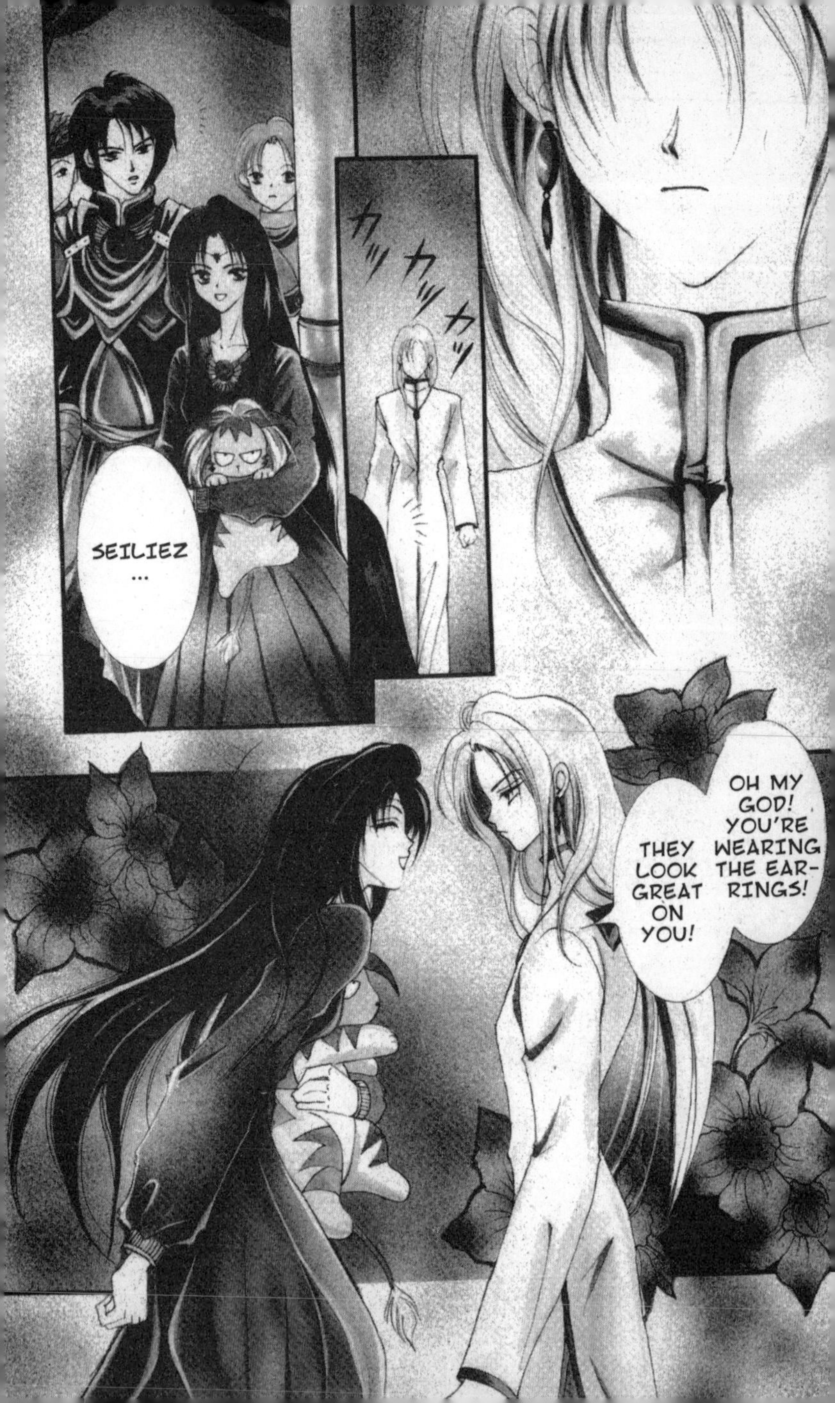
カッ カッ カッ
SEILIEZ ...
OH MY GOD! YOU'RE WEARING THE EAR-RINGS!
THEY LOOK GREAT ON YOU!

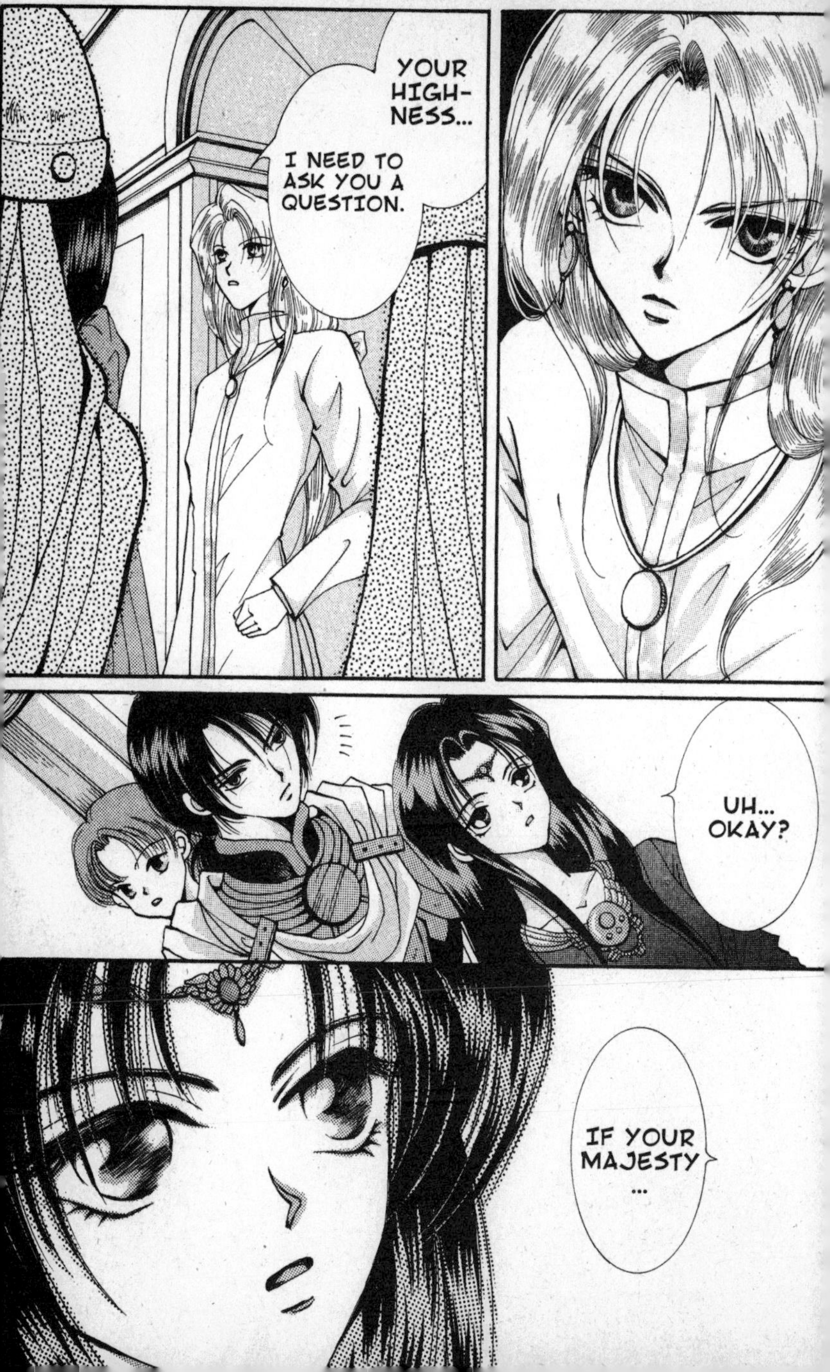
YOUR HIGH-NESS...
I NEED TO ASK YOU A QUESTION.
UH... OKAY?
IF YOUR MAJESTY ...

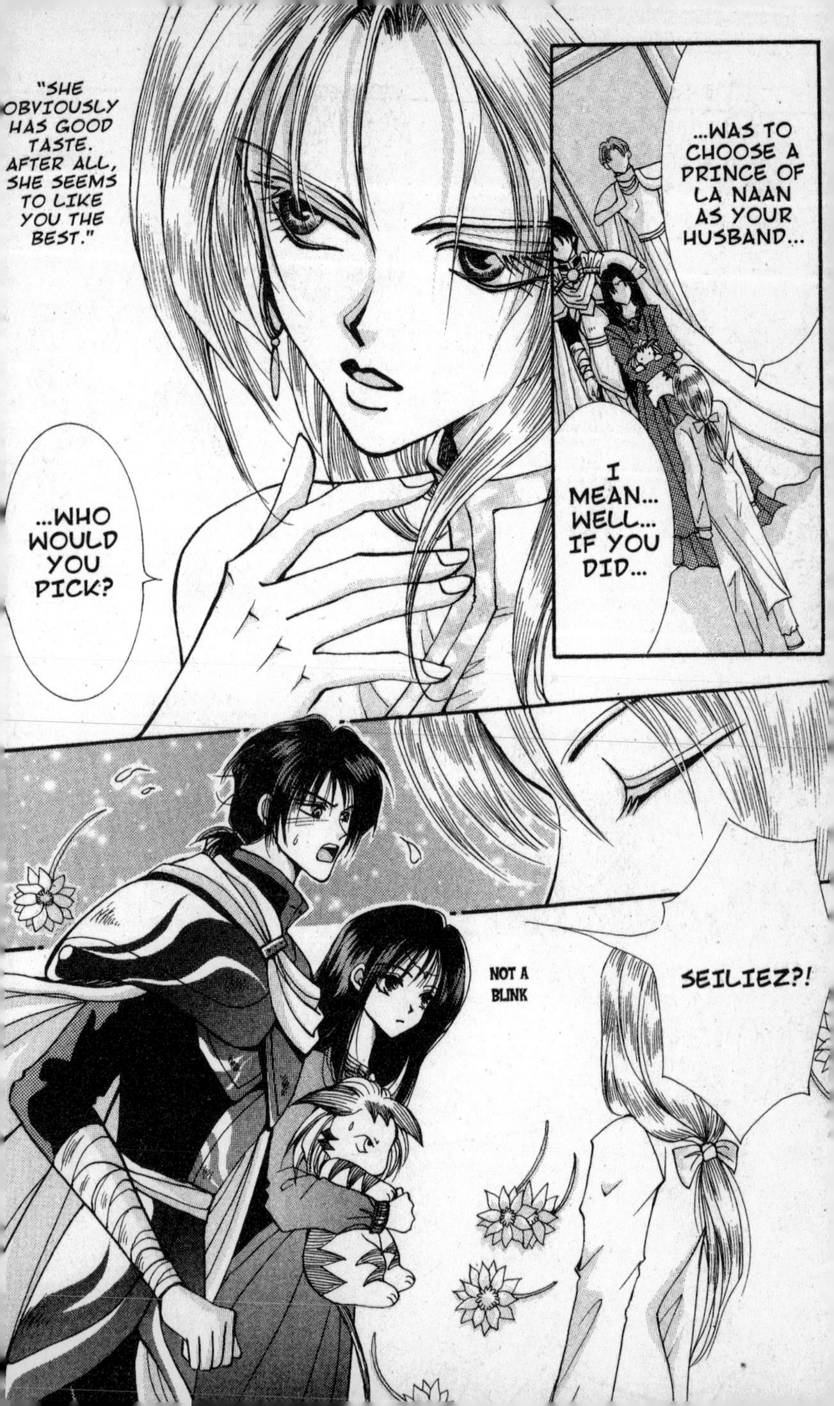
...WAS TO CHOOSE A PRINCE OF LA NAAN AS YOUR HUSBAND...
I MEAN... WELL... IF YOU DID...
"SHE OBVIOUSLY HAS GOOD TASTE. AFTER ALL, SHE SEEMS TO LIKE YOU THE BEST."
...WHO WOULD YOU PICK?
SEILIEZ?!
NOT A BLINK

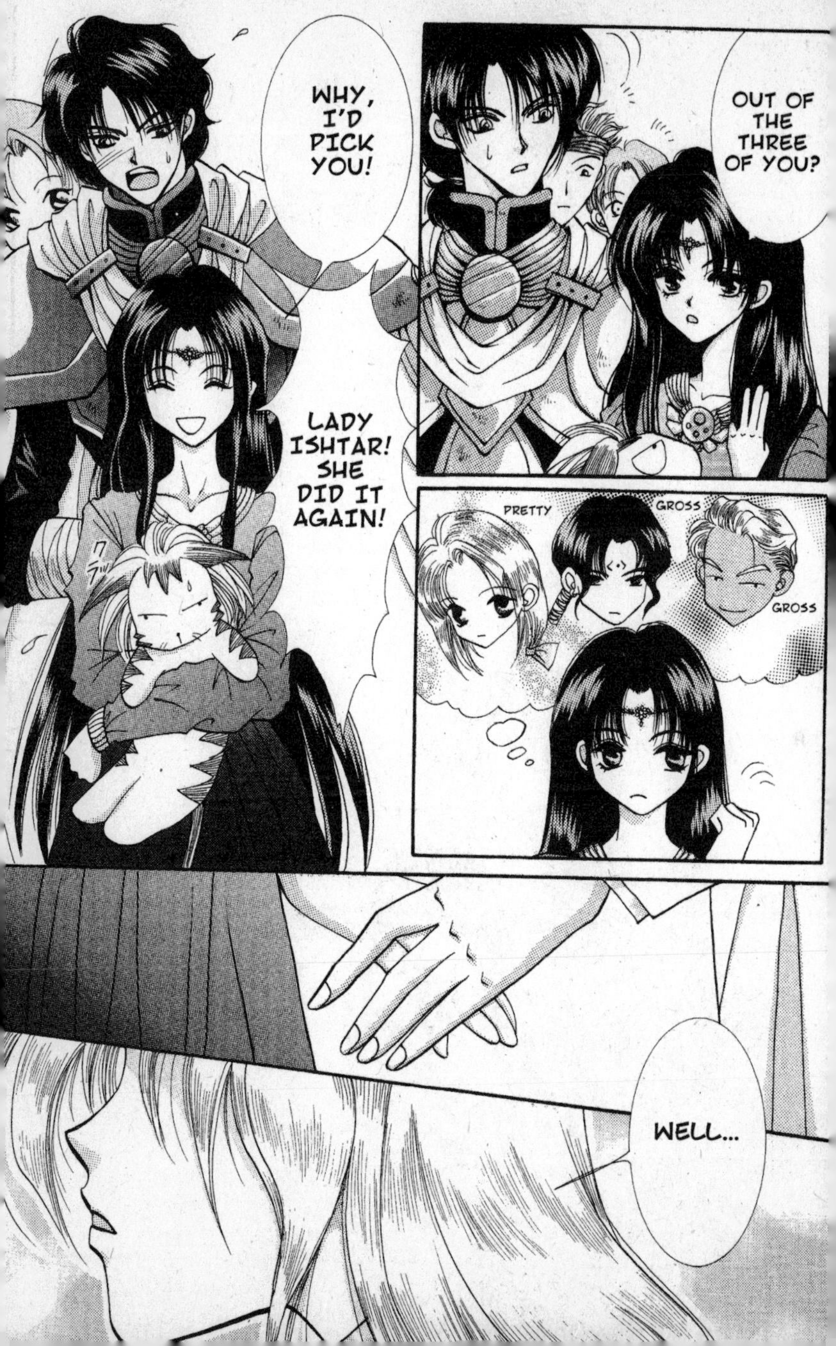
OUT OF THE THREE OF YOU?
GROSS
GROSS
PRETTY
WHY, I'D PICK YOU!
LADY ISHTAR! SHE DID IT AGAIN!
WELL...

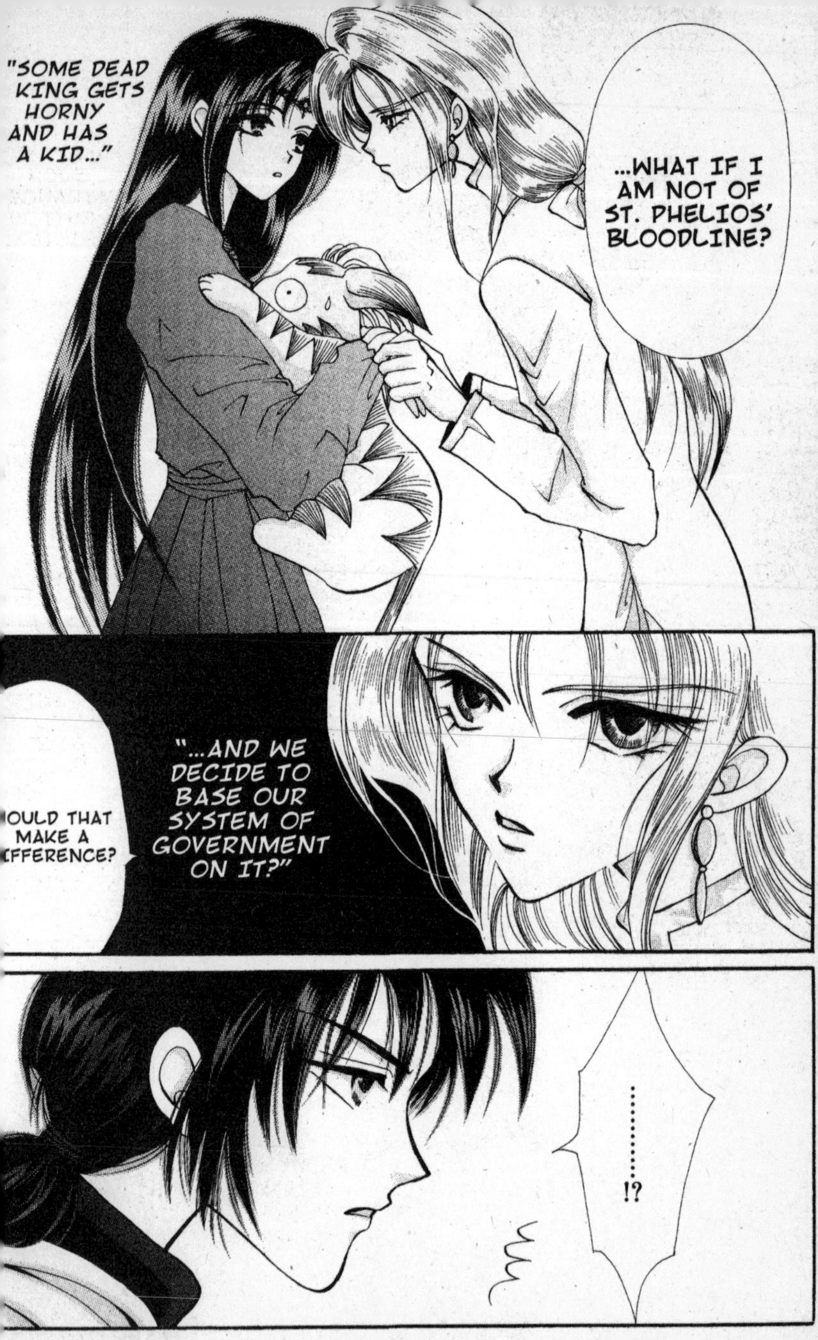
...WHAT IF I AM NOT OF ST. PHELIOS' BLOODLINE?
"SOME DEAD KING GETS HORNY AND HAS A KID..."
"...AND WE DECIDE TO BASE OUR SYSTEM OF GOVERNMENT ON IT?"
OULD THAT MAKE A FFERENCE?
......!?

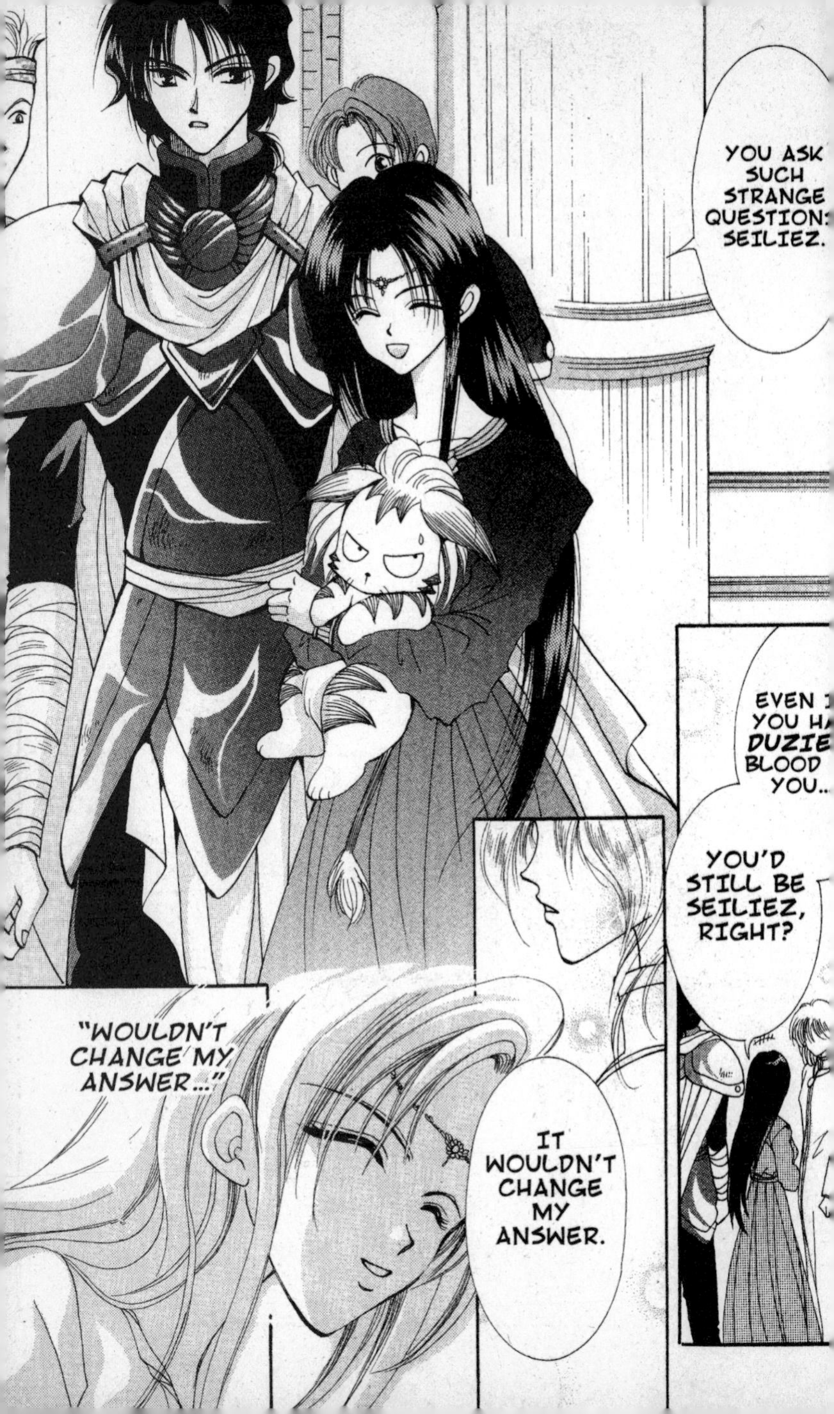
YOU ASK SUCH STRANGE QUESTION SEILIEZ.
EVEN I YOU HA DUZIE BLOOD YOU...
YOU'D STILL BE SEILIEZ, RIGHT?
IT WOULDN'T CHANGE MY ANSWER.
"WOULDN'T CHANGE MY ANSWER..."

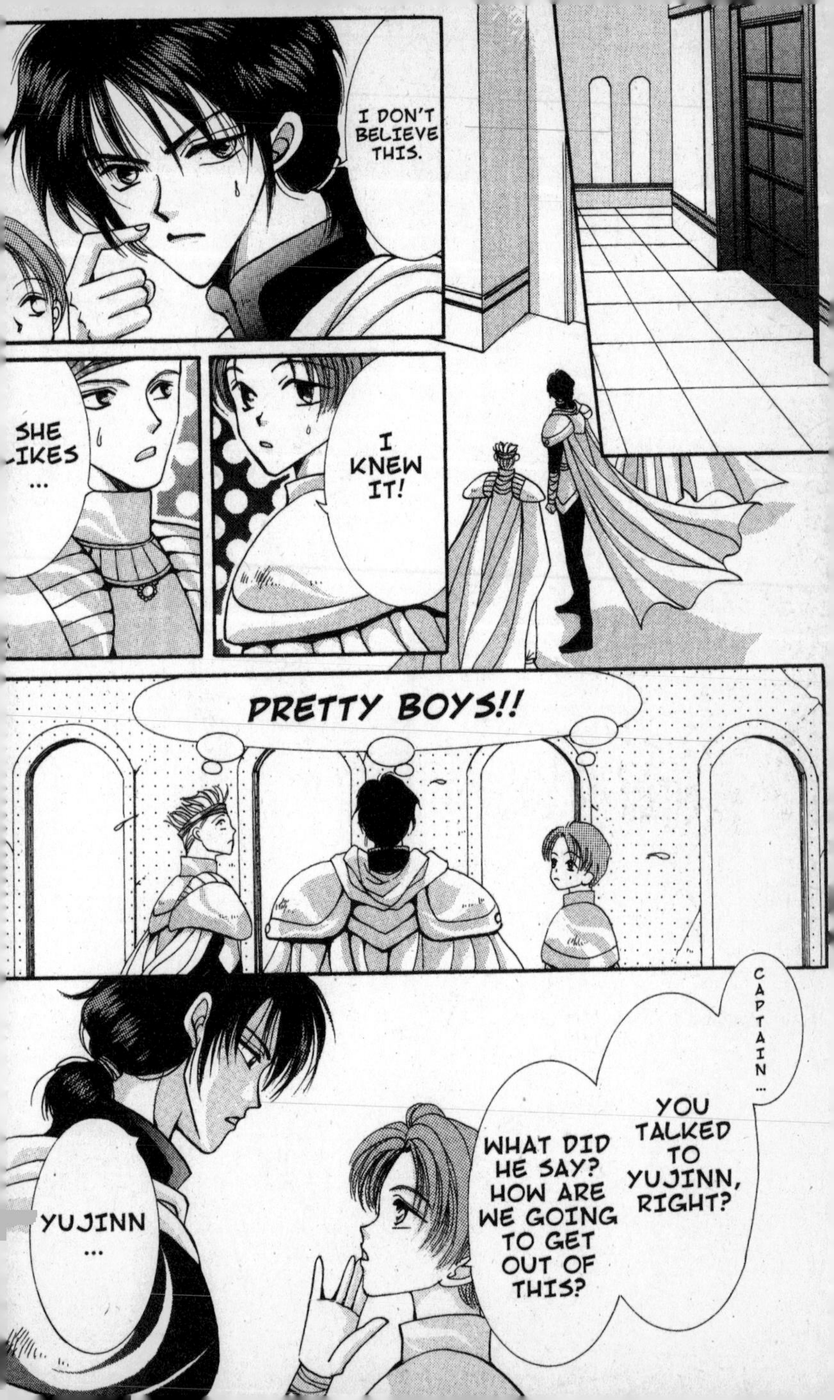
I DON'T BELIEVE THIS.
I KNEW IT!
SHE LIKES ...
PRETTY BOYS!!
CAPTAIN ...
YOU TALKED TO YUJINN, RIGHT?
WHAT DID HE SAY? HOW ARE WE GOING TO GET OUT OF THIS?
YUJINN ...

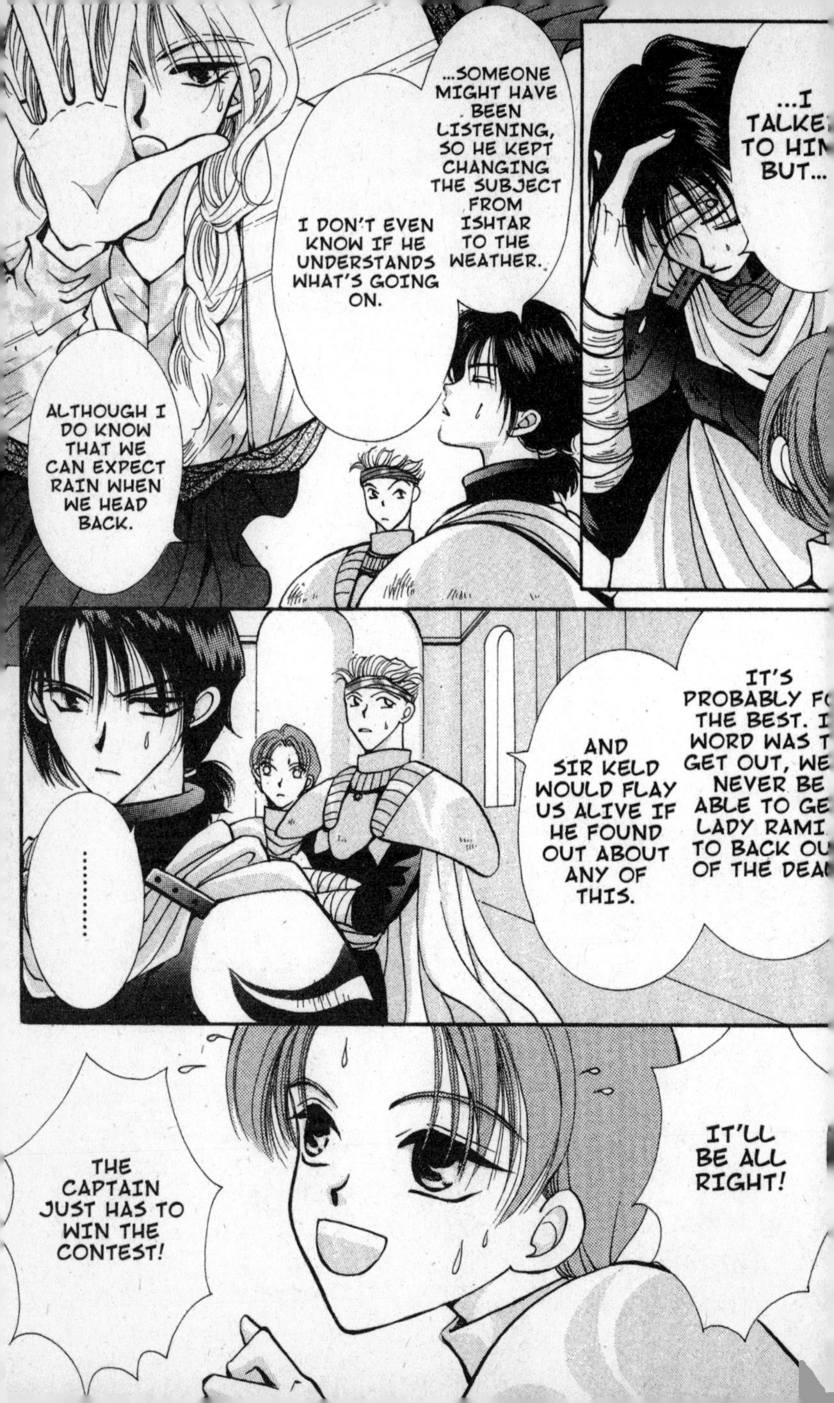

...I TALKE TO HIM BUT...
...SOMEONE MIGHT HAVE BEEN LISTENING, SO HE KEPT CHANGING THE SUBJECT FROM ISHTAR TO THE WEATHER.
I DON'T EVEN KNOW IF HE UNDERSTANDS WHAT'S GOING ON.
ALTHOUGH I DO KNOW THAT WE CAN EXPECT RAIN WHEN WE HEAD BACK.
IT'S PROBABLY F THE BEST. I WORD WAS T GET OUT, WE NEVER BE ABLE TO GE LADY RAMI TO BACK OU OF THE DEA
AND SIR KELD WOULD FLAY US ALIVE IF HE FOUND OUT ABOUT ANY OF THIS.
......
IT'LL BE ALL RIGHT!
THE CAPTAIN JUST HAS TO WIN THE CONTEST!

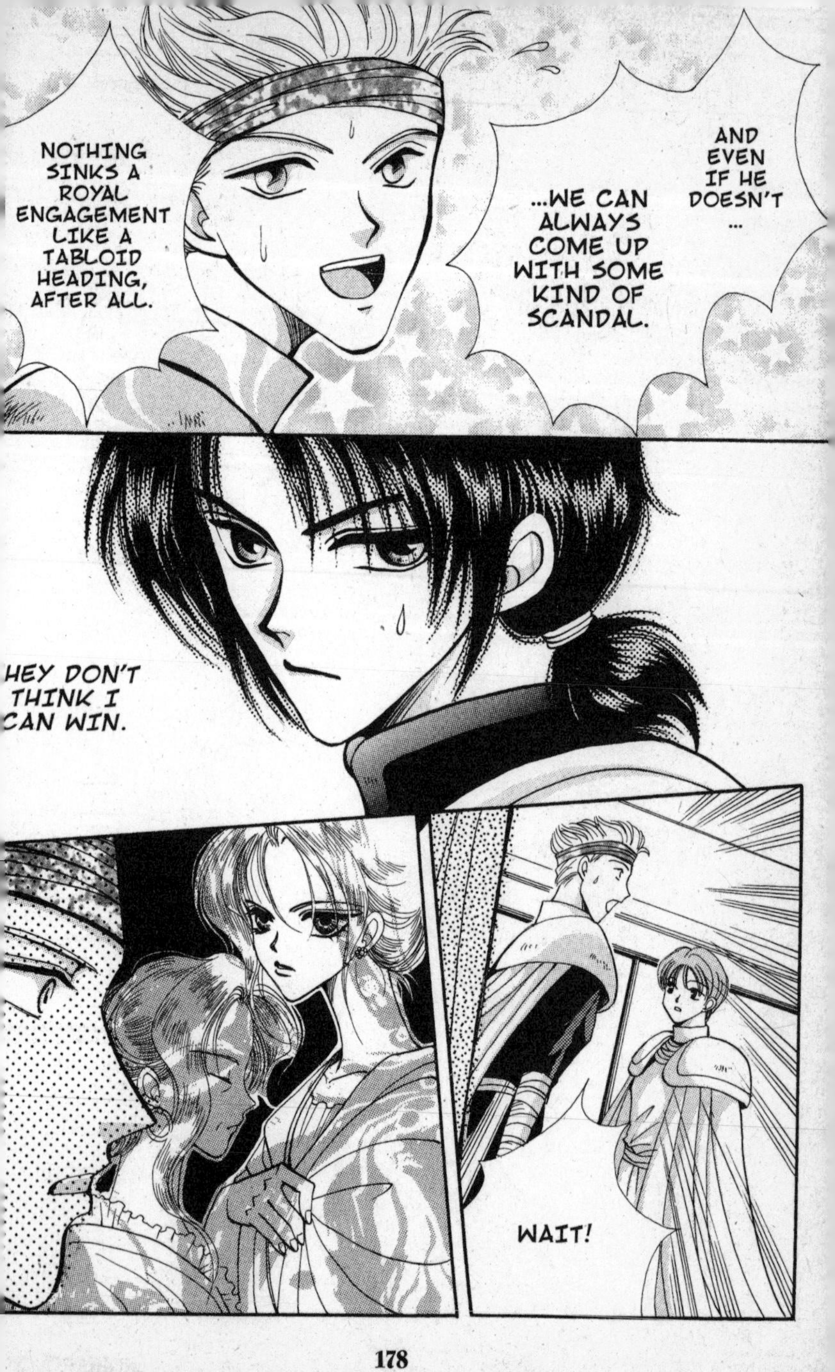
AND EVEN IF HE DOESN'T ...
...WE CAN ALWAYS COME UP WITH SOME KIND OF SCANDAL.
NOTHING SINKS A ROYAL ENGAGEMENT LIKE A TABLOID HEADING, AFTER ALL.
HEY DON'T THINK I CAN WIN.
WAIT!

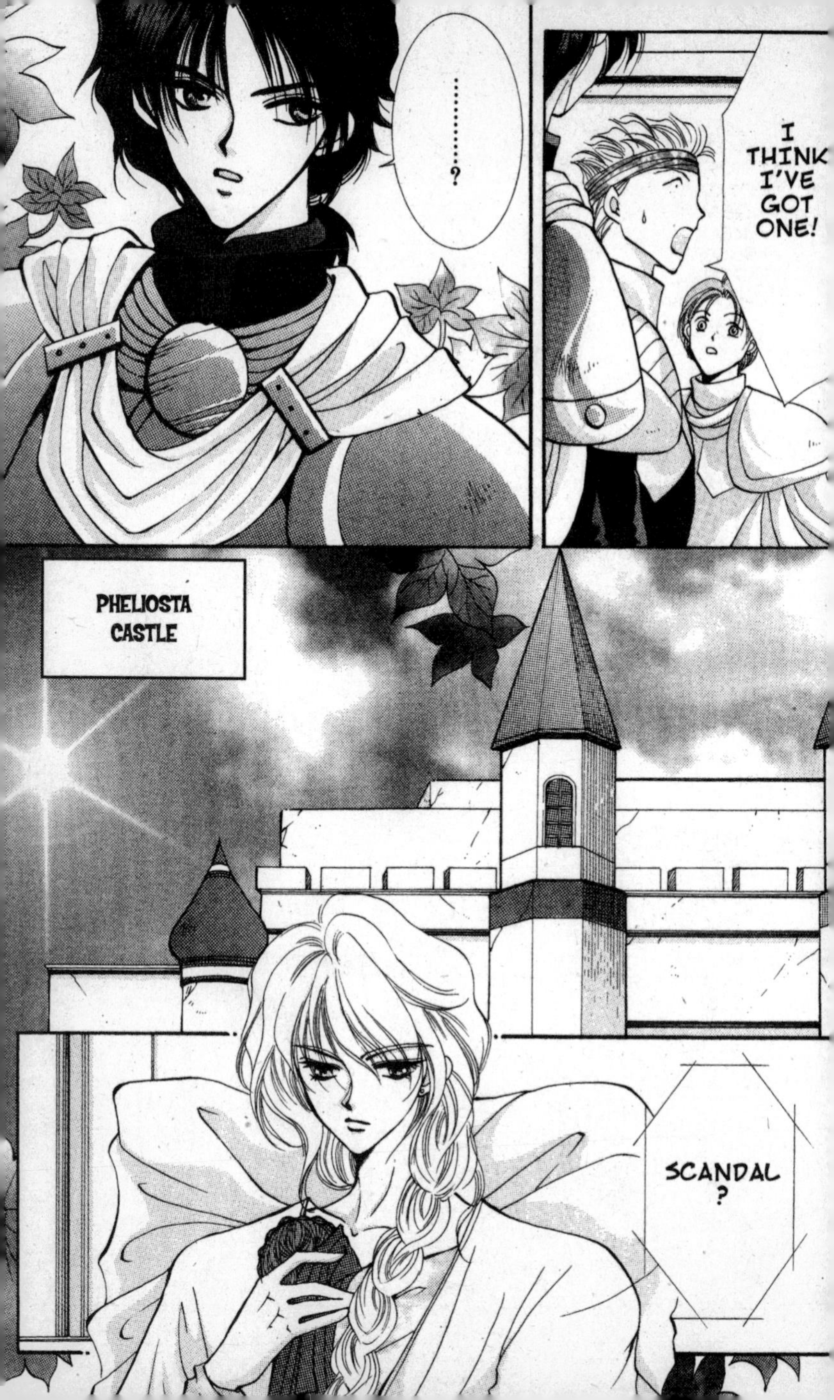
I THINK I'VE GOT ONE!
......?
PHELIOSTA CASTLE
SCANDAL ?

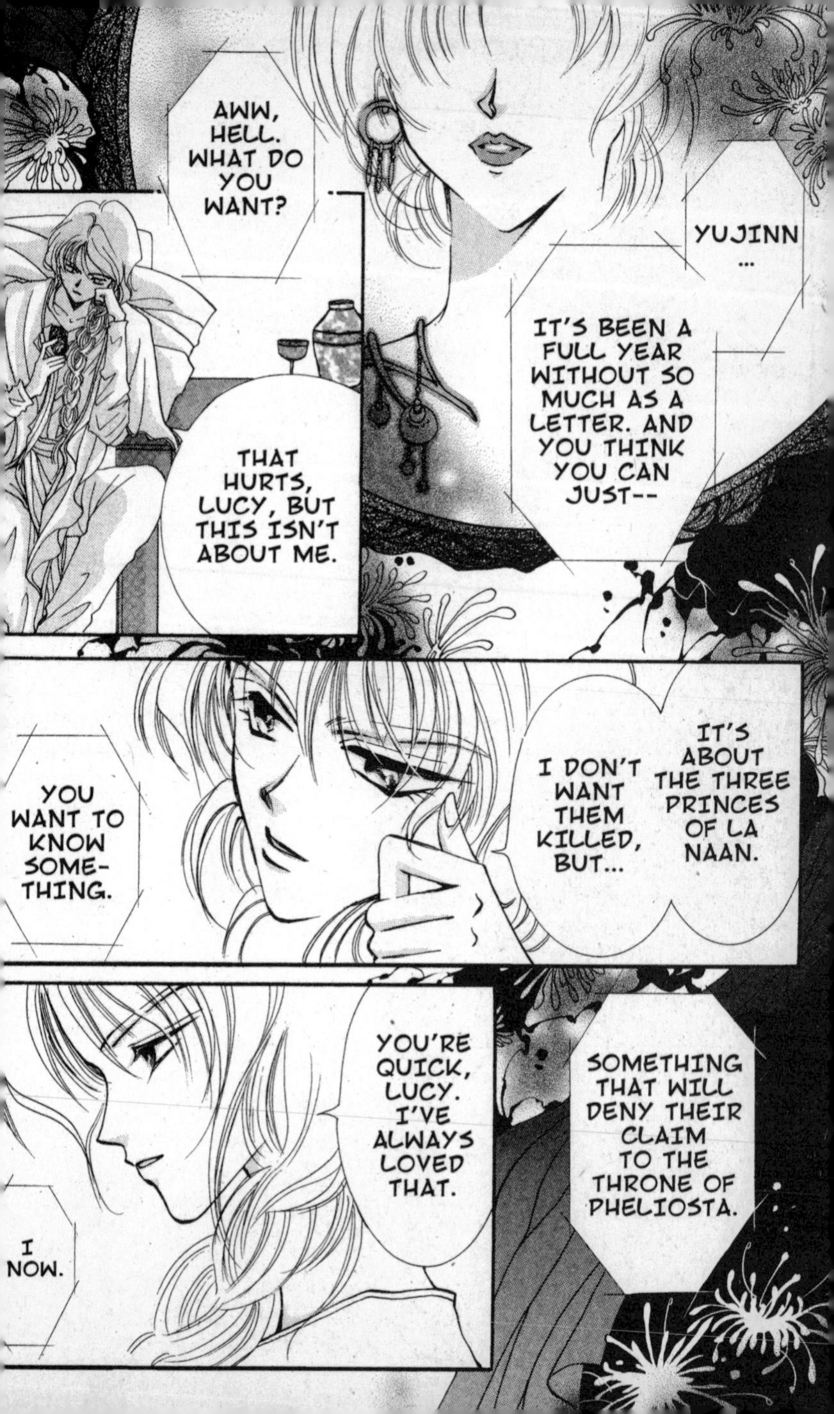
YUJINN ...
IT'S BEEN A FULL YEAR WITHOUT SO MUCH AS A LETTER. AND YOU THINK YOU CAN JUST--
AWW, HELL. WHAT DO YOU WANT?
THAT HURTS, LUCY, BUT THIS ISN'T ABOUT ME.
IT'S ABOUT THE THREE PRINCES OF LA NAAN.
I DON'T WANT THEM KILLED, BUT...
YOU WANT TO KNOW SOME-THING.
SOMETHING THAT WILL DENY THEIR CLAIM TO THE THRONE OF PHELIOSTA.
YOU'RE QUICK, LUCY. I'VE ALWAYS LOVED THAT.
I NOW.

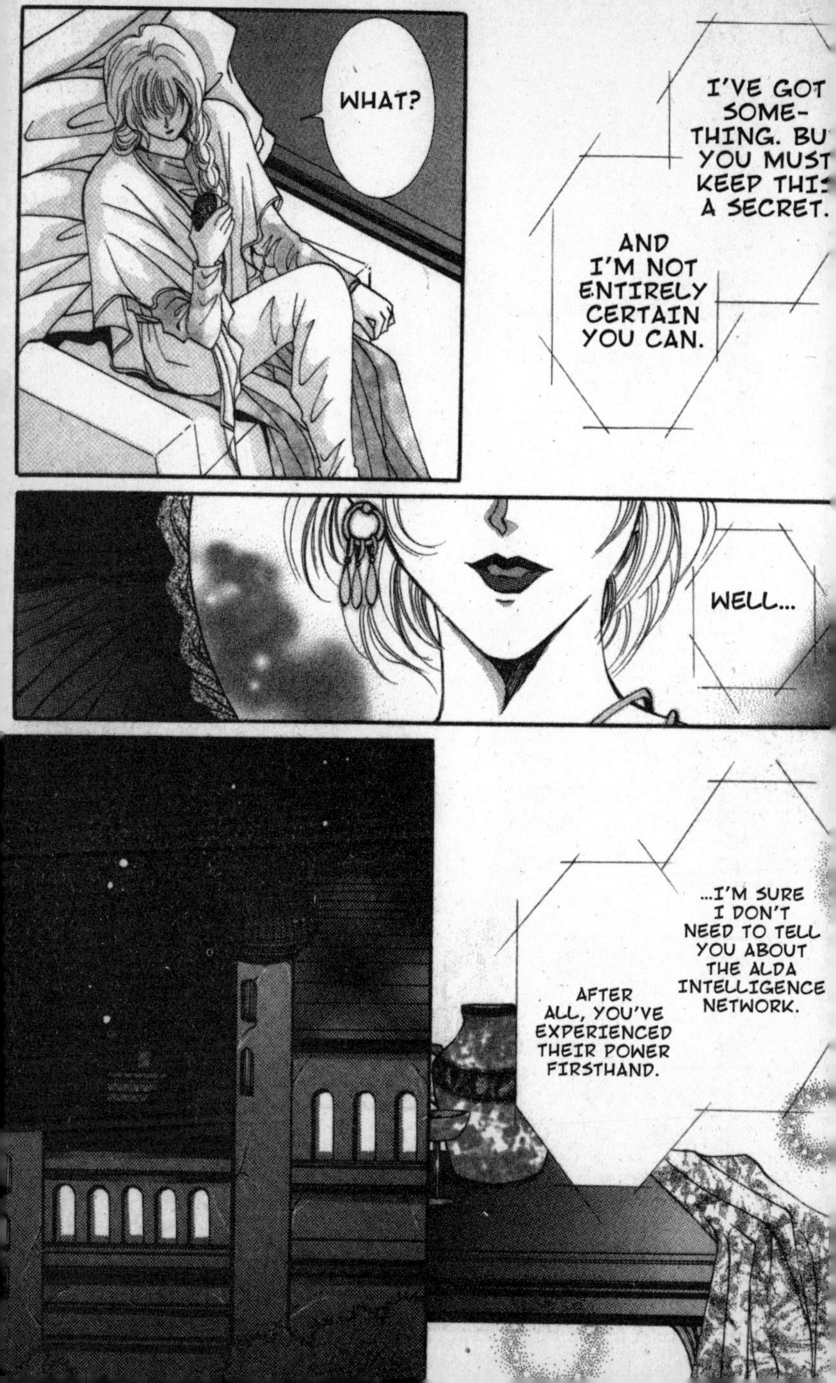
I'VE GOT SOMETHING. BUT YOU MUST KEEP THIS A SECRET.
AND I'M NOT ENTIRELY CERTAIN YOU CAN.
WHAT?
WELL...
...I'M SURE I DON'T NEED TO TELL YOU ABOUT THE ALDA INTELLIGENCE NETWORK.
AFTER ALL, YOU'VE EXPERIENCED THEIR POWER FIRSTHAND.

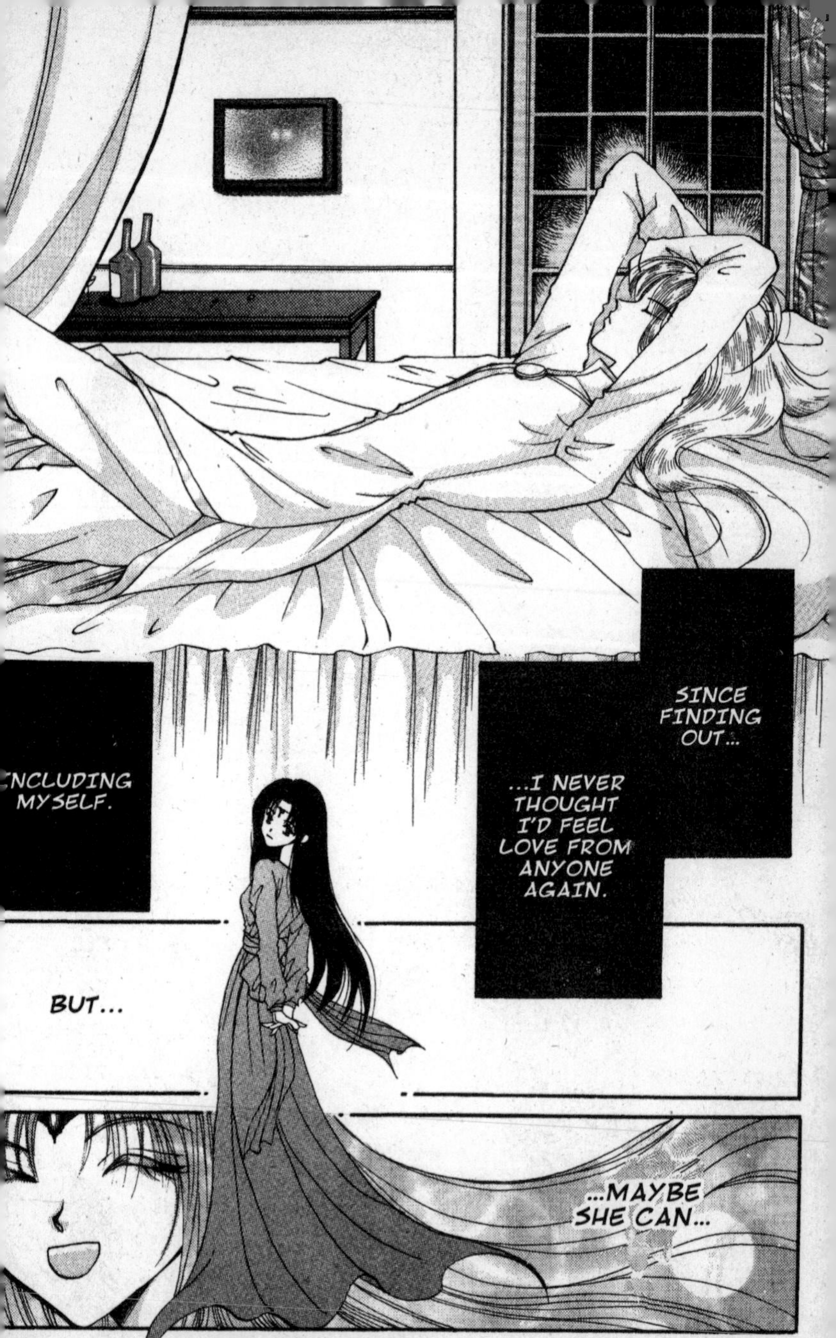
SINCE FINDING OUT...
...I NEVER THOUGHT I'D FEEL LOVE FROM ANYONE AGAIN.
INCLUDING MYSELF.
BUT...
...MAYBE SHE CAN...

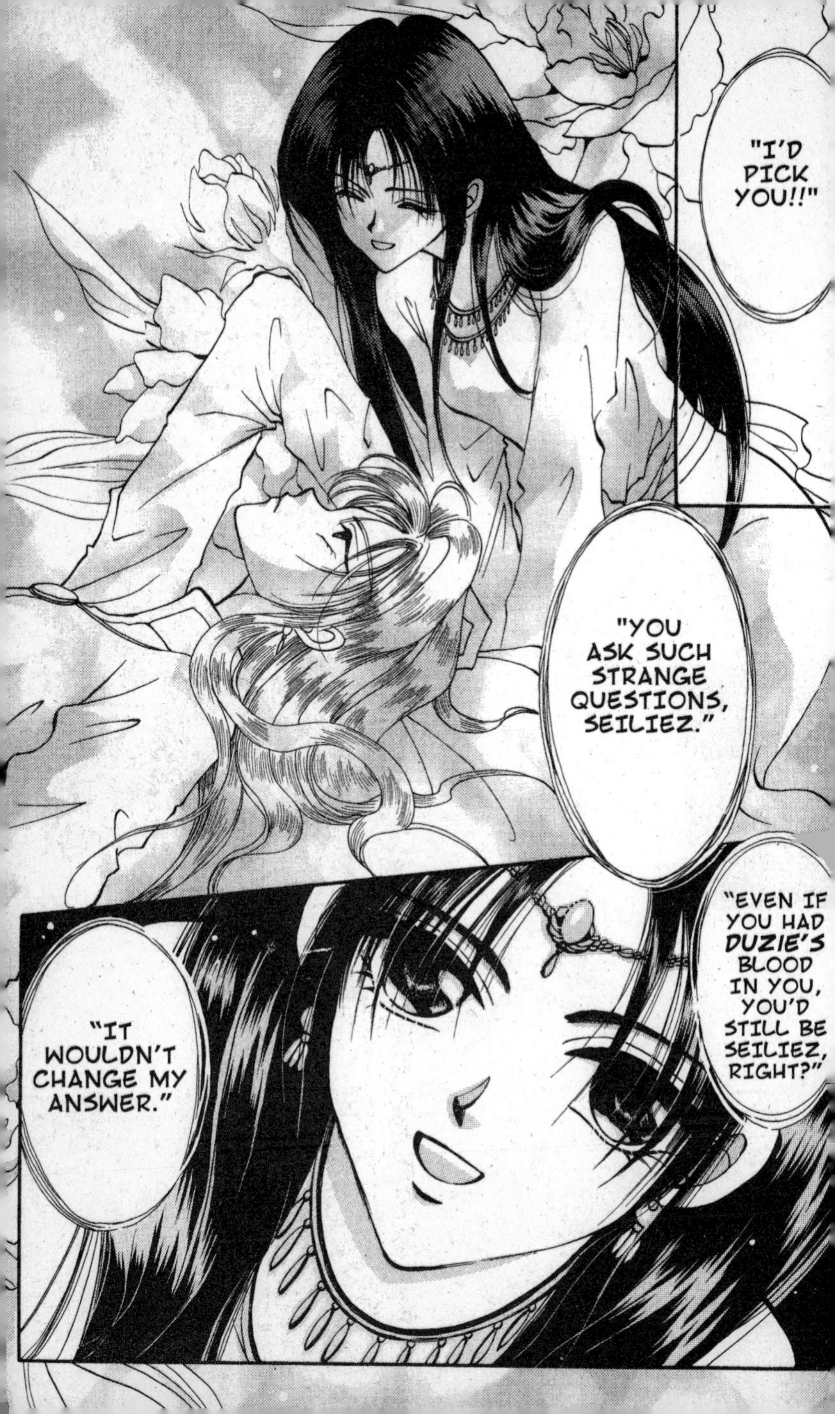
"I'D PICK YOU!!"
"YOU ASK SUCH STRANGE QUESTIONS, SEILIEZ."
"EVEN IF YOU HAD DUZIE'S BLOOD IN YOU, YOU'D STILL BE SEILIEZ, RIGHT?"
"IT WOULDN'T CHANGE MY ANSWER."

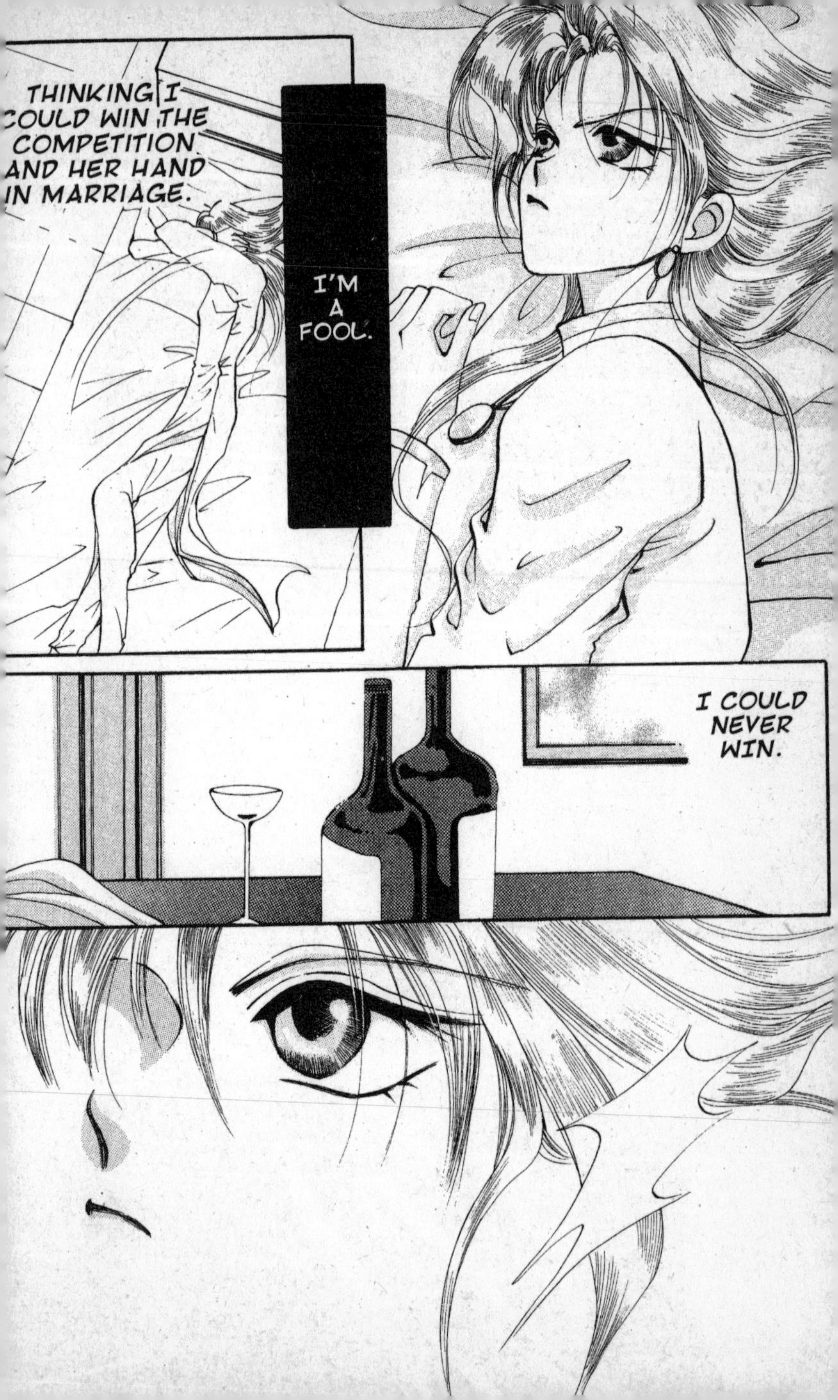

THINKING I COULD WIN THE COMPETITION AND HER HAND IN MARRIAGE.
I'M A FOOL.
I COULD NEVER WIN.

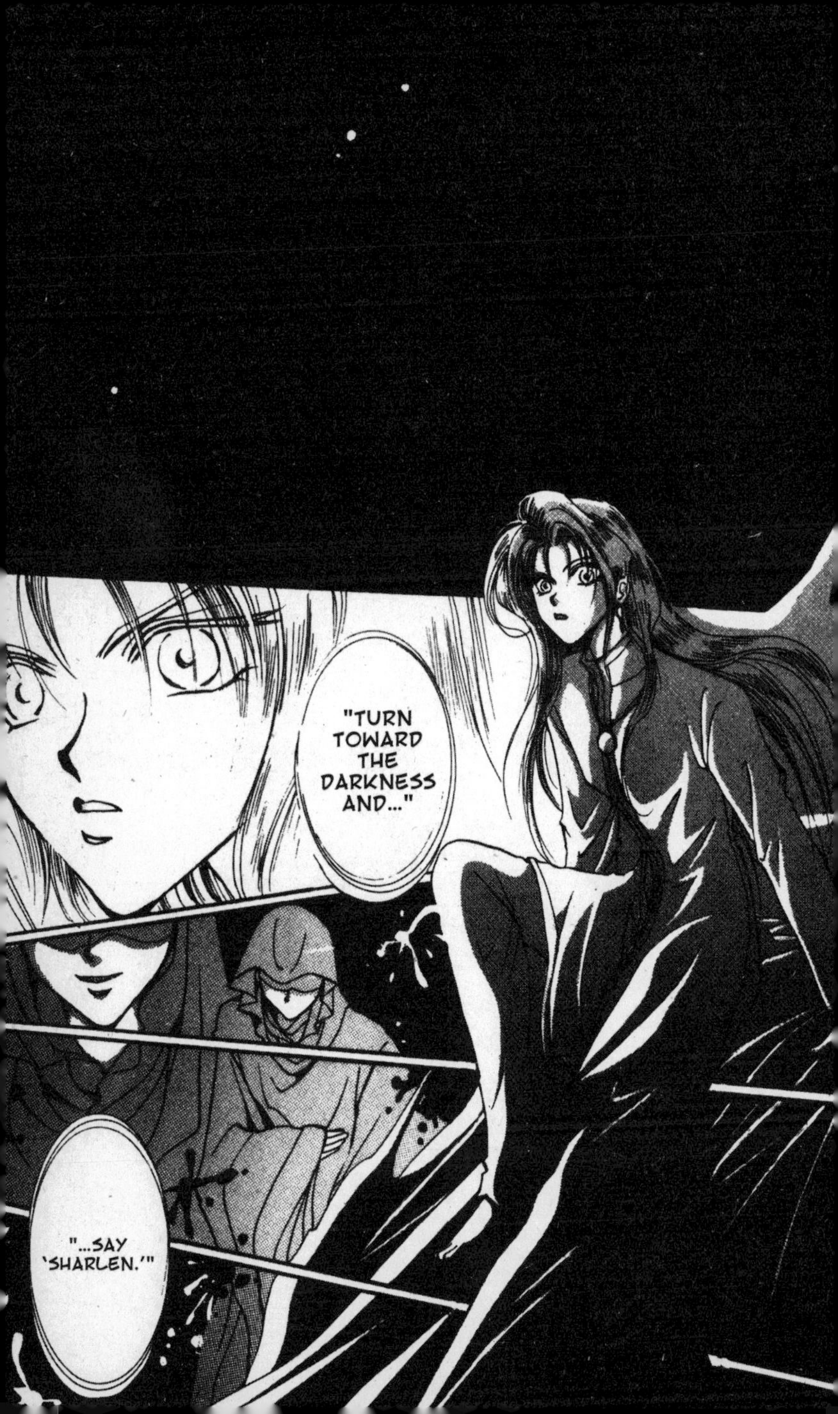
"TURN TOWARD THE DARKNESS AND..."
"...SAY 'SHARLEN.'"

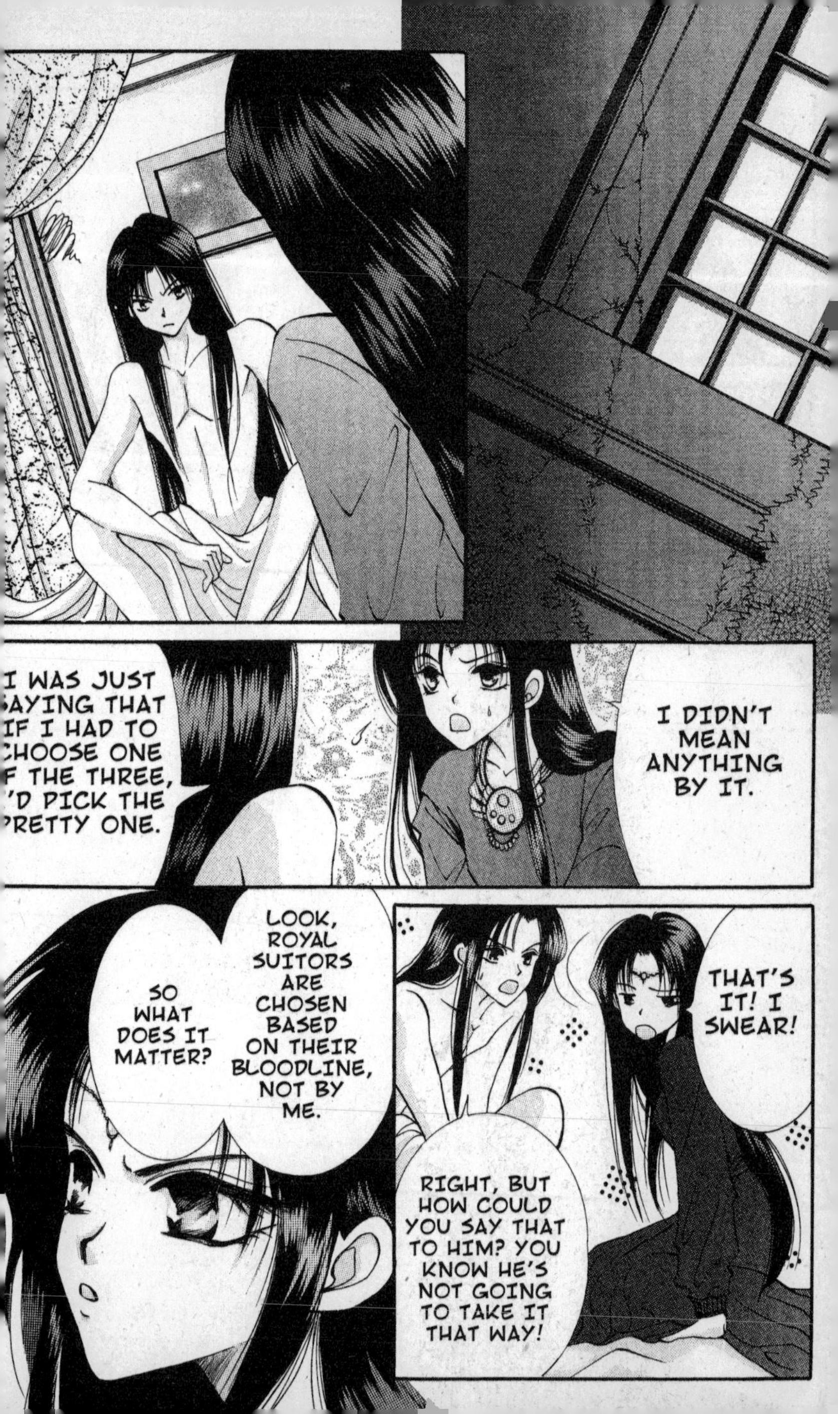
I DIDN'T MEAN ANYTHING BY IT.
I WAS JUST AYING THAT IF I HAD TO CHOOSE ONE F THE THREE, 'D PICK THE RETTY ONE.
THAT'S IT! I SWEAR!
RIGHT, BUT HOW COULD YOU SAY THAT TO HIM? YOU KNOW HE'S NOT GOING TO TAKE IT THAT WAY!
LOOK, ROYAL SUITORS ARE CHOSEN BASED ON THEIR BLOODLINE, NOT BY ME.
SO WHAT DOES IT MATTER?

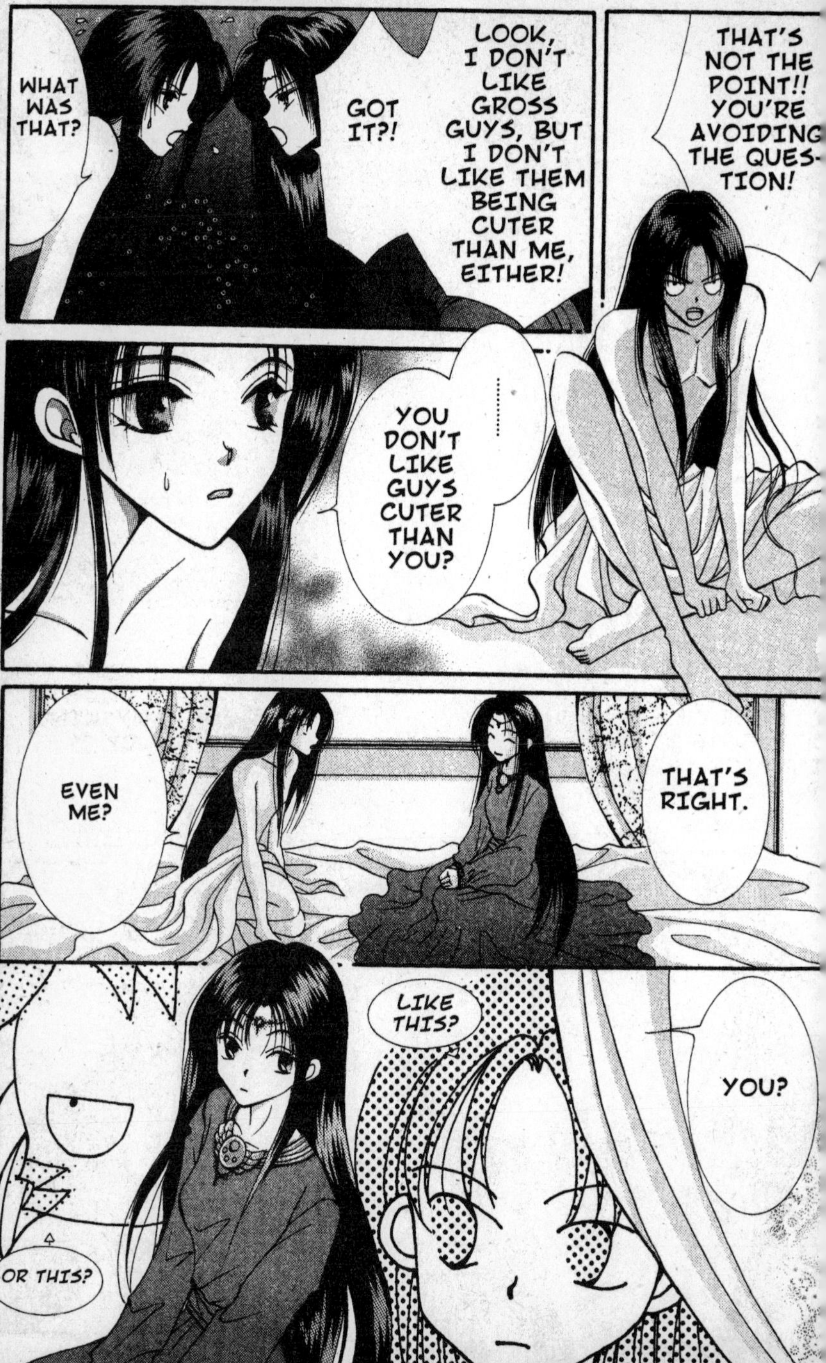

THAT'S NOT THE POINT!! YOU'RE AVOIDING THE QUES-TION!
LOOK, I DON'T LIKE GROSS GUYS, BUT I DON'T LIKE THEM BEING CUTER THAN ME, EITHER!
GOT IT?!
WHAT WAS THAT?
......
YOU DON'T LIKE GUYS CUTER THAN YOU?
THAT'S RIGHT.
EVEN ME?
YOU?
LIKE THIS?
OR THIS?

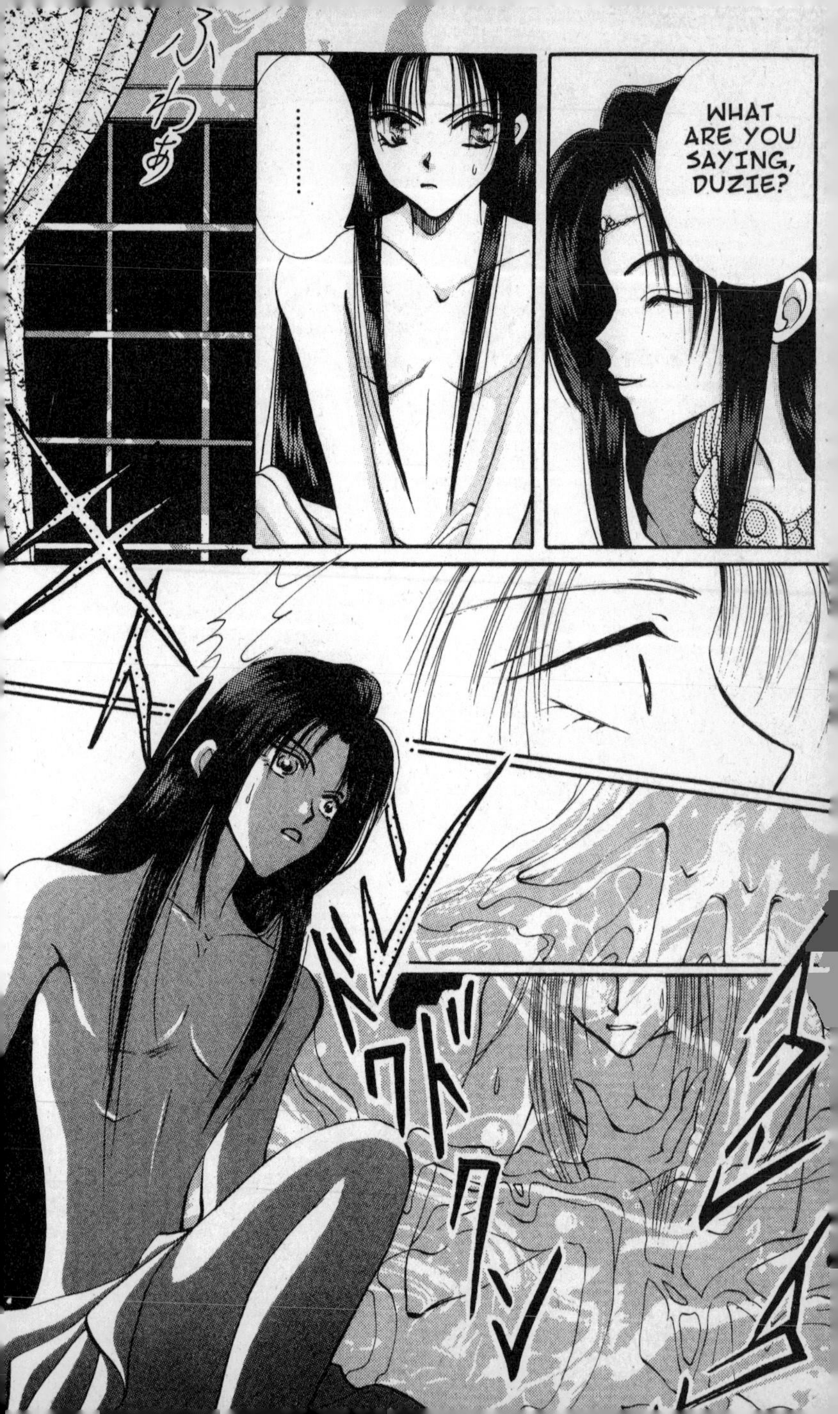
WHAT ARE YOU SAYING, DUZIE?
……
ふわぁ
ドクン

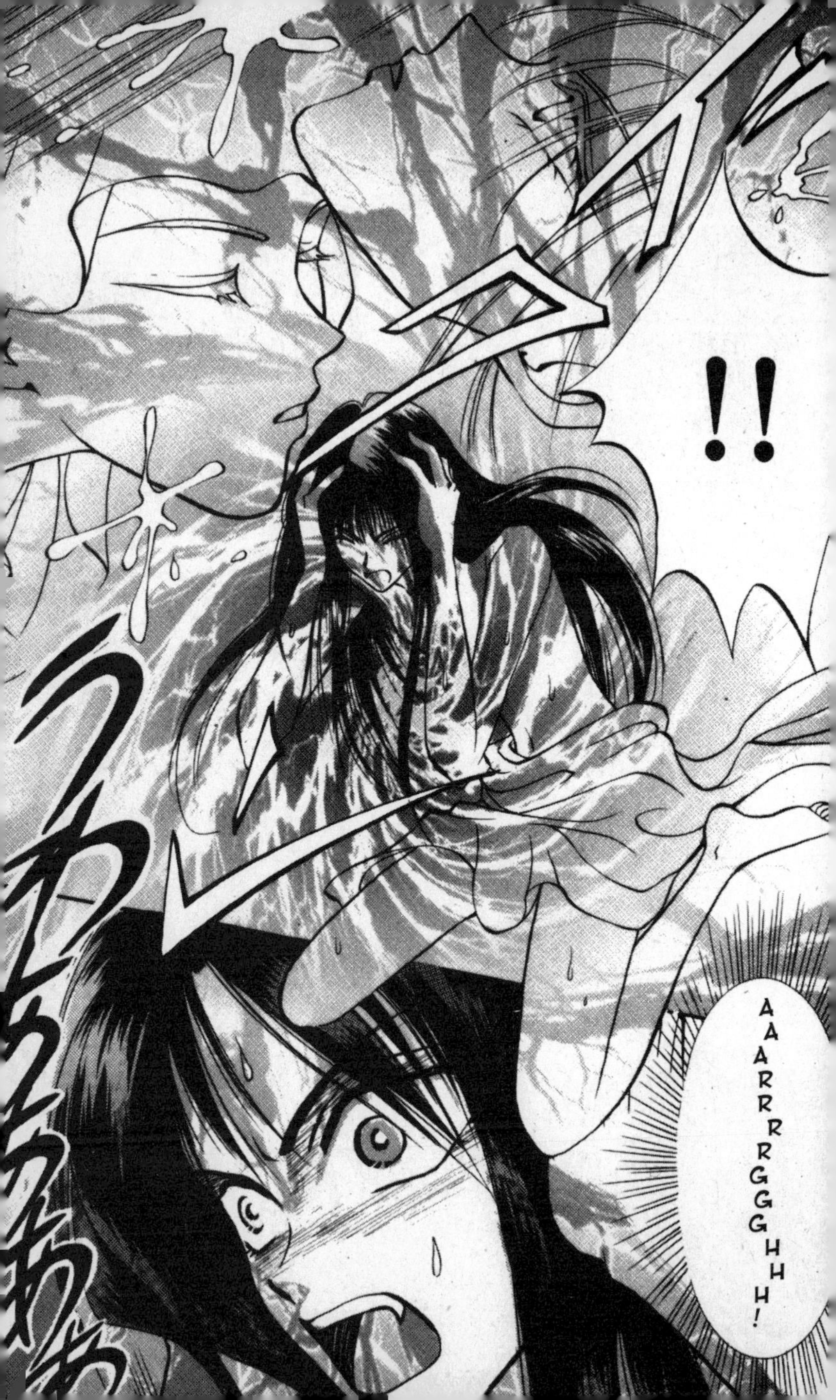
!!
AAARRRRGGGHHH!

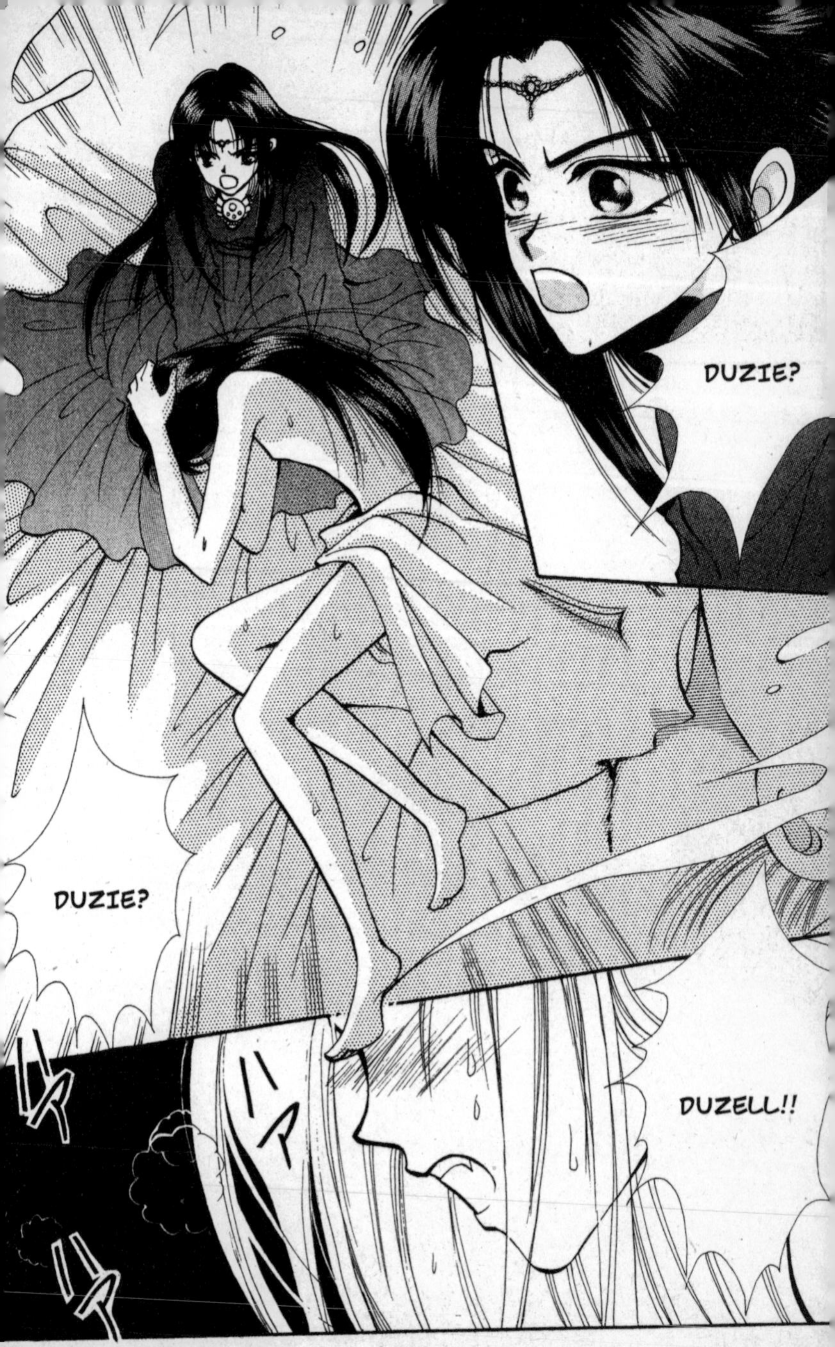
DUZIE?
DUZIE?
DUZELL!!

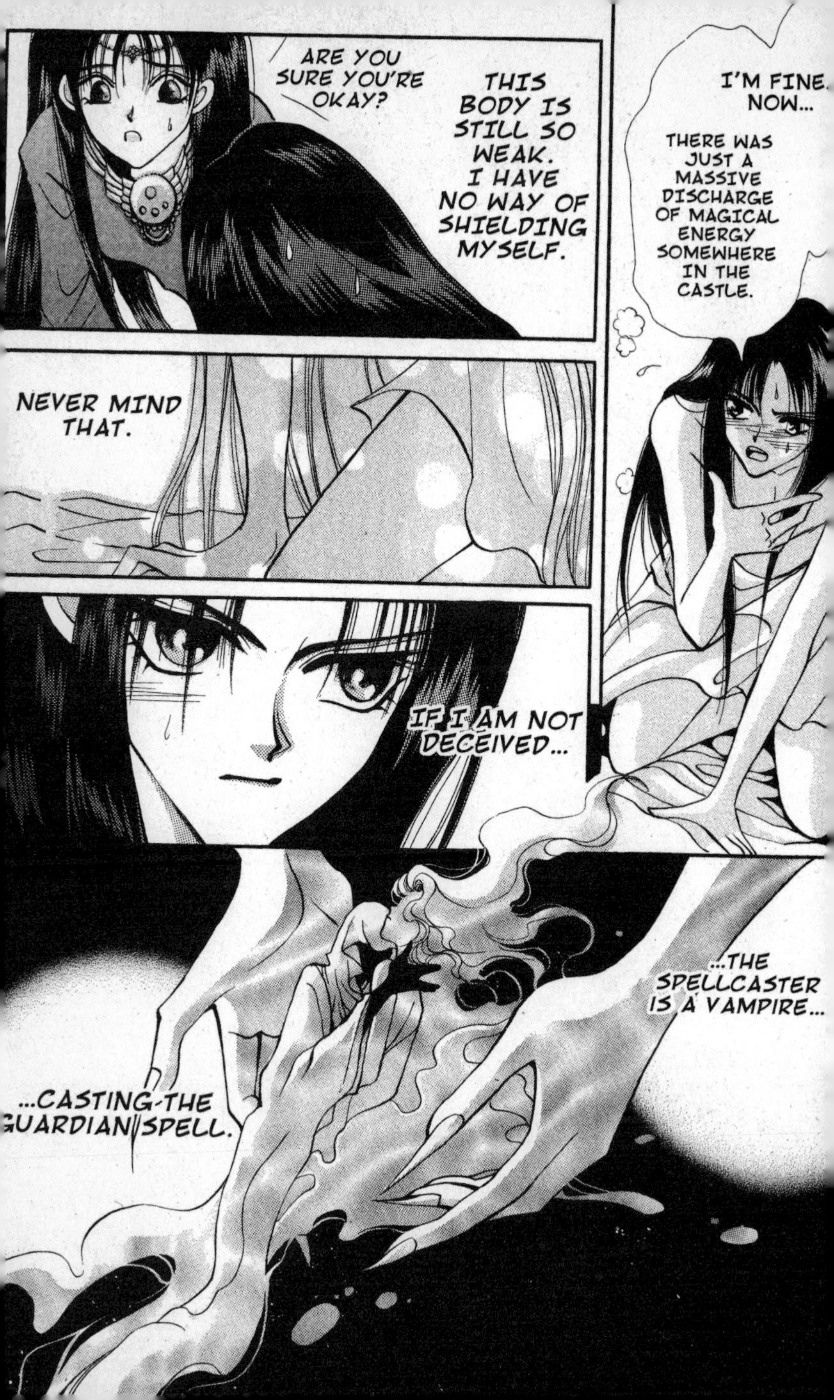
I'M FINE. NOW...
THERE WAS JUST A MASSIVE DISCHARGE OF MAGICAL ENERGY SOMEWHERE IN THE CASTLE.
ARE YOU SURE YOU'RE OKAY?
THIS BODY IS STILL SO WEAK. I HAVE NO WAY OF SHIELDING MYSELF.
NEVER MIND THAT.
IF I AM NOT DECEIVED...
...THE SPELLCASTER IS A VAMPIRE...
...CASTING THE GUARDIAN SPELL.

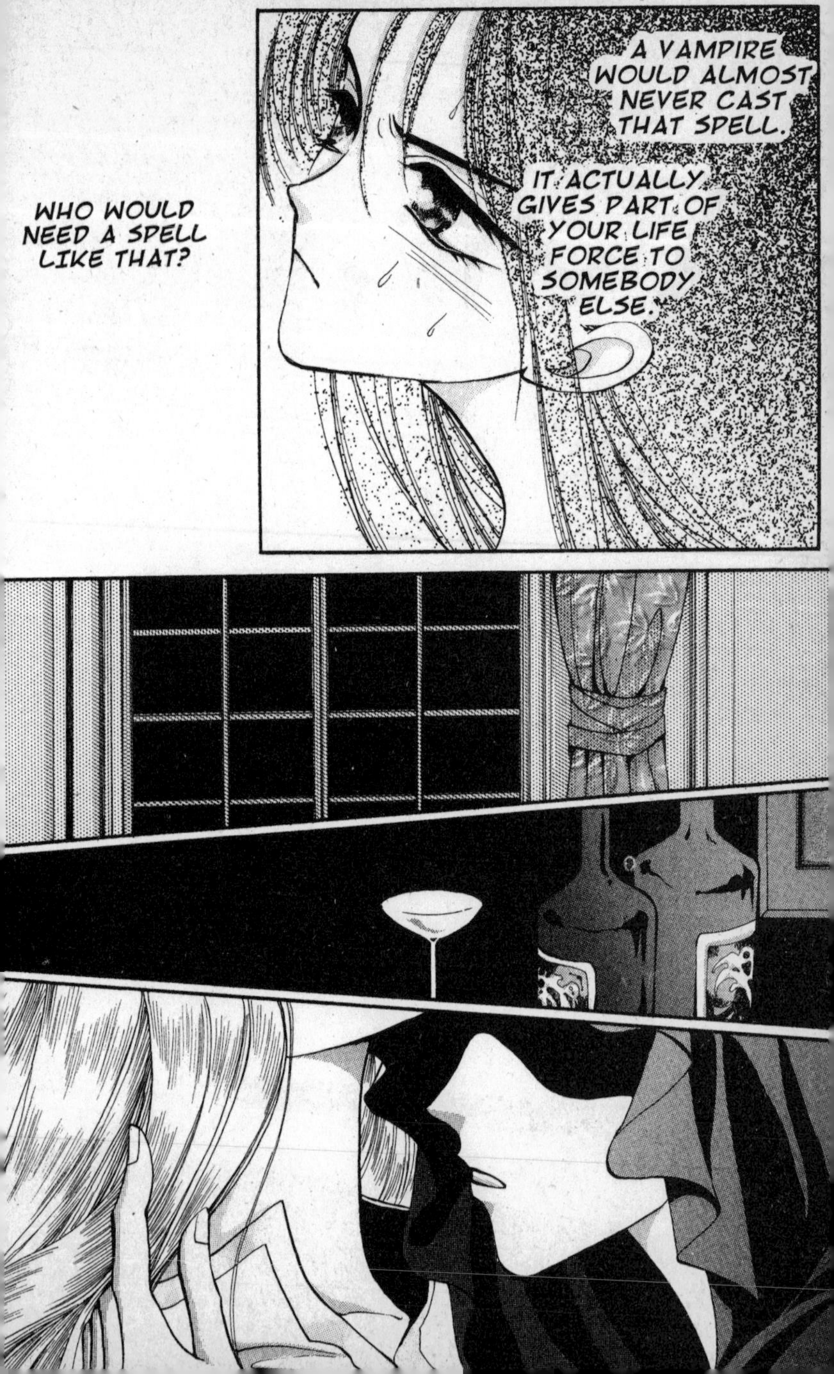
A VAMPIRE WOULD ALMOST NEVER CAST THAT SPELL.
IT ACTUALLY GIVES PART OF YOUR LIFE FORCE TO SOMEBODY ELSE.
WHO WOULD NEED A SPELL LIKE THAT?

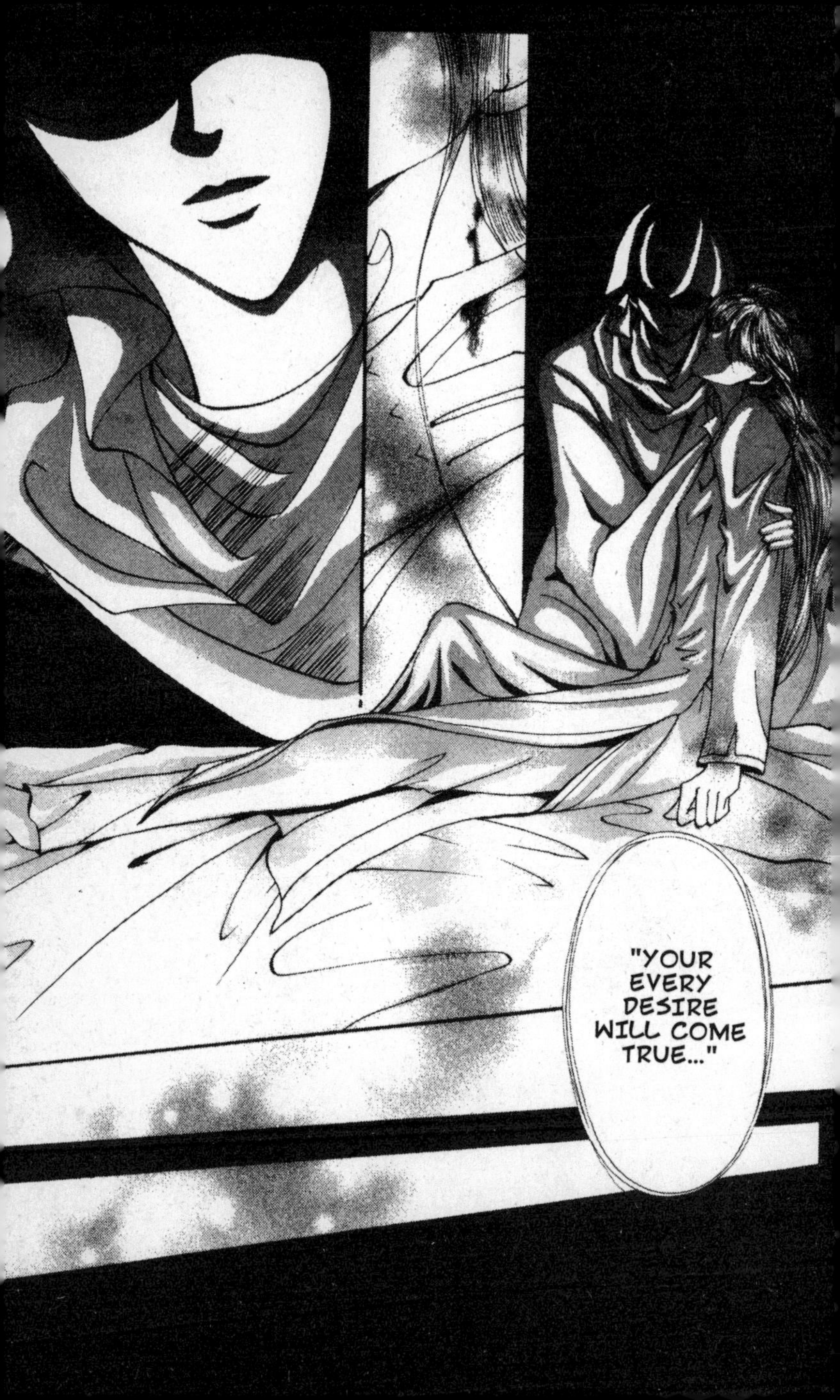
"YOUR EVERY DESIRE WILL COME TRUE..."

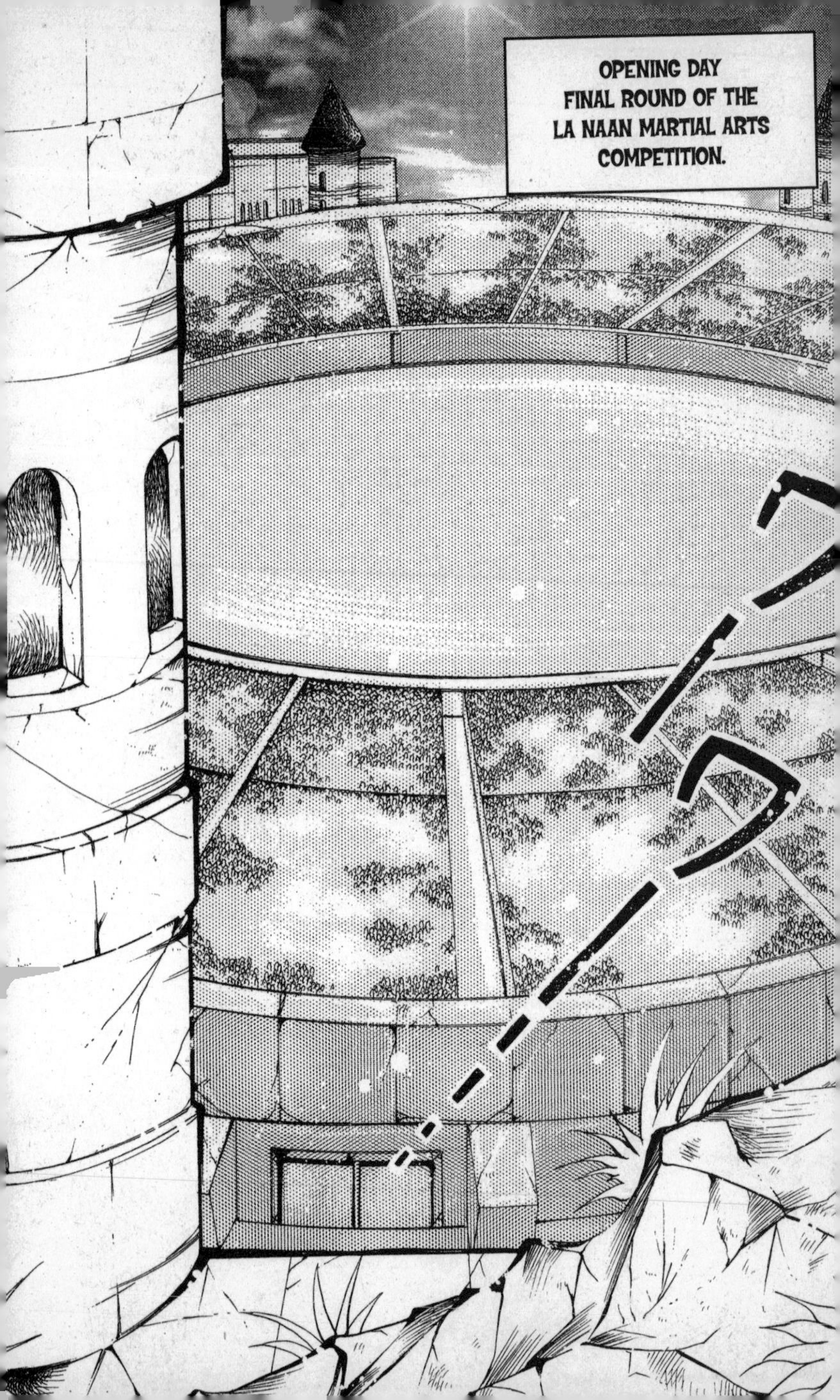
OPENING DAY FINAL ROUND OF THE LA NAAN MARTIAL ARTS COMPETITION.

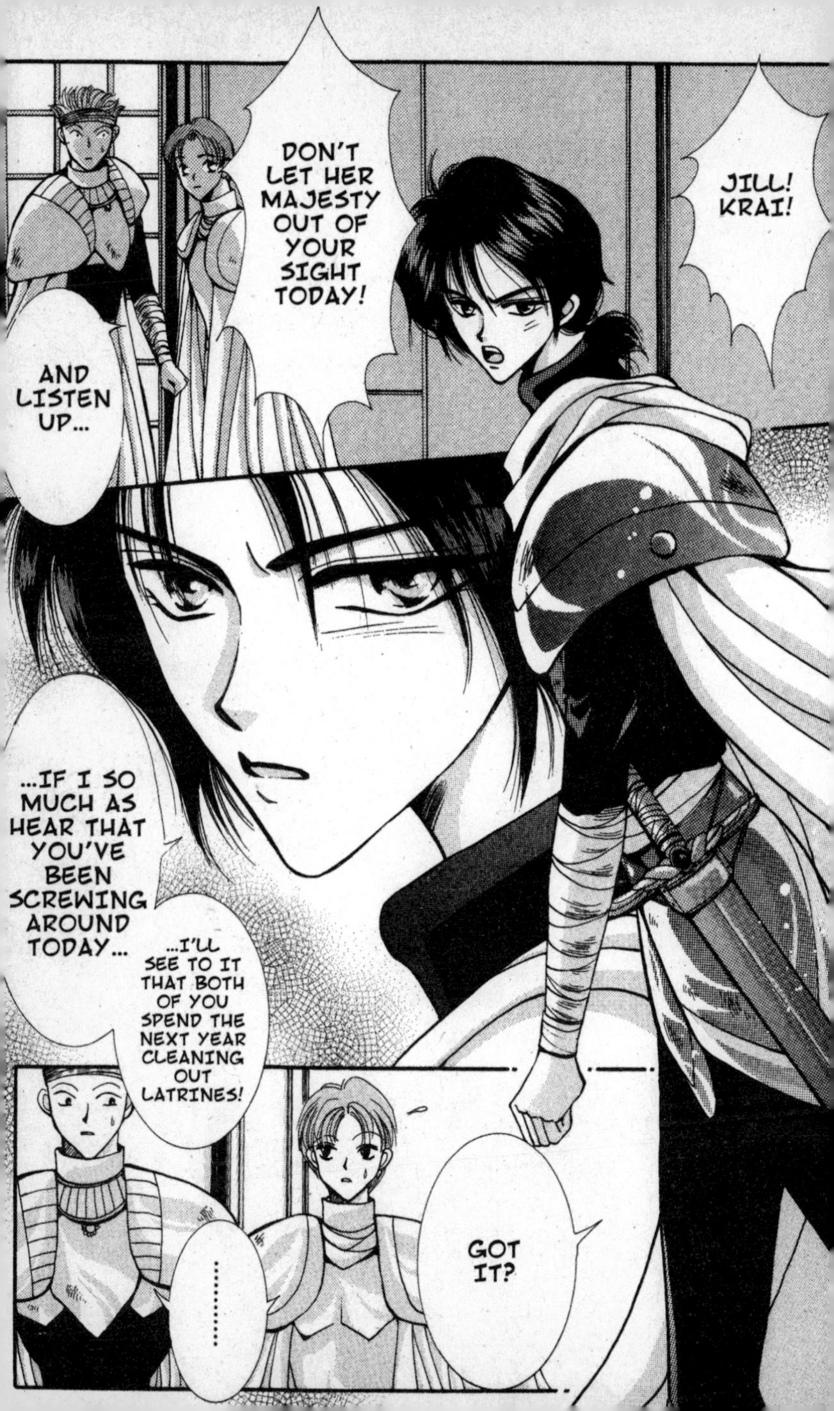
JILL! KRAI!
DON'T LET HER MAJESTY OUT OF YOUR SIGHT TODAY!
AND LISTEN UP...
...IF I SO MUCH AS HEAR THAT YOU'VE BEEN SCREWING AROUND TODAY...
...I'LL SEE TO IT THAT BOTH OF YOU SPEND THE NEXT YEAR CLEANING OUT LATRINES!
GOT IT?
....

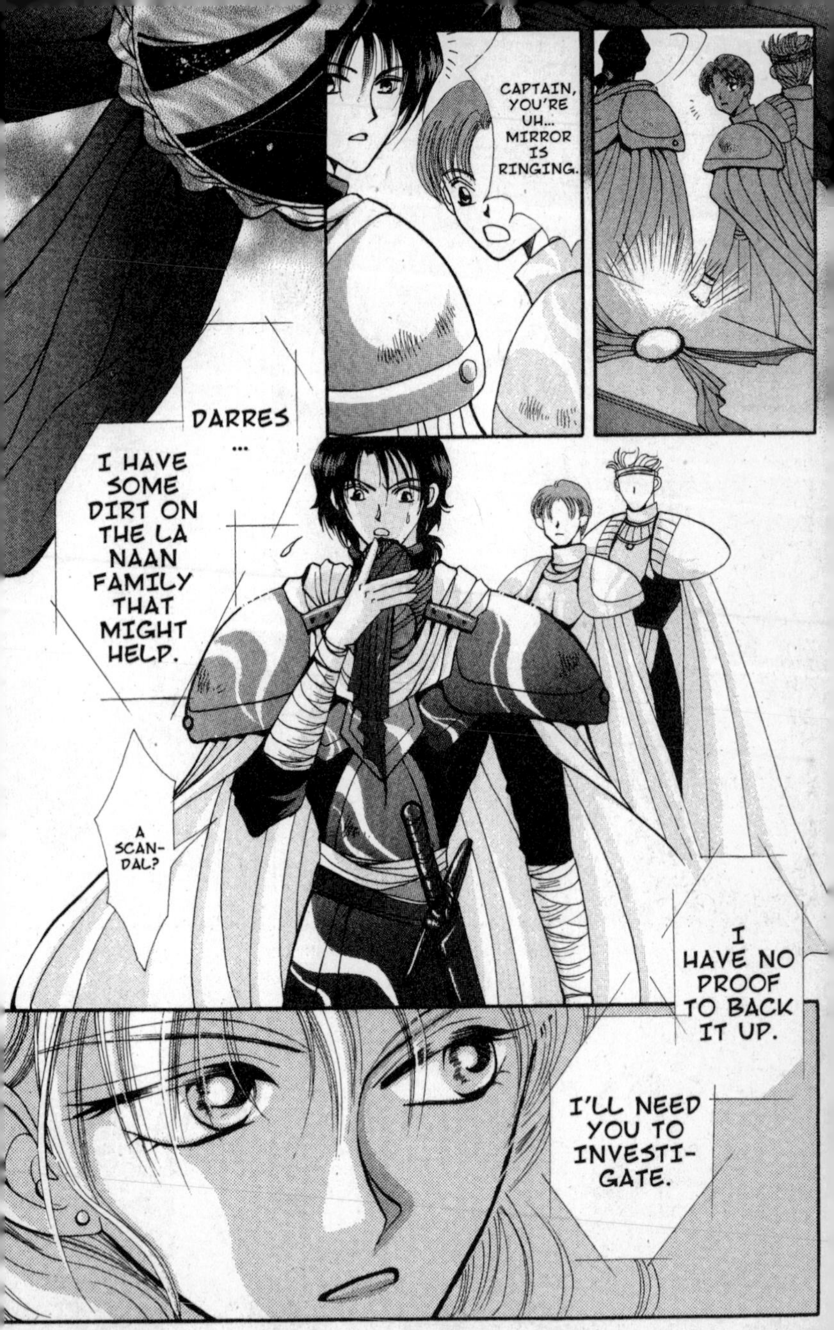
CAPTAIN, YOU'RE UH... MIRROR IS RINGING.
DARRES ...
I HAVE SOME DIRT ON THE LA NAAN FAMILY THAT MIGHT HELP.
A SCAN-DAL?
I HAVE NO PROOF TO BACK IT UP.
I'LL NEED YOU TO INVESTI-GATE.

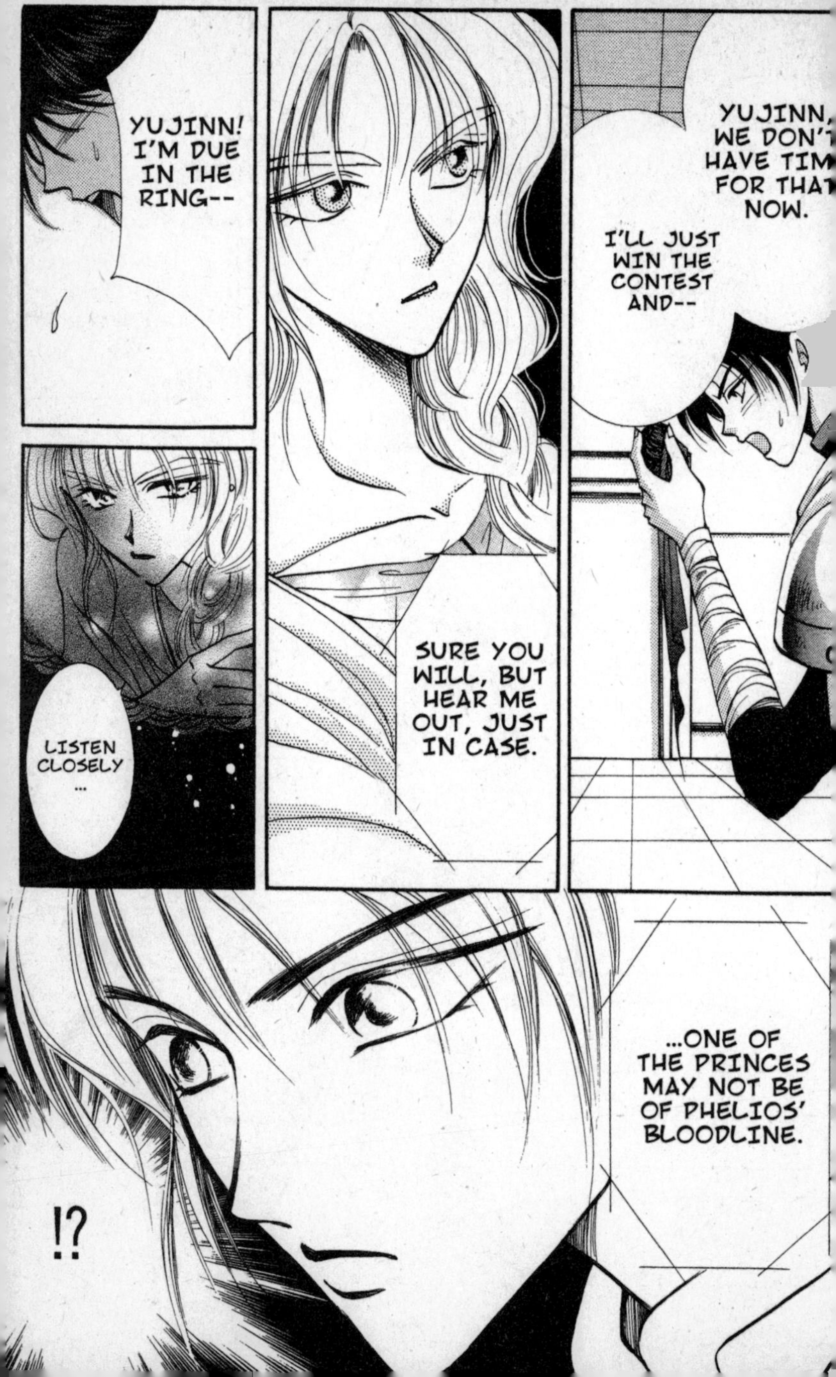
YUJINN, WE DON'T HAVE TIM FOR THAT NOW.
I'LL JUST WIN THE CONTEST AND--
SURE YOU WILL, BUT HEAR ME OUT, JUST IN CASE.
YUJINN! I'M DUE IN THE RING--
LISTEN CLOSELY ...
...ONE OF THE PRINCES MAY NOT BE OF PHELIOS' BLOODLINE.
!?

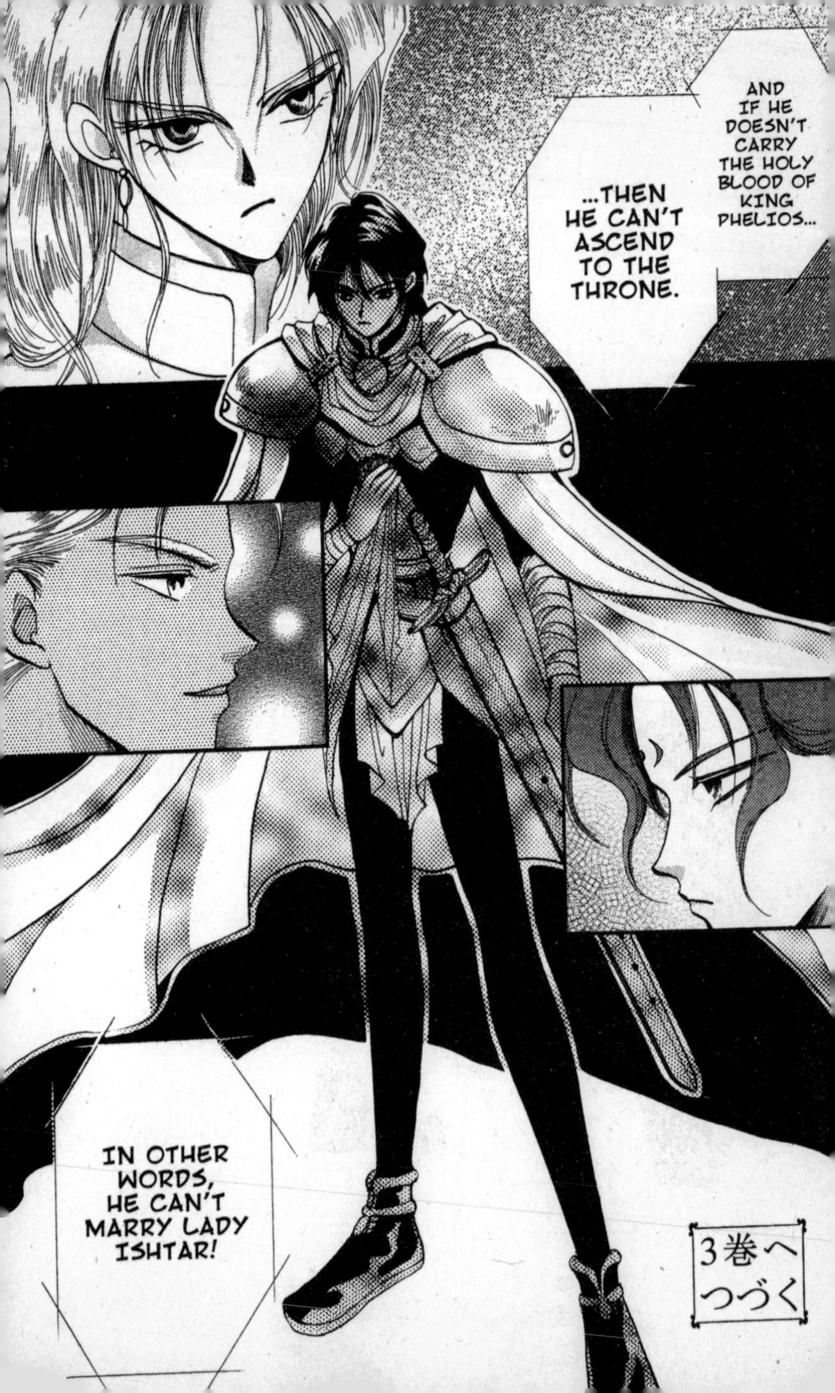
AND IF HE DOESN'T CARRY THE HOLY BLOOD OF KING PHELIOS...
...THEN HE CAN'T ASCEND TO THE THRONE.
IN OTHER WORDS, HE CAN'T MARRY LADY ISHTAR!
3巻へつづく

POSTSCRIPT

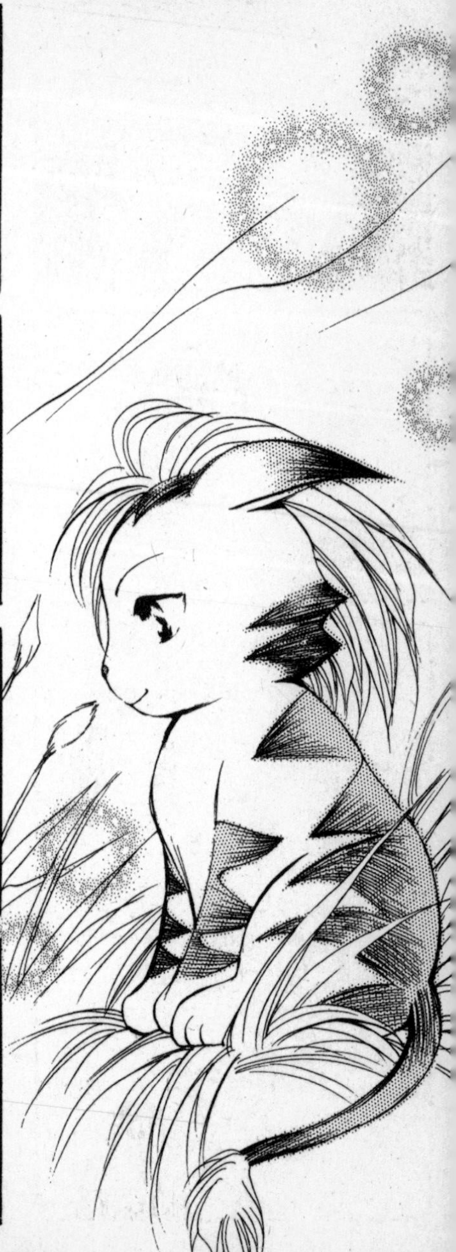

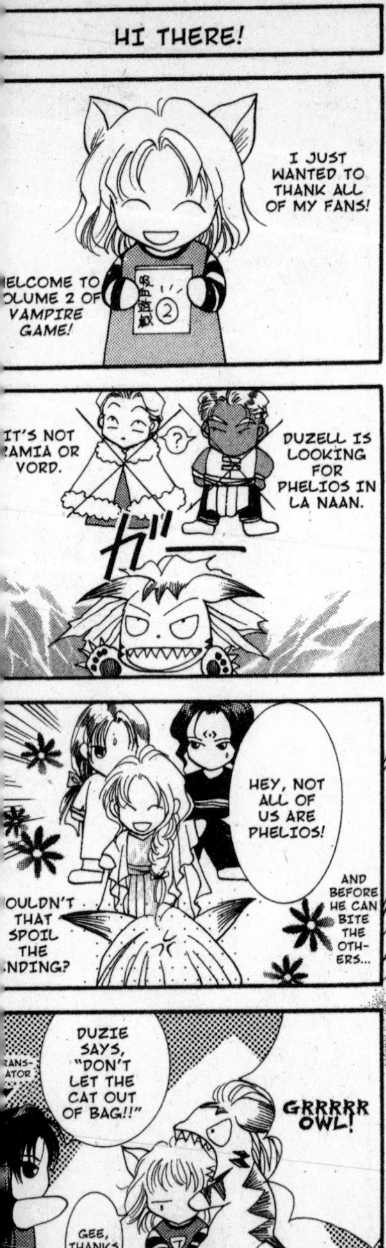
HI THERE!
I JUST WANTED TO THANK ALL OF MY FANS!
ELCOME TO OLUME 2 OF VAMPIRE GAME!
DUZELL IS LOOKING FOR PHELIOS IN LA NAAN.
IT'S NOT AMIA OR VORD.
ガー
HEY, NOT ALL OF US ARE PHELIOS!
AND BEFORE HE CAN BITE THE OTH-ERS...
OULDN'T THAT SPOIL THE NDING?
DUZIE SAYS, "DON'T LET THE CAT OUT OF BAG!!"
RANS-ATOR
GRRRRR OWL!
GEE, THANKS ...

ABOUT VORD

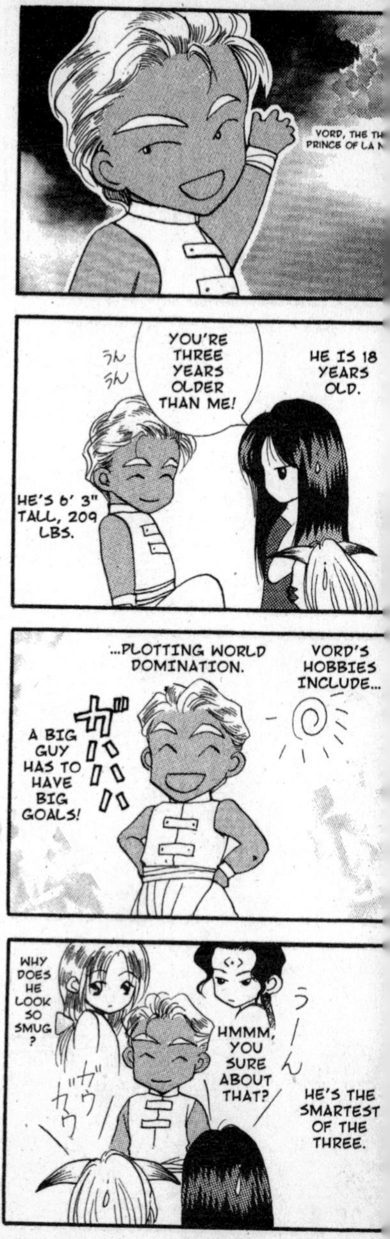
VORD, THE TH
PRINCE OF LA N
HE IS 18 YEARS OLD.
YOU'RE THREE YEARS OLDER THAN ME!
うんうん
HE'S 6' 3" TALL, 209 LBS.
VORD'S HOBBIES INCLUDE...
...PLOTTING WORLD DOMINATION.
ガーー
A BIG GUY HAS TO HAVE BIG GOALS!
HE'S THE SMARTEST OF THE THREE.
うーん
HMMM, YOU SURE ABOUT THAT?
WHY DOES HE LOOK SO SMUG?
ガウガウ

ABOUT SEILIEZ

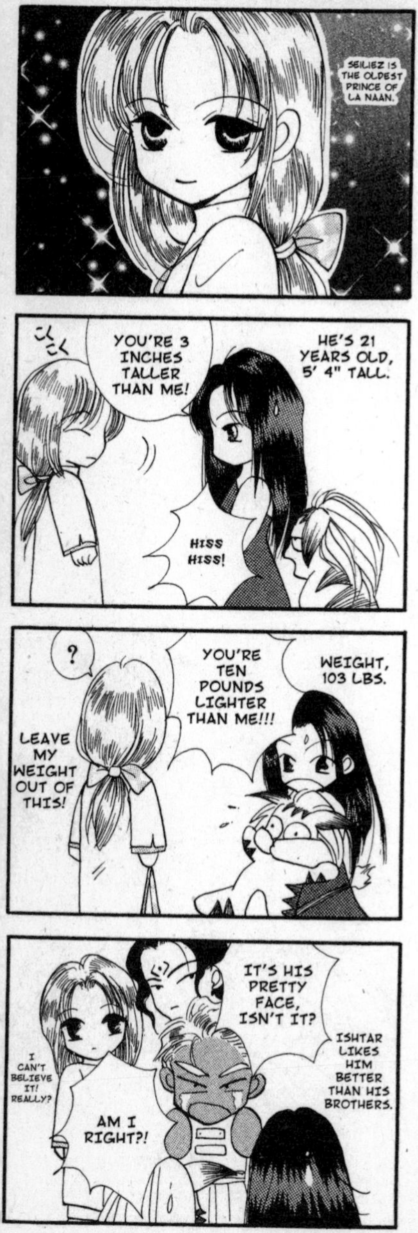
SEILIEZ IS THE OLDEST PRINCE OF LA NAAN.
HE'S 21 YEARS OLD, 5' 4" TALL.
YOU'RE 3 INCHES TALLER THAN ME!
こくこく
HISS HISS!
WEIGHT, 103 LBS.
YOU'RE TEN POUNDS LIGHTER THAN ME!!!
?
LEAVE MY WEIGHT OUT OF THIS!
ISHTAR LIKES HIM BETTER THAN HIS BROTHERS.
IT'S HIS PRETTY FACE, ISN'T IT?
AM I RIGHT?!
I CAN'T BELIEVE IT! REALLY?

ABOUT LAPHIJI

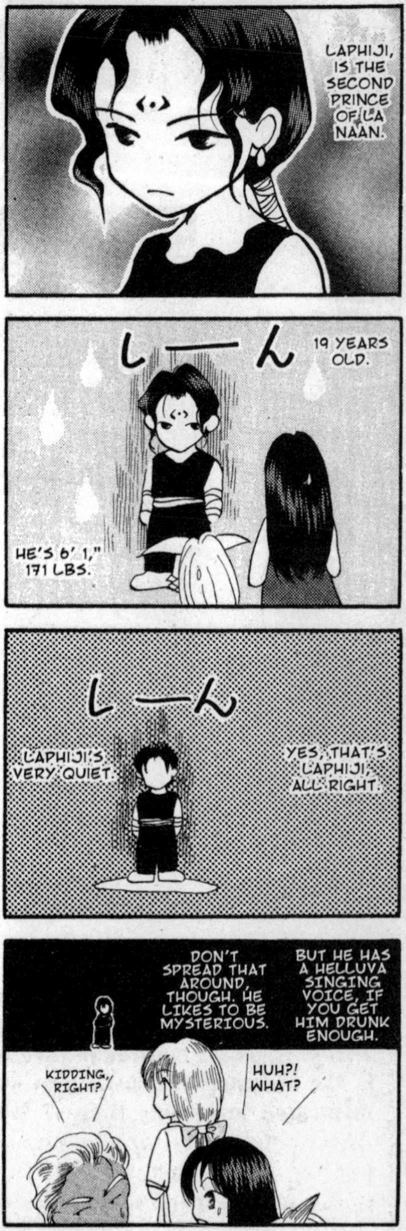

LAPHIJI, IS THE SECOND PRINCE OF LA NAAN.
しーん
19 YEARS OLD.
HE'S 6' 1," 171 LBS.
しーん
YES, THAT'S LAPHIJI, ALL RIGHT.
LAPHIJI'S VERY QUIET.
BUT HE HAS A HELLUVA SINGING VOICE, IF YOU GET HIM DRUNK ENOUGH.
DON'T SPREAD THAT AROUND, THOUGH. HE LIKES TO BE MYSTERIOUS.
HUH?! WHAT?
KIDDING, RIGHT?

CONCLUSION

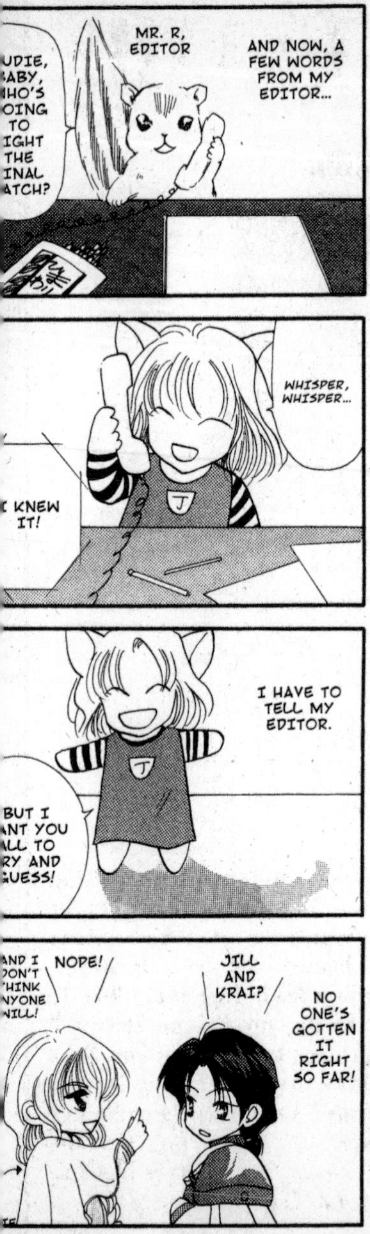

AND NOW, A FEW WORDS FROM MY EDITOR...
MR. R, EDITOR
UDIE, ABY, HO'S OING TO IGHT THE INAL ATCH?
WHISPER, WHISPER...
I KNEW IT!
I HAVE TO TELL MY EDITOR.
BUT I ANT YOU ALL TO RY AND GUESS!
NO ONE'S GOTTEN IT RIGHT SO FAR!
JILL AND KRAI?
NOPE!
AND I ON'T THINK NYONE WILL!

VAMPIRE GAME

Next issue...

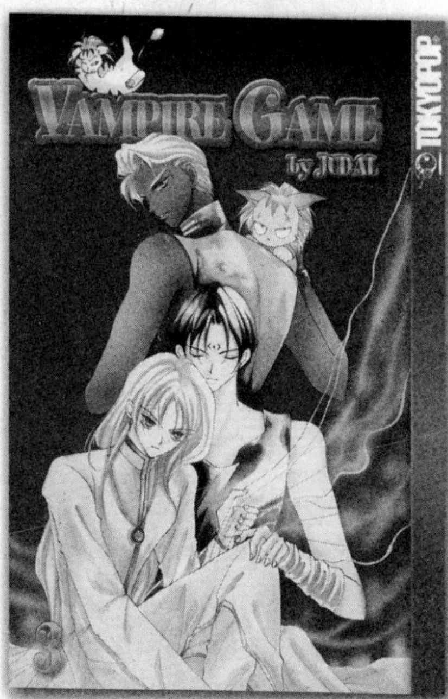

VAMPIRE GAME
by JUDAL
TOKYOPOP
3

Comic escapades meet with political intrigue and martial arts action in what may be the most exciting volume of Vampire Game yet! As the La Naan Competition enters its final rounds, Seiliez, Laphiji, Vord and Darres lock blades with the Kingdom of Pheliosta at stake. However, all is not what it seems. A tip from Yujinn leads Krai and Jill to La Naan's infamous Red-Lantern district to dig up dirt on the royal family, while the motives of the three princes become murkier. Why is the fortuneteller Sharlen so interested in Seiliez? Why is Vord interested in helping Darres? Why won't Laphiji say something? Anything! And as for our titular character, what is Duzell doing hanging out with a bunch of kittens? Discover the answers to these questions and more in Volume 3 of Vampire Game!

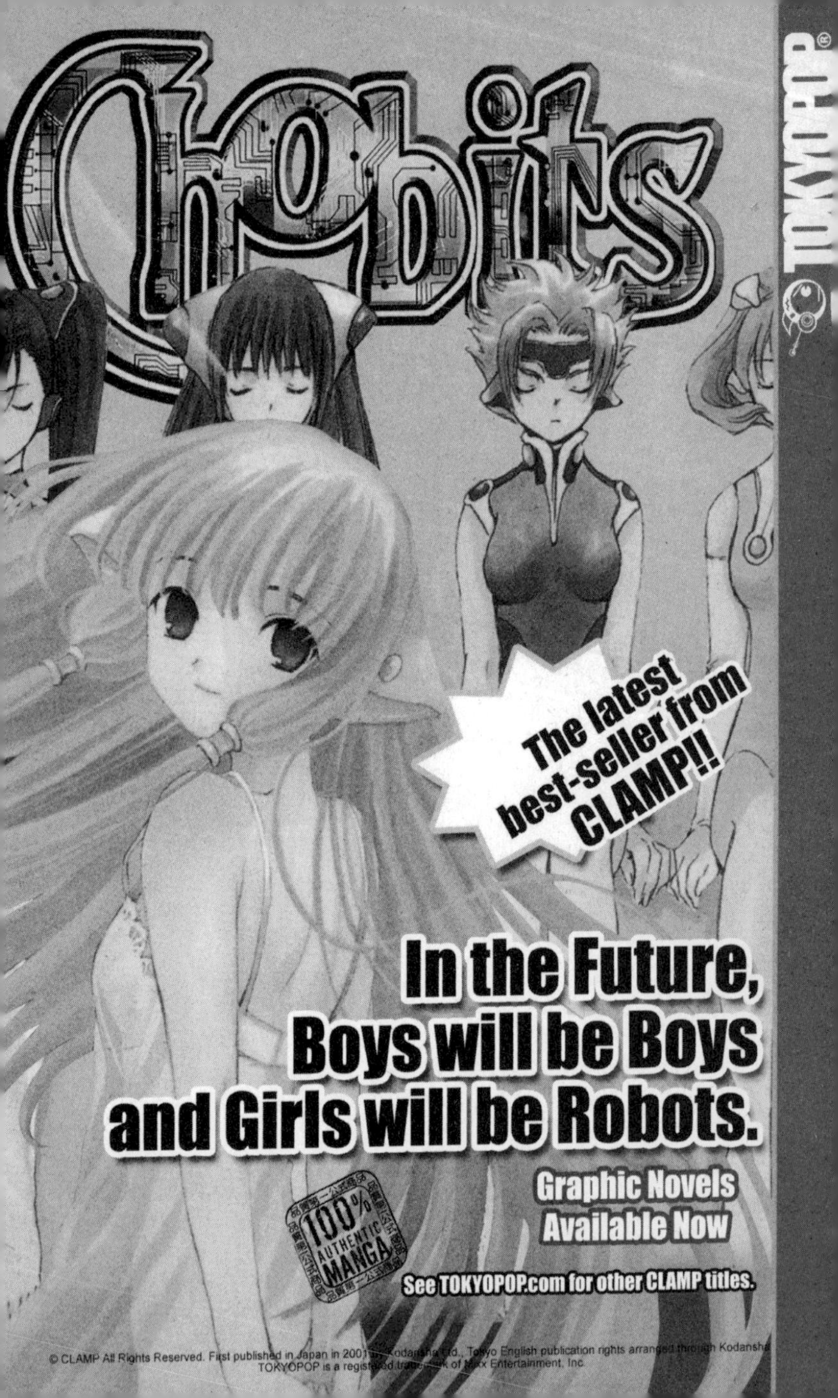

Chobits
TOKYOPOP®
The latest best-seller from CLAMP!!
In the Future, Boys will be Boys and Girls will be Robots.
Graphic Novels Available Now
100% AUTHENTIC MANGA
See TOKYOPOP.com for other CLAMP titles.
© CLAMP All Rights Reserved. First published in Japan in 2001 by Kodansha Ltd., Tokyo English publication rights arranged through Kodansha
TOKYOPOP is a registered trademark of Mixx Entertainment, Inc.

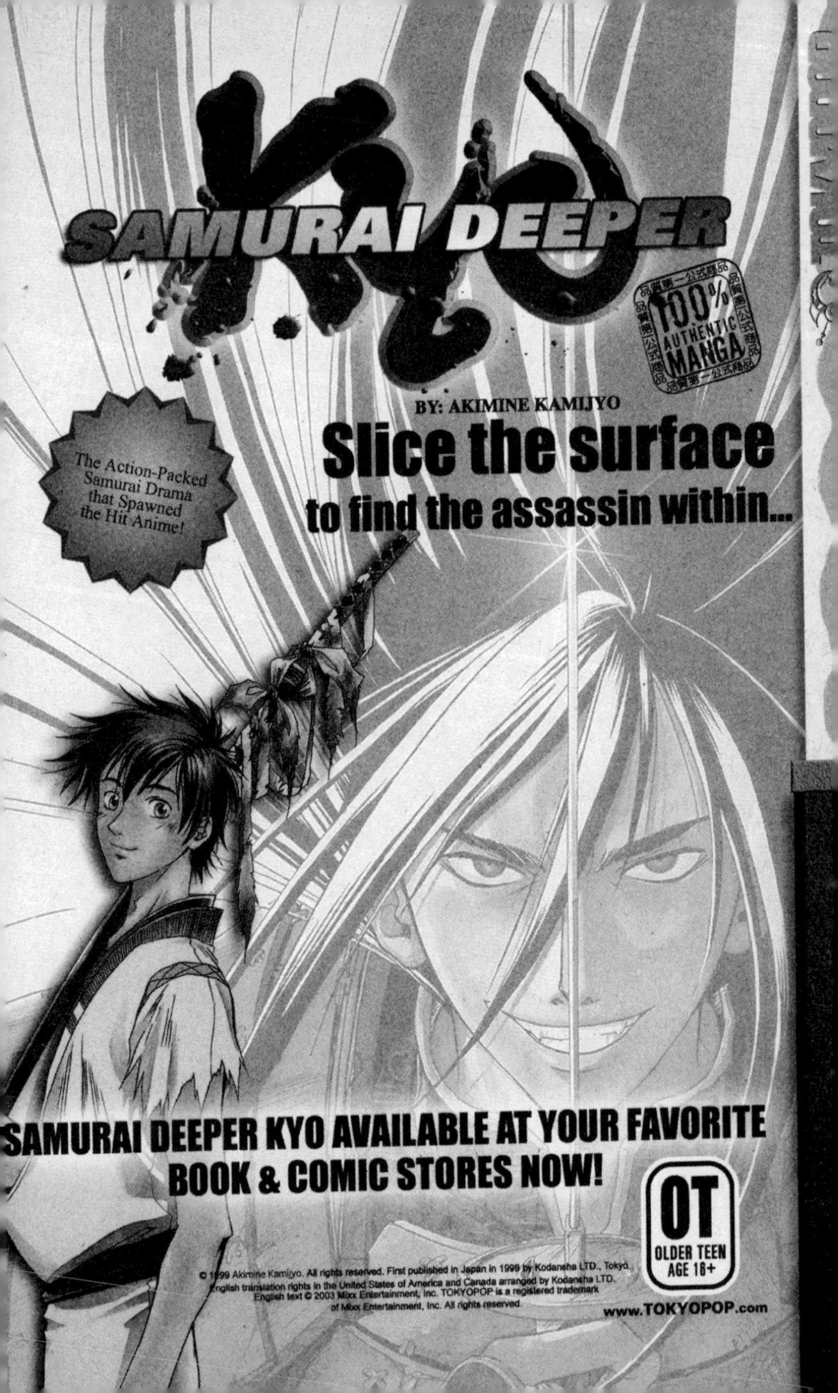

SAMURAI DEEPER KYO
100% AUTHENTIC MANGA
BY: AKIMINE KAMIJYO
Slice the surface
to find the assassin within...
The Action-Packed Samurai Drama that Spawned the Hit Anime!
SAMURAI DEEPER KYO AVAILABLE AT YOUR FAVORITE
BOOK & COMIC STORES NOW!
OT
OLDER TEEN
AGE 16+
© 1999 Akimine Kamijyo. All rights reserved. First published in Japan in 1999 by Kodansha LTD., Tokyo.
English translation rights in the United States of America and Canada arranged by Kodansha LTD.
English text © 2003 Mixx Entertainment, Inc. TOKYOPOP is a registered trademark
of Mixx Entertainment, Inc. All rights reserved.
www.TOKYOPOP.com

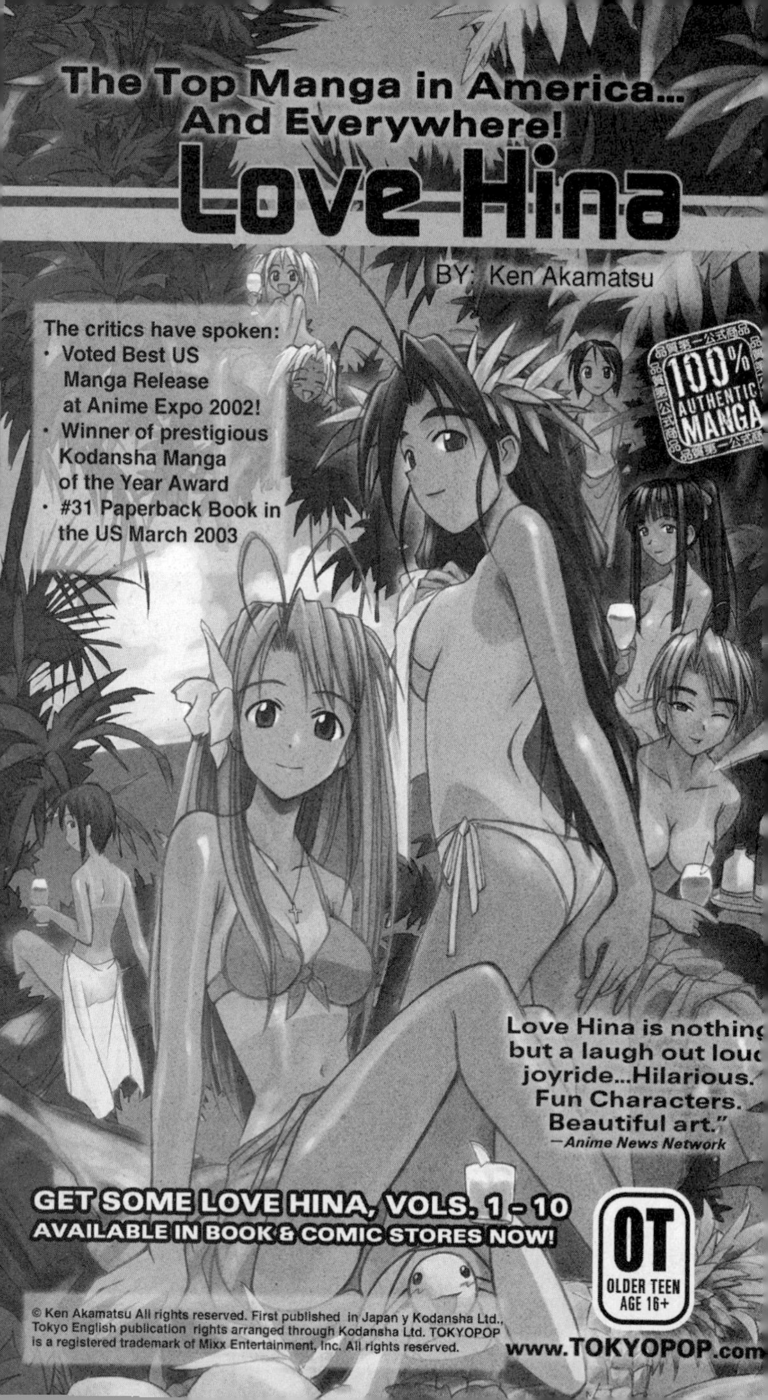
The Top Manga in America... And Everywhere!
Love Hina
BY: Ken Akamatsu
The critics have spoken:
• Voted Best US Manga Release at Anime Expo 2002!
• Winner of prestigious Kodansha Manga of the Year Award
• #31 Paperback Book in the US March 2003
100% AUTHENTIC MANGA
Love Hina is nothing but a laugh out loud joyride...Hilarious. Fun Characters. Beautiful art."
—Anime News Network
GET SOME LOVE HINA, VOLS. 1 - 10
AVAILABLE IN BOOK & COMIC STORES NOW!
OT
OLDER TEEN AGE 16+
© Ken Akamatsu All rights reserved. First published in Japan y Kodansha Ltd., Tokyo English publication rights arranged through Kodansha Ltd. TOKYOPOP is a registered trademark of Mixx Entertainment, Inc. All rights reserved.
www.TOKYOPOP.com

STOP!

This is the back of the book.
You wouldn't want to spoil a great ending!

This book is printed "manga-style," in the authentic Japanese right-to-left format. Since none of the artwork has been flipped or altered, readers get to experience the story just as the creator intended. You've been asking for it, so TOKYOPOP® delivered: authentic, hot-off-the-press, and far more fun!

DIRECTIONS

If this is your first time reading manga-style, here's a quick guide to help you understand how it works.

It's easy... just start in the top right panel and follow the numbers. Have fun, and look for more 100% authentic manga from TOKYOPOP®!